FRAGILE
GLORY

ALSO BY RICHARD BERNSTEIN

From the Center of the Earth:
The Search for the Truth About China
(1982)

Richard Bernstein

FRAGILE GLORY

A Portrait of France
and the French

THE BODLEY HEAD
LONDON

First published in Great Britain 1991
The Bodley Head, 20 Vauxhall Bridge Road, London SW1V 2SA
© Richard Bernstein 1990
Maps © George Colbert 1990

Richard Bernstein has asserted his right to be
identified as the author of this work

A CIP catalogue record for this book
is available from the British Library

ISBN 0 370 31587 1

Printed in Great Britain by
Mackays of Chatham PLC

To Judy and Joe, Jonathan and Michael

We'll become a big, dreary industrial country—
a kind of Belgium. The disappearance of Paris
will make France dull and stagnant. She will
have no heart, no center—and, I think, no mind.

GUSTAVE FLAUBERT, *letter to George Sand*

This pale, torn, bloody thing called France still
grasps a fold of the starry mantle of the future.

GEORGE SAND, *letter to Flaubert*

ACKNOWLEDGMENTS

Over the years there have been so many people, French and others, who have, intentionally or not, helped me with this book, that to name them all would be impossible. But I do want explicitly to thank several of the most important. A. M. Rosenthal sent me to Paris as the *New York Times* correspondent there and then, somewhat to my surprise, made me bureau chief after just a few months. My colleague and predecessor as bureau chief, John Vinocur, taught me a lot both in conversation and by the example of his own writing about the French. I owe a debt of gratitude along these same lines to my other colleagues in Paris: Paul Lewis, Judy Miller, Flora Lewis, and Steven Greenhouse. And then, of course, there is that exceptional group of people who formed the staff of the *Times* in Paris during my years there: Anne Aghion, Daphné Angles, Florence Radovic, Marie Pélétier, Marie-Françoise Denis, Jean Smina, and Nikolas Kamm. Among those who helped me learn the many things I needed to know were Meica O'Mara, Liz Young, Wendy Miller, and, again, Florence Radovic, who not only provided a personal tale that makes up the first part of chapter five but helped with her enthusiasm and knowledge in many other ways. Karin Blanc gave a careful and perspicacious reading to the first draft of the manuscript and helped with numerous matters both large and small. Caroline Marks gave me her sunny place in Paris when one was needed. Kathy Brynner provided remarkable hospitality in her remarkable home in Normandy when I was desperate for a quiet place to work, and Matt Cohen lent me his old stone house in Provence for a period of chained-to-the-chair writing.

Jonathan Segal, my esteemed editor and friend, took me to lunch one day in 1987 and inspired me to undertake this project. I've had my doubts along the way, but, several years and many pages later, I am sure his idea was a good one. I'll have to leave it to others to judge its execution.

And as for the French and others living permanently in France who opened their homes, offices, farms, and schools to a prying reporter; who welcomed me, argued with me, leaked to me, corrected my mistakes, answered my questions; who lunched and dined with me, suffered my prying and my curiosity; who engaged in conversation and argument, talked about restaurants, wine, politics, literature, and sex; who, in short, took an interest in a foreign journalist trying to learn about them— without them, of course, very little of this would have been possible. I have thought about listing those who were my instructors in the ways of the French, but I have decided that they know who they are and might even be embarrassed to be publicly thanked. So, I grant them anonymity even as I express my appreciation to them all. I want, however, to mention one special person and group, Françoise Stoll and the members of her large and splendid family, whose quiet generosity and kindness helped in more ways than they can ever know.

CONTENTS

———

III THE REASONS AND THE MYSTERIES OF STATE

FRAGILE
GLORY

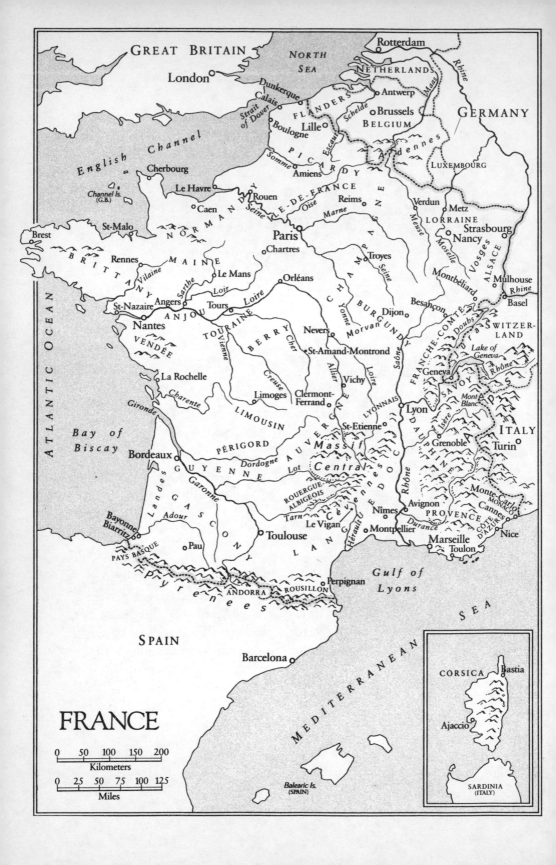

GREAT BRITAIN

NORTH SEA

London

Rotterdam

NETHERLANDS

GERMANY

Dunkerque
Calais
Strait of Dover

Boulogne

FLANDERS

Antwerp

Brussels

BELGIUM

LUXEMBOURG

Ardennes

English Channel

Cherbourg

Le Havre

Caen

Rouen

PICARDY

Somme

Amiens

ÎLE-DE-FRANCE

Oise

Reims

Marne

Verdun

Metz

LORRAINE

Strasbourg

Nancy

Channel Is.
(G.B.)

St-Malo

NORMANDY

Seine

Paris

Chartres

Troyes

Seine

Montbéliard

Moselle

Meuse

VOSGES

ALSACE

Mulhouse

Basel

Rhine

Brest

Rennes

BRITTANY

MAINE

Le Mans

Orléans

CHAMPAGNE

Dijon

Besançon

Rhine

Vilaine

Sarthe

Loir

Yonne

BURGUNDY

FRANCHE-COMTÉ

Doubs

SWITZER-LAND

Angers

Tours

Loire

Nevers

Morvan

Saône

Jura

Lake of Geneva

St-Nazaire

ANJOU

TOURAINE

BERRY

St-Amand-Montrond

Allier

Vichy

Geneva

SAVOY

Rhône

Nantes

Vienne

Cher

Loire

LYONNAIS

Lyon

Isère

Mont Blanc

ALPS

VENDÉE

ATLANTIC OCEAN

La Rochelle

Creuse

Limoges

Clermont-Ferrand

St-Etienne

DAUPHINÉ

Grenoble

ITALY

Turin

Charente

LIMOUSIN

AUVERGNE

Massif Central

Isère

Gironde

Bay of Biscay

PÉRIGORD

Dordogne

Lot

Rhône

Durance

Monte-Carlo

MONACO

Bordeaux

GUYENNE

Garonne

ROUERGUE
ALBIGEOIS

CÉVENNES

LANGUEDOC

Avignon

PROVENCE

Cannes

CÔTE D'AZUR

Nice

Landes

GASCONY

Adour

Tarn

Hérault

Nîmes

Le Vigan

Montpellier

Marseille

Toulon

Bayonne
Biarritz

Pau

Toulouse

PAYS BASQUE

Pyrenees

ANDORRA

ROUSSILLON

Perpignan

Gulf of Lyons

SPAIN

Barcelona

MEDITERRANEAN SEA

FRANCE

0   50   100   150   200
Kilometers

0   25   50   75   100 125
Miles

Balearic Is.
(SPAIN)

CORSICA

Bastia

Ajaccio

SARDINIA
(ITALY)

The Imaginary Country

"FRANCE," a character in Paul Claudel's play *Le Pain Dur* says, "nobody understands it."

The French, if truth be known, like to think of themselves as just a bit inscrutable, especially to outsiders. Not being understood gives them a benignly perverse pleasure. And yet perhaps the Claudel character is right, and nobody does understand either it or them. Why should comprehension—clear and distinct ideas, as Descartes might have put it—be so elusive?

Part of the reason lies in the habit of both the French and the rest of the world to locate the country someplace midway between a certain persistent dream and an immovable reality. The French, to paraphrase —and only slightly distort—a famous notion of de Gaulle, have a certain idea of themselves. It is, put briefly, to represent something beyond themselves, to light up the world, to glow with the torch of civilization itself. But at the same time, the French have a stubbornly sanguinary history, a gloriously unreasonable past. They have been a contentious people fragmented by conflicting interests, passions, and obsessions, on which the compromises reached, albeit with difficulty, in other countries have been smashed to pieces like wooden boats upon the shoals. The French twentieth century, moreover, has been something more than sanguinary, more even than morally agonizing, though it has been that as well, particularly the country's military and then moral collapse in the face of the Nazis. Before it, the French, for all their stubborn inscrutability, could at least bask in the certain knowledge of their global

greatness, the brightness of the torch they shone on the global civilization. In this century, the French have faced with a national clenched
fist the specter of their own decline, a dimming of the torch.

This does not mean that I have written a book about a country of
negligible importance, or that I spent three years reporting on France
for the *New York Times* on the assumption that it has come to figure
in only a minor sort of way back home. My belief, unchanged since I
first lived in France, spending a year there as a student twenty years ago,
is that it matters, in large part simply because of its role, sometimes
infuriating, often defiant, as the major ancient civilization in the Western
world that does not represent one or another of the products of British
imperialism. Still, I would be dishonest if I concealed my belief that one
of the most fascinating things about the French is the very ambivalence
with which they view their late-twentieth-century role.

The French present many paradoxes. One of them is that they have
emerged in the last several decades more stable and more democratic,
more unified and at internal peace, than ever before in their history. The
French no longer so conspicuously present that aspect of themselves
that, as Jules Michelet, the great nineteenth-century historian of the
Revolution put it, "strains toward disunion and discord." Strangely,
though, even as they have in the past quarter century solved the political
problem that haunted them for centuries, they lost the compelling presence they used to have when they were beset by earthshaking troubles.
France is no longer capable of throwing the world into turmoil. At the
same time, it has never been better off. The French themselves are not
sure which they would prefer.

I once heard of a wine grower in Bordeaux who had the rather odd
practice of requiring his children to view on French television the week-
day-morning broadcast of one of the American news programs—it takes
place Monday through Friday at 7:45 a.m. They would see, he told a
friend, how infrequently there was news about France in America. He
wanted them to know how unimportant France had become in the eyes
of the rest of the world.

To be sure, the wine grower's bittersweet resignation is not to be
confused with a belief that France has in reality declined in importance.
The French are not a people particularly known for the modesty of their
self-conception. And yet they harbor a mixture of feelings. The first
French reaction to such things as their failure to make news elsewhere
would be to think they are unjustifiably slighted by a world that has
forgotten to appreciate them. And then there would be an uneasy, sub-

terranean companion feeling that perhaps, after all, the changes in the world have made them a bit less deserving of attention. The very fact that the wine grower could utter his statement reflected at least some erosion of confidence. And that is the point. The idea of broadcasting the American news would have been anathema to the French in days of more unalloyed national glory, because after all, what is the assumption underlying the effort? It is that the American view of the world, as reflected on television news, is significant enough for France to occupy a half hour of its morning. Nobody would have the temerity to suggest that the inverse of this proposition is true. The real global news, the television initiative suggested, is American; the French version is a regional variant, a kind of picturesque dialect worth retaining but secondary to the standard language.

If the shift is thought of as a process by which the French have become a net importer of intellectual product, it is easy to see, in the country of Victor Hugo and André Gide, Proust and Sartre, how momentous, and sudden, it has been, how much the country of the 1980s had changed, even from the way I found it a few years earlier. I first came to Paris in 1970, fresh out of graduate school, where I had been exercising a durable taste for the exotic by studying, not France, but China, its language and its history, in the half-conscious expectation that the future lay in the East, in Asia—where, in fact, I spent much of the next ten or so years. I had stopped off for an academic season in France, where I hoped long afternoons reading *Le Monde* in cafés would impart to me some of the intellectual sophistication that I associated with France and its great figures. And of course, I had a vague notion that in France, that remarkably beautiful country filled with remarkably talented, self-assured people, I would surely absorb useful lessons in the connoisseurship of life itself. It wasn't an accident that the rest of the world admired the French so much. I admired them too.

Like most children of the 1960s, I had read Camus and Gide, Sartre and Malraux, not to mention Hemingway and Fitzgerald, who were Parisians in their way, as were Gertrude Stein and Alice B. Toklas, whom one did not so much read as read about. I had seen *Jules and Jim* and *Children of Paradise*, Charles Aznavour in *Shoot the Piano Player*, Jean Gabin in *Grand Illusion*, Louis Jouvet in *Drôle de Drame* and *Hôtel du Nord*. I thought I understood something of existentialism, postimpressionism, surrealism, even structuralism, that most difficult of the century's schools of thought, all of which were creations of the French mind. And even if I did not understand these things as well as I would have liked, I took as a given the preeminence of France's creative genius in the West. I assumed that to be *un homme du monde*, as they say, it wouldn't be a bad idea to know something about France.

The country was different then, of course, in the late 1960s, different from now in some of the same ways that the United States is different. The great leftist intellectuals, Sartre foremost among them, still held sway. France—or at least that part of France that went to the Sorbonne or drank coffee on the rue de Buci—was determinedly anti-American, pro-Arab, rhapsodic about the future programs of the revolutionaries in Vietnam and Cambodia, many of whom, after all, had drunk coffee sitting in the same Left Bank chairs in the same studiously drab cafés a generation or so previously. The students' own "revolution" of 1968 was still fresh in the memory, and every once in a while some renewed internecine strife would break out among university factions, and a classroom would suddenly be transformed into a battleground, with desks overturned, chairs hurled through the air, and the losing side in the struggle decamping through the windows and jumping into the street below. It was as Michelet said about disunity and discord. The great good fight, the just struggle, of those days centered around a magazine called *La Cause du Peuple*, a Maoist pamphlet favoring a "proletarian France," which nobody in particular read but which had been banned by the government, leading Sartre, when he was not giving exhortatory speeches to student groups about Palestinian rights, to become its editor in chief and to campaign on its behalf by selling copies of it in the streets. De Gaulle, as many knew, had once explained that Sartre could not be repressed by the police. "You don't put Voltaire in prison," he had said.

De Gaulle died a few months into that first of my stays in France, and he was, significantly, buried in the little town of Colombey-les-deux-Églises, where he had always retired when not in power. I could see the symbolic importance of the passing of the man who had made France great in the world again, after the humiliation and shame of defeat in World War II, even though his manner of doing so was often infuriating to France's allies. De Gaulle had already stepped down from the presidency of the Fifth Republic, which he had created in 1958, and the Élysée Palace was occupied by his handpicked successor, Georges Pompidou (whose own protégé, Jacques Chirac, became prime minister, first in 1974 and again in 1986). The newspapers and magazines announced with pomp and solemnity de Gaulle's departure from this world. But the fact was that both he and Pompidou were cordially hated by the students and the leftist intellectuals whose company I kept. I remember the anarchist satisfaction, the cries of glee—shameful to think back on it now—when de Gaulle's death was announced.

Perhaps it is only in retrospect that I now hear a certain hollowness, a phony bravado, in those claims of joy. One of the major differences between French and American students in those days was that the former were patriotic, proud of France, even though they did not talk about it that way. The latter were antipatriotic, their common ground with the French being their own anti-Americanism. The students and leftist intellectuals saw in de Gaulle the heritage of the vaingloriousness, the stuffiness, the privilege, the elitism, the deep and abiding conservatism, of France, and they disliked him for that, and for the distant, arrogant, unsympathetic attitude he had shown during the 1968 riots.

But to my foreign mind, there was also a tight knot holding the students and the Gaullists together. It was the essential, identifying idea that France was, despite its inner turmoil, a beacon of illumination for the rest of the world. After all, Victor Hugo, the nineteenth century's representative adversary of haughty political power, the sworn enemy of that premature, foolish Gaullist, the emperor Louis-Napoleon Bonaparte, had said: "Without France, the world would be alone." De Gaulle's similar comment was: "France cannot be France without grandeur."

So many of the predominant attitudes changed in the decade before I returned to France as a journalist in 1984. Sartre's politics had been put aside. Anti-Americanism had been replaced by an almost (not quite) unabashed admiration of the United States. The trendy armchair revolutionists of the Left Bank cafés had given way to what were rather grandly called the New Philosophers, the champions of a school of thought that proclaimed, in essence, the virtues of bourgeois democracy and condemned the dangers of totalitarianism—which, as has been pointed out by many, they had just discovered for the benefit of the rest of the world.

Despite the changes, however, the two strands of national pride earlier represented by de Gaulle and by the rebellious student masses had come together, and the embodiment of this process was François Mitterrand, de Gaulle's chief political enemy for many years, who became president of the French Republic in 1981. Mitterrand, the first Socialist ever to hold real, unopposed, full power in France, leapt into new government expenditures, trying to fulfill his campaign promise of more rewards for less work for the working class. But at the same time, he maintained what always appeared to me to be an entirely Gaullist conception, not only of France but of the French presidency. He remained aloof, reserved, politically above it all; publicly austere; overtly, stirringly patriotic.

The one thing that did not change in the decade between my two periods of residency in France was the consensual conception of the country as a fundamental force for good in the world, with the accompanying idea that nothing should be allowed to stand in the way of its national interest. Mitterrand, for example, pursued with enthusiasm the nuclear weapons program that the Socialists had denounced less than a decade earlier. He maintained the "special relationships" with the dictatorships of Africa that had once been colonies; he kept a careful distance from the United States, the allied superpower whose political and cultural might was seen, in many ways, as just as threatening as Soviet military power coming out of the East.

I remember visiting in 1986 a top adviser of Mitterrand's in a small private dining room at the Élysée Palace, access to which was granted to me from time to time by virtue of my duties as the *Times* correspondent in Paris. We ate surrounded by a certain faded imperial splendor—the Élysée, if truth must be known, is grand and imposing but also a bit tarnished, like Grandma's box of heavy sterling silver—and we talked, among other things, about France's refusal a few weeks earlier to allow the United States to overfly its territory on its way to bombing Colonel Muammar Gaddafi's Libya, a refusal that, on a personal level, had mightily annoyed me and seemed a classic sort of arrogant, uncooperative Gaullist reflex, one that had given a rare public unity to both the right and the left in the country.

"France is the only country in Europe that has not simply become yet another star on the American flag," the adviser said, not concealing a certain pride in this. "And we are the only country that can do this." Perhaps he was right. The Germans, while economically far more powerful than the French, have no nuclear deterrent and, in those days before the rush toward reunification, were the immediate stake in the East-West competition in Europe, and thus could not mark themselves off from American policy. Moreover, their role as aggressor earlier in the century might disallow them from being the political leader of Europe even after reunification is achieved. The British can afford to see American predominance as a natural extension of Britain's experience, which softens their own loss of influence. Only France has the capacity, and experiences the necessity, according to Mitterrand's adviser and many others, to design its own foreign policy independently of the United States.

. . .

MITTERRAND, like de Gaulle, put the stress on the national greatness—never on the national flaws. As president, he became as adept as de Gaulle at listing the national accomplishments, pushing the *idée fixe* of French greatness in the world. And he has reasons.

France, after all, is a nuclear power, capable of lighting the final conflagration. It has no empire anymore, but its power and influence extend into the Pacific and, more so, into its former empire in Africa, where French troops keep the peace and tens of thousands of French citizens still run almost as much of the show as they did in the full, unembarrassed flush of imperialism. French policy, pursued steadfastly and with considerable consensus within the governing class, defeated Gaddafi's designs on Chad in the mid 1980s. France, in concert with Germany, is still the spiritual heart of the European idea, the notion that the Common Market could one day be another sort of superpower—and at the same time, France over the years has done more than any other country to sabotage that idea in the service of its conception of independent action and glory. De Gaulle's idea that France, despite its defeat in World War II, could play a major power role was reflected as late as 1986, when Mikhail Gorbachev chose to come to Paris in his first official visit to the West—and the French were happy to have Gorbachev confirm the perception they already had of themselves.

The French developed the European high-speed train and the Concorde supersonic airplane—not to mention the Airbus, now the world's major competitor with the American aviation giants—and they are the leaders in the European space-launch program. They have a computerized information service, known as Minitel, that links millions of home and office telephone users to an extraordinary array of services, from looking for a mistress to making airplane reservations—something neither the Japanese nor the Americans nor even the West Germans have developed. Outside the political-technological realm, French culture, its political thought, its symbolism as an epicenter for both the style and the art of living, all mark the country as an important one. When the French change governments, when they have quarrels in the Middle East, when terrorists strike here (as they did, devastatingly, in September 1986), when students demonstrate en masse in the streets against an educational reform, when a chief curator of paintings at the Louvre Museum is indicted for allegedly trafficking in a stolen painting (he was subsequently exonerated), or when there is a debate over suggestions that a phonetic spelling system should take the place of current orthography, even when a jailed convict, developing a new method of evasion, escapes from prison in a helicopter piloted by his girlfriend, it can be, and has been, front-page news in America.

Moreover, the idea that France is no longer what it used to be should not take on the quality of a funeral oration. Never have I lived in a country whose standard of living was higher or where the overall quality of life was better. This reminds me of a standard line among many foreigners in the country, which goes something like this: "France is not what it used to be. There is nothing going on in the country compared to what used to be the case; but live someplace else? Whatever for? France is the only place where I would really be happy."

Among the elements in allowing for this happy living—and let there be no mistake, the French themselves love living in their own country —is that paradoxical transformation of the French in this century accompanying the slipping away of their global power. The French since the end of World War II have become happy. They are sensible, so sensible that it is difficult to imagine that a mere half century ago— indeed, up until the end of World War II with its collaboration and postwar *règlements de comptes*, the settling of scores—the French were torn asunder by their civil divisions. And yet despite this strife-ridden recent history, the most violent perhaps of all the European countries, France about twenty years ago abruptly dispensed with its most unresolvable divisions, so that today, irreconcilable class struggle seems far more common in Great Britain than in France, wrenching disputes over a country's role in the Western alliance more characteristic of West Germany or Holland. There is an extraordinary pragmatism among the French, often concealed by their love of debate; their delight in expressing their differences, in airy philosophizing; their sadistic pleasure in finding the other foolish. The French function well, even if they don't always think so. They have found a happy balance between the needs of individual initiative and those of collective welfare, and, perhaps more important, between the requisites of freedom and a shared sense of civic responsibility. The French, after all, while priding themselves on a certain anarchism of thought, have in the past generation or so rarely passed into anarchism of action. They fight bitterly among themselves with words and, at the same time, have reached a tolerant sort of consensus that they themselves rarely admit. France has universal military service and virtually no draft evasion; it places great reliance on nuclear power, both peaceful and military, but suffers from no antinuclear movement of any importance; it enjoys untrammeled cultural choice and openness but has fewer of the punks, skinheads, and other rebellious extremes so abundantly produced in England, Germany, Holland, and Sweden. It bursts with the leftover rhetoric of class struggle and labor strife, but if a strike lasts more than a few days, it is seen as an extraordinary occurrence. By almost any realistic standard in the world today, France is a success.

And yet, of course, there is no denying that the subversive notion of France no longer being what she was has a clear ring of truth. One of the themes of this book—perhaps its principal one—is that the major event of recent French history is the country's fierce, stubborn, and, I believe, even admirable battle against a lapse into a sort of great power's middle age. It is the French disinclination to stop believing in the country's preeminence. Alexis de Tocqueville, the nineteenth-century liberal, described France as having the memory of great power but no longer disposing of the means to exercise it—a contradiction that got the country into very serious trouble a bit after de Tocqueville's time, particularly in its vainglorious and self-defeating complacency toward Germany, which resulted in the utter, miserable debacle of 1870.

The French often refer to their country as the *hexagone*, which is more than a mere description of its roughly six-sided shape. It reflects the perverse satisfaction, suggested by the character in the Claudel play, in being incomprehensible to the rest of the world. The term *hexagone* suggests a spiritual condition, usually an exclusive one, meaning that only the French can really understand the French, that they are, in their difference and in their exoticism, unbridgeably apart from the rest of the world. Another expression suggesting the same sort of impenetrability is *franco-français*, Franco-French, which refers to something so determinedly and peculiarly French in nature as to be not merely mysterious but uninteresting to all other peoples. When a book published here is called Franco-French, it means that it is unpublishable, virtually unreadable, outside the *hexagone*, even if it was a major best-seller inside it. Conversely, the French, who used never to be able to learn foreign languages, have been making their adjustments to what they sometimes call "Anglo-Saxon hegemonism." Many French in positions of responsibility in business, government, cultural life, and elsewhere read the *International Herald Tribune* or the London *Financial Times* every day as accompaniments to their reading of *Le Monde*, *Le Figaro*, and *Libération*, the three most commonly read Parisian papers. But there is no international *Le Monde* being intended for publication in the lands of Anglo-Saxon hegemonism. It has long been an expectation of small countries, whether Sweden or Singapore, Israel or Iceland, that they will know others better than others will know them. The French now are acquiring that expectation.

In the summer of 1987, the newspapers were suddenly full of this theme, related to the frequent concern about their unexportably hexagonal character. The question, already asked a century ago by de Tocqueville, was abruptly being asked again: Is France in decline? The debate started, as far as I could tell, as a cover story in the newsweekly *Le Point*, entitled "Inquest into the Decline of France," which elucidated three stages in the French attitude toward the country's own relative world power. First, de Gaulle inspired in them the dream of great power, the magazine said. Then, in 1976, it recalled, President Valéry Giscard d'Estaing announced that France was a "middle-sized power." Finally, in the spring of 1987—we journalists tend to think of all things as specific events occurring at clearly identifiable moments—"they discovered, or, rather, they admitted to themselves, that it is not the first among the middle-sized powers."

Soon the theme was picked up by the politicians, especially Mitterrand, but only to provide a negative response to the question. "Decline? I don't believe in it," Mitterrand said on a trip to Normandy. "France has no reason to abandon itself to the inevitability of dangers." Raymond Barre, a former prime minister and a man who would like to be president, brought some attention to himself by labeling as "ominous" the whole debate. Barre, who had the advantage of being out of the government at the time, allowed that France in 1980 has been in the "second rank" among nations. "Now we are in the fourth or fifth rank, and we continue to slip," he said. Barre evidently would attribute the decline to the Socialist years, which began in 1981. Another major political figure, Chirac, would no doubt have liked to do the same thing. But Chirac at the time of the debate was, inconveniently, France's prime minister. And so, to combat the "morose" mood, the "pessimism" in the air, as he put it, he laid down the law. "France is not in decline," he said.

The press persisted, however, in raising the dread specter. A new though not very appealing word was created—*déclinose*, the disease of pessimism. *Le Monde*, still the most serious newspaper of France, began publishing commentary. "As soon as the subject of decline comes up, the politicians have to reject the worrisome spectacle, fearing to appear to lack confidence in their country," Alain Touraine, a distinguished sociologist, wrote on the newspaper's front page. "However, it is the rumor that is true, not their rather too reassuring speeches." A poll, also reported on *Le Monde*'s first page, showed that 56 percent of the French agreed with the statement "The decline of France is a reality." Asked by *Le Point* whether France was in an economic decline, 68 percent of the population replied in the affirmative.

The question, of course, should have been: decline in comparison to what? If it was to the eighteenth century, the answer would have to be yes, the country is no longer a world power, certainly not in the grand historical sweep, and certainly not now that the prospect of German reunification threatens to knock France a rung or two down on the comparative European ladder. Perhaps, though, if we limit our purview to this century alone, the rumored decline is a bit like the "new house" of Marcel Pagnol, which the great novelist and film director from nearby Marseille described, in *The Glory of My Father*, as having been new for a very long time. But the very fact that the French, who are great self-examiners, became gripped by the issue is a symptom of a certain loss of confidence, further evidence of the national effort to struggle against what that adviser to President Mitterrand saw as a variant of the English disease, an acceptance of a middle-level status in the world. De Gaulle himself, in a quirky and much debated remark, once referred to the Jews as "an elite people, sure of themselves and domineering." I have always found the remark strange because it seemed to apply so aptly to the French themselves—or, at least, to de Gaulle's own aspirations for his people, perhaps even his illusion about them. Since de Gaulle disappeared from the scene, followed a few years later by Malraux, in 1976, by Sartre, in 1980, and then by Raymond Aron, in 1983 and France thus seemed bereft of its larger-than-life twentieth-century figures, the French themselves have become collectively less sure of themselves but, at the same time, unwilling to accept anything less than a glorious fate.

B UT I F the French fret and worry about their decline, real or imagined, they do so in the service of a particular type of glory, one perhaps unique in history and one that, depending on how you look at it, can seem the epitome of arrogance and haughtiness, or an admirable quest to project values and ideas. Even in economic and political decline—if decline it is—the French insist that they represent something finer than mere wealth and power. More, perhaps, than any other European people, they have succeeded in creating an aura around themselves, accepted both inside and outside the country. It is that France is greater than the sum of its parts. It stands for things. The Declaration of the Rights of Man is one; the notion that French is the language of love and of civilization itself is another. De Gaulle's actual oft-quoted phrase was: "I have a particular idea about France." Exactly what the particular idea was, de Gaulle always left unspecified. And yet few can doubt what the general meant. It was that France was just that, an idea toward which reality should strive. And the idea was not only of glory and prestige, though it certainly was those things as well; it was also an idea of brilliance, genius, even conscience.

The issue, particularly when viewed by outsiders, has aspects both of the solemn and of the ridiculous. I remember that once when I was working in Paris for the *Times* there was a fire in an upper floor of the building whose ground floor housed Fauchon, the famous gourmet food emporium. For me, as a resident of Paris, the food capital of the world (another element of France's cultural centrality), Fauchon always seemed a highly overpriced and extremely pretentious grocery store patronized by the kind of people who buy for the sake of the label rather than intrinsic quality. Fauchon's, I felt then and still feel now, is not the Louvre, just as a great meal is not the *Mona Lisa*. But for the sober *New York Times*, acceding to the status of France as an arbiter of good taste and elegance, the Fauchon fire was a major event, front-page news. The store was viewed as more than just a store. It was an embodiment in its way of nothing less than the French vocation to instruct the world in the finer things of life. In this sense, the French do not merely like to eat well; they like to exaggerate the activity of pleasurable nourishment, transform it into a high cultural event in which they are the world's leaders—and the world acknowledges their right to the role.

There is something about even the trivial and frivolous sides of greatness that captures the spirit. When Mitterrand visited the United States in 1984, he was asked during a trip to California what he thought of the wine. Now, Mitterrand's visit there centered on California high technology; there was a discussion with some of the American leaders of Silicon Valley, during which the president of France seemed to be facing something new and daunting, a virtuoso combination of scientific genius and risk-taking entrepreneurship that simply does not exist in France, not with that scope or at that level of revolutionary vision. And yet the questions at Mitterrand's press conference were not about microchips or French software or the absence in France of private venture capital. It was rather a reverential one about wine. Did the California wines measure up according to the French yardstick of quality? The French president, who has always managed to combine a certain Gaullist hauteur with a highly democratic discourse, did not exactly answer the question. He let it be known that the California wines were enjoyable; they were all right, even in some instances quite excellent, he said. And then the conversation turned to French wine imports. There are a lot of countries that send their wine to the United States, Mitterrand said. Italy sends more than France does, he went on, adding: "But French wine is more expensive because it is more highly esteemed."

Esteemed. The word reverberates with the stylish side of that special French aura. Italian wines may be just as good. Surely many of them are in the same class as the best Bordeaux and Burgundies. But French wine, like French taste, is more esteemed. It is not by accident that the French, in keeping the world company, gave it such words as *savoir-faire* and *savoir-vivre*, which mean, in essence, skill and taste.

And then, of course, there is the grander part of the French image. It was the French, after all, who dressed their pursuit of imperial power in the nineteenth century—conquering Indochina and the western half of Africa, to add to the various scattered possessions around the world that were already theirs—in the vestments of a pretty phrase, *la mission civilisatrice*, "the civilizing mission," while more down-to-earth, less idealistic peoples, such as the British, the Dutch, the Germans, conquered with a good deal less fancy talk, simply to enhance their wealth and power. The country of the Enlightenment, of the Revolution, of the Declaration of the Rights of Man and Citizen, has at numerous times in its history pursued its grandeur as if it were a sort of rescue mission for the rest of mankind.

In 1984, Paris was in the midst of celebrating the fortieth anniversary of its liberation from German occupation, reliving history by, among other things, a giant sound-and-light show projected against the ornate facade of the City Hall. Never mind that the armies of Britain, the United States, and Canada, which had made the liberation possible, were barely mentioned in the celebrations. One of the great moments of forty years earlier, determinedly remembered during the festivities, was de Gaulle's entrance into the city a few days after it was freed and the speech in which he talked about Paris—"Paris saved, Paris free, Paris liberated by our own hands." Liberated by our own hands was certainly an incomplete, even a fanciful, description of the event, though the Allies did indulge the Free French forces and allow them to enter the evacuated city ahead of the larger armies. But de Gaulle was already projecting forward the need of France to resume what he saw as its place in the world, as a beacon as well as a power. Similarly, when Mitterrand, that self-proclaimed Socialist and, I believe, unproclaimed Gaullist, gave speeches in the summer of 1987 denying those persistent, troubling, obsessively repeated reports of the country's decline, he was not speaking merely of the gross national product. He was speaking of France as a light unto the nations.

In the final analysis, France, more perhaps even than my own country, is an idea toward which a great collective effort has tried to shape reality. The ineluctable element of size and the force of global homogenization are against it. So, too, are the forces of history. And yet both the French and the rest of the world believe now and will continue to believe in a certain imaginary country, a France of the mind, an ideal both to remember and to strive for.

"Our country," Michel Charzat, a Socialist parliamentarian, has written, "has been, all during its past, a history of illusion. Each generation has forged a certain image of France. . . . Few nations owe as much as ours does to the imagination and to the violence of its people." There are discrepancies between what is imagined about France and what actually exists, between the country's goals and reality, between esteem and unblinkered judgment. There is something at times pathetic and laughable, or perhaps it is only sorrowful, in seeing a country that no longer enjoys great power attempt to portray itself as a colossus. There is a sense in which the French live on a kind of past capital, nibbling unconsciously away at the foundations of their very imaginings.

I do not mean by this that I intend this book to be a portrait of a distressed people obsessed by a loss of stature and importance. The average Frenchman does not lose sleep over this issue. Not everybody requires his children to undergo the humbling experience of witnessing the near absence of France from American television screens. The French are too interesting, too diverse, too *hexagonal*, to be reduced to a single preoccupation. And indeed, this book was not written to prove any particular hypothesis; my aim is not to buttress a position, to foment an argument, to pin the French down, for I knew that the more I might have attempted to classify them, the more ungraspable they would become. I have tried instead to draw a somewhat interpretive portrait of them, hoping that in the end some notion of what they are really like and how they got that way would emerge.

At the same time, I don't want to fall into the relativistic trap that would make impossible any conclusive statements about them at all: to elucidate no characteristics, to arrive at no judgments about their culture, political, moral, or intellectual. I frankly do not like books that start out from the premise that matters are too complex to allow for any generalizations. You do need to keep themes before you. Thus it is that, not unexpectedly but without definite intention, one thematic result of the writing of this book has been the emergence of the contrast between the French consciousness of decline and the equally strong French attachment to the values of moral transcendence. The theme is appealing not merely because it reflects reality but because there is something awesome in it. Who, after all, is to say that owing something to the imagination does not call for a sort of higher reality, or, at least, that it does not stimulate the admirable ambition of a people to count for something? I am, even after quite some time living in France and reporting on it, perplexed over whether the phenomenon of a country that must possess grandeur if it is to be itself is inspiring or simply ridiculous. I even suspect that the French themselves, in the privacy of their hearts, are in these waning years of the twentieth century—particularly with the apparent end to the Soviet military threat and the disintegration of Communism in Eastern and Central Europe—tiring of the necessity to be great. And if I am borne out in this suspicion, its confirmation would be an aspect of decline unmentioned by the Cassandras cited above. Assuredly, it is clear that the effort to associate the nation with a certain glory, both material and spiritual, often against overwhelming odds, is a principal pattern discernible in French twentieth-century history. It accounts for much of the country's present nature and identity, its problems, even its political evolution and the way it confronts the scary ghosts of its past. It underlies much of the description that I shall attempt to make of what I like, in glib moments, to think of as "the imaginary country," meaning that place that exists in the sometimes feverish mind of the French as they strive to live up to an ageless aspiration.

I

――――

FRANCE DEEP AND FRANCE PARISIAN

Its white houses with their pointed roofs of red tile extend down the slope of a hill where clumps of vigorous chestnut trees mark the slightest bends. The Doubs runs several hundred feet below its fortifications, built long ago by the Spaniards and now in ruins.

STENDHAL, *The Red and the Black*

1

The Miracle of the Whole

THE PLACE is called the Mas Corbières. It is high up, perched near the crest of a valley overlooking a splendid terrain of terraced vineyards and gardens, goat trails, fruit trees, and a dozen small streams descending into the Hérault River, and it is about as good an example of what the French call *La France Profonde*, "Deep France," as you can find. I stumbled across it one summer during a walk through the *garrigues*, the scrubby green hills, of the Cévennes, a rugged, poor, wet, unfashionable district in the south, lying about fifty miles north of the Mediterranean, just across the Rhône River from the more chic and expensive, drier and more populated region of Provence. The *mas*, a term meaning roughly "hamlet, farmstead, small agricultural outpost on the outskirts of a village," lies along a stony path, lined with stunted chestnut trees and berry-bearing shrubs, between the village of Notre-Dame-de-la-Rouvière, a single-belfry habitation with one, all-purpose store, and the top of the valley wall.

It is a half-ruined collection of two-story stone buildings, about ten or twelve altogether, that seem to have built themselves up like coral on the cleft of the valley, the sort of arrangement that, when viewed from above, looks like the crackling on old pottery. A sign at the first hut along the pebbled path, overhung with wild apricots, says FRÈRES LIRON, referring, I learned later, to three bachelor farmers who live in spare circumstances on the premises. The detritus of subsistence agriculture is amply spread out around the *mas*, which reeks powerfully of manure. Goat droppings are everywhere; here and there a pot of bright begonias has been put on a window ledge. Roses climb a few of the walls, dropping petals onto passages of loosened stones. Earthen court-yards are shaded by heavy growths of vines.

Like most ancient rural habitations in France, the Mas Corbières is made entirely of stone, except for the roofs (where there are roofs), which are of slate or tile, the latter a faded rust color. Irregular, crumbling steps lead up and down through the collection of dilapidated buildings, which seems to have been constructed, one layer after another, over a long period of time, even as it was being worn down by the elements. A disused washing machine leans against a supporting wall, which is itself patched with dry yellow moss. A wooden table covered with an oilcloth stands in the middle of a yard. There are some pots and pans, an old, empty, dark-green wine bottle or two, a glazed earthenware jug in two tones of brown. A single electrical line goes from one building to the next. The walls of half of the houses are crumbling away. Roofs have caved in. Grass, shrubbery, purple and yellow wildflowers are interspersed prettily among the loose stones. Tawny chickens wander about, pecking the splotched ground. Some of the buildings have new roofs and windows and other signs of care and restoration. There is a sound of flowing water from one of the many streams that lead down from the top of the valley. This could be paradise, this cluster of pic-turesque stone ruins, inviting restoration, transformation into a little handicrafts colony, set amid green hills and valleys towering over spar-kling streams. But for now, and perhaps forever, it is poor, unkempt, malodorous, and backward—and about as far from the legendary glitter and glamour of France as you can get.

P ARISIANS use the term *La France Profonde* in a good-humored, bemused, condescending sort of way to refer to the many rural places where, it is assumed, a vaguely old-fashioned, obsolete system of values and habits has survived even in this most modern, progressive, and free of countries. Americans talk metaphorically about "the sticks"—Peoria, say, or places in the Deep South, which represent nonurban America, with its slower pace, its supposedly more ineradicable prejudices, its presumed social conservatism, its boredom, but also its comfort, its ease, its down-home authenticity, its simpler, easier, more wholesome flavor, of the sort that makes for good locales in the filming of advertisements for whole-wheat breakfast cereals.

The Parisian view of Deep France is similar but more pejorative, despairing, even if numerous urban French families have their roots and their country houses there. For the big-city sophisticate, Deep France is funny, crusty, truculent, ignorant, blinkered, and obedient to authority. There is no doubt that the Parisian mind is capable of distinguishing between an economically harsh rural landscape—such as that of the Mas Corbières—and a more prosperous rural setting, which would also make up part of that large, vague category known as *La France Profonde*. There are places entirely colonized by the Parisian way of life, where some local color, an old stone church or crenellated rampart festooned with vines, perhaps a medieval fortress squatting atop a hill, has been enhanced by the addition of a very pricey and ultra-chic three-star restaurant—Vézelay, in the heart of Burgundy, or Les Baux, in Provence, are examples—out of which, after lunch, emerge tipsy demoiselles wearing Cartier pins and leather pants. But *La France Profonde* as an intellectual category suggests something rather unrefined, naive, gloomy, often religious, hokey, and immutably unmodern, the sort of place doomed (or, for the nostalgics among us, blessed) to repeat age-old agricultural patterns of life, give or take a labor-saving device here and there.

During my years in France, whenever I was going outside one of the major cities, the reaction of my Parisian friends and contacts was a bemused "Ah, you're going to *La France Profonde*," as if my destination were on the other side of the earth. They refer to this distant place with mockery, embarrassment, and longing, all mixed together. They regard it as a place of origin that they have escaped, grown out of, like short pants; and indeed, one of the historical purposes of *La France Profonde* was to send forth from its very poverty the stream of rural emigration that enabled Paris to become one of the great cities of the world. Whatever emotion it evokes, Deep France is a real place for the French, a definite geographical entity, and that leads to certain questions. What does the concept actually mean? Is it merely a pattern of prejudice as outmoded and antiquarian as Deep France itself was alleged to be? Is it a smug assumption about the superiority of urban life and attitudes emerging out of Deep Paris? And if there is truth to the idea of a France lying out there in the depths, or perhaps in the heart of the country, that is truly different, stubbornly old-fashioned and parochial, a real and authentic France of habits and customs, values and beliefs, marking off an entirely different world from the urban part of the country, would knowing it produce an appreciation of the whole of a country of many parts whose Parisian nature not only has long dominated the overall image but determines the self-conception of the French themselves?

The whole of France, especially the spiritual whole, the idea of a single, centralized entity has always dominated our conception of the country. And yet any grasp of all of France has to start from the geographically evident proposition that it is a patchwork quilt, a jigsaw puzzle, of regions and localities, each of which holds its own particular qualities and pleasures. What, after all, would France be in the eyes of the world's Francophiles (myself included) without Burgundy or the Périgord, Champagne or Provence? And what gives these very different regions—besides their incorporation inside the same political boundaries—their Frenchness? The question is not an easy one, but I start here with *La France Profonde* because, whatever that notion may mean to supercilious Parisians, it is useful in framing a consideration of what France is, the relationship between the idea and the identity that it represents and the various parts that make it up.

I'VE IMAGINED a tour of the extremities of the country, a clockwise pilgrimage around the New England–sized territory of the forty million French that would be not only an entirely enjoyable excursion but also a short introduction to the heterogeneous array that makes up Europe's most politically centralized state. The regions of the periphery of France are neither more nor less French than the center, and I would not recommend visiting only them. You would miss too much if you did—the rolling wheat fields of Seine-et-Marne, the vistas and Renaissance châteaux of the Loire Valley, the rugged, gloomy, poetic scenery of Burgundy. You would miss the several landscapes that exist on the three-hundred-mile route between Paris and Lyon: first the pretty forested hills just south of the capital; then the sweeping wheat fields of Brie (famous for cheese), where you can see past the rows of poplars from one tree-shaded village to the next; then the undulating terrain between Berry and Burgundy; the vineyards and orchards all along the east bank of the Rhône to the ancient, discreet, Italianate town of Lyon. One of the remarkable things about France is, quite simply, its remarkable physical beauty, the special varnished glow of its landscape, the quality of light that inspired the impressionist painters, the wealth of the extraordinary endowment of its land.

France is the only country besides Spain that has long frontiers along both the Mediterranean Sea and the Atlantic Ocean (and, in the French case, the Atlantic's inner-European arm, the English Channel and the North Sea), a geographical fact that helps to explain France's spiritual and cultural mix of southern and northern European qualities, at once

Italian and Flemish, Dionysian and Apollonian, quick-tempered and calculating, austere and decorative, thrifty and extravagant, hard-working and hedonistic. The French over the centuries have shuffled and reshuffled themselves into the great national deck, so a predominant local personality is difficult to discern. And yet if you think of two great regions, north and south, the Loire River being the major climatic barrier between them, you do have the feeling in the former of a more austere character, one given form and substance by the rocky soil, the rawness of winter. The northerners are sparer, more private, restrained, unobtrusive, thrifty, prudent, laconic, compared to the more rambunctious, softer, extravagant, reckless, boisterous, sensuous southerners. The French, from Menton on the border with Italy to Quimper on the North Atlantic, love the outdoors, when the season permits. They are a people that adore the sun and the breeze. They are nature lovers, fishermen, hunters, gatherers around the al fresco café table. But given the climate, it is natural that the north is, by comparison, a largely indoor culture; the south, where the men gather under the plane trees for crepuscular games of *pétanque*, more exterior and extroverted. Walk along the quai in Trouville on the Channel, where the fishermen are stamping their feet on a misty morning selling their catch, and compare the scene to a fish market in Marseille. The one is a kind of French Maine, relatively subdued and quiet; the other is Naples, loud, colorful, full of hawkers' raucous shouts and cajolings. The first is in a setting of half-timbered houses and gardens, neat, calculated, dutifully tended, carved patiently out of the soil. The other is in the midst of burgeoning pastels, stained and unkempt buildings and yards, shops and cafés tumbling over each other without apparent plan or design.

France is a country of rivers that, augmented by canals, have made the country traversable by boat and barge since medieval times. It has several ranges of magnificent mountains and the remnants still of the montagnard way of life. It encompasses an inviting, fertile, well-watered temperate zone where some of the oldest cultivated land on earth is heavily sprinkled with the most enchanting villages and towns on the planet. Like other peoples, the French have ruined some of their natural patrimony with gas stations and tinseltowns, shopping centers and tank farms. But my subjective, unscientific estimate is that they have ruined it less. The Luberon Valley in Provence is an arid region of pastel colors, of mottled pink land, of olive and fig groves and vineyards that turn scarlet in the autumn, the ensemble of colors mingling harmoniously like those on the printed cotton cloth manufactured in the region; a few hundred miles away in Burgundy, the view from the basilica of Sainte-Madeleine perched atop the village of Vézelay is of a deep emerald green, of damp hardwood forests and icy streams. They are different but equally unmarred by human tastelessness. What joins them together aesthetically is a scrupulous attention to certain common details—the way, for example, that the roads are lined for miles by rows of trees, whether linden or poplar, oak or sycamore; the way the agricultural fields are defined by hedges; the way the villages are marked off by walls overgrown with vines, these same villages grouped around the church or cathedral and the market square like hands cradling pearls. These are characteristics common to the central regions of France and to the extremities. I choose a tour of the latter to stress the country's diversity, the miracle of its belonging to a single place and time.

One could begin, arbitrarily, in the northwesternmost part of the country, in Brittany, perhaps the most stubbornly different of the great French regions, similar in many ways to Wales or Ireland, with its seacoast towns and rugged promontories overlooking the Atlantic, its manicured villages of pristine white houses and sharply slanted slate roofs, and such Celtic names as Lannilis, Guingamp, Kernascleden. Because much of the region is within long weekending distance of Paris, it has been colonized by the owners of secondary houses, many of them small stucco affairs standing in curved rows in the midst of what once were cow pastures. But you can still find dairy herds grazing in vast expanses of heath running down to the sea, alongside of which are arrays of menhirs (standing stones) and burial chambers dating from the Neolithic era.

Breton nationalism has not been a genuine threat to the French nation since the counterrevolutionary uprising in Brittany known as the *chouannerie* took place between 1793 and 1796. The Breton women still wear idiosyncratic white hats, and there are summer folk festivals in places like Concarneau and Quimper, where traditional costumes are brought out of closets and stands sell delicious yeast pancakes called *kouign* unheard of in other parts of France. Still, as late as the early 1970s, local police banned bumper stickers with the initials BZH, an insignia for Breton nationalism. When the Socialists came to power in the 1980s, they wanted to give legitimacy to minority languages and cultures— these having become charming vestiges of yesteryear and no longer threats to the territorial or cultural integrity of France. The minister of culture, Jack Lang, reverentially citing "the right to be different," created an advanced degree in teaching that can be earned only in the Breton language at universities in Brittany.

Even that small step, which seems to have brought no major threat to French unity, was attacked as a blow to France on the grounds that—as a former Conservative prime minister, Michel Debré, argued at the time—such moves would "shatter the culture." By giving regional languages the "rank of official instruments of education and communication," Debré said, the Socialists were "working for the end of the nation, which is to say the end of democracy." The newspaper *Libération* took a more humorous view about the latest small sign of Breton difference. On its front page it published the phrase "my tailor is rich"— the opening line of the standard English primer in France—in six languages, including Alsatian, Occitan, Corsican, and Breton, in which it comes out as *pinvidik eo va c'hemener*. The newspaper's point was that a few people studying and teaching in Breton or in Occitan hardly mattered in France anymore. Debré's argument harked back to an older time, when the national unity could not, as it can today, be taken virtually for granted, when the forces of dispersion in diverse France seemed sometimes to be more powerful than the forces of cohesion.

Brittany is enormous, a great peninsula separating the English Channel from the Atlantic Ocean and, in itself, consisting of some 3.3 million people; it is a place that could threaten the national unity in the unlikely event the notion of regional autonomy or ethnic separateness ever took hold again. France, after all, could, if circumstances had dictated otherwise, be more like Yugoslavia, a network of Croatians, Serbians, Slovenes, Albanians, Bosnians, Montenegrins, and others, bound together more by outside pressures and internal coercion than by voluntary cultural and national association.

East of Brittany is Normandy, a lush, emerald landscape that is a mere two-to-three-hour drive on the *autoroute* from Paris and, like Brittany, a world unto itself. This, in fact, despite the near-constant threat of rain, is my favorite of the French regions—a difficult choice to make. There is something about the mists rising in the morning off the pastureland, the profusion of blackberry vines climbing over stone walls alongside nearly abandoned dirt roads, the view of the sea from the high road between Honfleur and Deauville, that make up for me the images of a gentle paradise. There are sleek thoroughbreds grazing in the fields of the wealthy, and near stolid manor houses surrounded by flower gardens and fruit orchards; elongated stone barns in the midst of impenetrable hedges; the foamy, dry, gently inebriating apple cider drunk from pottery bowls, accompanying the splendidly earthy taste, the noble putrefaction, of cheese from Pont-l'Évêque or Livarot.

Normandy itself is many regions, the most obvious distinction being that between the fashionable coastal resorts of such places as Cabourg and Deauville (crowded in the summer), with their casinos and cabanas, and the always quieter, frequently damp, undulating inland regions of farms, orchards, and half-timbered villages stretching from Rouen in the east to Mont-Saint-Michel in the west. I think of the two Normandies as literary settings. One is the seaside Normandy of Proust, who wrote *Within a Budding Grove* at the Grand Hotel in Cabourg and whose upper-crust characters passed the social season there; the other is the interior Normandy of Flaubert, where the stupidity of convention and the tragedy of unfulfilled longings are set in places entirely unknown to the likes of Proust's Baron Charlus. Now the coastal district is touristy and inauthentic, each of the towns a collection of chic, highly orna-mented shops selling the prestige designer products. The Norman char-acter is barely to be found here. Inland are the "real people," the ones who don't go to the beach: milk farmers, orchardmen, small distillers of cider and Calvados, which they advertise with signs outside their masonry houses, trying to attract purchasers from among the streams of sightseers making excursions from the beach.

Normandy merges in the northwest with Picardy, along the border with Belgium, with its flatlands and windmills, its slag heaps and stilled, bankrupt steel mills, along with its soft landscape of field and forest. The frontier then runs southeast along the several microclimates of the Ardennes and Champagne, the one an area of dense forest and the other of open fields sitting atop chalk formations where the famous grapes are grown—both among the chief killing fields of World War I. Beyond that, still moving clockwise, illustrating, more than anything else, the long, sanguinary, futile, mutually self-destructive history of conflict be-tween France and Germany, are Lorraine and Alsace. The one is an area of dark forests and verdant, well-watered fields, of districts like the Vosges, where the landscape seems, somehow, even larger, more au-dacious, than that of the rest of France. The other is the broad western valley of the Rhine, where some of the world's greatest white wines are produced.

Farther south again is the region that Stendhal called the most beautiful in France, the Franche-Comté (meaning "Free County"), incorporated after a long military campaign by Cardinal Richelieu in 1674. The Jura Mountains, due north of Lake Geneva, are wild and wet, covered with deep snow in the winter, dotted with lakes, crisscrossed by white-water rivers; there, poor farming and small-scale tourist villages cluster around churches with distinctive square belfries. Plunging farther on the perimeter of France, one comes to the Savoy and the Dauphiné, south of Lake Geneva, site of the great Alpine ski resorts and thus, in season, among the more Parisianized districts of France. The very wealthy might have two places of escape from the capital: one, for the summer, just outside Deauville; the other, the winter residence, a ski chalet in Val d'Isère or, perhaps, Courchevel or Megève, beneath the snowy peaks and glaciers and elevated meadows of one of the world's geological wonders.

Again illustrating the sometimes apparently accidental shape of France, the Dauphiné, bequeathed to the eldest son of the king of France in the fourteenth century (the reason why the heir to the French throne was known as the Dauphin), has been judicially incorporated into France almost since the French nation took form under the Parisian kings. The Savoy region, while heavily influenced by French culture, remained politically under the control of the Italian dukes of Piedmont—except for a brief period when it was annexed by Napoleon. It became a permanent part of France by the terms of an 1858 agreement between Napoleon III, the first Napoleon's nephew, and Camillo Benso di Cavour, leader of Italy's unification—an agreement that was, in a practice unusual for the time, ratified by a free plebiscite in Savoy ten years later.

Savoy and Dauphiné are far in every way from, say, Normandy or Champagne, geographically as well as commercially. But more interesting, perhaps, the two Alpine districts are in most ways, though not geographically, far from the region just to the south, the fabulous Provence. Somewhere on the lower slopes of the Maritime Alps, the mountains give way to an identifiably Mediterranean landscape of lavender and thyme, fields of garlic and figs, and, finally, the fabled and, these days, seasonally overcrowded Côte d'Azur, the "Azure Coast," more commonly known as the Riviera.

Provence contains several worlds of its own. It ranges from such entirely different coastal towns as Saint-Jean-Cap-Ferrat, symbol of luxury and exclusivity, and Marseille, a tough town emblematic of ethnic intermingling, organized crime, picturesque harborside sinfulness, and common bustle. Saint-Jean-Cap-Ferrat is the West Palm Beach of France, only smaller; Marseille is Phoenicia and Chicago rolled into one. Provence contains the Camargue, a vast stretch of salt marsh just west of Marseille; it has Avignon, the walled town on the Rhône whose summer theater festival is one of the world's best; it has the principality of Monaco on the Italian border, great Roman ruins in Nîmes, Vaison-la-Romaine, and Arles (where Van Gogh lived and painted for a time); it has gorges cutting through limestone cliffs, the so-called Grand Canyon of Verdon, the high hills peering over Mediterranean coves, the rushing fountain of the Vaucluse. There are gastronomical meccas like Mougins, perfume-manufacturing centers like Grasse, seasonal focal points of culture and business, like the annual film festival at Cannes.

There are little villages set amid scrubby hillsides, where old ladies wearing black sweaters and long skirts follow herds of goats up and down stony paths and where Marcel Pagnol and Jean Giono set some of their greatest stories; there are casinos and hilltop fortresses, medieval abbeys and cloisters, art and handicraft colonies, vast high-rise condominiums for Parisian retirees, old stone houses with swimming pools, inhabited by vacationing interior decorators from New York and senior State Department officials from Washington. They eat well in Provence, better perhaps than anyplace else in a country where elaborate eating is commonplace. You can enjoy simple fare like roast lamb with Provençal herbs and ratatouille; or you can blow a couple of hundred dollars a person on something more elaborate, perhaps a filet of Saint-Pierre steamed in lettuce leaf, followed by quail stuffed with goose-liver pâté, then herbed salad, an assortment of goat cheeses, a white Burgundy to drink with the fish followed by a lubriciously red Châteauneuf-du-Pape, and finally a large, shallow bowl of fresh fruit smothered in a zabaglione sauce and gratinéed under the grill.

Onward, continuing clockwise. West of Provence is the Cévennes, where the Frères Liron occupy their lofty, decrepit perch. Here, devout, plain-living Protestants inhabit France's entirely unmenacing, tolerant Bible Belt, where the believers in a fundamentalist creed nurture their beliefs quietly, unassumingly, like the pietist sects that long ago came to North America from Germany and England. As the Mediterranean coast curves southward there is Languedoc, another of the fabled, distinct regions of France, the capital of the ancient language of Occitan and the center of the thirteenth-century Albigensian heresy (cited in today's guidebooks as an example of the region's independence of spirit); in this place of mountain retreats, centuries after the eradication of the Albigensians, France's Protestants sought places of refuge, from which, though they were persecuted, they were never dislodged. These days, like much of the south of France, Languedoc has received a large number of non-European immigrants, many from Spain but a more controversial number from North Africa, fueling a renewal of xenophobic, nativist sentiment in an area already familiar with the values of the blood feud, clan warfare, hot-blooded vengeance. Along the coast, the sun pours down on such Roman-era cities as Montpellier, Sète, Narbonne, and

Perpignan, with their Italianate seventeenth-century buildings, their ancient universities, their shady boulevards and narrow streets, their cafés, wine bars, outdoor markets, churches and cathedrals, their feel of the Levant, with which they have been trading for two thousand years. The dish identified with the region is cassoulet, a rich stew of white beans, sausage, fowl, and smoked ham. They drink light, spicy red wines of the sort that rarely make it onto the export market—Madiran, Côtes du Gard, Côtes de Roussillon. They force-feed geese and ducks to produce foie gras; they hunt for truffles; they smoke numerous kinds of ham, make pastries flavored with almond paste and pistachios, and put garlic into almost everything.

The border of France is formed here by the Pyrenees, stretching along a line running west-northwest from the Mediterranean to the Atlantic and containing, among other things, the population of French Basques whose traditional berets are one instance of a mode of haberdashery that became a poster image for the rest of the country.

Up the coast are such Atlantic fishing industry towns and holiday beach resorts as Hendaye, Saint-Jean-de-Luz, and Biarritz, the last of them once made synonymous with high fashionability by the empress Eugénie, wife of Napoleon III. Biarritz is a magical place, sitting on a lovely stretch of uncrowded, open coastline. The hotels are less expensive than those on the trendy beach areas of the Riviera and the English Channel. I once spent an entirely agreeable summer week living in a rented cottage farther up the coast in Cap-Ferret, where a buffer zone of untamed sand dunes descended to an unspoiled sea.

Cap-Ferret (not to be confused with Cap Ferrat on the Riviera) is west of Bordeaux, the center of the fabulous region of wines that can cost when new and not yet drinkable as much as fifty dollars a bottle or more. It is no doubt safe to say that more has been studied and written about the few square miles of vineyards surrounding Bordeaux than about any other comestible-producing territory in the world. There are two lessons in this. First, a cultural one: Bordeaux, with its high-priced and, it must be added, extraordinarily delicious agricultural product, is synonymous with the image of France as a place of connoisseurship, a domain where life takes place at the sensuously cultivated height of the human register. Second, a lesson in geography: In Bordeaux, microclimate, soil composition, and the orientation of the land to the sun are everything, the essential difference—or so the wine growers say— between wine at fifty dollars and wine at five dollars a bottle. Within a few yards of a great vineyard there can lie a mediocre one. Between

Graves, south of Bordeaux, and the Médoc, perhaps fifty miles north of it, are hundreds of different combinations of soil and climate, each of them producing a slightly different taste and value from the grape.

Then there is the rest: the flatlands along the Atlantic known as les Landes; the region of Charente, north of the Garonne River, where cognac is distilled; the Vendée and Poitou, from whose main port town, La Rochelle, the early French explorers set out to discover their portions of the New World; finally, again, the southern part of the rocky coast of Brittany, completing this particular *tour de France*. It leaves out very large portions of the country: besides Burgundy and the Loire River Valley, there is Limousin, Auvergne, the valley of the Rhône, the great wheat-growing, cheese-producing plateaus of Beauce and Brie, the valleys of the Marne, Seine, and Saône rivers, and much else containing that combination of human artistry and natural beauty that has always made France every foreigner's favorite second country. Still, even a tour of the perimeter demonstrates that whatever non-Parisian, "Deep" France is, it is diverse and heterogeneous.

Indeed, the tour underlines not just the extraordinary fact that France, politically speaking, is a single country but that it all partakes of a common, powerful culture. Whereas other great European cultures, in particular the German and the Italian, remained until just a historical yesterday fractured and fragmented into dozens, hundreds, of kingdoms and principalities, their genuine unifications taking place only in the nineteenth century, France, despite its great size and diversity, was a unified kingdom by the sixteenth century, with most of its various current far-flung parts—and these parts were far more far-flung centuries ago than they are today—incorporated into the crown by the eighteenth. Paris, the seat of the kings, gradually spread out, annexing feudatory lands, imposing the power of its culture and language, eventually creating the nation so powerfully centralized three hundred years ago that present generations have lost sight of the monumental difficulty of the task.

It was not inevitable that it turn out that way. The very notion of a uniformity to *La France Profonde* is a modern-day conception, one that leaves out the very important fact that it took a good millennium and more for the various parts of the country to be absorbed by the forces of homogeneity so prevalent today. The grossest division of the country, into essentially Mediterranean and northern zones, is in itself a historically powerful one that could plausibly have left behind, not a single country with a memory of fissures, but two countries that strove but failed to unite. If twentieth-century France had turned out to be several small states tied together in shaky federal bonds, rather than the most centralized country of Europe, a confederation including Normandy and Brittany, Occitania, the Basque country, Provence, Berry, Lorraine, Alsace, and Savoy, the explanation accounting for that outcome would in many ways be easier than the explanation needed to account for the actual outcome, that of a free people sharing a certain, if elusive, common identity.

Fernand Braudel, one of the great members of the school of historians who pioneered the study of geography as a historical determinant, talks in his affectionate and brilliant book *The Identity of France* of the land of *oc* and the land of *oïl*, the one being the south and the other the north. *Oc* means "yes" in the original, nearly disappeared dialect of the *Midi*, the south. *Oïl*, now spelled as *oui*, is the "yes" of the north. Braudel's point was that Mediterranean France, the land of olives and vines, apricots and mulberries, is a different world from "Atlantic" France, with its wheat, apples, and oaks. But it is also that the land of *oui* eventually imposed its culture, the price of uniformity, on the land of *oc*.

What explains the unity that emerged from this diversity? The historians have speculated on that question for decades, and to tell the truth, it has baffled them and it baffles me. The learned Braudel himself admitted in *The Identity of France* that the concept of France itself has always remained elusive. Braudel, who died in 1985, was the twentieth-century Michelet, but whereas the great nineteenth-century historian was the practitioner of literary history, the brilliant raconteur of Great Events, Braudel's post-Marxist history stresses not so much events as impersonal forces and influences, the conditions of material life, geography, conflicting economies as well as conflicting ideas. Michelet, who did more than any other figure to establish the Revolution as the central, creative event of the French identity, claimed that he saw in France "a person, a soul." Braudel's view is more diffuse, more complex, more evasive.

"The unity of France evaporates," he writes. "One feels as though one can grasp it at first; it escapes us; a hundred, a thousand Frances are in place, long ago, yesterday, today."

One explanation for the existence of France, offered and then, in part, rejected by the dissatisfied, skeptical Braudel, is that France is Europe's narrowest isthmus, a peninsula between the Mediterranean and the North Sea, which, compared, for example, to Germany, was relatively easy to cross via an ancient system of waterways and plains. France, some historians have pointed out, in this sense linked up the two great commercial civilizations of ancient times, northern Italy and the Low Countries, and the links themselves breathed life into France, gave it not only its character but its common characteristics. Its transportation network, according to this thesis, girded the national unity. It made possible, as Braudel puts it, "the conquest and the use of the whole of the French territory," and it imparted the sense of France as an entity, surrounded by such "natural" borders as the Pyrenees and the Alps, the ocean, the sea, and, dividing it from the Germanic domain, the Rhine River.

The other explanation begins from Paris and assumes that France, rather than a natural, veritably predetermined geographic unit, was the political creation of the rulers of Paris. It was a kind of imperial conquest, a gradual encroachment of a dominant culture over a lesser one, not an inevitable coming together of diverse elements. In this sense, Paris bears a role familiar to other histories and France repeats a common historical pattern: the conquest of a softer southern people, accustomed to the gentleness of climate, the relative ease of life, by a harder northern people—other, more frequently cited examples would be the Mongols and the Vikings—used to the harshness of climate, hungrier, more ambitious. The heavily populated Paris region, it has been pointed out, was a rich agricultural terrain. It was suitable for oats, which were essential for horses, the key ingredient in medieval military conquest. And gradually, Paris did conquer, for centuries spilling the blood of its young men over outlying lands, expending fortunes, razing towns and building fortresses, a costly process that threatened at times to bankrupt the state but that also produced the country, part Nordic, part Latin, that the world knows and loves today.

And so the question remains: If France is a richly endowed, variegated territory painted over by a veneer of Parisian conquest, do there remain the two great zones so dear to the Paris imagination, the zone of the deep country and the zone of the metropolis? If the creation of France was a miracle, did it nonetheless leave behind a subculture of the hinterlands to be uncovered in valleys and hilltops of the sort inhabited by the Frères Liron?

2

The Persistence of the Parts

ONE OF THE first journalistic efforts I undertook after arriving in
France in 1984 was to visit three villages near the city of Bourges,
in the Berry, each of which was claiming, in what the delighted Parisian
press called "the battle of the belfry towers," to be the exact geographical
center of France. The argument centered on three far from grandiose
monuments, one put up in each village to mark the supposed exact point
in question. The issue amused Paris. Even the humble scale of the stone
markers in each village suggested that the argument was a classic example
of petty, parochial, archaic concerns of the countryside, far different,
smaller, and sillier than the matters that would arouse the tempers of
sophisticated Parisians. I visited each of the villages, finding, first of all,
that while necessarily cheek by jowl on the map, all of them in the gently
undulating country south of Bourges, they were extremely different. One,
Saulzais-le-Potier, was a genuinely rural hamlet. It was little more than
a row of two-story stone houses decorated with painted wooden shutters
and surrounded by agricultural fields.

The mayor, a man named Maxime Chagnon, who had been the village
cobbler for forty years, submitted to an interview across the well-worn
counter of his dark little shop in the center of town. He wore a beret
and a heavy leather apron over a short-sleeved knit shirt, spoke with a
powerful local intonation, seemed a rather shy man, a bit flustered by
the attentions not merely of the national press but of a reporter who,
strangely, seemed to have come a very long distance for what surely
would seem, to his readers, a rather remote and unimportant quarrel.
The mayor identified himself as a member of the Socialist party. He took

me to see the Saulzais monument marking the center as calculated by a
certain Abbot Moreux, director of the astronomical observatory in
Bourges a century ago. It was inconspicuously placed in a small, shady
glen just off a country road outside town and consisted of a tapered
unpolished stone-and-mortar cylinder about ten feet tall, set on a square
cement pedestal and bearing an inscription attesting to the geographical
importance of the site it occupied. M. Chagnon gave me the classic quote
explaining his village's determination to fight the battle to the last. "We
don't want to be the center that is cast aside," he said. I did not know
if the humor was intentionally understated or simply unintentional.

The second village, Vesdun, was affluent and well groomed, not much
larger than Saulzais but more spruced up, neater, the houses a bit more
ornate, the shutters more freshly painted. The village prided itself on its
avocational cultivation of flowers, displays of which in roadside flower
beds and window boxes had, residents said, won it several prizes from
a horticultural organization that conducted an annual national contest.
Compared to the other two places, Vesdun was chic, stylish, sophisticated. It had constructed on the edge of town a round, waist-high mosaic
depicting the French *hexagone* in green, yellow, and brown, with itself,a
red dot, in the center. A village official taking me to see the monument
was able to specify the exact number of octagonal enamel tiles—sixty
thousand, he said—that had gone into the mosaic, designed and built
by a retired factory manager named Guy Grandmaire. Vesdun was once
a farming village, but it had become largely a place of secondary residences and retirement homes for Parisians longing for the quiet of the
countryside. The mayor, who was out of town on the day of my visit,
was a member of the Rassemblement Pour la République, the Rally for
the Republic, or RPR, the largest rightist political formation in the country, which enjoys more support among the affluent than among the poor.
The town had no hotel, no shops, and only a single restaurant, but it
had the good sense to realize that being the geographical center of France
in the age of tourism might have considerable economic advantages.
The town council, an official said, was due to meet soon to authorize
the manufacture of postcards and other souvenirs that could be sold to
passersby.

The third village was Bruères-Allichamps, a flat, unattractive, dusty
highway crossroads vibrating with passing trucks and well endowed
with gas stations and roadside cafés. The mayor, René Larguinat, was
a man of solid girth, closely cropped hair, and a no-nonsense, straight-
forward, disabused manner, who said he was a member of the Communist party. Most of the inhabitants of Bruères-Allichamps worked for

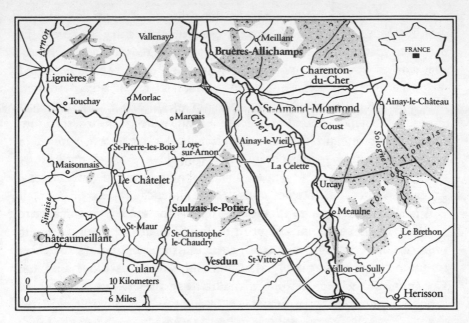

THE "CENTER" OF FRANCE

the railroad or in the Michelin tire factory in Bourges. The town was a kind of political red belt, as though a shard of the famous Communist party strongholds of suburban Paris, all sooty brick factories and sooty brick attached houses, had been transplanted a couple of hundred miles south. The monument that M. Larguinat took me to see was in the middle of the dusty, rumbling crossroads. It was an inscribed stone obelisk about ten feet high, atop a chipped plinth, but it was not all that Bruères-Allichamps planned as it strove to consolidate its claim to be the center of France. What made the town seem most deeply imbued with the hokeyness associated with Deep France was its intention to cover a fallow hillside overlooking the Cher River with a concrete abdomen, some forty-five by ninety feet in size, in which a spherical navel would presumably represent the town's pretensions in the ongoing dispute.

As the mayor put it: "For many years, being the center of France was our trademark. Now our neighboring villages are trying to take it away from us." M. Larguinat, though a Communist, had a clear commercial sense. Standing near the Café du Centre on the national highway, outside of which were metal stands selling the very sorts of postcards, tricolor pennants, and coasters in the form of the French *hexagone*, with a dot marking Bruères's location, that the town fathers of Vesdun were considering, M. Larguinat said the giant navel was necessary to protect the town's tourist industry. "In the last twenty years, the car has developed, tourism has developed, more and more people take vacations, so we have told ourselves that we have to do what we can to attract tourists here," he said. Already, Bruères boasted two pharmacies, two grocery stores, two butchers and two charcuteries, two bakeries, four restaurant-hotels, a doctor, and a mechanic's shop, all in a village of only 638 inhabitants. This vigorous commerce was made possible by the historic belief held by the rest of France that the village was the French geographical center—a status of considerable practical value.

And so here were three villages all roughly the same size, all eager to be seen as the geographic center of France, but each of them unique in political and economic character, their mayors representing the three traditionally competing political formations: Conservative, Socialist, and Communist. Their desire to win the battle of the belfries was colored with the sort of reverence, or perhaps absence of cynicism, that titillated the Parisians. The amused Parisian press assumed that the stakes in the struggle had to do with pride, glory, the longing for importance, when, in the Parisian mind, the striving for geographical distinction in itself marked what was parochial and small about Deep France. Paris, the spiritual center of France, does not need geographical preeminence. And indeed, there did seem to be an element of pride, a wish to be important, in the battle of the belfries, a yearning to partake, however much by unearned circumstance, of the overall French grandeur. But in fact, the issue for the three villages had just as much to do with practical matters as with the sort of modesty of ambition associated in Paris with Deep France. The authorities in each village knew that the geographical center of Paris, with a monument marking the spot, meant money, the sort of thing any Parisian can understand.

The differences among the three villages, their microclimates and microcultures, suggested the complexity of rural France; they reflected the diversity of the country as a whole, and that diversity, in turn, casts doubt on the Parisian notion of Deep France, raising the question: Is it possible to uphold a concept so vague, so subject to difference?

T HE PARISIANS, or at least many of them, insist that it is possible, even if they are a little vague on the definitions, even if, in this age of superhighways and television, certain aspects of the national French culture implant themselves ever more deeply into the rural consciousness.

Once I accompanied a French writer friend on a trip to Saint-Cyr-sur-Mer, near Marseille. Saint-Cyr-sur-Mer is just inland from what might be called the poor man's Mediterranean, well west of the expensive, more famous, and glittering destinations of the well-heeled, such as Antibes, Cannes, Saint-Tropez. It has something, however, that none of them have—an original iron cast by Bartholdi of the Statue of Liberty, the larger version, of course, being the one that Bartholdi made for New York. The statue, until some recent sprucing up of the town, stood partially obscured by trees on the edge of a pleasantly drab town square containing the driving school, the shoe repair shop, a hairdresser, and the Café de France, within which locals with mustaches play cards beneath shelves of football trophies and a calendar picture of a girl in a yellow bathing suit. The statue was part of the scenery, such that most townspeople were for decades unaware of the sculpted glory in their midst—until the Americans decided to make a big celebration of the centennial of their own Statue of Liberty in New York Harbor.

When they decided to celebrate their version of Liberty, the city fathers of Saint-Cyr-sur-Mer sent letters to Catherine Deneuve and Brigitte Bardot, France's most celebrated female movie stars, asking them to participate in the festivities, making it a point to assure them that both their travel expenses and their hotel costs would be covered by the town. And it was that touching, otherworldly bit of naïveté, summed up in the assurance that the Desmoiselles Deneuve's and Bardot's expenses would be covered, that suddenly struck my writer friend, until then a bit evasive on the definition of the concept, as the very quintessence of *La France Profonde*. "That's it," she said, lighting up with sudden revelation. She was talking about the worshipful parochialism, that openhearted ignorance of the way the world really worked, evidenced by the Deneuve-Bardot letter.

On the same visit to Saint-Cyr-sur-Mer, my friend and I went to see the local chatelain, the scion of the town's oldest family, still living in its most imposing mansion, thereby conforming to another stereotype of village France, which assumes the existence in every town of some remnant of the old feudal aristocracy living in the local château, holding a yearly reception for the townsfolk, being elected, as a matter of course, the town's mayor, renting out some land to tenant farmers, and clinging as much as possible to the old honors and prestige. The chatelain of Saint-Cyr-sur-Mer was elaborately polite, a bit stiff, and, in the view of both of us, rather opinionated (meaning that we did not agree with him). But what made him, for my writer friend, a denizen of Deep France was his use of the imperfect of the subjunctive, a peculiarity of speech roughly akin to an American speaking in iambic pentameter. The subjunctive, the elaborate form used to express doubt, uncertainty, surprise, or conjecture, is standard when used in the present tense among all educated French, whether Deep or Parisian, but the imperfect form disappeared along with dueling and ruffled collars among most of the French before World War II. In his movie *Manon des Sources*, Marcel Pagnol has the village schoolteacher use an occasional imperfect of the subjunctive as a way of demarcating himself from the simpler folk around him. But outside the homes of France's decaying rural aristocracy, it is rarely heard these days at all. Its reappearance in Saint-Cyr-sur-Mer in the mouth of the village chatelain struck my writer friend as another eruption of the archaic, perversely unmodern phenomenon I was trying to understand.

Farmers, according to some versions of what might be called Deepest France, sleep with their piglets in the winter in order to keep warm (I never understood if the piglets were supposed to warm the farmer or the farmer the tender piglets). Village idiots, squinting at the world through slitty eyes, are reported to wander the ancient, narrow streets in rather larger concentrations than one would normally find in the cities; they are the alleged products of centuries of inbreeding among close-knit family clans. Those who are not idiots are reputed to hoe and spade the soil during the day, wearing patched blue overalls, suspenders, dark plaid shirts, and berets roughly the color of the overalls, along with a heavy black coat that's hung over a fence post when the sun gets too hot. During the evening, especially during the summer, to escape their underilluminated and unventilated houses, they sit out on chairs by the side of the only road that goes through their village, the one that leads a few miles farther on to another village, just like it. These people are mostly elderly, since youth escapes Deep France to go elsewhere. They are weather-beaten and craggy; they are suspicious of "foreigners," by which they mean anybody not from the immediate vicinity, and they wear this suspicion in a sort of impassive stare when one of these "foreigners" should pass by.

It is these characteristics that create one of the most persistent Parisian beliefs about Deep France, which is that it never changes, or, at least, that it changes glacially. In truth, studies have shown that there is considerable mobility in France. The denizens of the villages are not necessarily able to visit the graves of their ancestors in the nearby church cemetery. But ethnically, the villages are less mixed. There are few synagogues or mosques there, not many Portuguese or Polish names. I have been a few times to a friend's house in Normandy, that blessed territory of half-timbered houses and emerald meadows where Madame Bovary lived out her tragic life. The town of Cambremer, population 915 (with 100 secondary residences), is typical of the apple-growing country, where the farmers ferment their own cider and distill their Calvados (an apple brandy), selling it to tourists. Here are the *l*'s and *m*'s, the two letters chosen at random, listed in the local telephone directory:

Regis Laffon	Lucienne Leprevost
Jean Lafitte	Therese Le Rumeur
Dominique Lafosse	Odile Lesachey
Maurice Lamare (boucherie)	Robert Le Saux
Philippe Lanos	Marie-Claire Leseigneur
Michel Lapièrre	Jean Lesenne
(pépinières de Cambremer)	Guy Letellier
August Lasseur	Bernard Levoy
Georges Lavalley	(boulangerie, pâtisserie)
Eric Laviec	Germaine Lie
Claude Labaillif	Remi Linant
(tapisserie, décoration)	Jeannie Longuet
Hubert Le Baron	Hubert Louvet
Aimée Le Breton	Jacques Maheu
Juliette Leclerc	Marius Mainfroy
Roger Lecoq	Maria Marcotte
Christian Lefebvre (transports)	Eric Marie
Marie Legrand	Denise Martin
Yvette Le Guern (hôtel, rest)	Jacques Martin-Gautier
Albert Lehericy	Alain Mathe
Olga Lemaitre	Claude Matrat
Marcel Le Masson	Jean-Paul Maurey
Genevieve Lemieux	Daniel Maurice
Annick Lemoine	Jean-Pierre Mezière (menuiserie)
Jean-Pierre Lemonnier	Bernard Monts
Charlotte Lenoble	Jean-Claude Morin (fleurs)
Jean Lepelletier	Jacques-Antoine Motte
Nicole Lepetit (bar, rest)	Pierre Mottelay

And so it is true that a certain traditional "Frenchness"—or, at least, a phonetic sort of Frenchness—is found in many of the villages, an ethnic homogeneity that some find very comforting. But the Parisian association concerns not only homogeneity. It has to do with an alleged primitiveness, one that has clear and accurate historic roots. In a scholarly book entitled *Peasants into Frenchmen*, the historian Eugen Weber has written: "There is a great deal of evidence to suggest that vast parts of nineteenth-century France were inhabited by savages." Professor Weber's thesis is that in the fifty or so years before the First World War, the French countryside changed dramatically, losing its untamed quality as well as its local customs, lore, and practices, and becoming integrated into Parisian France and the modern world. He cites numerous witnesses of the epoch, who describe not so much a Deep France as a Dark France, swampy, disease ridden, wild, inhabited by ignorant, superstitious, greedy, violent, dull, dispirited, and vicious cretins. Léon Gambetta, one of the heroes of the Third Republic, described the peasants as "intellectually several centuries behind the enlightened part of the country." There was, he said, "an enormous distance between them and us."*

The distance has, as Weber reports, narrowed considerably, but is it still enormous? There was, at least until recently, a strong cinematic version of rural France as a place of a certain inherent violence and cruelty, either presenting the possibility of escape to the Parisian world or imposing the necessity of stagnation, despair, futility, drunkenness, and insignificance. See one of the small-town films of Claude Chabrol, for example. One tells the story of a young man who returns for the first time in many years to his native village, especially eager to see the childhood friend he has left behind. The village is grim and forbidding, sinister and lugubrious, full of dementia and desperation. Even the local curé is deeply cynical. The prettiest girl in town is a slut, raped by the man who raised her. The childhood friend is drunken, brutal, and embittered.

It is not village France today, of course, but the images remained fixed nonetheless in the Parisian mind. In the summer of July 1985, the murder of a four-year-old named Gregory Villemin became a national obsession. The boy was found drowned in the Vologne River in the village of Lépanges, deep among the verdant hills and valleys of Lorraine, in far eastern France, near the German border. The mystery grabbed the French imagination as have few other recent events. There were countless magazine cover stories, television specials, and almost daily front-page newspaper stories for months. The murder had become a French obsession. I asked Philippe Séguin, the region's most influential national political figure, the reasons why. Among them, he ventured, was the fact that the drama had taken place against the background of a rural region "with

---

* Cited in Eugen Weber, *Peasants into Frenchmen: The Modernization of Rural France, 1870–1914* (Stanford, Calif.: Stanford University Press, 1976), p. 5.

its own mystique of remoteness and of the forest"—the mystique of a dark and mysterious place breeding a Faulknerian sort of nastiness. Other elements made the case fascinating—in particular, the way the police accused first one person of the murder and then another, the final suspect being none other than little Gregory's mother, Christine, whose name quickly became one of the best known in France. (She was indicted and jailed for two weeks, then released; the indictment still officially stands, but the trial has been postponed indefinitely, the French justice system often working in this mysterious way.) But I felt, with M. Séguin, that the crime tended to confirm some deep Parisian suspicion about Deep France as a place that was not merely conservative and old-fashioned but, as in that film by Chabrol, benighted, lurid, harboring an evil in its soul.

The Parisian view of things also attributes to the French village a clear and simple configuration of authority and a politics still rooted in nineteenth-century quarrels. The mayor, the notary, and the local doctor are the ones with the power and influence. The first has been in office since the beginning of time and is reelected as a matter of village tradition. The second takes care of all legal matters, title searches, bank loans, last wills and testaments; he is an informal real estate broker in the village, since he knows everybody who wants to buy or sell, and he takes a percentage of everything. The last is a man of science and in some places is one and the same as the mayor. The major political conflict, well illustrated by numerous literary examples, takes place between the village curé, the representative of miracle and authority, and the schoolteacher, usually a Socialist, sometimes a Communist—in the French version of this category, a person, not necessarily a Leninist at all, who believes in the necessity of radical social change and sees himself as the emblem of enlightened secular modernism.

During a national election campaign, I went to Cléry-Saint-André in the Loire Valley because the Socialist deputy from the region told me that in that town in particular all the archaic political habits of Old France were still visible. Cléry is a pleasant town with a twelfth-century cathedral and a long row of masonry houses with colored wooden shutters lining the main road. Its most noteworthy political characteristic was that for one hundred years it supported two separate marching bands, which during all the decades of French history had never agreed to play together. On July 14, Bastille Day, there had been occasional fisticuffs between members of the two *musiques*, as marching bands are called. But musically and socially, they had always been deeply divided by a chasm of contrary association. One of the bands, La Fanfare Republicaine, was the leftist group, the "red" band. It played the "Internationale." Its members voted Socialist, sent their children to public schools, and rarely, if ever, went to church. Indeed, La Fanfare Republicaine was so emphatically anticlerical that it refused to play inside the church, and it was on that point, according to village historians, that occasional efforts to heal the rift between the two *musiques* had always foundered. The other band was "white." It was—or is—L'Union Musicale, which splintered off from La Fanfare Republicaine a century or so ago because the latter was too leftist, disrespectful of legitimate authority. Its members remained supporters of the traditional rightist parties, went to church, and would rather leave the village of their ancestors than play the "Internationale."

There was more along these lines in Cléry-Saint-André, whose total population was about 2,200. There was a "white" café and a "red" café, both of them diagonally opposite the cathedral on the town's main street. Townsfolk who voted for the parties of the left went to the Café de la Gaieté; their political opponents tended to gather at the Brasserie de la Belle Image, just a few doors down the street. Socialist voters patronized one butcher, Conservatives another. One villager told me that when a shop opens, he first finds out the political affiliation of the shopkeeper, and if that fails to meet with his approval, he decides not to patronize it.

Political power, which is to say the mayor's office, alternated between the town's two doctors, one, Roland Delastre, a Socialist (out of office at the time of my visit) and the other, Michel Bridart, a rightist. The village itself, according to Dr. Delastre, tended to vote Conservative. In 1986, there were, for example, only seven Socialists on the twenty-two-member city council. The reason, he said, had to do less with genuine differences than with identification with certain traditions. "There's a certain medieval aspect to Cléry-Saint-André," he said, by which he meant that such age-old pillars of conservative authority as the major local château owner, who rented out land to many farmers, and the village priest were still strong and widely respected.

I spoke with one Socialist farmer, Roger Boissay, a member of the city council, who allowed that he voted Socialist both because his father voted Socialist and because "the privileges haven't disappeared, and I am in favor of equality." Here, too, the words alone marked the vestiges of long-term political struggle in the village—privilege and equality, terms invented during the revolution of 1789 and still holding their associative power. The other farms, M. Boissay said, cling to conservative habits of mind, just as they hold on to their parcels of farmland,

fearful of losing them to what they perceive as "Socialist collectiviza-
tion." (And after all, the Socialists, while leaving agriculture alone, did
nationalize major banks, insurance companies, and industrial corpora-
tions when they came to power in 1981.)

What was Deep French about this? My friend the writer thought it
was the stubborn clinging to convention, to an almost ritualistic pattern
in the waging of the political contest. If feuds between family clans were
an aspect of rural life in America—something that never happened in
more sophisticated urban areas—the stubborn, truculent cultural adherence to centuries-old political symbols constituted, to my Parisian
friend, one of the fusty, archaic characteristics of Deep France. It was
not so much ideology that counted in Cléry as habit, custom, the un-
willingness to change. The issues that created the old political conflict
in the village—loyalty to king rather than to revolutionary, acceptance
of privilege as a necessary alternative to chaos—disappeared long ago.
In the Parisian view, it would only be in the villages, in places like Cléry-
Saint-André, that people would still be living among the residues of
those defunct struggles.

I T   I S   P O S S I B L E, of course, that there is nothing to this, that the
Parisian image of non-Parisian France is utterly wrong and preju-
dicial, or, certainly, that Deep France is no deeper than rural America
or rural Japan. The national education system, after all, has wiped out
the brutal ignorance described by Weber. The national village has eliminated what Karl Marx called "the idiocy of rural life," which, in a way,
is another way of characterizing the hinterland culture of any country.
Still, if my own experiences—and places like the Mas Corbières—are
reliable indications, the notion of rural France as different and traditional, a bit sad these days, and, at the same time, at the origins of France
itself, is irresistible. After visiting the three villages in the Berry, for
example, I came back feeling that even if the Parisian idea was a bit
condescending and supercilious, each of the villages did represent something qualitatively different from Paris, something more than the commonplace difference between town and country. And even if the Deep
France of the Paris imagination no longer exists (if it ever existed), the
concept does, at the very least, help in an understanding of this country
in at least two ways.

In the first place, it was from stone farms enclosed by various lost
valleys that French manhood emerged in centuries past to make up this
country's international greatness, in particular the military prowess en-

joyed in past centuries, before it was eclipsed by that of Germany. Virtually every row of stone or masonry houses lining the two sides of every departmental highway in France has its monument to "our sons who gave their lives in the war of 1914 to 1918." Notre-Dame-de-la-Rouvière has one just in front of the Catholic church and behind a little fountain; it is festooned with moss, and there is a single wrought-iron cross above it. But the manhood—or, more properly, the late boy-hood—that flowed out of the villages and onto the regional highways that led, eventually, to Paris has been flowing since long before Richelieu and Colbert began the great work of centralization and Louis XIV's great armies went out, sometimes to victory, imbued with what the Italians, in a famous and oft-repeated phrase, called the *furia francese*, the "French frenzy."

In other words, Deep France has never been too deep to be excluded from conscription and taxes, not since the nation was born. The population of the cities came from the more impoverished areas of the countryside. Braudel has described the role of the Massif Central, the broad range of high hills in the country's center. Like a giant multi-directional headwater, the Massif Central sent forth its trickle of excess population to the several urban corners of France. It is, in this sense, the demographic cradle of the country. Certainly, for all the centuries that France was the biggest and most powerful nation of continental Europe, it was the fertile, sturdy peasantry that provided the blood and the muscle, and even a good deal of the heroism and dash. French literature is replete with tales of peasant adventurers who hustled and romanced their ways out of the hinterland to taste the glory and glamour of Parisian life. Julien Sorel, the tragic hero of Stendhal's *The Red and the Black*, is perhaps the best known. But many others besides the ill-fated Julien swept out of what was not yet known as Deep France to enhance the French *galant*'s reputation for reckless bravery, impetuousness, and pride.

The second useful element in the concept of *La France Profonde* is its ability to remind us that by contrast, for example, to England or to Japan, France was until relatively recently an overwhelmingly rural nation and that more, perhaps, than any of the other major industrial democracies, it has held on to the patterns of rural, agricultural life. That, in turn, explains the ambivalent longing the Parisians feel for vast stretches of supposedly old-fashioned, unchanging rural territory. It represents for them a place where the wholeness of the old ways remains unaffected by the glittery inauthenticity of urban life.

The just-yesterday quality of the pattern of rural life is striking all over France. These days only about 15 percent of the population lives from agriculture. France is not a rural country; it is a modern industrial power. And yet, you can drive for thousands of miles along hundreds of rural roads from north to south, east to west, in the rolling, verdant landscape of Normandy or the flatter, drier terrain of the Loire Valley, plunging into the green hills of Burgundy and, onward, out along the valley of the Marne, and beyond to the luscious stretches of countryside in the Vosges or the forests of the Ardennes, and you will barely see a factory of any size or importance. Village follows after village; and despite microclimates and microcultures, there is much that makes them similar, north and south, east and west, to each other. Each of them has its belfry tower, its Café du Commerce, with its single pinball machine and a couple of rickety tables set out close to the passing traffic; each will have its *boulangerie* and its *boucherie* and its pleasant collection of stone houses with wooden shutters painted a gray, a green, or a brown that has nicely cracked and faded over the years. No matter where the village is situated, in the Limousin or the Savoy, in Brittany or Provence, there will be the little post and telephone office, perhaps a communal grammar school, most often a restaurant or two, with rustic wallpaper and checked tablecloths, where the local people are indulging themselves in the national weakness for four-course lunches and dinners. Certainly, there will be the stone or masonry town hall, with the tricolor hanging on a flagpole outside and the famous old slogan LIBERTÉ, ÉGALITÉ, FRATERNITÉ etched into the stone up above the second-story windows, declaring the village attachment to the values of the *République* and demonstrating the commonality of the experience of the revolution of 1789 and its long and complex aftermath.

I have marveled as I have driven through dozens, hundreds, of these villages all over the country, in Beauce and Brie, in the Dordogne, the Languedoc, and Roussillon, at how deserted the streets usually are even in the middle of a pleasant springtime afternoon. You enter the village from one side and drive through the precariously narrow and venerable main street, practically brushing the houses lined up on either side, exiting past the gas station and a couple of posters advertising, perhaps, the Auchan supermarket or the Leclerc appliances emporium two villages farther away, and there will be almost nobody on the streets, only a false impression that the place has been abandoned—when, in fact, the truth is that the people are either at work in neighboring towns, or in their fields nearby, or, quite simply, at home.

In Alsace, in the magnificent green stretches of Lorraine; in the huge terrain of Auvergne in the south, or farther south again among the steep, wet crevices of the Cévennes; or in the stubborn, scrubby Provençal hills made famous by Pagnol; throughout the Périgord to the west; even in the legendary Savoy, and in the Jura range north of Geneva, and in the voluptuous, sunny territories of the eastern and western Pyrenees, it is much the same thing—enormous, scenically extraordinary stretches of farmland, much of it (not all) apparently not doing so well. Indeed, if France is indeed in decline, if many French are not so sure really if they are genuinely a modern country, one of the major elements of concern is the stagnation of the rural economy.

To be sure, France, even the France of the legendary depths, is too varied and complex to be reduced to such a generalization. I am not neglecting here the great, modern, prosperous farms of France, which produce the grapes and the wine, the 247 varieties of cheese, the apricots, the figs, the apples, and the cherries, the brandy and the Calvados, the spices, the truffles, the mushrooms, the foie gras, and the confit d'oie, that, taken together, constitute one of the bases of France's marvelous culinary art of living. But there is no doubt that France, more so I believe than the United States, for example, is a country of villages, perched on hilltops and lodged in valleys, settled along little rivers or nestled under clumps of sycamores and poplars surrounded by vast open fields. It makes up one of the fabulous charms of the country and inspires in me, and in much of the rest of humanity, at least two ardent hopes—one, that it will never change, and two, that I may one day have a nice little house and garden of my own in one of these places of magnificent antique habitations. It is no accident that the British in particular, but also the Germans and the Americans, scour the remotest corners of the glorious French countryside, trying to buy the little stone house, or perhaps an isolated *manoir* standing in its own patch of manicured garden, where they can very pleasantly put up for a month or so every year.

The impression one has traveling in France is that the archaic life of our grandparents has been slower to come to an end there than in its competitor countries. I don't know if there are farmers sharing their winter beds with piglets—one of the people who told me this widely repeated contention was Dr. Delastre in Cléry-Saint-André, who was in a position to know—but I can affirm from firsthand observation that this is a country where indoor plumbing is far from universal in rural areas, where people still pass their lives in earthen-floored dwellings with no heating system other than the fireplace, and farm land owned by the ancestors of the former feudal lord of the area.

I have a photograph of just such a pair of French farmers, taken in a village in the Loire Valley, that blessed, fertile territory of celebrated Renaissance châteaux and little hotels less than a three-hour drive south and east on the superhighway from Paris, the kind of place where Parisians can make easy weekend trips to their country homes. There, in the midst of evident prosperity, was this couple, a common part of the landscape of the area, living in a stone cottage that they rented, along with some surrounding parcels of land, from the local chatelain (who may or may not have used the imperfect of the subjunctive; I didn't speak with him). The couple were stout and stolid, callused and weatherbeaten; they stood stiffly in front of the dark doorway of their kitchen in the fashion of people unused to having their picture taken. They assumed what seemed to me to be a subservient attitude toward Dr. Delastre, who took me to see them. The house was dark, dank, low, and sooty, a three-hundred-year-old rural dwelling that seemed not to have been much improved on since being built. To be sure, the couple had certain conveniences. There was electricity and running water. They had modern medical care, which is a major element in reducing the difference between the rich and the poor of yesteryear. But I had the strong feeling, supported by my guide, that their style of life, their relations with each other, and even their degree of material comfort were not all that different from those of their great-grandparents in the last century. I have been to see farmhouses for sale in Normandy, occupied for decades by some recently deceased farmer, that had neither electricity nor running water nor indoor plumbing of any kind, where there was a stone well and a bucket at the end of a rope a few yards from the house, and where the former occupants went into the fields to take care of their physical needs.

A friend of mine in Paris, a pretty secretary for an annual art festival in the capital, seemed to me a nice example of the closeness, the just-yesterday sense of agricultural France. We'll call her Sandrine, and she is a modern girl in every sense, with her own apartment near the Place d'Italie, her live-in boyfriend, her wardrobe, her travels on vacation to the Mediterranean coast, where she has become proficient in sailing a catamaran. She is also the first of her family, which goes back many generations in the Loire Valley, to grow up in Paris. She loves to talk about her grandparents, who never came to Paris in their lives. She describes them with great affection, as simple, wholesome, happy people who do not need the accoutrements of modernism. They make all their own clothes. They never go to restaurants. When she visits them, her grandfather takes her fishing, and she is as adept at catching *brochet* as she is at manipulating the typewriter in her office. Sandrine talks about her origins in the "good old French peasantry," and there is no doubt that her own urban, late-twentieth-century life seems to be separated from that of her grandparents almost by centuries, not just by her parents' single transitional generation.

Sandrine reminds me, in fact, of myself as a representative of American life. My grandparents came from a Russian shtetl, a place that I have always imagined to have been dark and menacing, poor and benighted—something to escape from. Their lives were probably in many ways a good deal more different from my own urban and materially blessed existence than Sandrine's is from her grandparents'. A rapid, one- or two-generation jump from some sort of "deep" rural way of life to flashy, mobile urbanism is not exclusive to France. It is part of our century. But whereas my grandparents crossed oceans, leaving behind them all physical trace of their existence, their language, and much of their mentality in that spare, hard shtetl, Sandrine's origins are right there, three hours on the *autoroute* from Paris, for her to visit on weekends. In a bemused and accepting way, she still talks of herself as a peasant, fresh in from the farm.

Many of the French are like that. Indeed, to have some direct, intimate link with *La France Profonde* is part of the mystique that surrounds the most successful of the country's political figures, virtually none of whom claim origins in Paris, that spiritual entity diametrically opposite the France of the countryside. Every year, President Mitterrand makes a pilgrimage to a rural area called Sologne, where, surrounded by advisers and cameramen, he climbs a mountain so he can be seen communing with nature, reattaching himself to the soil. De Gaulle, anticipating, perhaps, a move to inter him in the Panthéon, in the middle of Paris, insisted that he be buried in Colombey-les-deux-Églises (whose very name resonates with a rich and mystical nostalgia), the town, now less than two hours from Paris, to which he retired during what are rather meaningfully called his periods in the political wilderness. One of the recent prime ministers of France, Chirac, is the mayor of Paris; but his parliamentary constituency is the district of Corrèze in the Auvergne, the approximate French equivalent to Appalachia. Giscard d'Éstaing, the former president, lives in an elegant bourgeois house on the rue de la Faisanderie in the Sixteenth Arrondissement (I like to call this Parisian quarter of sumptuous, grand apartment buildings *Le Seizième Profond*, "the Deep Sixteenth"); but his parliamentary constituency is in Saint-Chamond, another sign of an attachment to the rural origins, and thus the spiritual origins, of the country. The careful cultivation by all these highly urban Parisian figures (except for de Gaulle, who genuinely was uncomfortable with the idea of Paris) of that rootedness in Deep France is no accident. It is extremely common for a cabinet minister or an important parliamentarian in France to be simultaneously the mayor of the small town where, perhaps, his grandparents had spent their lives. It may happen to my friend Sandrine someday. The tradition shows the strong belief that to be truly, profoundly French in identity, you have to have that rural attachment.

PART OF the reason may be the simple sense of dislocation that rapid social change and modernism bring about, especially among a people like the French, who live (in contrast with a good percentage of Americans) in the territory of their ancestors. The idea of *La France Profonde*, even to the supercilious Parisians, is reassuring. It echoes of a period, probably largely imaginary, when life was simpler and less ridden with anxieties and traffic jams. And it has something to do with the grandeur of France as well. The verdant stretches of farmland that radiate outward from the very gates of Paris were the reasons for French greatness in the first place. Agriculture, the fabulous soil of France, provided the wealth that enabled the great centralizing monarchs of the sixteenth and seventeenth centuries to turn their country into the most powerful in Europe. The historian Pierre Miquel has said that France's kings were great, not so much because they had more arms or money than other kings, but because they had more wheat. And so there may be an intimate connection between the taste of the bread of France and the sense of national glory. Both are rooted, almost literally, in the soils of the deep country.

The paradox is that if French greatness came out of the countryside, to which the French remain so attached, modern times have turned that success into a problem. The French are like China in this sense. The very glory and might of China throughout history, the conviction of the Chinese that they were at the spiritual center of the world, made them inadaptable for a century to the arrival of the technologically superior West. The very extent of their historical success turned them into a failure. The analogy is far from exact in France, but the truth is that village France, in its failure in some places (by no means all) to adapt to modern times, its enduring primitiveness, is one of the great worries of the country's political leaders and one of the great causes of national unemployment (it's also one of the picturesque delights in traveling in France, but that is another matter). Perhaps the problem with Deep France, so seductive, so pleasurable, so quiet and peaceful, so slow in its rhythm of life, is its inability to shake free of the notion that life is a few cows or goats, a hectare or two under cultivation, and a few children, who, because times are changing, may not farm after all but may work instead in the local hotel, or find a job at the post office or repairing the rural roads or in the factory in the nearest city, which might itself not be faring very well.

It is the absence of ambition, of the questing, dynamic attitudes characteristic of urban dwellers, that sometimes preoccupies local and national leaders. I once visited the village of Le Chambon-sur-Lignon, a place legendary for some because of its record during World War II of protecting Jews and helping to spirit them out of occupied France to neutral Switzerland. The town is about one hundred miles southwest of Lyon, and I went there in 1987 to observe the local reaction to the trial in that city of Klaus Barbie, Lyon's wartime Gestapo chief. The person to see was the Protestant minister, in large part because the wartime minister, a man named André Trocmé, had led the village's efforts to protect the Jews. A single plaque on the wall of a small square, put up after the war by Jewish groups, commemorates the village's heroism. But the minister, who, like all Protestant ministers in France, came from outside his parish, spoke not of the pride of the townsfolk in their exploit but of what he called their embarrassment. Far from feeling satisfied or boastful about their role in saving Jews during the war, he said that the people of Le Chambon-sur-Lignon were rather painfully shy about it, unwilling to take credit, reluctant to acknowledge in the depths of themselves anything extraordinary or heroic. I myself had learned of Le Chambon years earlier, through a very good book by Philip Hallie, called *Lest Innocent Blood Be Shed*, which tells the story of the *pasteur* Trocmé and his commitment to save threatened Jews. (Later, there was a documentary film about it made by Pierre Sauvage, who was born there of refugee Jewish parents.) But M. Trocmé's present successor told me that the book had troubled the spirits of the people of Le Chambon, who, once again, shied away from any notion that they might have been unusual or great.

But it went beyond shyness. Le Chambon-sur-Lignon is also an economically stagnant place, even though it is not far from Lyon, which is growing and energetic. And the *pasteur* attributed at least part of the problem to a habit of thought that I associated with the modesty of village France. He talked about an inferiority complex, a deep sense of a lack of worth among his parishioners, arguing that the problem was particularly strong among rural Protestants in France—and Le Chambon is predominantly Protestant. "I see it in my church council meeting," he said. "When I ask somebody to do a reading for the following Sunday, for example, the response will be: 'Oh, but not me, I can't do that.'" The people he described were self-effacing, determinedly modest, lacking in ambition and in the notion that the world can be transformed by bold human effort. "I tell the young people that they will have to learn advanced skills, computers, the sciences, in order to compete, but their attitude is rather too often: 'Oh, I'll just get a job in the hotel or in one of the stores.'" And then he added, with a rueful smile, "I have a great fondness for my parishioners, who are marvelous people."

T HE ASSUMPTION underlying my own interest in grasping the essence of *La France Profonde* is that no country is so entirely divided into countryside and city that there can be no connection, no cultural similarities, between them, certainly not in Western Europe in the last few years of the twentieth century. The glamorous, urban France of the cities—and by the cities in France, one means primarily Paris—drew its sustenance and character ultimately from its rural origins, which, in the case of France, are relatively recent. And indeed, look at Paris closely and you will see the flavor and style of its origins. If France is the most rural of the great industrial democracies, Paris is the most village-like of the great European capitals. It is a very rich, ornate, highly decorated network of separate villages, with its narrow streets, its trees and parks, its resistance to building houses too high, its little cafés. Paris, of course, is far more than that. It is also the Champs-Élysées and the Louvre, the rue du Faubourg Saint-Honoré, the Musée Rodin, the Forum des Halles, and the Pompidou Center. But have you ever spent a day walking the neighborhood streets of Paris on a Sunday, wondering where the people are, experiencing its jewel-like emptiness? Take away the city's great monuments, and you have left a powerful, uneffaced residue of a typical rural village.

Perhaps that explains the bemusement, and sometimes the embarrassment, of the Parisians themselves at the idea of Deep France, a locality so fixed in their imagination that they frequently reminded me that that was where I was going whenever I set out for a village. It is a distant mirror of themselves. I always felt that to touch it at its core would be not to touch some irrelevant and archaic aspect of the nation as a whole but to touch its very essence, and that is why I persisted in my pursuit of the concept, going to numerous villages and towns, trying to see what was deep about them and what was simply French.

3

Villages

L E C H A M B O N - s u r - L I G N O N is in the great terrain of small
villages that stretch south practically from the outskirts of Lyon
through the vast, picturesque Auvergne—the very stereotype of *La
France Profonde*—and down through the Cévennes, where the Mas
Corbières, in the midst of the *garrigues*, is situated. I spent two weeks
there one summer, swimming in the Hérault River and driving through
the small villages of the region. I had the feeling that, entirely by coincidence, I had arrived at a crucial moment of transformation.

There is indeed a Deep France, just as there is a Deep America and
probably a Deep Denmark. In some places, perhaps, its characteristics
will change slowly, even given television and other culturally unifying
forces; this is likely to be the case in such departments as Lozère and
Haute-Loire, poor rural regions straddling the Auvergne and the Cévennes, and others where urbanites and foreigners rarely look for secondary residences. Other, less untouched regions of the French rural
domain are being swept away in the tide of modernization. I think of
Provence in this regard, the areas in the southeast around Avignon, Arles,
Aix-en-Provence, enriched both by tourism and by new industry. Once
I spent a few days in Aubagne, the birthplace of Marcel Pagnol and a
sort of Deep France legend, the setting of the movie classic *La Femme
du Boulanger* (*The Baker's Wife*), starring the great Raimu, in which
the aging baker stops working because his young wife leaves him. The
entire village, full of truculent, individualistic peasants, embarks on a
collective effort to find the baker's wife, so he will start baking bread
again.

The Pagnolian life was not so long ago as to have utterly disappeared, even if Aubagne itself these days is a place of suburban supermarkets and industrial parks. When you visit small towns in the Midi, all along the Mediterranean coast, it is the local accents that often give you the feeling of life imitating the movies, so similar are the real characters of present-day France to the film characters created by Pagnol, and this is true not only in the area surrounding Marseille but across the entire Mediterranean seaboard, including the Hérault region, about one hundred miles to the west. Throughout the crumbling stone towns of coastal Provence and the Languedoc, on the other side of the Rhône River, the whole set of local gestures, the phrases, the use of a kind of long, drawn-out *ehhh* to signify an "isn't that so," the French that seems to have been marinated in the spices of Italian—all of these make one think of Pagnol. And so do the little hilltop villages of crumbling stone, built over a small stream, where crooked women carrying wooden staffs lead their small herds of goats and sheep up into the hills every day.

And so, before I went there, I had an imaginary sort of Aubagne in my mind, as a place frozen by time, where the villagers sat around tables in the late-afternoon heat drinking *pastis* and waving away their wives' annoyed demands for them to come home. Aubagne, for example, was the place where, according to Pagnol, the mayor was elected because he was the only man in town who had a telephone. Pagnol also wrote about the political divisions of Aubagne, particularly the clash of church and state (the latter represented by the schoolteacher, who, as he explained in a classic memoir, *The Glory of My Father*, read by every French schoolchild even today, was his father). Left and right in Aubagne, like in Cléry-Saint-André in the Loire Valley, went to different cafés, frequented different clubs, patronized different butchers. A village elder named Lucien Grimaud, who has written books about Aubagne's history and legends, takes pilgrims on tours of the sites made famous in Pagnol's books and movies.

It was a series of magazine advertisements, showing a different sort of Aubagne, that made me want to visit there. Published in the leading newsweeklies, the ads promoted the town not as a museum piece of a vanishing past, not even as a tourist site for visits to the major Pagnolian shrines, Manon's Spring and the New House, but as a high-technology center, one of "the new style of cities in the south," a prime location for investment. One ad showed an astronaut suspended someplace in the darkness of space, with the city of Aubagne, its steeples, belfries, and ancient stone habitations, mirrored in the glass of his helmet.

The advertisements upset all earlier imaginings. Until then, I had been a bit like Arthur Waley, the great translator of Chinese and Japanese literary classics, who all his life refused to set foot in either country, knowing that his poetic illusions would be shattered. Nonetheless, I did go to Aubagne, met with M. Grimaud, with the mayor (a Communist), with the very capitalist owner of a factory installed in one of the town's two new industrial parks, and I realized again what was already obvious—that not all of village France is frozen in an archaic past. I strolled with M. Grimaud through Aubagne, whose ancient center has been beautifully preserved, and he pointed out the cafés that were once identified with the leftists or the rightists, telling me that while, yes, there was still a left and a right in Aubagne (the former being considerably stronger than the latter), the divisions were no longer visible in the cafés or in the social clubs, now thoroughly mixed. These old conflicts still existed, of course, but Aubagne was far bigger now, more impersonal, more oriented toward modern, competitive, high-technology industrial and commercial activity than it had been in Pagnol's day. The town of economic zones and advertisements showing astronauts whirling through space was no longer the simple agricultural community where mixing failed to take place. I went to see a local farmer, a grower of apricots, who spent weeks of his time studying modern farming in government-sponsored seminars and subscribed to magazines on changing techniques in the cultivation of fruit. M. Grimaud explained that apricots imported from North Africa were cheaper and had long ago harmed the local farmers. "The apricots from Aubagne are better," he said. "The problem is that there are more eaters of apricots than there are connoisseurs of apricots."

Outside town were suburban supermarkets and a network of highways linking the industrial parks with the port of Marseille, not even an hour away. The population had increased from ten thousand at the end of World War II, already a decade or more later than the town portrayed by Pagnol, to forty thousand in the late 1980s. When the filmmaker Claude Berri was preparing a remake of one of Pagnol's classic novels, *Jean de Florette*, he couldn't film in Aubagne itself. It didn't look the part anymore. There was something about a town with a modern sports complex, a new theater, a technical college, prosperity, that no longer looked right, and Berri had to find instead a much smaller, less prosperous town, lost in the hills of Provence. Even the town's tourist office promoted its archaic image with modern skills. Brochures and maps had been printed up showing how to travel to the sites made famous by Aubagne's most famous son, Marcel Pagnol.

"There are days when you want to dream and days when you want to work," the owner of a factory in one of the industrial parks said. The factory owner manufactured all sizes and shapes of plastic tubing. He was steely-eyed and efficient. He reminded me of a group of civic boosters I had once met in Marseille, who bemoaned the Pagnol legacy, believing that it encouraged outsiders to attribute troglodytic characteristics to the entire region. The Marseille boosters had invited some journalists to a fabulous lunch of bouillabaisse and white Bandol wine in a restaurant overlooking the Mediterranean. They had laid on a program of helicopter rides over Marseille's industrial districts, visits to such big-time industrial centers as Aerospatiale, the French airplane and helicopter manufacturer, and when I bungled into the subject of Pagnol, thinking that I would evoke some nostalgic, reverential comment on the famous local son, I was surprised to find a certain irritation with the writer as the propagator of obsolescent images. Similarly, the factory owner put the image of crusty peasants, lazy and scheming, out of his mind. "There are a lot of people in Aubagne who want to work," he said.

IN THE Cévennes, by contrast, instead of modernization and change, one observes something closer to a regional depopulation; there is not so much an alteration of the old rural way of life, represented by such places as the Mas Corbières, as its disappearance altogether, its simple lack of economic viability. The local residents themselves say that this part of the Cévennes, not conveniently near a good port and industrial center like Marseille, is in danger of becoming an empty country, a territory deserted by its original inhabitants and left to the transient, seasonal cares of the owners of summer houses.

The entire region is in what was know historically as the Languedoc, whose local dialect, similar to Provençal, produced its own considerable literature—analyzed in a fascinating book by Emmanuel Le Roy Ladurie called *Love, Death, and Money in the Pays D'Oc*. It is the kind of place that has no flat land at all. Village after village is located underneath some steep valley floor next to a fast-flowing stream, surrounded by profuse vegetation. Grapes and wisteria vines overflow their trellises. It is a damp and, in the summer, even steamy place, a haven for butterflies, dragonflies, lizards, centipedes, grasshoppers, flies, and small scorpions that, I was told, are relatively harmless. The sound of water flowing is never far off, behind a row of houses, alongside the road, trickling

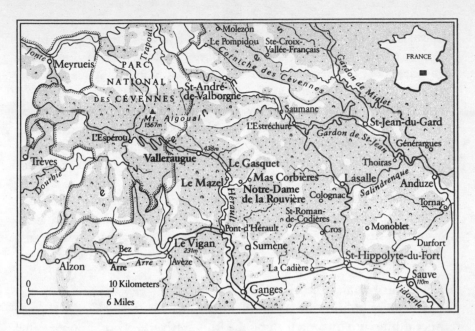

CÉVENNES

through the rocky meadows. Roads all curve crazily as they make their way up and down the hills, running past narrow, semicircular terraces that are buttressed by millions of stone ramparts, a testimony to the hard labor of years past. Everywhere there are views of valleys flowing between successions of green hills, and in the early morning and evening, they are shrouded in mysterious blue mists. Many of the village houses are large and square and imposing but show signs of dilapidation, suggesting that the families living inside them had once been wealthy but have since fallen on harder times, or moved away altogether, leaving the old homestead of the valleys to the mercy of the rain and the wind.

Anybody from the area, which stretches westward from Nîmes to Le Vigan, will tell you that its former prosperity was based on orchards, particularly apples, on vegetables such as onions and potatoes, and, most of all, on the production of raw silk thread, which fed the legendary weaving plants of nearby Lyon. The great square houses, whose roofs reminded me vaguely of Asian temples, belonged to the important silk growers, and they are scattered densely through the entire region, backed by the scrub-covered hills, often alongside pleasant streams next to the laboriously terraced fields where mulberry trees, whose leaves were used to feed the silkworms, were grown. The houses now are sometimes empty; or they have been bought by city dwellers who come to them on weekends; or they are inhabited by descendants of the original silk growers, who have managed to hold on economically in the region in some less refined occupation. Each house has an upper story lined with square windows that are smaller than those below. These are the attics, where, until just after World War II, the silkworms were fed so they would produce their precious cocoons. Along the Hérault River, in the tiny village of Le Mazel, stands an immense five-story building of gray stone, looking like an abandoned monastery or a barracks, perhaps a prison. This was one of the factories, employing several hundred local women, where the cocoons were first softened in very hot water and then unwound onto bobbins for eventual shipment to the weavers of Lyon.

Silk was a major factor in the economy of the city, which treats the now defunct industry as an essential part of its legacy. There is a magnificent museum on a quai along the Rhône River in Lyon, showing the various patterns of brocade created over the centuries, when the city was linked through trade, banking, and commerce to Geneva and Florence, selling its production of silk to both. One of the historical heroes of the city is Joseph-Marie Jacquard, who in 1804 invented a new and revolutionary loom that utilized coded cards and enabled one weaver to do what it had taken five weavers to do before him. The new loom was too big for the narrow houses of what is now called the Old City, a charming district on the right bank of the Saône River, consisting of narrow, pastel-colored houses built around Italian-inspired loggias, and so the manufacturing of silk moved up a hill to La Croix Rousse, where its feeble remnants can still be seen.

Both Lyon and its agricultural hinterland, the Languedoc, were necessary components of a complicated, modern commercial activity that made fortunes for some and was one of the bases of French economic greatness. The industry, however, like so much industry of contemporary Europe, was savaged by Japanese competition, so that today in the little villages along the Hérault, the very evocation of Japan can bring sharp expressions of anger. I met one man—we'll call him Jacques—from the tiny town of Le Gasquet, which is a collection of perhaps eight or ten large stone houses built on either side of a bridge over the Hérault. Jacques, in his late forties, comes from one of the silk families and can go on at considerable length about the techniques of raising mulberries, feeding silkworms, and extracting the precious thread from the cocoons, all of which he remembers from his boyhood. But in Le Gasquet, he is the only person his age left. Half the houses of the village are empty. Among those that are inhabited, one belongs to an elderly retired couple who originated in the village. Another, a magnificent spread surrounded by terraces of fruit trees and grapevines, is used on weekends by the descendants of one of the local silk families. A third has been bought by a young couple who commute to work elsewhere. And there is the one lived in by Jacques and his wife; it stands on a stone terrace overlooking the road that runs along the river and is backed by the steep side of the valley. A single mulberry tree grows in the garden, a memento, he said, of past days.

"We had better silk than the Japanese," he said, venting his annoyance at the competition that, he believes, destroyed a way of life in France. "We got only one harvest of mulberries each year, while the Japanese got two, but because our leaves were richer, our silk was of a higher quality." Jacques speaks French with the musical accent of the south, so the words come out longer than those of the Parisians, with extra syllables appearing here and there and somewhat more stress on the consonants, less of that nasal glide common in Paris. "But what can you do? People buy. They look at the price, not the quality, and how can you compete with the Japanese?" he went on, speaking more from emotion than from a grounding in the facts about the rival country. "They don't have any social security. They don't take vacations. They work fourteen hours a day. Their whole lives are based on work, and they don't care so much about the pleasures of life. There's no way you can compete with people like that.

"Well, this region needs something else. We could develop tourism, since we've got the mountains and good weather five months a year. Some people went into *gîtes*," he said. (A *gîte* is a rural cottage rented out on a weekly basis to city families who want to restore their connections to the countryside or simply have a vacation.) "But they were badly done, too primitive. People didn't like them. I was always saying, 'You've got to give people all the comforts of home, since they're used to them, and if they don't have them, they won't come.' Now some of the *gîtes* are better. But people need more than just a pretty view. They need tennis, golf, things like that. The problem is we're too hilly for a real golf course. We don't have the space. Maybe one of those small golf courses that don't take up too much room. I hear they're pretty popular."

Jacques, who operates heavy road-repairing machinery, speaks with a certain melancholic tone and, at the same time, with a sort of conviction that his region of great beauty can be saved. Once, we passed by a patch of raspberries ripening in the sun, and before I knew it, he had plunged into the thicket to pick the berries, correctly extolling their virtues. He spoke about his mother, a paramedical volunteer who used to walk for miles along rural paths in the day before many of the present roads were built in order to give vaccinations to the remote farmers. "It sounds utopian, I know," he said, "but that's the way she was." I talked about Deep France, my constant obsession, and he laughed knowingly. He was familiar with the concept, and he confirmed it in both its negative and its positive aspects. In the Cévennes, he said, people help each other, or at least they know each other. Paris, he said, is a place where you might live on the same landing as your neighbors for years but never get to know them, whereas here, in the commune of Valleraugue, which stretches for miles through remote valleys, he personally knew virtually every inhabitant.

He could tell you, for example, which people had been to Paris and who had only gone as far as Nîmes in their lives. He knew who was married to whom. He confirmed the Parisian suspicion that the populations of small villages have been intermarrying for so long that, as he put it, "some new blood would do us some good." He was talking at this point of the emergence in Valleraugue—which, he said, had a grand total of one family of Arab origins—of the extremist anti-immigrant National Front party, a development that he deeply disapproved. There were considerable numbers of Arabs in nearby, larger Le Vigan, perhaps fifteen hundred of them, he said, which explained the formation of the National Front in the area. Like elsewhere, the far-right anti-immigration party came about in reaction to the Arab presence. But as far as he, Jacques, was concerned, he had never known Arabs to cause any more problems than the French. Jacques pointed out that one of the reasons for the depopulation of some villages was the simple failure of people to marry. "They are shy," he said, "or they don't have much money and they figure they need it all for themselves, so they don't take on a wife. It's selfish." A presumed miserliness is a central ingredient in the Parisian notion of Deep France.

Jacques took me to a place called Ardailles, two exquisite stone villages overlooking the valley of the Hérault. The separate villages are a heritage of the days when the entire region was divided into Catholic and Protestant quarters, since these mountains, like many of the hilly regions of France—Le Chambon-sur-Lignon is another example—were the kinds of places where Protestants settled. Ardailles used to have twelve hundred head of sheep in the days when agriculture was prosperous. Now only a few of the sheep are left, and all but five or so of the houses are inhabited part of the year, by city dwellers who come for weekends. He pointed out the old schoolhouse, now unused, because there aren't enough children. Grammar schools have been closed all through the valleys of the Cévennes, so that children are bused to the few remaining schools in the communal center—Valleraugue for the children of Ardailles. Down the hill is an old château nearly in ruins, formerly owned by someone Jacques identified as "a count from Paris." The count sold the building and its land for something like fifty thousand dollars to a young architect who plans to restore it.

Jacques goes to visit all the people who buy houses in the region to tell them he is available for help if they need to get a phone installed, for example, or to hire a carpenter. But he has another reason. It's part of what I realized was a quiet, inconspicuous effort to keep the territory alive, accepting that farming inevitably will die out but hoping that it will be replaced by a combination of tourism, secondary residences, and, eventually, some small-scale industry. (When Jacques first came to visit me in my rented stone cottage, he was wondering if I was a possible investor in the region, and was disappointed, I think, to learn that I was a mere scribbler, not an industrialist.) "It's much better when there are people living here," he said. "Otherwise, nobody cares for the gardens. The brush gets thick, and when it gets dry there are fires, which destroy the area altogether. If people take care of the place, it can be preserved, but if the area is depopulated, the land itself will be destroyed."

Valleraugue's mayor of thirty-two years, Claude Bitte, the son of a farmer, is a Socialist reelected each year with something like 80 percent of the vote (he is opposed by the Communists on one side and what the French call the "diverse right," various independent conservatives, on the other). He became a Socialist, he said, because he knew from experience what economic difficulty meant and because he believes in collective efforts to help the needy—in other words, in the attitude that goes by the name *solidarité* in France. M. Bitte is a soft-spoken man with a heavy meridional accent. I found him one day during my two weeks in Valleraugue cutting the grass with a scythe at the municipal campsite. "Somebody has to do it," he said.

"I think that when a region is in difficulty, there is more solidarity among the people, because they know that it's better to stick together when you're in trouble," he said. "Everybody knows everybody else," he went on, "so when somebody is in desperate shape, it's easily known, and we try to find some way to help." He gave the example of a farmer whose house burned down and who had no insurance to cover the construction of a new house. The town lobbied at the local Farmer's Mutual Insurance Company to provide money for a new house. "More often, it's a matter of the town hall providing wood or charcoal so people can stay warm in the winter," he said. "We don't have that many cases, but when there's no other way, the municipality itself provides the means.

"In the city," he said, "the counterparts of our farmers would be among those anonymous people for whom nothing is done. That's the advantage of a small place." Then the mayor gave his own definition of *La France Profonde*, which, almost exactly the inverse of the Parisian conception, put a value on the earthbound experience of the countryside, compared to the fine, affluent abstractions of the city. He spoke for the putatively benighted peasants of the Cévennes by proclaiming, in his modest way, a kind of higher enlightenment, coming from the reality of experience rather than the pleasures of pure reason. "*La France Profonde*," the mayor said, "is the France of practical experience. It's the France that is not enlightened but that has to think practically, because peasants have a rhythm of life that enables them to reflect on their problems." People in the city, he said, don't have time to reflect deeply on their problems.

And then there is the question of freedom and what he called the farmer's deep attachment to it. "In the wars of religion, the people of this region went into rebellion to fight for freedom of religion," he said. "And during World War II, they were strong supporters of the resistance, because they wanted to fight against the German occupiers. We had Jews who took refuge in this area, and they survived the war here. We knew that if they were turned in, they would have been killed; nobody here turned anybody in.

"These are good people," he said of the farmers of Valleraugue. "They don't accept the suffering of others without trying to do something about it. This is a place where parents take care of their children and then children take care of their parents. Nobody is left alone here."

UP THE VALLEY from Valleraugue, which lies along the Hérault River, a winding, narrow road leads to the town of Notre-Dame-de-la-Rouvière, where it joins another valley, called Loisières. The road runs through Rouvière (a Catholic village, by comparison to Valleraugue, which is Protestant) and then above the valley floor for a few miles; a left turn onto a narrow, nearly overgrown paved track brings you, after a mile or two, higher up to the Mas Corbières, which, its own inhabitants say, represents a way of life that is quickly disappearing, the end of at least one part of Deep France.

On one of my walks there, I met René Liron, who saw me with a small pack on my back, about to take the trail through the *garrigue* that leads to the top of the valley, and he stopped to talk. We talked once and then again; I bought cheese from M. Liron, who is one of the three bachelor Liron brothers, all of them lean, sunburned men, with large foreheads and an indentation of the face that seems to cut it in two parts at the bridge of the nose, so that top and bottom were like the opposing sides of a hinge. M. Liron brought me to the dank cellar where he ages his goat cheese on top of oat straw (he specified that it had to be oat straw, not wheat straw or rye) inside closed wooden boxes. I bought a pound of his product, mindful of his warning that it needed to age about a week before it would be ready to eat. He told me to keep it on the bottom of the refrigerator—"don't let it freeze, or you'll have goat's rocks," he said, "and don't let it sit in the sun, or you'll have more goat's rocks." He spoke in the same musical accent as Jacques, but he put exclamation points at the end of his sentences with sharp brief whistles, as when he warned me about the danger of creating goat's rocks, shaking his head simultaneously and drawing a horizontal line in the air with his hand, as if to indicate the border between happiness and disaster. Later, we went into his kitchen and I drank some of his homemade wine, which was powerful and bitter. "If you're afraid of a little bitterness, this wine is not for you," he said.

Liron's dark, windowless kitchen was neat, clean, and cool; a door opening onto a cement terrace outside was covered with long colored strips of plastic, designed to keep the flies out. There was a refrigerator, a radio, a telephone, and a bare light bulb suspended from the ceiling. Peasant houses are often kept dark, presumably to save electricity, but so, too, are the apartments of the *grande bourgeoisie* in Paris. Indeed, I've always been struck by the crepuscular gloom that pervades such spacious, affluent habitations, and I wondered in the Liron kitchen if that permanent Parisian twilight wasn't part of the French peasant inheritance. Two pots were simmering on a stove, and M. Liron told me he was making rhubarb and raspberry preserves (not very many raspberries this year, he said). I seized the occasion of his hospitality to ply him with questions, about his way of life, the situation in the Cévennes, how he made the cheese, how many goats he had, and what the future held in store.

"It's almost over for this area," he began. "From now on we'll live here off vacation houses and visitors, but as far as farming is concerned, it's becoming a dead countryside. After I'm gone, there won't be any more people coming up here to buy goat cheese. I've been here for sixty years, born in this house. So were my parents. We had potatoes, onions, oats, eggplants, grapes, apricots, apples, and the cheese, of course. Now it's all over except for a little bit of cheese. We'll go out and get some chestnuts later, since it's the season now. We used to sell them all the way to China. You put them above a slow fire for about thirty-six hours to dry them, and we sold them that way. But no more. It's no longer profitable. The young people don't want to stay here anymore, so they go elsewhere, looking for work. You see down there—that building down there?" He pointed to a large, squat house along the winding road a dizzying distance below. "That used to be the school, but no longer. It was closed a few years ago.

"My parents left by the wrong side," he went on, meaning that they were dead, "but the young people today leave because they're not willing to work the way you have to in country like this. There's no possibility of using machines here. The valley is too steep, so the terraces are very narrow. If you try using a tractor, even just one of those small ones, you'll ruin the terrace walls. There's no point. You know, every bit of seed, all the fertilizer, is carried up to the terraces on your back, and every piece of the harvest is carried down on your back too. There's no other way.

"Well, I'm sixty now, and in a few years I'll retire, not that I'm going anyplace, because where would I go? But if I did go someplace, I'd like it to be someplace flat, where you don't have to build any terrace walls. I've built thousands of them in my time and wouldn't mind if I didn't have to build any more.

"A German bought one of the houses next door, and he's been fixing it up. He speaks French better than I do, but once I heard him speak German, and I'll tell you, it's a good thing he speaks French, because I was lost. Isn't it true that American is kind of similar to German? And in America, do they have goats like here? It's more cows in America, I think. I tell you, if you spoke American, I wouldn't understand a word. We have our patois here too. It's a little like Occitan, but not exactly. I have to speak French to you, but if I were talking with some of the peasants, you would be lost.

"No, I've never been to the capital," M. Liron said, when I asked him if he had ever traveled to Paris. "I've been here pretty much all the time. Three bachelor brothers, where would we go? Yes, all three of us are bachelors. There were eight of us in the family: three brothers, three sisters, and the mother and father. The three sisters are all married. One lives down the valley. One of them went to Montpellier. But the three boys stayed here. I can't go anyplace; I've got sixty goats to take care of. Who's going to take care of them if I go up to the capital? You'll find lots of people who've never been to the capital, especially the older people, but the younger ones, they go. Maybe after I retire I'll take a little trip or two, but I don't think I'll go as far as that.

"The important thing is freedom. That's the main thing, even if you have to suffer for it in a countryside like this. I get up at six a.m. to take care of the goats, and I have a nap in the middle of the day, because it's often not until eleven p.m. that I get to sleep. Sometimes, I tell you, it's midnight, and I haven't had supper yet. And then you've got to get up at six a.m., because the goats won't wait. But it's a free life. There's no looking at your watch and saying, 'Oh, I have to be here and here because it's this time or that time.' There's suffering here, but it's a free life. Maybe when I retire I'll have a bit more time, but let it not be retirement in a chair, sitting all day because you're too old and sick to move. I like to put a little pack on my back like you and wander up into the hills, and if I'm not strong enough for that, then there's no point, is there?"

While M. Liron talked, sitting in his dark kitchen or standing under a grapevine in front of it, neighbors came by, dark and grizzled like him, and very curious. One of them sat on the stone stairs leading into the yard and stared at me, tilting his head and closing one eye as if he were looking down the sights of a telescope. He was wearing the standard peasant's garb, the black beret, the plaid shirt, the blue heavy cotton pants. His shoes were rubber. M. Liron's brother came cheerfully down from hoeing a patch of onions and disappeared into the depths of the kitchen, where he was joined by another man over a glass of the bitter wine. Three bachelor brothers are hard to find in France these days, but rural bachelorhood, as Jacques acidly pointed out, is nonetheless something of an economic tradition, stretching back centuries amid a people who believed they lived too close to the margins to afford wives and families.

I asked about politics in the Mas Corbières, which was administratively a part of Notre-Dame-de-la-Rouvière, and provoked heated discussion, the gist of which was that there were what they called two clans in the village, one Catholic and the other Protestant, and they apparently alternated in their control of the town hall. When one clan was in power, it placed its family members in all the good jobs, removing the others. Did that mean that the wars of religion persisted up here? I asked. "Oh, no. It's not wars of religion," M. Liron said. He explained by way of proof that though he had been born a Catholic, there were five, no—wait a minute now—six Protestants in his family. "One thing I can't stand," he said, "is fights about religion, which they certainly had in this region in the past. Let's be honest. All the religions are the same, and there are so many of them in the world."

THE DAY after my talk with Liron and company, I drove down to Montpellier, about fifty miles to the south on the Mediterranean coast, to pick up some friends who were spending the weekend with me. I had some free time, so I drove out to see the beach, which, like a great deal of the Mediterranean coast of France, has been turned into an endless esplanade of ugly low cement housing blocks, fast-food joints, and all the other unpleasantries of downscale seaside development. It was the middle of July. The newspapers were full of headlines about enormous traffic jams in France, with three million people having left for their annual holidays on that weekend alone.

The coast near Montpellier is, like Saint-Cyr-sur-Mer, another district of the poor man's Mediterranean, a relatively inexpensive place where a factory worker, or a postman, or a grade school teacher, or a small shopkeeper, can rent a couple of rooms for a few weeks and take his family on holiday. The paved road, lined by interminable rows of cement blocks with balconies, was crowded with pale people, with painfully red people, with peeling people, with already tanned people. There were women massive with cellulite and gleaming with lotion, bowlegged men with hirsute paunches sagging like sacks of rice over their bathing briefs, roving bands of teenage boys with long hair and single earrings, sputtering past on motorbikes. The sound of the mournful sea mingled with the ratatatat of the bikes and the whoosh of tires on pavement and the sloughing of sandals on the sidewalks as the vacationing multitudes headed back from their afternoon by the sea. Already many people were framed in window casements mounted in studios perched above the pizza stands and overlooking a stream of traffic. There was no smell of the Mediterranean. It was rather an odor of frying food, automobile exhaust, Vaseline, garlic, air-conditioning vents.

Were there, among the crowds of modern French enjoying their modern vacations, some residents of the Lirons' valley, some of those farmers in heavy overalls who have made thousands of terraces in their lives, even as the mulberry cultivation followed apple cultivation into oblivion? No doubt, some of these vacationers sitting in the greasy air on this violated beach were the young people mentioned by M. Liron, the ones who left Deep France to become residents of the modern country. The Liron brothers weren't here, though. They belonged to what Braudel has called "the time and space of yesterday," to that disappearing France where you can still hear "strange music, the sound of sheep bells, a dog barking, a man calling out commands, and the flock traveling past, gradually moving away into the silence."

I know that chiming of bells and the accompanying tapping of a heavy stick on the rocky soil as a shepherd leads his flock into the hills. It is a pleasant old-fashioned sound, like the clop-clop-clop of a horse drawing a carriage through the streets of a village, the sound of the unrecapturable past, whose pleasures are not always wholly imagined by the urban sentimentalists of today. I drove away from the beach at Montpellier feeling sad for the bachelor brothers of the Mas Corbières, certainly not envying them for their Deep France existence and yet sensing how lost and alienated, how trapped and hemmed in, they would feel on this strip of vacation homes. The scene in Montpellier is, in a sense, the metaphorical alternative forged by a modern economy to the Lirons' way of life: an urban existence and an occasional vacation whose questionable aesthetic properties do not come from bad taste or ignorance of something better—these people on the beach have, after all, all heard of Saint-Jean-Cap-Ferrat—but arise out of economic reality. This is what they can afford. The vacationers, of course, would hardly know how to exist up on the Liron brothers' impoverished hillside redoubt. The Lirons would be lost down here in Montpellier. I hoped for the sake of all three of them, cordial and full of their homespun wisdom as they were, that they would stay where they were, enjoying what René Liron aptly called "a free life," until they too, as he put it, have to leave by the wrong side.

4

Paris the Conqueror

THE MOMENT comes in the spring in Paris when the weather starts to get a bit warmer, and suddenly, every morning, there is the sound of metal scraping on concrete as the café waiters put chairs and tables in the open air. Making a different sound, the Parisians also emerge from their winter hiding places. They sip little cups of coffee or *citron pressé* at the vast square in front of the Opéra, or perhaps on the Place de la Contrescarpe, a shabbily genteel little square in the Latin Quarter, or under the budding plane trees in the Place Dauphine, or perhaps out beyond the Bastille, at one of the cafés placed along the Canal Saint-Martin. They appear on the little footbridge that crosses the Seine opposite the Cour Carré of the Louvre; they stroll on the asphalt walkways—obediently keeping off the grass—in the Luxembourg Gardens and the Parc Monceau. Miniature, remote-control sailboats operated by small children crowd the basin in the Tuileries. Swarthy men wearing white skullcaps put out used goods for sale on the broad divider in the middle of the boulevard de Belleville, while farther to the east, where the boulevard de Belleville becomes the boulevard de Rochechouart, single men of all ages appear for an odd rite of spring. Still in the morning and lasting all day, in front of tents all along the boulevard, girls in skimpy outfits strut under strings of colored lights while barkers with amplified voices invite you inside to see them, upon payment of a small entrance fee, entirely *au naturel*.

The outbreak of spring is an annual reminder that Paris is everybody's favorite city, the world's most beautiful, the one you have to know in order to be a man or woman of the world. And it is a place of remarkable charm and interest, a place that has more of everything—more museums and movies, more bookstores and restaurants, more intellectuals per square inch, more distinguished men and beautiful women, more shops selling designer clothing, more grand monuments and historic places than just about any other great urban conglomeration in the world. That alone might very well seem to mark the basic difference between it and the rest of France, between the France that is Parisian—and this category exists not only in Paris but in Avignon, Lyon, Saint-Tropez, Cannes, and the ski slopes of Val d'Isère—and the France that is "deep." In fact the charm of Paris, the things about it that have drawn people to it for centuries, cannot be dismissed. But they are not the main things that make Paris different. Nor is that to be found in the distinction between the modern and the old-fashioned, the sophisticated and the naive, in the touchingly hopeful letters to movie actresses from the one and the hotshot theatrical agents from the other. But if these distinctions have been erased by the apparatuses of the modern world, what are the differences?

They involve several component parts of the French capital. First, Paris has what came early in this century to be called the beau monde, which is a variation on what in English we came in more recent times to call the "beautiful people"—the smart set, the crowd that sets the fashions, both material and intellectual. The Parisians also talk about *le tout Paris*, everybody important in Paris, and while there is also a *tout Deauville* and a *tout Lyon*, the plain fact is that they don't count very much on the national scene; only *le tout Paris* is the national beau monde. Second, Paris is the place where the working class of France achieved its self-awareness and fomented revolution, and where its now less revolutionary spiritual center remains in such artifacts as the modern—one is tempted to say Stalinoid—massive headquarters of the Communist party. Third, Paris is the *lieu* of the avant-garde, not the artistic avant-garde of the *Belle Époque*, of Fauvists, Dadaists, and Surrealists, all of whom have largely disappeared as Paris has lost its status to New York, London, and Tokyo as the place where things happen in the world of the arts; but still, Paris is the place of concentration in a country of concentration, the place of the elites in a country that grants its elites the status of royalty. Paris decrees fashions, ideas, trends—more so in France, where Paris is the only truly great city, than the great urban conglomerations of other countries do, even more so than New York, which is rivaled in various aspects of cultural and intellectual life by such places as Los Angeles, Chicago, Cambridge, and Washington, D.C.

And yet the distinction between Deep France and Parisian France, so important to the Parisians, so talked about in the provinces, does not seem satisfactorily accounted for by these factors. For even if Paris has the beau monde and the provinces do not, even if Paris is the center of the class struggle in France and the venue of the avant-garde, the city might not yet embody a fundamental, qualitative difference of the sort that would justify the certainty of the Parisian view of the world as divided between themselves and the others. These are largely quantitative distinctions. France is France; Paris is France also in this sense, only more so. And it is justly renowned for being more so. But Paris, that great village on the Seine, that overgrown version of Le Chambon-sur-Lignon, of Valleraugue, of Aubagne, is not distinct from the rest of France because it represents a higher form of enlightenment than the deeper parts of the country.

Paris is different because it alone stands for Frenchness as we know it today. It created it, molded the concept to its own specifications. Greater France is a vast territory, a broad isthmus (as the historians have called it) between the Mediterranean and the North Sea, whose separate parts were too various for the whole to have a common identity. During the past thousand years or so, Paris threw its net over the territory; it gained suzerainty over the rest, first politically, then linguistically and culturally, finally morally and aesthetically. The rest of the isthmus is a Parisian colony, a subdued land, even if the wounds received during the process of subjugation, which was often violent, healed long ago. Paris's image as the City of Light, the special center of civilized behavior, of high culture and immutable values, emanated outward to encompass the rest of France. The historian Jules Michelet wrote that "Paris conquered France: and France the world." There could be no better encapsulation of the city's meaning. Paris is different because it is the conqueror of France and through France of the rest of us.

Various scholars have tried to account for this extraordinary and essential phenomenon, which saw a village on an island in the middle of the Seine become the greatest city of continental Europe. One of the theories is that the Arab expansion of the eighth century forced the kings of Carolingian France northward, where they made their base on the bend of the Seine. Eventually, Charles Martel put together the armies needed to stop the Arab hordes in Poitiers in 732. The Carolingians, who created the first French monarchy, chose the area of Paris, as we have seen, because it was at the center of a rich agricultural region, where horses could be raised on the oats that grew there. The horses, used with stirrups, an essential innovation, were the basis for the French cavalry and gave the Paris basin its military advantage.* Starting from its military and political ascendancy, the city of Paris, at its height the most populous in Europe, exercised a kind of spiritual hegemony over France, using the strength and wealth of the entire country to boost its claim of being mankind's universal city, its moral heart.

And so Paris is not merely the largest town in France, not merely the political and intellectual capital where all the smartest and most ambitious people from the provinces go to seek fame and fortune. If the origins of many of the Parisians lie in *La France Profonde*, the origins of the French identity nonetheless lie in Paris. *Le tout Paris* in this sense means something more than the gathering of the small number of people in town who count most socially, though of course it does mean that as well. It also suggests that to be Parisian is to have an identity that transcends social class, economic distinction; it is to belong to a world apart, to an intellectual and moral category, not of class, race, or gender, but of a qualitative difference from the rest, an essential worldliness, a heightened expectation—as F. Scott Fitzgerald put it in a different context—of the possibilities of life.

Many people, foreigners who belonged to Paris and Parisians exiled from it, put it their own way. Rainer Maria Rilke, the German poet, identified Paris as the place where the *élan vital*, Bergson's phrase for the life force, is stronger than elsewhere. "*Élan vital*," Rilke asked, "is it life? No. Life is calm, vast, simple. It is the desire to live in haste, in pursuit; it is the impatience to possess all of life right away, right here. Paris is full of this desire; that is why it is so close to death." Victor Hugo, the great novelist and poet, exiled for many years of his life, meant the same thing when he wrote: "Ever since historic times, there has always been on the earth what we call the City. . . . We have needed the city that thinks. . . . We have needed the city where everybody is citizen. . . . Jerusalem unleashes the True. Athens the Beautiful; Rome the Great. Paris is the sum of all three of these great cities."

And yet there is a question: Is Paris still great? Or has it become

---

*I have drawn here on Fernand Braudel's posthumously published book, *The Identity of France* (New York: Harper & Row, 1989), in which the historian provides a summary of several theories accounting for the paramountcy of Paris.

something of a living museum, a relatively quiet place living on the enormous accumulated capital of past glory? If France in the twentieth century has faced the agony of its own relative decline in importance, is Paris the capital of that decline?

It is easy to run into the sentiment that all is lost for Paris. You have only to get into a taxi at the airport for the drive into the center of town, get caught in a traffic jam, and start talking to your driver—assuming that he is not a recent immigrant—and you will uncover this view.

"There are no Parisians anymore," one such taxi driver told me, though he need not have been a taxi driver; he could have been a worker at the Renault plant in Boulogne-Billancourt or an *écailler*, an opener of oysters, at the shellfish bar of the Brasserie Lorraine on the Place des Ternes, or a science teacher at the Lycée Louis le Grand. But he happened to have been a taxi driver, about sixty, small and wizened, born and raised in Paris. He was listening to French operettas on his car's cassette player and remarking to me that "that is music, monsieur, real music ... that is singing, not like today, where the music is loud and barbaric. ... Today's music drowns out the words. ... The music doesn't accompany the singer anymore, but the singer the music.

"There are no Parisians anymore, monsieur," he repeated. And when I asked what makes a Parisian, he said: "It used to be different, monsieur. We all knew each other in the old days. There were neighborhoods like little villages, where when you went out into the street, you saw people that you knew. You talked to people. People went to church on Sunday, not like today. And there weren't so many foreigners. Not that I'm a racist, monsieur. Not at all. I don't vote Le Pen [a reference to Jean-Marie Le Pen, the president of the anti-immigrant National Front party]. But look at what's going on, in Belleville and the Thirteenth Arrondissement; there are neighborhoods that are entirely Arab; others are Chinese. I've got nothing against Arabs and Chinese. I don't think we're better than they are. But why should they be here? No, monsieur, there are no Parisians anymore. You know what we've become, monsieur? Anonymous. That's it. Anonymous. We're all just small people in a city that doesn't have its personality anymore. We're being swallowed up. We've lost a lot. There's no doubt about it."

I pressed this taxi driver, this lover of operettas and cozy neighborhoods. What makes a Parisian a Parisian? What are his characteristics? Perhaps they are those of the wrinkled, ageless petit-bourgeois couple, the husband and wife sitting together at a little café called À La Marquise on the rue Simon Bolivar, he hunched over a little espresso, she drinking a *chocolat chaud*, the two of them a bit small, a bit sad, a bit *usé*, as the French say, a bit worn down, like that famous café couple in the painting by Degas. Or perhaps Paris is represented by a young woman, very casual in a black skirt and a silk blouse with a scarf, having dinner with a somewhat older man in some classic café, say the Brasserie Stella on the avenue Victor Hugo, and looking as though she could transform a cowgirl's outfit into an instance of haute couture, because in her case, it is not the clothes that make the woman but the Parisian woman who makes the clothes. Maybe it is the mustached man in a white apron presiding over a hundred different kinds of cheese at his store on the rue Lévis, dispensing expertise, speaking of cheese the way an art history instructor might talk about paintings, as an element in a refined existence.

What makes a Parisian? A certain style? An intonation of language? A way of speaking? For the taxi driver, apparently, a Parisian can be distinguished from another sort of Frenchman by the way he looks and talks, by the way he spends his day, by a certain connoisseurship of life, an appreciation of the quaint charms of Paris's beauty. This person would like a Paris whose lists of names resembled that of the Cambremer telephone directory. His nostalgia derived from an image of his city similar to one of those naive paintings that became the rage in the 1980s, showing a little Parisian square from the point of view of a child's innocent eyes, with all the ideal elements in place: the grouping of narrow houses with wrought-iron balustrades and gray slate roofs and dormer windows, clustered around a small green space with plane trees and a café, along with a *boulangerie* and a couple of people passing by on bicycles. It is Paris as picture postcard, Paris as an imagined bit of space-time where life was whole, simple, predictable; the touching, wholesome Paris of sweet little movies like *The Red Balloon* or searing dramas like *Hôtel du Nord*, but a Paris that was wholly, uniquely, unmistakably, unalloyedly French.

But that's just it. The Paris that the taxi driver imagines, the city he believes is disappearing (and they have all through this century believed that Paris was disappearing), is not Hugo's city of the world or Rilke's place that lives close to death. Many Parisians, like the taxi driver, have always been struggling against the essence of Paris, not realizing that what they saw as decline, as the growth of impersonality, as the increase of foreigners, as the sound of music that was not real music, was really their city's greatness, the thing that made it unique in the world.

Paris, to be Paris, must be the place where the great moral dilemmas of mankind are identified and where the experiments in the life of thought—if not of action—take place at the highest register. Paris should be infuriating, as it must have been to millions when, for example, Édouard Manet painted a naked woman lunching on the grass, or when Antoine Artaud philosophized about *le théâtre de cruauté*, "the theater of cruelty," or Samuel Beckett wrote about the theater of the absurd, or François Truffaut said in *Cahiers du Cinéma* that the films being made then were merely pale replicas of books, not true films. Above all, for Paris to be Paris, it has to be free. The question thus is not: Are there too many Arabs in Belleville, too many Chinese in the Thirteenth Arrondissement, too many neighborhoods that have lost their character? The question is: Will the fear that there are no longer any Parisians lead the inhabitants of the great village on the Seine no longer to fashion a place that matters to all humanity? Will, in fact, Paris become indistinguishable from France itself, just the capital city of a medium-sized country, or will it shine with its particular luminosity, guaranteeing greatness to France no matter what its size?

T HERE ARE of course several cities called Paris—the city of great monuments and the city of separate arrondissements, each with its own history and character, its social classes and cultural styles, each mirroring an element in the life of France itself. You could draw up a kind of map of the human geography of Paris, a list of the kinds of people one would see in different places. Like the imaginary tour of the perimeter of the entire country, the map would show, above all, variety. You could start in the Sixteenth Arrondissement or in the Seventh, the two locales of the haute bourgeoisie, where the apartments are grand and the shopping expensive. The general belief is that the Seventh Arrondissement is the venue of old money and the Sixteenth of new. No matter. In both places dwell gray-suited bankers and businessmen, doctors and lawyers, living within heavy, ornamented walls. This is the Paris reputed, in the oversimplified view of the average American tourist, to be on the snooty, unfriendly, brusque, and impatient side. I lived for a time in what I called *le triste seizième*, "the sad Sixteenth," mocking my neighborhood's formality, its absence of commercial vitality and charm, its dark, formal dining rooms, where *les dîners en ville*, "dinner parties in town," are held. There are, of course, delightful people in the Sixteenth and the Seventh, but it would be fair to say that there is a heavy dose of the entirely fashionable, status-conscious rich as well. You won't see very many of them, however, if you stroll the streets. Perhaps if you drive by the private grammar school on the rue de Lota, just off the avenue Victor Hugo, you might see slender, well-dressed mothers dropping their young, well-dressed children off in the morning, or picking them up at night. But in general, one of the major characteristics of the Sixteenth Arrondissement is its absence of street life, the village-like silence of its streets. And there is indeed a sadness to these districts, evacuated on weekends by the large numbers of residents who have houses in the country. I have felt a melancholy, strolling areas of so much beauty and so little visible life. It is not good to be a foreigner in the Sixteenth.

To view members of motorcycle gangs and their molls with orange hair you might try the Champs-Élysées around midnight or, perhaps, the district around the vast Pompidou Center and the Forum des Halles, in what used to be the working-class district known as Beaubourg. The Champs-Élysées was once an elegant avenue of grand private homes, the wealthiest in the city, a former Sixteenth Arrondissement. It is now a broad strip of shopping galleries, movie theaters, automobile showrooms, advertising and film studio offices, racy nightclubs like the Lido—a place boasting mostly Scandinavian and American bare breasts and the most elaborate stage machinery outside of the Paris Opéra—game parlors, and no fewer than eleven fast-food joints, with names like Quick-Élysées, Free Time, Pop-Inn. When Fouquet's, the elegant eatery that for years still offered its basic nineteenth-century menu, closed down in 1989, the last vestige of the avenue as a center of style disappeared with it. The Champs-Élysées relinquished, perhaps forever, its status as a venue of upper-bourgeois life. But for observing the Parisians, it has a bit of everything: conservative financiers and moneyed matrons during the day, students going to first-run features at night, beggars, pickpockets, traveling salesmen, mustached off-duty café waiters in leather jackets, the guys in from the suburbs; everything.

The area encompassing the Pompidou Center and the Forum des Halles has become Paris's carnival district, the place for street performers, the scruffy young, many of them arriving on the new ultrarapid subway, which extends its sinews into the grimy working-class suburbs, where the stained, high-rise subsidized apartment blocks, so carefully excluded from the pristine precincts of Paris itself, blot the landscape. Beaubourg is an odd area, with the playland glitter of the shopping and exhibition centers and the slightly too adorable manicured pedestrian malls standing cheek by jowl with ancient working-class quarters, where you can still see unionized railroad workers or post office employees having their morning *ballon de rouge*, goblet of red wine, in the neighborhood café, while other guys, cigarettes drooping from their lips, two-day growths of beards on their faces, hunch over the pinball machine.

Immutable, classic Paris comes in the Sixth Arrondissement, the area alongside the Luxembourg Gardens on the Left Bank, which is the seat of less showy but nonetheless very chic addresses and shops and the kind of charm normally associated with Paris. Here, too, is the solid Parisian bourgeoisie, but the type of urban professional more likely to be seen in a sweater or jacket with an open-collared shirt than in pin stripes. Here you can see authors and editors, journalists and publicists, descending the narrow stairs of the bar in the Hôtel Pont-Royal, where they will expect to meet their friends at the end of the afternoon. The publishing houses are here; the antique shops; many of the art galleries. The old Latin Quarter, just to the east, has become a mixed domain. There remain some of those creaky, intricate, nicely aged neighborhoods where a few hold-out intellectuals in studiously drab brown corduroys continue to live, or at least where they go to the many film-revival houses in the area, but much of it has become a rabbit warren of shops and inexpensive restaurants catering to the huge crowds of rowdy young people who come for the food and atmosphere.

Southward is the area of extraordinary demographic change of such concern to that taxi driver, the Thirteenth Arrondissement, Paris's ever-burgeoning Chinatown. Here you will see Vietnamese boat people and Chinese immigrants and the Caucasian clients of the Vietnamese and Chinese restaurants. On the Right Bank of the Seine, the demographic picture becomes more complicated and changeable as one moves eastward. The Marais, for example, a quarter of narrow streets and ancient habitations just east of the Pompidou Center, was the original Jewish quarter of Paris. There are kosher restaurants and religious bookstores, men with beards and skullcaps, small children emerging from Hebrew schools, blond Sephardic women selling hummus and eggplant salad in ethnic delicatessens. The Marais is still one of the Jewish quarters, there being several in the city now, but it has also become a district where ever more expensive, often rather small apartments are being renovated by young professional couples. The chic restaurants have arrived, the decorators and frame shops and art galleries. The people here have that young and hungry look.

Indeed, these days, if you have upwardly mobile friends in Paris, people with good educations and excellent prospects who are in the early to mid stages of a career, they are far less likely to live in such glamorous districts as the Sixth Arrondissement and more likely to be in the Marais or in the small streets ranging north of the Forum des Halles, or out along the avenue de la République beyond the old site of the Bastille— that is, in the higher-numbered arrondissements, the Eighteenth to the Twentieth, those on the outer edges of the city rather than at its center. The area called Belleville is perhaps the best example of the transformation of one of the old *quartiers populaires*. For centuries, this north- easternmost section of Paris was one of woods, fields, orchards, abbeys, and vineyards, lying well outside the actual, de jure city limits. There is a 1904 photograph showing a man with an Old Testament beard and a black suit standing near a stern-looking woman in a long, black, stern- looking dress, both of them tending what the caption identifies as the last of the vineyards of the area, which was becoming a crowded work- ing-class district by the early nineteenth century. A particular institution called a *courtille* flourished in Belleville and the long hill alongside it, known for centuries as Ménilmontant. It was a drinking establishment arranged in open fields, where tables were put under bowers and lovers of the fruit of the vine could taste the various products of the district. Workers of the Faubourg Saint-Antoine passed their Sundays in the country in such places.

By the early eighteenth century, with the outskirts of Paris invading the Belleville countryside, the favored entertainment spot was the famous *guingette*, an immense dance hall, where, according to a guidebook of 1928, "you can dance, you can dine, you can make love, you can throw away your cares, you can pour out your heart, you can sup, and all of it in the most pleasant way in the world." Between 1840 and 1860, the population of Belleville quadrupled from fifteen thousand to sixty thou- sand people. Retired merchants, small landlords, other members of the bourgeoisie, occupied the houses that spread out on top of the hill of Ménilmontant. Workers came to the quarters at the bottom of the hill. Belleville, still not administratively a part of Paris, became the third- largest city in France. Its lower portions, called Bas-Belleville, became known to social crusaders and investigating journalists as a seat of squa- lor and misery, a cradle of radical sentiment, a major recruiting ground for the proletarian disturbances that rocked Paris throughout the nine- teenth century, including the famous, sanguinary Commune of 1871. The final pages of that extraordinary episode took place in Père Lachaise Cemetery, where, under a mournful rain, hundreds of desperate Com- munards were bayoneted by the soldiers of the government. Until well into this century, Bas-Belleville was viewed as an unsavory, dangerous place full of thieves, radicals, and other lowlifes.

What places like Belleville gave to Paris in the past was a large part of its political consciousness and turmoil. Today Belleville represents Paris's status as an immigrant city. It is a place where Chinese restaurants with roast ducks hanging in their windows are just down the street from Serge Hannouna's kosher butcher shop—the former representing the wave of Indochinese boat people who came to France in the 1970s, the latter the large numbers of Sephardic Jews from Algeria, Tunisia, and Morocco who have been arriving for the past thirty years. And then, outside Hannouna's on the broad, tree-lined rue Belleville, there might well be a bearded Moslem in a white skullcap selling Oriental rugs, or perhaps fresh stalks of parsley and mint, on the sidewalk. The Parisian snob is said to have found himself years ago in the midst of some American or British visitors in one of the city's good neighborhoods, a situation that led him to utter the sardonic question: "Is this still Paris?" Now the Parisians, like our taxi driver, look at places like Belleville, and they ask the same question. The answer is: Yes, this is Paris.

THE HUMAN geography hints at but does not encompass something else about Paris and its meaning. Paris is ever-changing and enormously varied, and it always has been. But what has not changed is the city's embodiment of the glory of the French self-conception. I don't mean that the Parisians pass their days aware of the light of history glancing off their shoulders. The Parisians live and struggle for livelihoods, security, and love like all other people, and they are not always bewitched by the properties of their place of abode that make it the foreigner's favorite city. People commit suicide in Paris; some are lonely, poor, and unhappy there. I have been to apartment buildings in the *quartiers populaires* on both banks of the Seine where the citizens of the world's most glamorous city climb five flights of rotting wooden stairs to arrive at their little apartments, where the "Turkish toilet"— a small round hole at the far end of a ceramic basin embedded in the ground—is in a fetid closet on the floor below and where the sound of squalling children and the smell of frying garlic from the neighbor's place in the alley across the street never disappears. There is the district known as the *Goutte d'Or* (Gold Nugget), a menacing slum inhabited largely by African immigrants, where an American friend of mine was chased by a gang of youths, barely escaping with his life, after he took out his camera to take a snapshot. That, too, is Paris.

But the truth is that in inventing Paris to be the crown of civilization, its people became well aware of the marvels they were creating. The city's special qualities can be enumerated: its remarkable beauty; the liveliness of its many neighborhoods; the temerity of its scale; its physical glory, which, in a sense, mirrors the yearning for glory that has been a central motive of national policy for centuries; its status as a place where both the high arts and the arts of day-to-day life have flowered as they have, perhaps, no place else. Paris is, indeed, a movable feast, as Hemingway cleverly called it. It is still worth a Mass, just as King Henri IV thought upon his conversion from Protestantism to Catholicism in 1593, which enabled him to take the throne of very Catholic France. To explore Paris is to see in it the characteristics that the French most value. It is a physical mirror of their soul.

For as long as I lived in Paris, I never completely accustomed myself to its remarkable beauty. If you stand on the Thames in London, you will see on the north side of the river a kind of undistinguished urban sprawl that does not reflect the city's greatness. The center of Paris, by contrast, is a consistent work of art, a chiseled piece of urban sculpture, a place that has been created over the centuries to be lovely everywhere. London, again by way of contrast, is smudged and stodgy, its architecture pleasantly plain and utilitarian. Paris is ornate, embellished, as sumptuous as the interiors of the city's great brasseries, filled with polished brass and amber lamplight.

If you stand on the little footbridge across the Seine near the Louvre and look eastward, the view of the Île de la Cité, dominated by the Cathedral of Notre-Dame, decorated by exquisite masonry houses overlooking the water, anchored by such other marvels as the fourteenth-century Conciergerie (where Marie-Antoinette was imprisoned in 1792) and the spires of Sainte-Chapelle arising from the courtyard of the Palais de Justice, the main courthouse, cannot help but take your breath away. Or you might wander into the Place Dauphine, the triangular little park under plane trees just opposite the Palais de Justice, for a small brown cup of foamy espresso, or wander through the flower market just next door to the hospital called Hôtel-Dieu, and Paris will ring in your ear like a finely tuned bell.

On the Left Bank, running in a semicircle just off the boulevard Saint-Germain is a little street called the rue de Buci, which I would recommend on a late Sunday morning. An outdoor market runs down the major part of the street, in front of the Hôtel Louisiane, a simple, inexpensive place where modest writers stay and, during the major fashion shows each year, some of the models—making the rue de Buci a good place to view striving intellectuals and young women who don't seem to have to strive at all. The market is one of the city's best, a cornucopia of fish and crustaceans, meats and fowl, game and inner organs, vegetables, fruits, wines and liquors, preserves, pâtés, cheeses, breads, pastries, chocolates, and other edibles for the refined Parisian palate. Many—not all—of the French eat well, but the Parisians arguably eat better than the others. It is another instance of the city's paramountcy. Sit at the Brasserie Le Muniche in the closed terrace, where the windows open onto the shelves of shellfish just outside and where the *écaillers* are doing their work with quick, lethal turning motions of the wrist. On the rue de Buci will very likely be an accordionist, which is something of a cliché. But you can eat oysters—which the Parisians consume with reckless abandon, producing daily mountains of dank shucked shells—drink white wine, and listen to the music. The cliché is so perfectly conceived that it transforms itself into a post-modernist entertainment.

Paris began on the Île de la Cité in the sixth century, and slowly it expanded, spreading out on both sides of the river (before embarking on its subjugation of the rest of France), and its development of both sides of the river simultaneously gave rise to two opposing symbols of the universal urban spirit. The Left Bank, in large part because it was the site of the Sorbonne—founded by one Robert de Sorbon in 1253 as a refuge for sixteen poor theology students—has always been the locus classicus of intellectual life, though the intellectuals have become far more scattered throughout the city than ever before. To this day, the Left Bank retains a smaller scale than the Right. It has fewer monumental structures, more narrow, twisting streets, greater charm—though, after all, it does have its share of monumental architecture in such buildings as the Palais-Bourbon (where the National Assembly meets), the Panthéon, and the Invalides, the former military hospital (and Paris's most beautiful architectural masterpiece) built by Louis XIV, in which Napoleon is buried. The Left Bank, eventually a worldwide symbol of a certain antiestablishmentarian, bohemian way of life, was all along a residential area, and the houses are on an entirely human scale, relatively modest, built around inner courtyards, the homes of thinkers, artists, writers, and others who eschewed the opulence and architectural pretension of the other side of the river.

The Right Bank, by contrast, was the seat of government, of royal power, and it has always carried a certain style of visible authority. If the Left Bank was, perhaps, Greenwich Village, the Right was Rome, or Washington. The inner square fortress of the Louvre was built on the Right Bank in 1190, and for the next eight hundred years it was altered and expanded, forged into an ever grander and more imposing edifice with each addition, as was deemed suitable for a place that was, at times, the actual residence of Europe's most powerful kings and, always, their symbolic abode. The Louvre, whose wings are each just about half a mile long, sets the tone for Parisian magnificence. Sharing its bank of the river are such other colossi as the Palais-Royal, the Hôtel de Ville, the Arc de Triomphe, the Place de la Concorde, the National Library, the Grand Palais and the Petit Palais, the Tuileries Gardens, along with such grand avenues as the Champs-Élysées, arguably the world's most celebrated street. All of it was created, consciously, to reflect French glory and prestige, under both the monarchy and the country's various republics.

When, in the mid-nineteenth century, an engineer named Baron Georges-Eugène Haussmann began, under Napoleon III (who deemed himself an emperor), to reorganize and modernize Paris, carving out of the helter-skelter network of lanes and alleys the broad, straight avenues and parks of today, many were dissatisfied, criticizing the city's new design for what they saw as its ungainliness, its aspect of a Babylon on the Seine. (One of the characteristics of Paris, as we shall see, is that no architectural innovation comes without intense controversy.) Today Haussmann's redesign of Paris seems to have increased the city's intentional grandeur. Note that the buildings on the five streets that end, with geometrical precision, at the Place de l'Opéra are all mirror images of each other. Paris is big and imposing because it was designed to be so. When private people, particularly the wealthy bourgeoisie, built their homes in the outlying areas of the Right Bank, they naturally mimicked the city's royalist style of ornamentation. The vast stretches of ornate, carved buildings, such perfect squares as the Place des Vosges, the Place François I, the Place Vendôme, all with their sculpted facades, immense windows, and wrought-iron balustrades, their statuary, their columns, their steeply pitched roofs, also emblemize the temerity of the French self-conception.

I happen to love looking at the Eiffel Tower, particularly from below, as it soars with its particular spindly power, its great legs leaping across the earth, while its new illumination from the interior gives it an eerie, orange sort of glow at night. The tower, built to mark the centennial of the revolution of 1789, was, after all, the very symbol of progress in the late nineteenth century, a physical symbol of the positivist optimism that mankind, liberated from the shackles of the feudal, royalist, superstitious, clericalist past, could soar metaphorically into the sky. In this sense, the Eiffel Tower, though not appreciated as such by most of the tourists who ride the elevators up its great legs, makes as good a representation of the French self-conception as any.

The great tower and the other splendid monuments of the city, its incorporation as a place of beauty and grandeur, are at the center of the city's global mission. Or, at least, they make up one part of it, the other part being that ever-endangered commitment to the values of the Enlightenment, which has always made Paris not just a magnificent place but a certain place of the spirit as well. The monuments show the audacity of the French, their grandiose sense of themselves. When François I embarked on the reconstruction of the Louvre in 1527, part of the process of transforming it from a medieval fortress to a Renaissance palace, he was declaring himself to be not merely the king of France but the monarch of the globe, one whose reign would extend over the concept of grandeur and civilization itself. The audacity of a city, to constitute itself as the locus of so much splendor! "Power in this country has always meant a château," the historian Emmanuel Le Roy Ladurie once said. Paris is the architectural embodiment of the imaginary country, its numerous great buildings extensions of its grandiose view of itself.

Some 450 years after François I, when the Socialists came back to power in 1988 after a two-year Conservative interregnum, a newly defined ministry was created for the man who, in the earlier government, had been only the minister of culture. He became the Minister of Culture, Communications, the Great Projects, and the Bicentennial. The bicentennial was that of the French Revolution, to be marked as a great development in the evolution of the human spirit. The Great Projects referred to several large-scale construction endeavors the Socialists had put in place in earlier years, including, most notably, the construction of a glass pyramid at the center of the once again renovated Louvre. Could there be such a cabinet-level position, a Secretary of Great Projects, in the United States? Would even Britain, with a bit of a tradition of self-importance itself, create such a post? I don't think so. It seemed always to me to reflect that particularly French notion that certain elements of the nation were of transcendent importance, enabling France to be larger than itself, greater than the sum of its parts.

There is, of course, pretension in the notion of Paris as the pampered seat of French grandeur. For one thing, it seems a bit obsolete as a concept at the end of the twentieth century, when France itself, its culture, and its ideas no longer shake the world as they once did. In the nineteenth century, when Paris held a grand exhibition—as the British historian Alistair Horne pointed out in *The Fall of Paris: The Siege and the Commune, 1870–71*—it was one of the events of world history, a high-water mark of technological and cultural civilization. And in the early to mid twentieth century, when the Parisians and the immigrants to the city propagated a series of ideas central to our intellectual history, Paris was the place the world watched. There is a kind of parlor game in Paris that consists of comparing the city today to the grand, legendary past epochs, during which its current incarnation always comes out lacking. For the fact is that Paris has an extraordinary past to live up to. It is no longer the exciting center of world intellectual and artistic revolt, as it was for much of the nineteenth and twentieth centuries. Neither Pierre-Joseph Proudhon (remembered for that catchy, pre-totalitarian slogan "Property is theft") nor Louis-Auguste Blanqui, nor Louis Blanc nor the "red virgin," Louise Michel, any longer stalk its streets. The Fauvists and the Cubists, the Dadaists and the Surrealists, the devotees of the *nouvelle vague* in film and the *nouveau roman* in literature, the existentialists and the situationists, are all gone, leaving the Left Bank cafés to sentimental literary tourists. There is a school of extraordinary historians; there are the post-structuralist literary critics, particularly the deconstructionists, the most important of whom were French, not to mention the post-Freudian psychoanalysts, but intellectual life, still fascinating, does not have the revolutionary vitality that was Paris's alone for several decades. And so the players of the parlor game called comparative history conclude that Paris has lost one of the major roles that gave it its mission to mankind—its status as the seat of the avant-garde.

Perhaps this is an unfair judgment. One might argue, indeed, that the world itself in its post-modernist phase—where the trick is not so much to invent something new as to comment wryly on what has transpired in the past—is not as inventive or as revolutionary as it was several decades ago. And yet it cannot be denied that over the years, France has lost to the United States its role as the world's chief intellectual protagonist. Who outside France reads new French novels anymore? What are the great current French films? Who in the current French firmament can compare to the likes of Artaud, Gide, Sartre, Malraux, Camus? When in 1985 the novelist Claude Simon became the first Frenchman to win the Nobel Prize for literature in twenty-one years, very few even among the French had heard of him. The previous French winner, Jean-Paul Sartre (who, in an act of ultimate reverse snobbery, declined it), was world famous.

The Parisians have responded in contradictory fashion to this long-term loss of international presence. On the one hand, there is discouragement. The writers of best-selling books who cannot get American publishers for them complain that they have become too *franco-français*, incomprehensible to the rest of the world. There is a certain bewilderment that French concerns are no longer universal ones. At the same time, the Parisians and their leaders fight a persistent battle to maintain their city's grandeur, its place as a world capital of meaningful events. The battle is forced at times, even a bit tragicomic. So much of what happens in Paris and so much of the way it happens, the manner in which controversies unfold and projects and events are announced and planned, are touched either by a reflexive, unexamined belief in the global Parisian importance or by a defensive effort to maintain the city's luster.

There are many examples making up part of the texture of Parisian life. When President Mitterrand in 1984 asked the architect I. M. Pei to design a master plan for a newly redesigned Louvre Museum, it unleashed one of those furious Parisian quarrels that can come only from a citizenry's jealously guarded love for the image of its city. Mr. Pei, who designed a controversial—and now completed—glass pyramid to stand at the center of the reorganized museum, said that when he presented his plan to a committee of French experts, he was stunned and shocked by the virulence of their response. Indeed, the pyramid unleashed talk on a whole host of subjects, talk that had a particular Parisian flavor, precisely because of the belief among the Parisians that part of the city's essence and mission is to be without blemish. The constant references, tinged at times with racist resentment, to Mr. Pei as being of Chinese origin seemed rooted in a consternation that no French architect had been deemed worthy of being given the task. And the entire debate about the Chinese-American's design, whether it was an elegant solution to a perplexing problem, as Pei maintained, or whether it was, as the critics charged, a desecration in the form of an Egyptian death image, had that special Parisian quality of intensity, cleverness, and fervor, which could come only from a concern that something deeply sacred—the very appearance of Paris itself—was at stake. Other cities have their debates about architecture, but it is probably safe to say that only in Paris would such an issue have produced quite that quantity of spilled ink, quite that scope of impassioned commentary. Three art historians, operating in the pamphleteering tradition of Voltaire, the Abbé de Sieyès, and Émile Zola, wrote a kind of "J'accuse" in the form of a sarcastic, witty, learned, and ultimately foolish little volume entitled *Paris Mystified*, whose main argument was that Mitterrand had dragged the Louvre into a "politics of prestige in which immoderation is the rule and overstatement the spirit." The political element in the debate produced some of its best wit. Mitterrand, accused of wanting to erect a lasting monument to his vainglory, was called Mitteramses I or the pharaoh François. Was it by coincidence that most of the commentators who lined up on the political right were against the project, while those for it were pro-Socialist in their political persuasions? When the monument was completed and opened to the public, the debate suddenly vanished. The Parisians seemed proud to have in their midst another edifice of world significance.

These are the things that give Paris some of its style, its weight, the sense that everything that happens in it is laden with significance. In 1987, for example, there was the intense discussion about an ultra-modern sculpture, created by Daniel Buren, which was eventually, and after a controversy that stretched across two French governments, installed in a courtyard, formerly used as a parking lot for government functionaries, inside the compound of the Palais-Royale, placed between the wing that belongs to the Ministry of Culture and the one occupied by the Conseil Constitutionnel, the closest body France has to a Supreme Court. Again, there was no question that removing the cars from that exquisite spot, that jewel of the monarchy just around the corner from the Comédie-Française, was a good decision. But the Buren sculpture was an odd thing, a difficult concept to grasp, consisting of several rows of black-and-white posts of various heights set into a large asphalt square that, in turn, ran over a mostly underground fountain that was visible, in part, through ground-level grates. As with the pyramid, the debate was lively, and it involved politics as well, since the Socialists, those fuzzy-headed slaves of innovation for the sake of innovation, had commissioned and approved the work. When it was continued by the Conservatives, it was done with a grudging tone; the reason it had to go ahead, the new minister of culture, François Léotard, said, was that it was already under way, and therefore "the rights of artistic creation" needed to be protected.

During the debate, Minister of Culture Jack Lang, whose office overlooked the eventual site of the sculpture, took me on his terrace and explained the project, pointing out, above all, the ugliness of the parking lot. After the sculpture was installed and had become part of Parisian life, no longer an object of debate, I happened to pay a call on Robert Badinter, the president of the Conseil Constitutionnel and a former minister of justice. We talked of several things of the sort that one would want to discuss with so highly placed an individual—politics, justice, the law. Before the discussion began, Badinter took me out on his balcony across the square from M. Lang's to say that he had, after considerable observation from his conveniently situated terrace, figured out what was wrong with the sculpture. The posts, he pointed out, were too small for two people to sit on comfortably and slightly too distant from each other for conversation to be easy for people sitting on adjacent ones. And therefore, he contended, one of the major goals of the public project— "to enhance the human contact," if I remember correctly, was the way Badinter put it—was not being fulfilled.

To be sure, both Lang and Badinter have offices overlooking the work in question, so their personal interest was natural. And yet I found it nonetheless significant that two cabinet-level officials had thought it appropriate to spend their precious time talking to an American journalist about a piece of Parisian sculpture. The work by Buren, like the I. M. Pei pyramid, and like the Eiffel Tower before them—itself the subject of intense argument at the time—was an issue that merited the attention of *le tout Paris*. Everyone was involved; everyone expressed, often in portentous, intemperate tones, an opinion; and everyone was seen to be involved in expressing these diverse opinions, exercising the relentless scrutiny inevitably generated by any planned addition to or deletion from the city's public places, those venues of taste, meaning, and history.

To some extent, what gives Paris its character is its sense of community, however disputatious and contentious the community may be, the sense of belonging to a unique and special place, unlike any other. Observers of the city noted long ago that, in contrast with New York or London, Paris is a place where worlds intersect, where people from one domain tend to know those in others and there is no tendency for different occupational or professional segments to create their own specialized hermetic worlds. "In Paris," wrote Maurice Sachs, a deeply flawed individual, a pro-Nazi Jew and collaborationist who nonetheless had some useful nonpolitical insights, "it seems that each state of society, each class, each chapel of the spirit, has delegated several of its members to a kind of *états généraux*, a senate of pleasure and knowledge." Beyond a certain point of success, which, Sachs points out, is reflected in financial terms, "an affiliation with *le tout Paris* necessarily results." But what draws *le tout Paris* into its sense of community is the common denominator provided by the city itself, its status as everybody's avocation, everybody's interest, everybody's passion.

As with the great buildings of Paris themselves, there is an insolence in this notion of *le tout Paris*, a braggadocio; there is temerity in believing that an association with Paris, as opposed to an association with Stockholm, Chicago, or, perhaps, Prague or Berlin, confers a distinction; but that is part of the magic of the imaginary country. I have attended award ceremonies in the Élysée Palace when the president of the Republic—always called the president of the Republic on these occasions, never just the president—gives out *Légions d'honneurs* to those who have, in his view, achieved something of particular note. There are usually several people—perhaps a film director, a foreign writer, a journalist, a wine grower, a businessman, perhaps a restaurateur, a scientist, a professor or two—grouped together in the ornate reception chamber of the palace, surrounded by friends and special guests. The president arrives, usually a half hour or so late, accompanied by his closest counselors and a few ministers of state, and while the crowd of perhaps a hundred or two forms a horseshoe around the ceremony, the president of the Republic, standing at its open end, makes a brief extemporaneous speech—a bit on the philosophical side, showing that he, too, is a person of reflection, like the other members of the assembly—citing the achievements of each of the recipients. Then he pins the medal on each of them, kissing them in turn on both cheeks. There is a champagne-and-smoked-salmon reception under the chandeliers of the *grand salle*, where *le tout Paris* mingles with the president, the cabinet ministers present, the special advisers, the award recipients, and their invited guests. France has done its duty, to confer its recognition on people of merit. *Le tout Paris* has witnessed it.

This kind of thing, to be truthful, has a certain aspect of parody, as political figures try a bit too hard to establish their credentials as latter-day Medicis, the patrons of the arts and the sciences. Under the Socialists—whom I speak of here merely because it is they who have been in power since I have known France from up close—the habit developed of holding grand international meetings of intellectuals, always in Paris. Within months of taking power in 1981, François Mitterrand, who has written a dozen or so books and, in contrast with heads of state on the other side of the Atlantic, is believed to read the books of others, called together a conference of cultural figures from around the world, everybody from William Styron to Sophia Loren, to mark his accession. Mitterrand had said early on that the Socialist project was "above all a cultural project." I never heard anybody explain what that meant, but I always assumed it had to do with the notion that there was more to life than the thirty-nine-hour week. In any case, the convocation provoked some sullen commentary to the effect that France no longer had the cultural brilliance to warrant such a gathering. In subsequent years, the Socialist government continued its efforts to summon to Paris the great of the world. The French love most of all to bestow badges of recognition, but they are given to a certain hero worship as they do so. It is a kind of grandeur by association, perhaps merely a need to have great personages within the boundaries of their great country. Elizabeth Taylor, for example, did not win the Nobel Prize, but she is lionized, adored, worshiped in France, and not merely by the glossy magazines. She is received and feted by the minister of culture and the president themselves when she comes to Paris. But the real attention is paid to the Nobel Prize winners. In 1985, in an exercise of a certain drawing power, the government, under the direct supervision of Laurent Fabius, the prime minister of the moment, held a conference, parts of which were televised live, of a group of winners of the Nobel Peace Prize, including Bishop Desmond Tutu of South Africa and Mother Teresa of India. A couple of years later, Mitterrand himself hosted a gathering of all sorts of Nobel Prize winners, some seventy-five in all, for no apparent purpose other than the prestige of their company. And why not? Why should the country of Voltaire and Diderot, Sartre and Malraux, not convene the intellectual giants of the twentieth century to the city of Voltaire and Diderot, Sartre and Malraux? It establishes Parisian centrality, or, at least, it breathes a bit of life into the idea of Parisian centrality. Whatever one may think of the idea—and I have to admit that I always saw a certain hollowness in it, a desperate quest for reflected glory—it reeks of the Parisian self-perception.

So, too, does another of those revealing French customs, the awarding of an extraordinary number of literary prizes—probably, though no statistics are available on this, the largest number per capita of any country—all of them designated in Paris in front of the usual beau monde. Each year there is the Goncourt, the Femina, the Interallié, the Medicis, the Renaudot, and others. They are highly sought after. Parties are planned at the publishing houses, in anticipation of the announcement of a winner. The party goes ahead if the news is as expected; otherwise, it is canceled, though that rarely happens, because insider intelligence on this sort of thing is pretty accurate, the major publishing houses tending usually to have at least one of their own authors, an earlier prize-winner, on the jury. The complaints about this, needless to say, are many, including that the whole business is implacably clubby and arbitrary, which it is, and that the small, ingrown tribe of judges considers not the whole gamut of works published in a given year but those published by certain houses, especially the holy trinity Gallimard, Grasset, and Seuil—Galligrasseuil, as one discontented chief editor at one of the other houses put it one year in an essay in *Le Monde*. Still, they signify something, though perhaps it is not first and foremost excellence. The prizes signify an aspect of the self-conception of the groups that make up Parisian society. They represent invitations to others to join in; they are tangible signs of membership in the city's most exclusive club—not the Automobile Club or the Jockey Club, where entry is by wealth and social position, but the Club of the Order of Merit, which embodies the republican idea. It is open to all and marks Paris's role as arbiter of excellence and good taste. As I said, there is temerity in this. A city that takes itself as seriously as Paris does needs to be audacious.

V ARIOUS writers have tried to discern how Paris has imposed its will, its tastes, its preferences and standards, and even its prizes on the rest of the world. Here, again, it is that concept of *le tout Paris*, the people who count, who make up the explanation. Leo Ferrero, writing about the city in 1931, traces Paris's global influence to the period of monarchy, when it "instructed the world in the magnificent rites of royalty." In a strange perpetuation of custom, the same city then instructed much of the world in every other sort of political system and idea imaginable, from bourgeois revolution to working-class insurrection, parliamentary republic to empire. In the same way, while at times weakened and fearful, living in a sense off the capital accumulated by Louis XIV, the French, led by the Parisians, have managed to remain closely watched. The word used by the French to describe the Parisian influence is *rayonnement*, which means something more than its standard translation—radiance. It is more active than that. It has to do with an extension of the light. And it was always the quality of the Parisian elite that allowed this extension, this radiation of the rest of the world from a central beacon. Paris, in the 1930s, Ferrero wrote, "continues to attract men and to send them back again into the world as carriers of its message." That is the deeper meaning of the prizes, the stamp of approval gained at one of those semiroyalist ceremonies at the Élysée Palace.

The elite itself also owes its origins to the days of the monarchy, when a small number of cultivated noblemen, wealthy members of the emerging bourgeoisie—whose deepest interest was not so much money as the titles and the honors the money would eventually gain for them—philosophers, particularly those who, in the eighteenth century, begat the Enlightenment, and, not to be dismissed, the society ladies who organized the fabulous "salons" where the rest of the beau monde could meet, created the standards observed by the rest of the world. Despite their predilection for occasional insurrection, the rest of the Parisians—called "*la multitude*" by Ferrero—accepted the elite's prescriptions in the domains of art and taste. The Parisian elite, born to determine standards, had a passion for judgment, for determining the values of things, for deciding who and what were to be esteemed, celebrated, honored—or, as Ferrero puts it, "to discern the men of the first order from the men of the second and to assign to them both their official places in the immense table of values that it was always creating."

"It is said that the public has a passion to admire wherever great men are to be found," Ferrero remarks. "I am tempted to reply that the great men are born where the public has the passion to admire them." Otherwise, how explain the diversity of the Parisian taste, its capacity to give its coveted medals of honor to different people of entirely contradictory characteristics. "The Parisians experience such an ardent need to admire," Ferrero writes, "that they do not fear being inconsistent. They admire for all sorts of reasons." Citing examples of people, some of whom are now unknown, Ferrero goes on: "They admire Pourtales because he comes on time, Fargue because he comes late; Poincaré because he answers letters; Gide because he does not answer; the countess de Noailles because she talks, Joyce because he keeps quiet; Alain because he is surly, Maurois because he is amiable; Mauriac because he is crabby, Catholic and urchin-like, Valéry because he is bemused, tired and polite. They admire certain mistresses of the house because they receive with elegance and majesty in salons that are immense and well-lighted like aquariums; others because they pile up their guests in an inconvenient hole, squat on the floor and abhor the conventions."

The sense of quality, and the related valuation of elegance, are part of this Parisian élan, what makes the city different. It is also the value that the city puts on skill, what the French call *métier*, translated best as trade, perhaps as profession, as knowledgeability in one's role. To know, for example, how to be a good *écailler*, an opener of oysters who looks like an opener of oysters. It is a *métier*, and like so much else in Paris, it should not only be performed well; it should be done by a certain type of person. You couldn't have a good brasserie without one; the choreography of the place depends on him, just as the presence of the beau monde is the necessary accoutrement of those Élysée Palace awards ceremonies. The link between these two diverse aspects of Parisian life is the assumption of a kind of excellence. To be a writer, to be an opener of oysters—neither can be done by just anybody; both are given their recognition by the Paris that sets the standards, that arbitrates between the authentic and the false.

The waiters are another such group. In France in general, but in Paris in particular, to be a waiter in a café is also a *métier*, a bit like that of the butler in England, requiring that you move fast and gracefully, that you carry your uniform—short black jacket or red vest and bow tie—well, and, above all, that you cultivate a demeanor of proud professionalism, of brisk, no-nonsense courtesy. As a waiter, you have to establish the authority of your establishment. You have to be able to intimidate a bit if the clientele itself is not up to snuff. And so there is none of the little-girl charm or the boy-next-door friendliness of American restaurants. In Paris, the waiter does not introduce himself by name. He doesn't smile a great deal or spend a lot of time in ceremonious *politesse*. You sit at a café correctly, which means that you manifest a certain composure; you don't gawk at the passing world, and you know what you want to be served. And then you are served correctly, with a quick, nimble formality and an economy of motion, by a practitioner of the *métier*, who knows how—oh, so subtly, with just a hint of condescension in his *oui, monsieur*, or a hard stare that lasts just a moment too long, or perhaps a sudden departure just before your business has been transacted—to put you in your place if you seem to be inadequate to the ritual. I prefer not to explain how I know this.

Every year in Paris, as if to establish the seriousness of the *métier*, or, at least, its existence, there is a race of café waiters down the boulevard Saint-Germain. It is, of course, also a comical affair. Wearing their black jackets and bow ties, or their red jackets and white shirts, and holding their small round trays with a glass and a bottle on them, the waiters huff and puff down the broad street, their normal, requisite coolness, and much of their usual agility and lithesomeness, dissolving with the exhaustion of the unaccustomed effort. And yet even with their shirttails hanging out and the bottle and glass on their trays toppled over, they manage to retain one aspect of their normal demeanor, a frosty composure, an attitude of indifference to public opinion. The crowds that line the boulevard cheer them on.

Perhaps the importance of all this is the public nature of each of these elements of the French capital, from the awarding of the *Légion d'honneur* to the waiters' race. Oyster openers and waiters, like cooks and barmen, *sommeliers* and *maîtres d'hôtel*, are the accoutrements of a life that, to be Parisian, needs to be seen, to be open to public view. The café and the restaurant, in this sense, are more than charming places that add their dimension to the pleasures of urban life. In Paris, these are the gathering places where the barriers are broken down, where the sense of community is established, where intellectual life goes on in the form of gathering and discussion. There are a few places in Paris that have achieved great fame and exclusivity because of this, the Brasserie Lipp on the boulevard Saint-Germain, just across from another establishment, the Café de Flore, renowned for much the same thing, being the epitome of the type. To be recognized at Lipp is to have arrived in the beau monde. It is the city's highly sought after seal of approval, like the Prix Medicis or Femina, a sign of membership in the club.

In *The Banquet Years*, his remarkable book on the avant-garde epoch in Paris, Roger Shattuck describes the "gaiety and scorn for convention," the wild, carnivalesque atmosphere, the heretical aspirations, the buffoonery and the foolishness, the "full aliveness to the present moment," that together created "the setting for a great rejuvenation of the arts." He points to London, where the likes of Wilde, Aubrey Beardsley, and Max Beerbohm were also pursuing "newness for its own sake." But the difference was that these Englishmen "found no surroundings in London equal to a Paris café." Only in France—so socially conservative that the heretics took protest to an extreme degree, turning it into a life-style, an end in itself, because they did not believe it would really change anything—could an extreme bohemianism coexist with earthbound convention.

The avant-garde disappeared with the beginning of World War I, but the combination of political threat, social conservatism, and protest, the search for new, authentic modes of expression and ways of life, remained the Parisian contribution for later generations, which seemed to suck from Paris a certain sustaining force. The question now is: Is anything of it left, except the streets themselves, the monuments, the museums, the libraries where the creations of those generations are stored?

I don't know. I suspect at times that in some ways Paris's long moment has finally passed. The Parisian giants have gone, and the new giants are emerging elsewhere. In art and literature, drama and film, Paris neither produces nor attracts the sort of genius it once did. That, too, marks the difference between it and Deep France. When Paris declines, France declines; nothing that happens elsewhere can matter. I was always a bit envious of my journalistic predecessors in this respect. When Janet Flanner covered Paris for *The New Yorker* in the several decades following 1925, her articles—many of them collected in a marvelous volume, *Paris Was Yesterday*—covered civilization itself. The events she wrote about, whether François Mauriac's acceptance into the Académie Française, André Gide's 1937 statement of disillusionment about the Soviet Union, or the death of Maurice Ravel, seemed to be within the local sphere of interest in New York. There are echoes of that remaining, to be sure. But they are echoes. My own coverage in the middle 1980s was about a country and a city striving to retain their place.

But if there are no Parisians anymore, the ones who are missing are not those who disappeared from the cozy corner of our taxi driver's imagination. And this is the irony. Paris's greatness has become one of style and comfort, of way of life rather than creative audacity. The very picturesque life that the taxi driver believes to be a thing of the past is, in fact, what remains—the markets, the cafés, the bistros, the neighborhoods, the galleries, the curio shops, the elegance, the voluptuousness, the beauty. They are still there. The Parisians lead the Western world in enjoyment, while they add, in the remaining nooks and crannies of their beautiful city, new works in their already considerable collection. Having made France and conquered the world, the Parisians worry about their decline even as they bask in the rewards of their success. Meanwhile, the Parisians, proud and energetic, quick-witted and bright as icicles, continue to define the French and Frenchness, thereby opening up an entirely new area of inquiry into their nature, one concerning the ways, not that the Deep French might be different from the Parisians, but how all of them might be different from us.

II

THE FRENCH:
WHO THEY ARE

Intelligence is nothing without delight.

<small>PAUL CLAUDEL</small>

5

Blood, Names, and Identity

HER REAL name was Mignon, but everybody, more by necessity than choice, called her Florence. The reason is that Florence, the name of one of the Catholic saints, was a suitable baptismal name and therefore a legal, authorized French name, while Mignon, according to a certain functionary of the state, the one who rejected Mignon's own preference in the matter, is not. The questions arising from this are: Are there illegal names in France? Can parents not give their children whatever first names they choose, drawing them from whatever heritage, traditions, ancestors, languages, and values are important to them in their free and democratic country? The answers, which may be surprising to some, are yes and they cannot. And even though it does not affect the choices of very many people, and it certainly does not call into question France's attachment to human rights, rule by law, or personal freedom, the obscure, private saga of Mignon/Florence does help to answer the question of who exactly the French are, or who they think they are.

Mignon Radovic, or, as I always called her, Florence Radovic, is a thirty-three-year-old French citizen born in Yugoslavia, whose French-speaking Serbian parents wanted to call her Mignon, which happens to be both the title and the name of a character in an 1866 French opera by Ambroise Thomas. The Radovic family fulfilled their lifelong ambition of moving to Paris, and when little Mignon was five years old, her parents took her, as French law requires, to be registered at the local Parisian town hall. The clerk there accepted the parental choice, regis-

tering the little girl as Mignon. This happened in part because the Radovics had gone to the foreigners' section of the births, marriages, and
deaths registrar, which is more lenient than the French section in per-
mitting non-French people to register the names of their children, allowing newborns with names like Mohammed, for example, to be duly
inscribed on the state's complicated social services registers, which, given
the system of family monetary allowances for each registered child, is
important.

When Mignon went to school, however, the teacher of her class believed that she spied a grammatical mistake. The little girl's name could
not be Mignon, which is a masculine adjective; it had to be Mignonne,
which is the feminine form of the same word, meaning "cute" in English.
The teacher refused to listen to the argument of the Radovics—who
were very likely more knowledgeable about French culture than she
was—that Mignon is not only the eponym of the opera by Thomas but
also the name of a character, and a female character at that, in one of
the lesser-known novels—*Modeste Mignon*—of none other than Honoré
de Balzac, who was no Serbian. Accusing Mignon's father of being a
bad speller, the teacher insisted on Mignonne or some other "correct"
name. Mignon, she decreed, was wrong.

And so Mignonne it was. Several years later, when Mignonne needed
a suitable name for her baptism—she couldn't use Mignonne because
that is not a saint's name—she chose the name Florence, becoming
Mignonne Florence Radovic. Florence, at the age of twelve or thirteen,
stubbornly identified herself on her school papers as Mignon Florence;
they always came back corrected as Mignonne Florence. Eventually, she
dropped the effort with Mignon and called herself simply Florence,
becoming later a student of political science both in New York (where
she learned to speak English with native fluency) and in Paris, where
she returned to live. In the meantime, however, when she was in her
mid-twenties and still theoretically a Yugoslav national, she decided to
get the French citizenship papers to which she was entitled. She went
to the *préfecture de police* for the formalities involved in that process.
"I'd like to take this opportunity to get my real name back again," she
said. What is it? she was asked. "Mignon," she replied, mentioning, in
defense of her desire, the Thomas opera and Balzac's little-known novel.
The argument fell on deaf ears. She was told she would have to be
Florence.

Mignon/Florence did not, however, let the matter rest there. She set
out to rectify what she viewed as a minor but annoying injustice imposed

by virtue of the arbitrary power of a *petit fonctionnaire* who refused to recognize the authority of Balzac or, for that matter, the wishes of the individual involved in the matter. Florence became something of a lay expert in this question of names. She learned, among other things, that ever since the reign of François I in the sixteenth century—the exact year was 1539—parents have had the legal obligation to register their children's names with a state functionary known as an *officier d'état civil*. Until the Revolution, these civil status officers were always priests, who accepted as a legitimate French first name only that of one of the Catholic saints. In 1792, the civil status officers were secularized, and a wider choice of first names became available. Still, in 1802, the newly invoked Napoleonic Code prohibited the use of first names other than those "in use in various calendars [that is, the traditional Catholic calendar and the new republican one] and those of great names in ancient history."

The practice as it evolved over the century points up the fact that first names in France are not regarded as matters merely of personal choice. They are within the domain of the public interest and are considered to weigh on the general order of things. Furthering this concept, the Napoleonic Code made first names "immutable." A citizen cannot legally bear a name other than the one he or she was registered with at birth. In more recent years, the immutability principle was slightly relaxed. Three conditions were established by which an individual could go to the French civil courts and demand a change in his first name. One covered the cases of adopted children whose new parents want to give him or her a new name. A second concerned foreigners acquiring French citizenship. These people would be permitted to *franciser* their names —make them more French—so that, presumably, our hypothetical Mohammed could decide to call himself Maurice or Michel but not Mahsourd or Muammar, which are Arabic names. The third condition covered those people who had what a new law called a "legitimate interest" in a name change. In one case, for example, the courts approved the change of a name from Sarah to Suzanne, because Sarah claimed to have been persecuted as a Jew during World War II.

Whatever the rules, Florence, at the age of thirty or so, became determined to change her name from Florence back to Mignon. "It's a French name, and it's my name," she said, "so why not?" She knew she would have to prove a "legitimate interest" in the change. She hired a lawyer. Months passed. These things proceed slowly in France, as legal matters do in most countries. As of this writing, it was still unknown whether Mlle Radovic would legally become Mignon or whether she would be obliged to remain Florence. The state would decide.

THE MODERN justification for this control over names—far more relaxed, certainly more secular, than in centuries past, but still slightly obstructionist, intrusive, potentially and, sometimes, actually disrespectful of personal choice—stems from the French adherence to a certain ideal Cartesian logic, which maintains that a public rationality must supervise private decisions so as to avoid possible cruelty done by parents to children, in, for example, giving them ridiculous names. This Cartesianism itself can have its ridiculous applications. There arose in the 1960s, for example, the case of a family with the last name Le Goarnic who moved some years ago from the outskirts of Paris to Moëlan-sur-Mer, a small coastal village in Brittany, where the original language, still spoken by a few crusty old oystermen and their wives but by few other people—certainly not by the masses of Parisians who have week-end homes there—is Breton, a variation of Celtic. The Le Goarnics had six children while still in the region of Paris. They gave each of them Celtic names—the first one, for example, was called Adraboran—and they were allowed to register them all at the foreigners' window at the local city hall, where what were called "foreign-sounding names" had a better chance of being accepted. (So much seems to depend in this matter of names on the mood and attitude, perhaps the aesthetic preferences or the degree of chauvinism, of the particular functionary on the other side of the *guichet*, a heavy glass partition with small holes to talk through.) Everything was fine.

In 1955, however, new ministerial instructions were issued, closing down the foreigners' sections at the city halls and urging the *officers d'état civil* to refuse first names with a specific "local character." The Le Goarnics moved to Brittany. The next time they brought in a new baby with a Celtic name, they were turned down. Anne Le Goarnic, the mother of the brood, reported that the functionary told them, "You can call your children 'Brouette' if you want to, but you can't use any more Celtic names." Brouette, which means "wheelbarrow" and might be seen as exactly the sort of practical-joke name that any good Cartesian would want to avoid, is included as a name day in the republican calendar issued during the Revolution to replace the calendar of the saints; it should therefore be deemed a legal first name just like Églantine (a kind of rose) or Amandine or any of the other name days in the republican calendar. Despite this problem of names, the Le Goarnics continued to have children, six more of them altogether. The local authorities, not wanting them to be nonpersons, eventually registered them all without first names. Still, at a certain point in this saga, because, according to Mme Le Goarnic, the press was talking about the issue and the government was embarrassed, the authorities in Paris during de Gaulle's presidency relented, and such Celtic names as Maiwenn and Morgann and others the Le Goarnics had given their children were at last accepted.

Still, the earlier contretemps had been so fouled up with suits and claims against the government, and countersuits and counterclaims by the government against the Le Goarnics, that even after all the children were fully grown up, lawyers were still fighting out the left-over matters in the courts. These seemed to involve not names but rather substantial sums of money—sums demanded by the Le Goarnics in various indemnities, sums demanded by the government in claimed unpaid taxes. "France is not a nation," Mme Le Goarnic said over the phone one day, talking in particular of her hiring a lawyer and pressing ahead with her suits and claims. "It is just one big administration, which is utterly static and stupid. Taken individually, civil servants might be intelligent. But put them behind a desk, grant them anonymity, and they will act in a totally arbitrary fashion." In this, Mme Le Goarnic was expressing a view commonly held in France, even among people who dutifully name their children Chantal, Suzanne, Françoise, Micheline, Jean, Jean-Philippe, François, and Bernard.

W HO ARE the French? Their ancestors, they believe, were the Gauls, as the textbooks used to say, but obviously that is too simple. The French, as the historian Braudel wrote in his final book, are a "condensation" of the people of Europe, a people poured into a funnel blocked by the Atlantic on one side and the North Sea on the other. The very complexity of the French identity has led to all sorts of theories, sane and malicious. There was, to cite one example of the latter kind, a racist-reactionary theory in France current in the first half of the nineteenth century, a time when the class struggle was particularly acute, according to which there would always be a racial conflict in France between two constituent parts of the population. On the one hand were the original Gallo-Roman inhabitants, the salt-of-the-earth peasants; on the other, the Germanic conquerors, who stood as a natural aristocracy. This distinction between noble-blooded blond beasts and stolid peasant clods is, of course, nonsense; moreover, it is generally considered non-sense in these enlightened times. But the French for decades have wrestled from time to time with the racial and other characteristics of Frenchness, trying to determine what names, habits, customs, beliefs, common experiences, and blood types give them their national identity. And this wrestling has become more intense in recent years, for two reasons.

The first—having to do with concern over the larger than ever numbers of non-European immigrants, especially Arabs, coming to the country —is obvious and acknowledged. It is a defensive reaction, a desire to establish a notion of primary Frenchness, to know what distinguishes a "real" French person from one who merely becomes French. This concern took on an ugly aspect, reminiscent of those early-nineteenth-century theories, when the National Front began to attract support from a portion of the electorate with its "France for the French" platform. I attended a few rallies given by Jean-Marie Le Pen, the far right's demi-god, who was traveling through the towns on the Brittany coast, giving speeches every night. At each of the rallies, the crowds were warmed up by a singer, one of whose chants evoked the dangers of *le sang de Barbarie*, "the blood of Barbary," coming into France.

In a less provocative but still telling way, the Conservative government in 1986 made its own effort to deal with this issue of Frenchness, tampering briefly though unsuccessfully with the legislation that determines exactly how a non-French person gains French citizenship. Until then, anybody born of two foreign parents in France became a citizen automatically after five years of residence. The proposed new law would have required such people—about eighteen thousand of them had become citizens each year under the old law—formally to demand citizenship when they reached age eighteen, doing so in front of a judge, who could refuse them if they had criminal records or did not speak French well. While perhaps not a major change, the idea provoked an intense debate in France, where it fed into an already existing quarrel concerning openness to immigration and racism. Opponents of the proposal, which was eventually dropped, argued that it would "marginalize" thousands of young people who, in any case, had no other country to call their own. The measure's proponents contended that in reality, virtually nobody would be denied citizenship who would have gotten it previously; but they felt some symbolic gesture, some act of choice, would give the notion of Frenchness great meaning, more gravity.

The second reason for the more intense French wrestling with the meaning of Frenchness, put here as conjecture, stems from the larger

French search for a place, a role, an identity, in a world in which they are becoming a less compelling and powerful presence. This has several manifestations. More history about the French past is being written than ever before. The French are dwelling increasingly on past events as they search for themselves. So, too, is there more exploration of their habits of mind and body, more effort at self-definition. They scrutinize themselves relentlessly and compulsively. The weekly magazines contain all sorts of polls and surveys, often collected in annually produced volumes, which, taken together, seem to reflect a deep, veritably unconscious sense that as the world itself knows less and less of them, they themselves need to know more and more. The poll data, constantly trumpeted with banner headlines, is a form of pop sociology, not to be taken too seriously—representing in this regard a lowbrow preoccupation with identity very much at variance with the new historical studies, which reflect the more probing, highbrow preoccupation. Still, the pop-sociology data is often fascinating and revealing about the self-image of the contemporary Frenchman. It concerns what this imaginary average person does and feels, what he and she like and dislike, how they behave, dress, eat, drink, make love, wash, shop, cook, bathe, and think, each of these activities being described statistically. Noting the phenomenon of *sondomania*—from the word *sondage*, meaning "poll"—the magazine *Le Point* reported in 1987 that in the realm of electoral politics alone, there were on the average two polls published every day in France—a world record! Part of the reason is merely the French preoccupation with politics. Another part, however, is what the magazine described as a collective insecurity. "The French," the magazine quoted sociologist Jean-Marie Cotteret as saying, drawing a rather unflattering portrait of his countrymen, "don't like to discover themselves; they hate individual commitment. By contrast, they are very happy to know what the other French are thinking. They thus recognize themselves by virtue of the polls and then commit themselves collectively."

There were several newly discovered characteristics of the French that the magazine linked with this yearning for a collective identity. One of the words of recent seasons has been *nombrilism*, a fascination with the self—*nombril* meaning "navel." *Nombrilism* soon became virtually synonymous with *hexagonal* and *franco-français*, terms that themselves reflected the deeply ambivalent feeling that the French were so steeped in their own peculiarities as to be incomprehensible to the rest of the world—with consequent poor showings for their books and movies abroad, these cultural products afflicted with so *hexagonal* a character that nobody outside the country could possibly enjoy them. This was both the pride and the anxiety of the French, who want at the same time to be gloriously, stubbornly different and safely, securely the same. *Le Point*'s argument was that *nombrilism* was an expression of the Frenchman's disinclination to be eccentric, his desire to have close at hand a mirror in which he can observe himself and compare himself as he is inscribed in a society where appearance counts above all else. The obsession with polls thus provides the French with the standard image of themselves that they crave. *Sondomania* reflected a deep curiosity about the national character, or, at least, a desire to know whether or not there was a national character, one that was expected somehow to emerge from a potpourri, an onslaught of statistics, details, habits, attitudes, that, taken together, would give an idea of aspects, both weighty and trivial, of the French character.

As the experience of Mignon / Florence shows, the French—to begin this composite sondomaniacal portrait—define themselves in part by the names they choose for their children. And while there are more Mohammeds, Mahsouds, Muammars in France than ever before, it is a country—not particularly unusual in this regard—with a limited number of commonly chosen given names. France for centuries was a vigorously, aggressively, and almost exclusively Catholic country, one whose identity was virtually synonymous with its religious affiliation. A historian, Colette Beaune, in a book entitled *La Naissance de la Nation France* (The Birth of France as a Nation), has described how the medieval image of the average Frenchman was drenched in religious imagery. "To be French and Catholic," she writes, "was virtually the same." And while powerful strains of republican anticlericalism have been on the scene since the Revolution, and while the number of the French who go to church these days is small and shrinking, the names chosen by parents today still reflect that Catholic past, in much the same way that the predominance of Mohammeds, Muammars, and Mahsouds in Arab countries shows the Islamic heritage. The major French governmental statistical office, known by the initials INSEE, showed in a report of 1986 that 29 percent of girls and 32 percent of boys bear the top ten given names for each sex. This represents a wider choice than in the 1930s, when ten first names covered 45 percent of the male population. Still, INSEE concludes that "at any given moment, parents make their choice within a relatively limited spread." For boys, the common names over most of this century have been Jean, Pierre, André, René, Michel, Claude, Jacques, and a few others. In recent years, there have been vogues for Thierry, Christophe, Stéphane, Sébastien, and Nicolas. For girls, Marie was the given name of choice for much of the first quarter of this century; then it was Simone, then Jeannine, then Monique, then Danielle, followed by Martine, Brigitte, and Sylvia. In the early 1980s, a few previously neglected names came into common use for girls, among them: Céline, Aurélia, Émilie, Virginie, Sandrine, and Stéphanie. Does this limited choice reveal an insecurity in France? It does show French parents cherishing a certain sameness, a desire to stamp their children with a label that will be familiar and recognizable to all, rather than to search for the different, the original, for the name that will attract attention by its unusualness.

The French can and do describe themselves in many other ways, including physical size. An annually produced volume known as *Francoscopie* claimed in 1988 that on average, French men were just a bit under 5′8″ and weighed 165 pounds; women were 5′3″ and 132 pounds. Forty-two percent of the population wear glasses; 58 percent of them cannot correctly identify the author of *The Charterhouse of Parma* (the nineteenth-century masterpiece by Stendhal). *Francoscopie* reveals that the French as a whole spend more total time watching television than either going to school or working. Eighty-six percent of them say they are happy; 96 percent maintain close relations with their families; 45 percent of them believe that God exists; 25 percent believe that the sun revolves around the earth; 36 percent smoke; 57 percent of them claim to have had sexual relations with their partner inside a car. Twenty-two percent of the men have been to a prostitute at least once. Fifty percent of the women, but only 19 percent of the men, have had only one sexual partner in their lives. Forty-two percent of men over forty have some difficulty, temporary or permanent, in achieving an erection. The number of couples living together outside marriage doubled between 1975 and 1985, from 446,000 to 975,000.

A poll in *Le Monde* in 1987 recorded the authors most recognized by the French, and here, if cultural purists are looking for adherence to a national literary essence—*Le Monde* called it a "hexagonal literary narcissism"—they will not be disappointed. Asked to list the greatest writers of the twentieth century, the French included in significant numbers only three foreigners, and in doing so, they did not show a remarkable literary culture. The three were Hemingway, Agatha Christie, and Solzhenitsyn. The writers the French had most often heard of were

Sartre, Simone de Beauvoir, Christie, François Mauriac, Albert Camus, Colette, Marcel Proust, Marguerite Duras, and, at the bottom of this list, Hemingway. The purists comforted by the list of known authors would have been discomfited by the list of the authors the French have actually read. Here, two novels by Hemingway, *The Old Man and the Sea* and *For Whom the Bell Tolls*—in translation, of course—took the top two places. Several novels by Camus, including *The Stranger* and *The Plague*, were highest on the list of French fiction.

There is a gleeful self-deprecation in some of these surveys, a near-masochistic delight taken by the purveyors of poll results in showing the French in an eccentrically unfavorable light, as though the opinion researcher were obligated to shake his head in mock despair as the statistics pour in. Much, for example, has been made in the newspapers and magazines of the poll showing that the French do not wash very much, compared to other Europeans. At four bars of soap per capita per year, their consumption of that commodity is supposed to be very low, half that of the British, for example (though others point out that a common variety of kitchen soap, known as Marseille soap, is not included as soap in this survey, so that the result is subject to serious doubts). Still, further studies show that only 19 percent of the men and 32 percent of the women say they take a bath daily. Worse, according to *Francoscopie*, 52 percent of the French go to bed without brushing their teeth. (I have observed nothing to give this troubling figure credibility, but *Francoscopie* is supposed to be reliable.)

The French enjoy certain statistical firsts among the major countries of Europe. They have, at 75 liters per person per year, the highest alcohol consumption; also the highest consumption of bottled water. Proportionally speaking, they own the largest number of pets, with 10 million dogs, 9 million domestic birds, 7 million cats, for the 50 million people living in the country. This mania for *animaux de compagnie*, as the French call pets, costs a total of 30 billion francs or, roughly, $5 billion each year. In 1986, there were more than 12,000 suicides, proportionally among the highest in the industrialized world, with 71 percent of the victims being male, often single or widowed, living in the countryside or in small towns. A total of 49,328 people were in prison in France in 1987, 73 percent of them French and the rest foreigners. There were 2,286 murders that year, 6,508 instances of armed robbery, 1,557,000 other thefts.

As if to show that France is still divided among economic and social classes, the compilers of statistics stress differences among them. They note, for example, that a senior bureaucrat on the average will be 2¾ inches taller than a farmer, 2 inches taller than a worker. White-collar workers are ten times as likely to divorce as farmers, though, as *Francoscopie* usefully points out, when a farmer marries a white-collar worker, the divorce rate is fifty times higher than it is among couples where both husband and wife are from farm families. Farmers tend to marry in April and September, white-collar workers in July and December, workers in April and July. Among farmers, 37 percent met their spouses at a dance, compared to 16 percent of the French as a whole. Members of the bourgeoisie are more likely to eat beef than workers, whose favorite meat is pork.

The magazine *Nouvel Observateur* once published a lengthy study of the correlations between preferences for wine and social class, region, and political ideas. Altogether, the article noted, only 28 percent of the French abstain from wine consumption, meaning that 72 percent drink it, the vast majority of that 72 percent liking red wine more than white wine, rosé, or champagne. The French have a general preference for Bordeaux over Burgundy and Côtes du Rhône, but rightists drink more Bordeaux, which is comparatively expensive, than do leftists, many of whom drink a category called "other French wines," meaning neither Bordeaux, Burgundy, nor Côtes du Rhône but the stuff produced in the less prestigious wine-growing areas, such as Bergerac, Cahors, or Roussillon. Those most likely to drink wine only at dinner are upper-level bureaucrats and professionals (a category that the French sometimes call PLCS (for *professions libérals et cadres supérieurs*). Something like 28 percent of the French drink wine with all their meals (excluding breakfast)—which is a smaller percentage than some of the stereotypes might suggest—with shop owners, artisans, and retired people heavily concentrated among them.

Francoscopie, and other compilations, include figures and statistics reflecting the obvious fact that the French belong to the modern industrial world and partake of its trends and patterns. They are marrying less than before, divorcing more, getting married less often in church. They spend more money on meat and less on bread, have more cars, stereos, refrigerators, and televisions, and spend more time on vacation. There is more concentration on the self, more purchasing of beauty products, cameras, Walkmans (the guardians of linguistic purity in France have invented the word *balladeur* for this Japanese-made device, which is a deft neologistic translation), compact disc players, and home video recorders—paying for these items twice or more what an American would pay because of high luxury taxes, inefficient retail distribution, and, I suspect but cannot prove, informal price-fixing practices among merchants. They go more often than ever before to health clubs and spas, ski resorts and beaches—which they rather grandly call *stations balnéaires*—to riding stables, parachuting clubs, mountaineering associations, and foreign countries. In these aspects of life, the French are, quite simply—though this is rarely mentioned by the interpreters of the polls—becoming more like other people living in the democratic West or Japan. The obsessive search for a particular identity only turns up the worldwide process of cultural and material homogenization, a virtually inevitable phenomenon that the French, with a note of despair, call Americanization but which is actually modernization itself.

D IGGING deeper into the question of who the French are, bands of historians have been studying with intensifying interest the forces and concepts that produced modern France in the first place, the country's origins in the experiences of centuries and millennia past. In historical writing in particular, there was clearly visible in the 1980s a return to national history, away from the sorts of universal, transfrontier histories popular in the 1950s and 1960s. The publisher Gallimard, under the direction of an extraordinary editor, Pierre Nora, issued a four-volume collection of essays called *Les Lieux de Mémoire* (The Places of Memory)—which, consistent with earlier tendencies in French historiography, eschewed standard chronological history, the histories of events and persons, and focused instead on a list of institutions, monuments, and cultural landmarks—the places of memory—that were both expressions of a unique, though generally inclusive, Frenchness and, at the same time, creators of that Frenchness.

The reference is to monuments like the Panthéon, where France's republican heroes lie buried, to the Larousse Encyclopedia, that standard reference work of all educated French persons, to the "Marseillaise," the national anthem. Nora included as "places of memory" the Paris Exposition Universelle of 1889 (the centennial of the Revolution), the creation of the Fourteenth of July as the national holiday, the funeral of Victor Hugo as a crystallization of a set of political and moral values, the celebrations of the centennials of Voltaire and Rousseau—all of them anchorages for the consciousness, the common experience of a nation whose events often reveal more conflict than commonality. In conversation, Nora talked of the shaping of a new historical consciousness for France, which in itself reflected the new realities of the country's situation.

In part, the diminution of France's role in the world has forced a reevaluation of the country's past and the search for the common symbols of identity. At the same time, the lessening of civil conflict, the end of the great ideological debates, have produced a coalescing around a single great idea, which, in essence, replaced the earlier great unifying idea of French history—namely, the absolute monarchy as embodied by Louis XIV. The new idea is, quite simply, the Republic, the hard-won governmental form that, today, gives the French a common political nature. For two centuries, the idea of the Republic was a battleground. Slowly it became a domain of peaceful consensus, fostered by those places of memory that Nora's imposing volumes both celebrate and describe—the Panthéon, the Exposition Universelle, the Fourteenth of July, and other seminal events, monuments, symbols, and personalities to which the French have attached themselves.

The point is that the identity of a Frenchman is a created thing, a shared historical memory, selected to buttress a particular self-image. Nora undertook his great labor precisely out of the belief that France is experiencing a crisis of memory, which is the same thing as a crisis of identity. A nation, he likes to say, remembers those things that it wants to preserve for its future. But in France, the changes of the past three decades have come so fast that there has occurred a "brutal tearing away" of the French from the standard places of memory, which is to say, the farm, the family, a certain notion of national greatness. Two generations of peace is in part responsible; there has been the commercialization of life; there are new problems, most notably the problem of immigration and, in response to that, the resurrection of a far-rightist, nativist political phenomenon.

"If we talk so much of memory and origins these days," Nora once told an interviewer, "it's because they have disappeared." The old categories by which the French defined themselves, such categories as revolution, progress, reaction, are obsolete, and there is great uncertainty over what categories can replace them. "We no longer see very well what we can restore of the past; we no longer believe in progress, and we have finished with the idea of revolution," Nora said. The very absence of the old quarrels has diminished the passion to remember, which may explain why Nora's particular places of memory have rarely if at all been treated by scholars before.

And yet the very fact that they have, in a sense, been taken for granted reveals the extent to which they are buried clues, insinuations, intimations, answers to that question for which there can never be a total answer: Who are the French, anyway? They are a people with a shared history and memory, the people begotten by the people who massed on the streets to mark the passing of Victor Hugo, poet and republican, whose remains lie in the Panthéon, in the heart of Paris. The French, or at least the majority of them, are republicans, believing deeply in the priority of merit over birth, opportunity over privilege. They are the inheritors of Cartesian clarity and the mysteries of Pascal, of the political thought of Montesquieu and the grand visions of Napoleon.

Are they also a race? a culture? Do the French have common ethnic origins? Can we speak legitimately of French blood? Of a French essence? Of a national identity arising mystically out of the union of a certain people—their ancestors the Gauls—with the rich earth of France? Can a foreigner become French and be regarded by those born French as just as French as they?

Throughout their history, certain Frenchmen have tried to tie their identity to blood, to race, to a tribe. These are men like Édouard Drumont, who, in the nineteenth century, wrote that "because of Jewish action the old France has dissolved and is now decomposed." There were others, like Maurice Barrès, who proclaimed, during the Dreyfus affair, that "foreigners do not have the same kind of brain as Frenchmen." There are Maurras, Drieu de la Rochelle, Brasillach, Céline, Laval. Today there is Jean-Marie Le Pen, the head of the anti-immigrant National Front. All of them believed or believe in some purity of the French essence that can be contaminated from abroad. The assumption, shared by many who do not otherwise associate with the far right, is, essentially, that the French identity is something, not that you have exactly to be born with, but that at least has to be inculcated early on in life. If the names that the French give to their children reflect the Catholic heritage of France, so, too, do the associations in the minds of the exclusionists on the subject of identity. They have a deep preference that a Frenchman be white and Catholic (or, in a pinch, Protestant) and that he not have immigrated within very recent generations.

Of course, there are exceptions. The definition has flexibility and can encompass certain people for sentimental or political reasons. I once asked Jean-Marie Le Pen, not a person I admire but one who seems to embody the most restrictive definition of Frenchness, what he would do about the so-called *harkies*, the North Africans, mostly Moslems, who fought on the side of France during the independence struggles of the former French colonies. Are they French, while other North African immigrants are not? In essence, Le Pen's answer was yes, the former are French, the latter will always be foreigners. The *harkies*, he said, threw in their lot with France when a choice had to be made; they were ready to sacrifice for their identification with the French nation. Le Pen, it seemed to me, included the *harkies* in his exclusive club because they chose Frenchness in war, that great bonder of men. Others, no matter how fully they absorbed Frenchness, no matter how well they spoke the language and absorbed its culture, would never be accepted by the National Front and those many Frenchmen who, on this question, agree with it.

The best of the historical writings reveal, nonetheless, that the yearnings of some of the French to establish an ethnic or a racial homogeneity have no foundation in the history of the country, which has always involved, not a tribal union, but a reconciliation of diverse peoples. Frenchness has always been the product of a common memory and a common experience of culture, rather than of some natural affinities among like-blooded people. Indeed, the recent approaches to national history show how astonishing a phenomenon France is, how surprising it is that a single nation, rather than several nations, exists in its hexagonal space.

"France is named diversity," Braudel writes, quoting another historian, Lucien Febvre. The very notion of "our ancestors the Gauls" appears ridiculous in the face of the facts of history, which show that "our ancestors" consisted of the entire European community, drawn in, forced to mix and to mingle.

The major characteristic of France beginning with its prehistory is that it was a crossroads, a confluence of peoples—Celts (otherwise known as Gauls), Romans, Germans, the diverse waves of immigration coming both from the Mediterranean and from the Danube. There is a still respectable theory, developed by philological researchers in the nineteenth century, that France, in its origins, was a derivative of Germany, the word *français* itself, meaning "French," basically the combination of a Frankish root (and after all, Charlemagne, the king of the Franks, spoke both a low form of Latin and an early dialect of German) and a Latin suffix. In prehistoric France, population levels were already remarkably high, made possible by the development of open-field agriculture on the country's rich land. Throughout the long prehistory and history of the country, according to some scholars, more individual human beings have died within its current territory, proportionately speaking, than in any other place. The historian Pierre Chaunu, cited by Braudel, estimates that the soil of France contains the mostly invisible tombs of fifteen billion people, who lived and died over the course of two million years of human habitation. As early as the Neolithic period, the population that settled in the country had become "decidedly modern," containing the kind of racial diversity that is characteristic of contemporary France. "What counts," the historian says, "is the mass, the majority in place. In the long term, everything loses itself within it." France today, and the French, are "the unconscious bearers of this prehistoric legacy."

Braudel's description of French prehistory as an early melting pot, a condensation of Europe, is aimed at providing current-day reassurance. Things, even with non-European immigrants, have not changed. New peoples have all along continued to layer over existing French society, which consisted of older immigrants, the products of previous migrations, the funneling of various clans and races into a rich territory beyond which it was both impossible and undesirable to go. There were waves of immigrants from Poland, Italy, and Belgium in the mid-nineteenth century, when French commerce and industry needed laborers. Another modern wave came after World War I, from such places as Portugal, Algeria, Spain, and, again, Italy. In the period between 1956 and 1976, there was a third massive influx, largely from North Africa and including both Arab and Jewish immigrants. In the end, Braudel seems to have a political lesson in mind in his description of a French identity that is diversity itself. For millennia, the newcomers have been absorbed into the nation, into the French "mass." The process can continue, and the treasured French identity will remain. Braudel writes:

"So many immigrants, for so long, ever since our prehistory and until our recent history, have succeeded in getting stranded inside the French mass without making too much noise, that it is possible to say, to amuse ourselves, that all of these French, if our glance carries back to the centuries and the millennia that preceded our time, are the sons of immigrants."

More than anything else, perhaps, Frenchness is an association with and at least a partial mastery of a powerful culture and a history. It is a question of education and, in the case of foreigners, of choice. When Jews or Moslems in France name their children Jean-François or Marie-Laure, they are acknowledging the power of "the mass in place," its homogenizing force. There are minority groups in France, and they insist on certain differences, such as religious observance. But by contrast with the general tendency in the United States, they do not generally celebrate that difference, demand that it be given equal status with the dominant group. Immigrant groups do not demand bilingual education for their children; there is no foreign-language advertising in the subway, no pressure for university reading lists to reflect the contributions of the Portuguese, the Arabs, or the Africans. There is here an acknowledgment of the belief that the French share a language and a history and a body of arcane knowledge—of geography and grammar, poetry and cheese. To be French is to adopt a certain appearance as well as to attempt to embody a set of values and ideals that, taken together, give meaning to a turbulent and often bloody history.

But that, of course, remains a bit general, abstract. Along the course of their centuries, the French have picked up a reputation for certain things: elegance and combativeness, naughtiness and brilliance, sentiments of monarchy, glory, liberty, and fraternity, a love of the finer things in life—food, wine, beautiful women, the arts, philosophy, language, and argumentation. They are seen as aggressive, anti-Semitic, chauvinistic, haughty, intelligent, refined, sybaritic, impatient, elegant. The European "condensation" created a culture whose specific characteristics have been the targets of both an unadulterated admiration and an unalloyed contempt on the part of others, who have, very probably, grasped one part of the personality but not another. The portrait of the French, that "mass" living in the westernmost isthmus of Europe, sandwiched between the Latin Mediterranean on one side and the cold Atlantic on the other, involves many aspects, some well known, some veritable clichés of the international mind, all of them bearing further scrutiny, a weighing of realities against images, particularities against abstractions.

6

The R5 and Other Complexes

I CALL MY favorite theory about the French the R5 complex. It is a half-serious, somewhat satirical effort to encapsulate a key element of their behavior and to describe their self-image in these waning years of the twentieth century. The R5 complex derives from the way the French drive, and in what.

The former can be described as quickly, aggressively, unsparingly. Anybody who has experienced, from behind the wheel, the great traffic circle at the Étoile, around the Arc de Triomphe, will know what I am talking about. Twelve avenues converge on the circle, which is a great hub dominated by the monument Napoleon commenced building in 1806 to celebrate the glories of the empire's armies. By law, cars entering the circle from the right have the right-of-way—*la priorité*, as the French, who study the complicated rules governing this concept in order to pass their driver's license exams, call it—so in essence, anybody coming into the Étoile can cut in front of anybody already there. The resulting scene, particularly when the traffic is heavy, comes directly from the philosophers' manual on the brutishness, the ungovernability of untrammeled mankind. Those who have the right-of-way barrel into the Étoile at full speed, trying to cut off those already in the circle, who in turn try to avoid, if they can, their legal obligation to yield. Cars assume collision courses, the one without the right-of-way attempting to get the other to make an exception, which the other usually refuses to do, causing the first to give way an instant before metal meets metal. Distances between cars are reduced to centimeters. There are a great number of rapid changes in direction, sudden veerings, short stops, quick starts, and gnashings of teeth as the noisy and noisome, highly polluting free-for-all around the Étoile is waged. The same observation could be made at numerous other similar, if smaller, intersections in the provinces, from Menton on the Italian border to Concarneau in Brittany. The French objective is to get ahead, to be first, but to do so cleverly, stressing speed and maneuverability, those necessary attributes of the physically less powerful.

Chivalrous Frenchmen, their traditions in personal comportment deriving directly from the feudal days of yore, gentlemen who are delightful to have around the dinner table and who would lay their coats across a puddle to prevent a strange lady from getting her feet wet, will cut off their dinner host or that same lady if the two of them are driving rival cars. I have had the experience of stopping for a red light, only to see a driver behind me—this one wearing a tough-guy leather jacket and displaying a two-day growth of beard—pull around and ahead so he would be in front of me and able to cross the intersection first. As a pedestrian, I have seen little French cars, driven by fine-looking gentlemen in tweed jackets and silk foulards, their eyes fixed determinedly on the road ahead, speed up so that they can pass, closely, in front of me, rather than slow down to allow me to cross the intersection. The objective is to cut ahead; the French rarely yield. I have an image fixed forever in my mind of young, blond, admirably coiffed, and chicly clothed young mothers in the driver's seats of Renault 5's (the other part of this encapsulation of the essence of Frenchness)—a Stuyvesant or a Virginia Slim or a Blue Blush by Helena Rubinstein held firmly in their lips (otherwise they would be biting them), a scarf by Hermès caressing their lovely necks, their Louis Vuitton bags by their sides, and two well-dressed small children strapped into the back seat—bearing down on the Étoile like tank commanders, shaking their hands with irritation (hand held palm upward, fingers splayed, and shaken up and down) at some offending other driver. *Mais, qu'est-ce que tu fous?*— What the hell are you doing?—they mutter under their breath as the battle ensues. *Ta gueule, salaud*—Up yours, you bastard (very rough translation)—they say.

For quite some time, even in the face of the everyday evidence, I still wondered if the French really did drive recklessly, with uncalled-for aggressiveness and an appalling lack of manners, or whether it was my Anglo-American imagination, an unjustified ethnic irritation. Once I even wrote an item in a language column about the absence in the French language of an exact equivalent for the word "reckless," which I found a strange lack among a people who produced terror and chaos daily around the Arc de Triomphe. The word *casse-cou* exists as a noun, meaning a reckless person—literally a breakneck—but the standard dictionary equivalents for the English adjective "reckless"—*imprudent, insouciant, téméraire, irréfléchi*—suggest, by their failure to convey the word's sense of heedless abandonment of caution, that perhaps, as some of my French friends maintained (in the face, I believed, of much evidence to the contrary) neither the Parisians in particular nor the French in general drive so badly.

Then *Le Point*, the large-circulation weekly newsmagazine, came to my aid. *France: l'Inconduite au volant* was the headline of a cover story in July 1987—"France: Misconduct Behind the Wheel" (there is a nice little pun in this in French, since the word *conduite*, pronounced "cone-DWEET," means both driving and behavior). "More than 100,000 deaths in ten years on our roads," the subheadline read. "More than Germany; more than Great Britain, more than Italy. Unavoidable? Come on. Highway insecurity is in France a matter of (bad) behavior."

The article went on to point out that 450,000 French people had died on the roads since 1945—compared to 600,000 who died in the last world war. Nine million were injured—three times the number wounded in World War I, France's most costly conflict ever. Highway deaths in France occur at twice the rate per kilometer driven than in the United States. The then minister of equipment and transportation, Pierre Méhaignerie, put the issue in dramatic terms: "Highway insecurity reflects a level of civic sense, of responsibility, and, certainly, of democracy. There is something in this French hit parade that we should be asking ourselves about."

Was it Méhaignerie's contention that bad driving showed the absence of a democratic spirit? I'm not at all sure that such is the case. Nonetheless, it must say something about the French that they have a substantially higher number of accidents, per kilometer driven, than any of their great neighbors, except Spain. (It says something also that Paris has the highest rates of lead and carbon monoxide pollution of any major European city, according to a 1988 article in the *Wall Street Journal*, European edition.) *Le Point* went on to argue, as I do here, that there must be some deep psychological and sociological reasons for the high accident rate, though the article said that no study had yet shown what exactly these reasons might be. It did point out that 80 percent of the traffic accidents were due to the behavior of the driver—

"excess speed, dangerous maneuvers, committing traffic infractions, improper use of the car"—and that seemed to me proof of attributes I had already identified with the French: that they are impatient, confident, sometimes overconfident, that they have an exaggerated sense of their locus of control, that they don't think it is going to happen to them. A certain heedlessness of danger is involved, a tendency to give priority to immediate gratification, and a keen, competitive desire to get ahead and to stay ahead of others, as well as selfishness and a depersonalization of the other, since drivers behave toward anonymous others as they never would toward people they know. Also indicated are a solipsistic personality, the absence of a sense of civic virtue, of the notion that life can be rendered far more pleasant for everybody by a prevalent reflex to insist on the priority of the other, rather than to take daily life as a bitter contest during which the other is to be defeated or, at least, ignored.

Le Point listed the most dangerous types of drivers. Significantly, the worst offenders were not young hotheads of the sort found in every country, who brandish their automobiles to impress their friends, though these were named as part of the problem. Even "socially marginal" types, in particular alcoholics, were not seen as mainly responsible for the *insécurité routière*. The worst danger on the road, the article said, was posed by middle- or upper-level white-collar workers, even the presidents of their own companies, aged between thirty-five and fifty, who work and drive a great deal, who have no time to lose, who buy what the French call "nervous"—meaning, in this instance, fast—cars, and who believe themselves to be skillful enough to avoid accidents even when they drive way beyond the posted speed limit: in short, by the ambitious and the successful.

Of course, the French, who are as attached to their cars as any other people, love big, elegant, and expensive models. BMWs and Mercedes-Benzes and the larger Peugeots and Citroëns are common on the road, costing $20,000 to $50,000 and more (the luxury tax alone on new cars is 28 percent). I myself during most of my years in France had the use of a Mercedes, and I must say I enjoyed being able to drive far faster than American law would have allowed. I liked also the extra "nervousness" that the Mercedes gained in not being saddled with a catalytic converter, even if I did thereby make my own contribution to the layers of lead and carbon monoxide that menace the Parisian lung. I drove along at a good clip on those long, straight, beautifully maintained roads that sweep through the countryside, as well as on the *autoroute*, where few people go less than 80 miles per hour and many go well over 100

—the speed limit there is 130 kilometers, or 81 miles, per hour, but it is only sporadically enforced. A common experience is to be moving along at 85 or 90 on the *autoroute* and to be passed constantly, or to be racing along at a good 60 or so on a country road at night, only to find another car bearing down from behind, its headlights assaulting your rearview mirror, tailgating treacherously, looking for an opportunity to pass. (I was interested enough in this phenomenon to look up "tailgating" in my French-English dictionary; it translates *coller à son pare-chocs*, "to stick to his bumper.")

What is striking is not that the drivers of big, powerful automobiles comport themselves in this way. The most popular car on the road for many years was the Renault 5, a compact, boxy little devil, a powder box on wheels, that has no problem at all doing 85 on the superhighway. In recent years, the R5, as it is called (pronounced in French as "air sank") has given way to a similar-sized car, the Peugeot 205, which is advertised as far more *pérformante* than it looks—and it is. The *deux cent cinq* slips through the tightening rings at the Étoile like an otter, a weasel, a mongoose; it and the R5 gobble up the miles on the *autoroute*, *maman* and *papa* in front, the two kids and the poodle in the back, and the family skis, or maybe two bicycles, or a wind surfer, tied to the roof. But it is the R5 that for years (since 1989 it is no longer produced) was the quintessential French car, the one that some years ago replaced that determinedly crusty but extraordinarily long-lived stylistic throwback known as the *deux chevaux*, the Citroën 2CV—the one that *Nouvel Observateur*, another weekly magazine, in another article on bad French driving, said "has a bit of the countryside parish priest in it, the nostalgic hippie, the far-out poet." The magazine called the R5, by contrast, *le sans-culotte*, the "most neutral, the most common, the most modest, the most sympathetic" of the French cars, the "most average car belonging to the most average Frenchman," the car that "everybody has driven, is driving, or will drive." Its top speed: 143 km/hr, or 90 mph. Price: 44,500 francs, or just over $7,000.

A year after that *Le Point* article, the issue of unsafe driving became a national one as the French embarked on new campaigns to get people to drive more safely. *Nouvel Observateur* had a cover story in October 1988 that was timed to coincide with the All Saints weekend, normally one of the most murderous of the year on French roads. "An Inquiry into France Behind the Wheels: The Nobodies," it was titled.

The magazine spoke of the French love of speed, of quickness. It quoted disapprovingly the leader of a group called Auto-Défense (I had never heard of it, but it claimed to have 500,000 adherents), who contended that speed limits were "petty measures, concocted by petty people for petty people." I was reminded of the love in France, a country not generally very attached to sports, of Formula One race car driving. The French follow football rather avidly, but sports, particularly among the middle and upper classes, are not the essential ingredients of life that they are in many other countries, which I always thought reflected on the French love for more serious pursuits, perhaps even the literary life. But turn on the radio any Sunday, and the lead item on the hourly news, no matter what else has happened in the world, no matter what wars, coups d'état, elections, earthquakes, or revolutions might have occurred, will be the excitedly announced continuing progress of whatever big-time car-racing event is taking place somewhere in the world. And so, when the president of Auto-Défense spoke against speed limits—and his comments were directed specifically at comments made by families who had lost loved ones in road accidents—he seemed to be speaking for a certain constituency. In its article on "the nobodies," *Nouvel Observateur* noted that "France is one of the rare countries in the world where a lowering of the speed limit could produce a debate worthy of the Dreyfus affair." The magazine had questioned some famous people in France about their attitude toward cars and driving. Political figures generally said they drove very prudently, although a friend of President Mitterrand testified that the head of state himself drove "with only distant reference to the code of the road but refuses to listen to the slightest criticism of his manner of driving." The prize comment, however, came from Françoise Sagan, the author of *Bonjour Tristesse* (Hello Sadness). In a paragraph cleverly entitled "Bonjour vitesse" ("Hello speed"), she enunciated what might be seen as a kind of existentialist coda to be appended to all definitions of the R5 complex. She allowed that she'd almost lost her life in a car accident when she was twenty-five, had had her skull bashed open, received last rites. She recovered. And then: "I immediately started driving again, and I love speed, which is less dangerous now than it used to be, just as much as before. At night I sometimes go over 200 (125 miles per hour). Anything is possible. You can die getting hit on the head by a flowerpot. But to die suddenly in a car, that's a fabulous death."

Even allowing for a large measure of poetic license, that statement shone a bright light on the R5 metaphor. Not physically large, not, at least since the era of Napoleon (speaking of small stature), impressive in military might, a people whose numbers, influence, power, and importance have been, with some complicated bumps on the graph, declining for most of this century, the French are a people of quickness and cleverness and are fascinated by fabulous deaths. History has bequeathed them a small but nimble car, and they drive it for all it is worth, getting everything they can from their maneuvering skills. They need this method of driving to get ahead in the world—and they are determined to get ahead, both as members of a nation and as individuals, whatever the danger. This encapsulation of the French is similar, though not identical, to a metaphor invented by the French writer Alain Duhamel, who published an affectionately despairing account of his countrymen a few years ago, suggesting not the R5 complex but the Asterix complex, a reference to the much-beloved cartoon character of that name, a small, feisty, impertinent, valorous, ready-fisted inhabitant of Brittany.

Asterix, whose name is supposed to summon up remembrances of ancient kings like Vercingetorix, is an original Gaul, doing constant battle with the large, ungainly, witless Roman centurions who occupied the country. He and his cohort were invented by two French cartoonists, Albert Uderzo and René Goscinny (the latter died in 1977), with the idea, M. Uderzo said on the twenty-fifth anniversary of the comic strip, of finding something completely and uniquely French that would be able to compete with the American-dominated world of cartoon characters. They turned to ancient Gaul, "the Wild West of our civilization," as Uderzo put it, inventing, in essence, the theme of a small, beleaguered people, facing a nearly omnipotent foe, but fighting, against the odds, for freedom.

Asterix's virtues are the ones the French most admire. He makes up for what he lacks in size and power by being clever, adroit, tenacious. He is also fiercely independent, full of pride and prickliness, though at the same time generous and courteous. This imaginary prototypical Gaul is a cartoon character intended to make children laugh, and so it contains a powerful degree of self-mockery, at which the French excel—witness the films of Marcel Pagnol, Jacques Tati, Jean Renoir, all of whom, in their way, turned the French love of caustic wit on themselves. A major character in Asterix, for example, is Obelix, an overweight gourmand, brave but not bright, who devours wild boar in the same passionate way the French now eat *foie gras de canard* and, occasionally, knocks some Roman heads together. And so there is also something very humanly lovable, entirely fallible, about Asterix, and that, too, makes up part of the French self-conception. But it is the stubbornness, the quickness, the mental aggressiveness that dominate in this view of them, whether the

Asterix view or the one I call R5. Duhamel, who is talking primarily of the French political temperament in evoking the Asterix comparison, lists his countrymen's traits as follows: "pugnacious, manic-depressive, courageous, ironic, discontented, generous but chauvinistic, active but moody, intelligent but fiercely individualistic, much taken with prowess and glory, skeptical in the face of authority, allergic to conformity, fiercely attached to his village and convinced that nothing in the world could equal it, intrepid and superstitious, enthusiastic, then discouraged, sentimental and misogynous." He then cites an earlier French writer, Jacques Fauvet, who summed up the collective temperament in three traits: individualism, intellectualism, and conservatism.

What does this explain? The French, like other people, are varied and various. Volumes have been written about them, and in perusing them, I have always had the conviction that they could, in most respects, have been describing just about anybody. The whole notion of an easily identifiable, quickly encapsulated French national character is invidious, an exercise in stereotyping and oversimplification, one that in other contexts, used against other peoples, has provided the basis for much intolerance and persecution. Yet I stick to my R5 complex, not so much as description but as a lighthearted metaphor for a people struggling scrappily against certain limitations of size, against even the tides of history, a people that feels, collectively, if not beleaguered in the way ancient Gaul was, at least reduced in importance by the might of a rival civilization, notably the Anglo-American one. The R5 complex is a good overall concept to keep in mind also as one examines some of the various common notions held by both foreigners and, to some extent, the French themselves, notions about the nature of the country and its people.

7

Gallic Shrugs and Other
Supposed Imperfections

THE REFRAIN about the French, spoken from the heart by many
an American tourist, expresses the common resentment. The French
are incredibly impolite and supercilious, it goes, not at all nice, especially
the Parisians. They are superior, cool, smug, unfriendly, and they have
utter contempt for anybody who speaks imperfectly, or not at all, that
extraordinary instrument of elegance and precision—that trumpet to
the world, as one writer put it—the French language.

I myself have not in my various sojourns in France run into the nasty,
unsympathetic French person of American legend—certainly not often
enough to make me think that the list of attributes in any way sums up
the national character, even if it does sum up the occasional Frenchman
or Frenchwoman. If anything, I would accuse the French of a kind of
too professional courtesy. Anyone who has shopped for daily necessities,
making the rounds of bakers, butchers, dry cleaners, *fromageries, charcuteries, crémeries*, opticians, tailors, *traiteurs*, and other small merchants, cannot possibly think that the French, as a whole, are less polite
than any other people. The problem for the short-term visitors to France
is that they do not come in contact with this aspect of life. They do not
go to the rue Lévis, or the rue de Buci, or the rue Rambuteau, to chat
about vegetables with the mustached man in the apron who stands before
his several kinds of lettuce, his pumpkins, his artichokes, peppers, potatoes, endives, radishes, fennel, carrots, celery, garlic, thyme, rosemary,
shallots, and parsley, joking to the young housewife not to make fun of
old people like himself, while he slips her child a nice dried apricot.

They aren't handed their guinea hen in aspic by the *traiteur* (delicatessen owner), who sends them off with a cheerful, musical *Merci beaucoup, monsieur-dame. Bonne journée.*

The French in general are elaborately, almost ritualistically polite, an attribute that accompanies their attachment to elegance, with which *politesse* is linked. They are among the rare people who use the slightly formal but nonetheless entirely courteous sir, miss, and madame as they address people with whom they are not familiar. There is that subtle and much discussed distinction in French between the *tu*, which is the familiar form of "you," and *vous*, which is the somewhat more formal "you." The shifting rules governing this linguistic ceremony, the determination of when the *tu* is appropriate and when you can't do without *vous*, would fill volumes. The moment when two acquaintances slip inconspicuously, almost by accident, or perhaps with one shyly, a bit uncertainly, opening the curtain, from the latter to the former marks a delicious, delicate, newborn intimacy, the silent collapse of a barrier and the equally silent but unmistakable erection of a new barrier, this one between the newly inaugurated "us" and a redefined "them." Moreover, once the change has been made and the more familiar form adopted, it is in itself a kind of rudeness to return to the formal form, a kind of rejection, a distancing, so that when somebody mistakenly uses the *vous* after having crossed the frontier into the territory of *tu*, an apology is called for.

It is one of the small agonizing decisions of people in public life when somebody they have known and addressed as *tu* for years becomes, say, president of the Republic or prime minister. They have to determine somehow, without ever talking about it, whether to regress to *vous*, as the president's or the prime minister's hierarchical dignity would seem to require; or do they continue with *tu*, or does one of them, the one with the exalted rank, stick with the *tu*, while the other resurrects a more respectful *vous*? Personal preference, individual character, play a big role in this. I have been reliably told that President Mitterrand addresses almost everybody around him with the *vous* and, naturally, is likewise addressed. Still, the *tu* has been intruding steadily into the domain of the *vous* as France itself becomes less formal. Except for Mitterrand himself, just about everybody of rank at the Élysée Palace uses the *tu* when talking to one another. If you went to school with somebody, the chances are you will continue to address that person as *tu* whatever position he may ascend to, and however much higher it may be than your own position. Students, when talking to other students, almost automatically skip the *vous* stage and career directly to the *tu*, which is not exactly the same as having sex on a first meeting but would, with only a small exaggeration, be seen as such by the generation of their parents. In the old days, when men dueled, had mistresses, and spent their evenings at their clubs, living the life so artfully presented in classic films like Max Ophuls's *Madame de . . .* , husbands and wives called each other *vous*, never *tu*, the latter form reserved almost exclusively for children and servants. Even today, it is relatively rare for parents-in-law to be addressed as *tu* by the husbands and wives of their daughters and sons. But that is one of the few remaining barriers. I remember visiting a vacation club in the Alps and feeling somehow offended that the service personnel used the *tu* form with me right away. I am not a formal individual. I much prefer the *tu*. It is friendlier and also grammatically less complicated than the *vous*, requiring as it does a somewhat simpler verbal inflection. But I had been in France long enough to begin attaching some value to the distinction and to view its annihilation at the Alpine ski club as creating a fake informality, a vulgar affability.

In any case, as a journalist working all over the country, I have been received by mayors and factory managers, farmers and professors, prime ministers and police chiefs, with unfailing courtesy, openness, and helpfulness. I've dropped in on mayors' offices, newspaper bureaus, cafés and restaurants, asking for help, information, directions, documents, and have almost never encountered the special sort of personal unpleasantness or linguistic disdain for which the French are supposedly known.

And yet there are those continuing tourist complaints; there is what is known as the Gallic shrug—I have heard an annoyed American diplomat refer to it as "the arrogant Gallic no." There are, to be sure, those icy cool store clerks, the sniffity concierges; there is a tendency, quite noticeable among the French, not to look strangers in the eye. I used to go in Paris to something called the Gymnase Club to exercise, and I noted that while everybody there shares a common purpose and interest, the only people who talk to each other are those who arrived together. Strangers are rarely acknowledged. There is a tendency of each person to stare straight ahead, to maintain an invisible shield of privacy and unapproachability around himself or herself, to signal aloofness and reserve. Years before I went to the Gymnase Club I was a student in Paris and used to eat at the *restaurants universitaires*, where subsidized lunches and dinners could be had for derisory prices. These, by definition, were student places, large halls filled with tables for four or six or eight.

Many was the time when I found myself, alone, sitting opposite another student, who was also alone, and following some strange ritual of privacy and formality that I am sure filled neither of our hearts with joy, we would avoid each other's eyes, look mostly at our plates, and say nothing at all.

Years later, it fell to me from time to time to attend large dinners where I knew nobody at my table. These are painful experiences in France. There are sometimes friendly people, of course, people who talk with strangers who happen to be sitting next to them, or across from them, at a banquet table, which is a more intimate setting than the weight-lifting room at the Gymnase Club, people who even, eventually, become friends, welcome you into their homes, come to yours for dinner. But it is rare. More often than not, unless formally introduced to me (this introduction performed, often, by myself), my fellow diners on these occasions rarely said a word. Everybody sits in his own zone of privacy, chewing and drinking. I have had the experience of being at a table where everybody knew everybody else, except me, and I sat through an entire meal unspeaking and unspoken to.

The French are shy and they are formal—it is not that they are unfriendly in the condescending or smug way sometimes attributed to them. They are uncomfortable with people whom they do not know, foreigners particularly but other French people also. There is a common explanation given for the French attitude toward personal relations, one used often by the French themselves. Americans, they say, setting a basis for comparison, are very friendly; among them it is easy for a stranger to penetrate the outermost circle of acquaintanceship, though difficult to go beyond that outer circle to deeper inner ones, precisely because the whole notion of American acquaintanceship, according to the French, is so superficial, so lacking in gradations and degrees, in *tu* and *vous* distinctions, that there is no inner circle. The friendliness is false, the French believe, false in the same way that a French person can be false if he uses the *tu* with somebody he barely knows; there is a lack of meaning in it, precisely because it can be transferred so easily from one person to another. The French, by contrast—or so goes the explanation—take longer to form personal relationships. They need time. You don't get into the outer circle very easily, but once you do, there is great meaning attached to it, because membership there cannot be transferred.

The explanation is too schematic, because it does not sufficiently account for variations among the French themselves. But there is something to it. Even among young, casual people, the kind with orange hair and bangles that group around the Forum des Halles in Paris to watch the street jugglers and musicians, there is a certain formality, and a tendency to form closed groups, to build that isolating shield around the self.

This question of formality cannot be too quickly passed over. Perhaps it is a heritage of the feudal tradition, in which the social rites were elaborate and linked to power, and the nobleman who was privileged to hold the king's towel as he stepped out of the bath enjoyed a distinction, a favored status, compared to the nobleman who was not so privileged. Government offices and senior functionaries, even of the most democratic and unpompous personal manners, seem to surround themselves with a certain ceremony that comes across as distance. I remember at a cocktail party meeting Michelle Aliot-Marie, who was at the time a deputy minister of education, and largely to make conversation, I asked her about some minor item in the news that involved her public life. Granted I was a journalist for the *New York Times*, but given that I was at a cocktail party hosted by a common friend, I was taken aback when she replied imperiously: "If you wish to interview me, you may call my press attaché and make an appointment." This reaction on Ms. Aliot-Marie's part is not necessarily the rule. There is no rule. Other senior officials or junior officials might well have established a tone of intimacy, even confidentiality, invited me to lunch, asked my own opinion. This did not happen in the case of Ms. Aliot-Marie; and yet I think her approach to the situation arose out of a sense of the ritualistic priorities; it was a reflex of formality and decorum more than arrogance or unfriendliness.

There is something about the very architecture and interior decor of public life that leads at times to this formality. Government ministries and offices are housed in what can only be described as palaces, or former palaces, with dizzyingly high ceilings, elaborate moldings, curlicues, cornices, curved balustrades, and sculptured window casements. It is an architecture designed to suggest hierarchy and to give the occupant a sense of his own power, and it does both these things admirably. Function follows form here. When the Socialists, who are generally a bit more casual, less formal, than the Conservatives (though here, too, I can think of exceptions on both sides), came into power in 1981, they talked breathlessly of the light finally penetrating the darkness. But the Socialist ministries maintained the ushers in morning coats, who behave with all the warmth and casualness of a classic English butler as they receive you, take your coat, and show you to your princely waiting room, where somebody else will eventually appear to announce you formally, ritualistically, to the official who may then greet you with his feet up on the furniture.

I have spent a certain amount of time observing Jacques Chirac, the mayor of Paris and a friendly man given even to a certain point of indiscretion in speaking his mind. I once traveled with him on his private airplane during a campaign trip, at the end of which he personally ensured that every person in the entourage had a lift home. He was friendliness itself. There wasn't a hint of formality, not an alloy of pretension. I have seen him also talking with visitors in a small, unpretentious office at the Hotel Matignon, where he has twice served as prime minister, and where he also was direct, affable, unassuming, even modest. But at the monumental Hôtel de Ville, the City Hall, where he holds court as the mayor of Paris, a certain frigid ritual prevails, a stiffness immediately becomes apparent, a distance is maintained, not so much because it is in Chirac's nature but because the occasion and the environment seem to call for it. Chirac's office there is immense and gilded, breathtaking in its monarchical splendor. A visitor sits stiffly in a chair, and so does Chirac, and the two of them speak, if not stiffly, at least formally to each other. Upstairs in his private quarters, where he holds dinners for friends and acquaintances, a certain forced casualness wars with the solemnity of the occasion. The conversation is free, but the tone is deferential. There is a distance that could be construed as a kind of arrogance of position, a sense of the hierarchical priorities of the court. But it always seemed to me to be independent of personality, outside the control of individual wills. It is inherent in the very structure of social life in a country with France's interior environments and traditions.

There is another aspect of the French reputation for rudeness, which cannot be too quickly dismissed. The rude ones are often the lower-level state functionaries; the people who sell tickets in the metro; the clerks behind the *guichets* at the post office, or the railroad ticket window, or at your local branch of the Banque Nationale de Paris. This is to some extent merely an illustration of the well-known fact that people who run their own small businesses are more polite to their clientele than are people who work for large, impersonal organizations from which they draw their salaries. The comparison between the reception of customers at the neighborhood butcher shop and the district supermarket, with its cuts of meat prewrapped in cellophane and its checkout counters, is a striking lesson in the virtues of small business that has little to do with the French character. But with the French, there is something else to this. The French, including the people who work at these institutions, feel an anger within them, and some of their brusqueness, their impatience, their apparent chauvinism, is a sublimation of that anger. I was once working on an article about the newspaper *Libération*, a formerly far-leftist, prorevolutionary daily pamphlet, founded by Jean-Paul Sartre, which in the early 1980s remodeled itself into a politically independent, generally high-quality, sometimes brilliant but always irreverent, often snide and cutting daily publication, full of sly puns, clever headlines, and an overarching, very French distrust of institutional power. The style is mocking. "Behind the headlines," the philosopher Alain Finkielkraut once told me, trying to describe *Libération*'s particular brand of breezy sarcasm, its occasional snickering tone, "lies the audible chuckle of the journalist." Who reads it? I wondered.

Jean-Paul Aron, the late sociologist and historian of ideas, told me that it was the newspaper read, paradoxically—and, obviously, among others—by the *petits fonctionnaires*, people behind the *guichets*. They read it, he said, because it satisfied the primordial French resentment against employers, the establishment, the way things are—a resentment, it should be quickly noted, that coexists with a deep and abiding conservatism in personal habits, dress, and, often, even political ideas. And so, while the garden-variety nasty functionary was not a big part of my life, whenever I did run into one, I took him to be an expression on the personal level of the anarchist spirit of Ravachol—executed as a terrorist, which he was, at the end of the nineteenth century—that both terrifies and seduces the French, who want a safe, predictable world of their own, their little spot behind the *guichet*, but like to rail against their lot in life by, in part, behaving contemptuously toward their customers. As M. Duhamel said in *The Asterix Complex*, the French are dissatisfied; they like to complain. Moreover, they complain from positions of safety. They are protected by law against dismissal. They work thirty-nine-hour weeks. They get five weeks of vacation a year. They receive monthly allocations from the state to help with their children. Medical insurance covers virtually all their health costs. They have their R5 in the garage, and they drive it with the same annoyance against interference that they sometimes manifest toward American tourists speaking French badly— or more likely, speaking English. *Libération*—which claims that nearly 60 percent of its readers are white-collar workers—gives them at least the illusion of a certain distance from the tawdry institutional world in which they are, by economic necessity, small cogs. Rudeness to tourists, in a way, accomplishes the same purpose.

But I wouldn't want to leave the question there, for it would preclude the numerous, undemanded kindnesses that I have received in France, the courtesies extended, the invitations home, the gratefully accepted offers of friendship, the eagerness to talk, to exchange ideas, and to debate on the part of a people who, above all else, love stimulating, intelligent discourse. Perhaps the difference between the French and others, particularly the Americans, lies in varying notions of family life, which in France includes outsiders with greater difficulty than its American counterpart does. Part of this derives from the French reluctance to make children a part of a social event—say, a dinner party at home—a fact that, for many, sharply demarcates family weekends from weekday intercourse. I have been invited to dinners at the homes of French friends whom I have known for months and years without ever once seeing their children. This is because I am invited for weekday dinners, not Sunday family gatherings. And on the occasions of adult socializing, there is none of the cooing over baby, none of the time-consuming waving at a tiny tot while his parents encourage him to "say nite-nite," that is part of the American ritual. The French do not impose on others the obligation to adore their children, which I have always felt to mark a pleasing sensibility, a capacity for empathy. But the very fact that the family is a tight-knit, closed entity that restricts outside participation can be taken as unfriendliness by outsiders.

Once, at an American embassy dinner, a French captain of industry at my table was being attacked by some of the Yanks present because, they said, they were so rarely invited to the homes of the French people they met. I always remember, just to put a bit of perspective on this issue, getting my visa to go to France as a journalist at the consulate in New York and hearing two consular officials complain bitterly that though they had been in my city for years, they had almost never been invited to an American home. I found myself making excuses for my fellow New Yorkers. It isn't that they are unfriendly, I said. Certainly they are not anti-French. Housing is expensive, and people don't have the space to entertain the way they once used to, I argued, thinking, to some extent, of my own situation. They are busy with work and other obligations. The days pass and one does not get to many of the things that one would like to do, I concluded. A couple of years later, I watched the distinguished, English-speaking, and extremely friendly French businessman put into a similar situation, making the same point I had made in New York but giving it a specific French flavor.

"I have been married to my wife for thirty-five years," he said, "and during that entire thirty-five years, except for periods when I was traveling outside the country, I have spent every weekend either going to my in-laws' house or my own parents' house, or receiving family members at our house. Every weekend for thirty-five years, and this is not unusual. It isn't that we don't like other people; it's that we have to spend our leisure time with the ones we are related to."

The captain of industry solved a kind of riddle for me. Many times have I wandered the streets of villages, and of Paris itself, particularly on Sundays, wondering about the reasons for the eerie emptiness I felt. Where are all the people? I would wonder, looking up at the facades of the buildings, dimly lit or shuttered tightly. Across the street from my apartment on the rue de Lota in Paris's Sixteenth Arrondissement, there so often seemed to be nobody left alive. The buildings opposite me were lifeless, the street empty but for the two armed police who guarded the embassy of the United Arab Emirates across the street. Where is everybody? They are visiting their families, spending the weekend at their houses in the country, being a private people already tightly woven into a fabric of blood ties and obligations, which, whether the French really want it or not, whether they are rude or friendly, forms a closed circle, a sealed familial ring into which the outsider penetrates only under certain happily exceptional circumstances.

8

The Myth of the
Anti-American

THE FACT is that, despite an established reputation for it, the
French are not anti-American. But they manage to be pro-American
without seeming to be. Indeed, they seem to be contemptuous, disdainful,
finicky about the United States, as though proximity to the great American ally carried the risk of a contagious disease. I am reminded of that
diplomat's comment on "the arrogant Gallic no." It was occasioned by
the French refusal in 1986 of the American request that warplanes based
in Britain be allowed to fly over France on their way to a punitive
bombing mission in Libya, a refusal that provoked enormous anti-French
sentiment, well reported by France's foreign correspondents, in the
United States. The United States had requested the overflight permission,
demanding an immediate answer, and the French had turned them down.
What is interesting in this is not so much that the diplomat was annoyed.
But why the expression "Gallic no," instead of simply "arrogant no"?
The diplomat perceived something particularly persnickety, character-
istically "Gallic," in the negative French government reaction. The phenomenon that bothered him was, no doubt, a derivative of what goes
by the name of Gaullism. It derives from the general's determination,
after the humiliating defeat at the hands of the Germans in 1940, to
make France felt in the world again, and what better way to make it
felt than to snub its nose, occasionally, at the very great power that had
restored its freedom and independence?

De Gaulle, of course, was opposed in practically everything he did by
the philosopher Jean-Paul Sartre, but it is odd to see how the separate
approaches of these two larger-than-life postwar figures in France agreed

on the necessity to tend toward anti-Americanism. De Gaulle saw it as an imperative of genuine French independence. For Sartre, it was part of his hatred of the bourgeoisie; in the class struggle, Sartre, whose relationship to Communism was complicated, contradictory, and ambiguous all his life, sided with the working class. In the 1950s, for example, Albert Camus broke with Sartre over the latter's refusal to condemn the Soviet labor camps. Sartre, according to his biographer Annie Cohen-Solal, did not want to appear to provide the United States with ammunition for its Cold War guns. The dislike between Sartre, the Voltairian, leftist dissenter, and de Gaulle, the imperious rightist, did not prevent them both from wanting a glorious role for France as the leader of a European entity, one of whose main purposes would be to dilute the dangerous polarization of the world into two enemy camps. Sartre's idea was that European unification was too important a task to entrust to political leaders, like de Gaulle. He saw it coming about through the near-mystical spirit of fraternity of the European masses. Sartre was among the first to raise the specter of an American cultural hegemony over Europe. A master all his life of the semi-informed generality, the euphonious but spurious distinction, Sartre once wrote that European writers were characterized by their struggle "against power, against established ideology, and for social justice." The American intellectual, by contrast, is pessimistic. Thus, regenerating European culture within a framework of European political unity, Sartre thought, was a noble and necessary effort to save the world not only from World War III but also from the Yankee onslaught, which, he seemed at times to think, was the more dread of the two dangers.*

And so, for France's two "great men" of the postwar world, a certain distancing from the United States—even if it meant, for Sartre, a closeness to the Soviet Union, which he had to repudiate after the invasion of Hungary in 1956—was part and parcel of French greatness. But genuine greatness among the cynical, worldly French was often only the stated goal, not the real one, as other leaders pursued the fashionable anti-American verbal trends. Georges Pompidou, not particularly known for his sense of humor, once quoted Jean Giraudoux to the effect that "We are fated to be the nuisance of the world." The French, desiring to be taken seriously, refuse simply to go along, not so much because their national interests on some specific issue dictate a go-it-alone policy but because being an *emmerdeuse*—Giraudoux's word, meaning actually something a bit more profane than "nuisance," something more

* Annie Cohen-Solal, *Sartre: A Life* (New York: Pantheon, 1987), pp. 298–311.

like pain in the ass—involves being taken seriously, imposing oneself. Mitterrand loves nothing more than to insert a French disagreement into the works during European and international summit meetings, as in 1986 when he alone among the leaders of the seven major industrial powers refused to put terrorism on the agenda. The difference is that when France now asserts itself, the world tends to shrug resignedly, saying to itself, There go the French again, and then to go about its business much as though the French did not exist. The world has learned that French stubbornness is an expression of weakness, not of strength. But in striking contrast, things were decidedly not viewed that way when de Gaulle made that first and still most important assertion of a particular French interest against the majority views of its allies. Early in 1966, the general, who more than two decades earlier had watched nervously from his exile in London as the Americans, the British, and the Canadians fought to free his country, announced to a shocked world that he was withdrawing France from the integrated military command of NATO. In other words, no French soldier would serve under anybody other than a French commanding officer.

Who knows what deep sense of humiliation de Gaulle was reflecting as he caused the NATO headquarters to be moved from Versailles to Belgium. Could he have resented that the Free French forces during World War II were ultimately commanded by Dwight Eisenhower? The French, he said, did not need or want an "American protectorate" anymore, even if such had been necessary in the years immediately after the war, when Europe was not strong enough to protect itself. But the major theme pressed by de Gaulle—who was, unintentionally, echoing Sartre's defiance of American cultural power—was that military integration for France meant subordination, and the French were not born to be subordinate. Their sovereignty and national independence were the issues to de Gaulle, who ignored cries on the other side of the fence to the effect that national sovereignty was only a phrase, and a meaningless phrase at that, if you didn't have the means to defend it. "It is the will of France to dispose of its own fate," de Gaulle said. The presence of American troops under American command in France diminished French independence.

If this is anti-Americanism, it has many sides, most of them having to do with an instinct to compensate for the natural limits of a country, the limits of population, national strength, the capacity to project power and influence beyond one's borders. The plain fact is that the height of French power, relative to its neighbors, came in the 150 years between the reign of Louis XIV, when France was the world's most powerful nation, and the short-lived Napoleonic empire, when ideological fervor and imperial ambitions combined to create a frenzy of expansionism, a veritable, and almost successful, effort to conquer all Europe. But France has been in relative decline since Napoleon's defeat by the Russians in 1812, a defeat confirmed three years later at Waterloo, when Napoleon, at the head of his armies again after escaping from exile, was beaten by the hated British. Following that, there were other defeats, mostly at the hands of the Germans; there was the debacle of the Franco-Prussian War of 1870, the near disaster of World War I, and the crushing, dispiriting, humiliating loss to the Germans in 1940, which led to the darkest period in all French history, the Hitlerian occupation and the collaborationist Vichy government in the southern half of France.

The record since Napoleon raises a fascinating question: Why, given France's considerable size, scientific genius, and national wealth, has it performed so badly on the battleground, its successes coming against far weaker colonialized peoples in Africa and Asia but never against Europeans? The issue is all the more puzzling given the country's military tradition, culminating in the awesome might of Napoleon's armies. Among the explanations is one based ultimately on the collective French preoccupation with the soft delights of culture and civilization. During the ages when manpower, the size of armies, determined national strength, France, as Europe's most populous country, was also its militarily strongest. When technology came to take precedence over the number of men under arms, the historic French failure, by comparison with the British and the Germans, to appreciate the absolute importance of science and technology led to its military undoing. In his book on the Franco-Prussian War and the Paris Commune of 1870–71, Alistair Horne tells of the great curiosity that attended the display of some steel cannon by a certain Herr Krupp of Essen at the Crystal Palace Exhibition of 1851. In the Paris Great Exhibition of 1867, Krupp sent over a fifty-ton gun capable of firing shells weighing as much as two small cannon. The French military failed to take the steel cannon seriously, believing, in any case, that the Prussians were, as Horne puts it, "a nation of comic professors and beer-swilling bombasts." When war came, of course, the French cannon, still cast in bronze, sent out shells that "burst noisily but harmlessly in the air," whereas the "Prussian percussion-fused shells exploded with demoralizing effects at the foot of their targets."*

* Alistair Horne, *The Fall of Paris: The Siege and the Commune, 1870–71* (New York Macmillan, 1965), pp. 4–5, 40–1.

French military defeats have in any case not diminished but increased the nation's determination to make itself felt in the world by other means, to be taken as a great power less by war than by politics. In recent years, the French have striven in numerous ways to play a significant role in the world, their initiatives including the testing of nuclear weapons in the Pacific (despite the fierce opposition of Australia, New Zealand, and the tiny states of Oceania); the effort to maintain especially close relations with the Arab world; the continuing special ties with West Africa, where France's former colonies are concentrated. The most conspicuous aspect of the French rearguard battle against decline can be seen in their attitude toward Britain and, in part by extension, toward the United States, which the French see as an embodiment of Britain in the New World. There have been polls showing which people the French most admire and which they most dislike. Strangely—or, at least, this has seemed strange to me, even a bit unsettling—opinion polls always show the French naming the Germans as the people they feel most akin to and the British as the ones they most dislike—that is, among the World War II allies. British Prime Minister Margaret Thatcher has long been the foreign leader least well liked by the French. The lesson here could be that old rivalries take precedence over more recent ones. The French have been fighting the British since the medieval Hundred Years' War. Joan of Arc is still, for many French, the ultimate heroine, the "purest symbol of patriotism," as the historian André Maurois put it, a fighter against the British and Britain's French lackeys. The modern era of the old rivalry goes back to the eighteenth century, and particularly to the era of what we in American schoolbooks call the French and Indian War, and the French call the Seven-Year War. It was a global conflict, the result of which was that the French lost most of their holdings in North America and India.

The mere fact that the United States became a kind of extension of British cultural influence, through both the English language and the special relations between the United States and Britain, leads the French to feel themselves in danger of being engulfed in what Sartre liked to call Anglo-Saxon hegemonism. In fact, the French use the term "Anglo-Saxon" to refer to what might properly be called Anglo-American. They lump together Britain and the United States into an indistinguishable mass that way, using a tone of voice that is unmistakably but unprovably pejorative. There is, for example, the Anglo-Saxon press, meaning the British and American newspapers. The French talk about Anglo-Saxon culture, or, very simply, about the Anglo-Saxons themselves, as though they constituted some ethnically homogeneous national group, like the Swedes or the Japanese.

I occasionally used to issue mild protests about this, based on my idea that "Anglo-Saxon" means something entirely different from what the French think it means, referring as it does to the peoples of Anglia and Saxony in northern Germany, many of whom migrated to the British Isles and therefore make up a tiny fraction of the overall American population. "I'm no more Anglo-Saxon than you are," I would say, thinking of my Russian-Jewish and Hungarian-Jewish ancestry. I don't think black Americans or Chinese Americans or Polish Americans think of themselves as particularly Anglo-Saxon, I used to argue. It was to no avail. In France, the term "Anglo-Saxon" still refers to us all.

WHAT of it? There is a nasty aspect of petty resentment to this, but it doesn't amount to very much, and it does not conceal the basic fact that France is enormously admiring, even adoring, of things American. In 1975, the French National Assembly, in a silly gesture of defensiveness, passed a law forbidding the use of untranslated English words for any commercial purpose in France, such as in advertising or package labeling. An organization called AGULF, an acronym for Association Générale des Usagers de la Langue Française (General Association for the Users of the French Language), partially funded by an official, state-supported organization known as the High Commission for the French Language, began to bring civil suits against offenders, asking for damages. Various companies had to pay what amounted to token fines. Trans World Airlines paid the equivalent in francs of five hundred dollars for issuing English-language boarding passes at Charles de Gaulle Airport; the Paris Opéra was fined for selling English copies of a program for a performance of *Bubbling Brown Sugar*; the Evian bottled-water company was brought to court for calling a new product "le fast drink des Alpes." Generally, the companies caught in this infraction of the law did not take great pains to defend themselves, since the sums involved were small and, after all, the law is the law. A furniture manufacturer named Hugues Steiner, however, decided to fight back when AGULF, in its role as avenger of an abused, linguistically baffled public, brought its prosecutorial powers to bear against an advertising brochure in which M. Steiner used the term "showroom." All sorts of human rights issues and linguistic questions emerged from the courtroom battle. The official French equivalents for "showroom" were *salle d'ex-*

position and *hall*, the latter, as Steiner's lawyers pointed out, coming from English and having, for some reason, been accepted into the French language, while "showroom" had been arbitrarily excluded.

Steiner accused AGULF of dictatorial tendencies; the methods of language control, he said, in an open letter to President Mitterrand, "evoke a certain dark period in the life of our country," an allusion to French collaboration with Nazi Germany during the war. The issue was a confusion of "the legitimate defense of the national heritage by inquisitorial and authoritarian means," he said. AGULF's attempt to impose restrictions on his ability to choose any language he thought commercially beneficial in the pursuit of his business affairs was a violation of his rights. M. Steiner went further. He believed that AGULF was run by people whose ultimate ambitions were the aggrandizement of the national power through a repudiation of the entire mechanism of French international entanglements. They wanted to separate the French from the Anglo-Saxon world and reorient it toward such "natural" partners as Africa and the Arab countries of the Middle East, thereby building up a special zone of power and influence. The language activities were, in Steiner's view, designed to further this broad anti-Atlanticist scheme, not merely to protect French from the intrusions of English.

I went to visit officials of AGULF, which was a small organization with two lawyers and a secretary, and a chairman named Philippe de Saint-Robert, who was also the chairman of the High Commission for the French Language, and their argument was simply that the defense of the French language was not a matter of dictatorship, nor a question of petty chauvinism. It was a sensible way to preserve the national means of communication and prevent the French people from becoming foreigners in their own land.

In the case of "showroom," M. Steiner won his case in court, and AGULF was even obliged to pay him a small fine for his trouble. But the effort to defend the French language against "Anglo-Saxon hegemonism" continued nonetheless, by means that nobody could reasonably argue were either mean-spirited or hateful.

One part of the effort, waged on an international scale, goes by the name Francophonia, and it is a campaign, furthered by whoever is in power in France (thereby having the rare status of a policy initiative that provokes no angry national debate between left and right), to bring together French speakers from around the world, particularly from countries where it is an official language, to Paris for conferences and speeches and promotions of the idea that efforts need to be made worldwide to preserve and develop French language, education, and culture. This is a remnant of that special attribute of the French effort to colonize much of the world, the notion of the civilizing mission. Whereas the British educated some of the subdued local people in the English language and the English way of doing things because they needed them to help run the colonial civil service and the army, the French wanted the natives to become French, at least culturally—though the French also wanted to keep these nonwhite, non-European converts to Frenchness at a distance. The classic example of the attitude is the grammar school textbook once used in Paris and Lyon as well as in Bujumbura and Abidjan, Ougadougou and Dakar. Its first line began "Our ancestors the Gauls." Or there were those World War II Free French army songs sung by the colonial troops, with words like "Your empire will save you, you the country of the great heart" or "*Marchez toujours, marchez quand même/ Jusqu'à la fin, jusqu'à la mort*"—"March on, march always/ Until the end, until death." The "country of the great heart" here was not Burundi or the Ivory Coast, Upper Volta or Senegal, Tunisia or Morocco, but what was called *La Métropole*, the mother country.

The civilizing mission now takes place at the occasional Francophone summits, held in Paris or in another capital every so often—what *Libération*, casting a mocking, linguistically mangled glance on the effort, called "Le Sommet du French Speaking" when such a meeting was held in Quebec in 1987. The Quebec meeting got together the heads of state or government of thirty-nine countries, and while, as *Libération* rather sourly put it, "the battle against the empire of English was lost a long time ago," the participants "tried to define the minimum friendly ties to which the users of the same language have the right." *Libération* summed up the entire business with a cartoon showing President Mitterrand barging into the room of his prime minister, Jacques Chirac, while the latter was wrapping himself in a towel from the shower. "What does 'Do not disturb' mean, Jacques?" Mitterrand asks, pointing to the English sign on Chirac's door.

Some other commentators, also rather skeptical of the event, pointed out that among the ostensibly Francophone countries, a large number, indeed, a clear majority, were far from democracies—by contrast with France's main rival in postcolonial institutions, the British Commonwealth. The definition of a Francophone country itself took a bit of stretching and included just about any country where France once had considerable influence or control, even if the sad reality was that French as an everyday language hardly existed. They included, for example,

Lebanon, Egypt, Vietnam, and the Seychelles. In twelve African countries among the thirty-nine countries attending the summit, French remains the sole official language, mingling with local tribal languages. French, *Libération* reported, came in sixth in the world's "language hit parade," behind Chinese, English, Spanish, Russian, and Arabic. The practical benefit for the Third World participants lies in an organization, created in 1970, called Agency for Cultural and Technical Cooperation, with money provided mostly by France, Canada, and Belgium going for development projects in poorer ostensibly French-speaking countries.

Lurking behind "les sommets du French speaking" is the longing for national glory, and not surprisingly, when this longing enters the area of language, it is the "Anglo-Saxons" who emerge as rivals, giving the entire enterprise, like so much in the French attitude, its superficial gloss of anti-Americanism. It has been a long time since French was the international language, when it was what Russian aristocrats spoke to each other, instead of plebeian Russian. English today is the language of diplomacy, of science, even of jet-set snobbery (though here French probably holds its own, at least among the Anglo-Saxons themselves). And so the French, who for decades were famous for not speaking English, have gradually gotten used to it as a necessity of the modern world. Even the political leaders these days, with the stubborn exception of President Mitterrand—who might indeed not have understood a Do Not Disturb sign—can handle interviews in English, and they do so with evident pleasure and pride. With French having, as *Libération* cruelly pointed out, lost the linguistic battle in the international world, the struggle has become a domestic one, with such organizations as AGULF striving at least to maintain a certain purity inside France itself.

There are in fact, under the auspices of the High Commission for the French Language, men and women who labor full time to invent French equivalents to English phrases that have invaded (the correct word from the French point of view), or threaten to invade, the French language, becoming what is widely known as Franglais. It is a prolonged effort at the creation of neologisms and has produced some inventive solutions, solutions that gain the force of a kind of law when they become required modes of expression in all government ministries, the previously used English equivalents being banned. One year, for example, the Secretariat for Technology and Communication published a list of one hundred new words, mostly covering the world of show business, replacing "one-man show" with *spectacle solo*, "disc jockey" with *animateur*, and "hit parade" with *palmarès*. In 1985, shortly before the AGULF-Steiner battle, the High Commission published a dictionary of some fifteen hundred neologisms, many of them covering technical and scientific terms. The French word for "computer" was decreed to be *ordinateur*; "software" became *logiciel*; the English word "brainstorm" became *remue-méninges* (meaning literally "stirring the brain," not to be confused with *remue-ménage*, "commotion" or "hullabaloo"); "a blackout" became *une occultation*; and the word created for "digital switching" was *commutation numérique*.

The belief is widespread in France that the intrusion of English words into French would be a disaster, depriving the language of Voltaire and Flaubert of its beauty, its purity. There are some scholars who disagree, arguing that the "purist" approach is misguided, that the imagined threat does not exist. Just around the time of the Quebec summit meeting a linguist named Claude Hagège published a book in which he argued that while French is indeed losing ground as an international language, it is not itself threatened by the much-feared English invasion. Word usage has been affected by the contact with English, though of course, as he pointed out, the contact has led a large number of French words to be absorbed into English—and indeed, the capacity to absorb foreign words is one of the main reasons for the vitality of English. But the "hard core" of French, the rules of grammar and syntax and word order, have not been influenced at all. Hagège put his finger on the political implications of this. "From François I to General de Gaulle, passing by Louis XIV," he wrote, "it is a tradition solidly established in France to see in the purity of the language the image of the grandeur of the state."

Mixed, or perhaps just negative, feelings about the "Anglo-Saxon" linguistic invasion, however, seem entirely justified. For even if French itself is not threatened, it is hard to see the use of random English words as a help, particularly, as the historian Jacques Barzun has pointed out, when a perfectly good word already exists in French. The French word *smoking*, which means dinner jacket, is not only ugly when thrust into a set of French phonemes (all the words ending in "ing" stick out like sore thumbs in French), it is unnecessary. Moreover, as Professor Barzun has written, it defies "the common forms of handling"—"the gender, the plural, the combining, and often the spelling of Franglais words follow individual choice." There are two deeper problems here, at least one of them having to do with the French conception of themselves. The plain fact is that it has become chic in France to use English words, even when they are like grit in the salad of French. Cultural pride has yielded to mediocre fashion, to snobbery. Barzun has written that this is not a question of useful linguistic borrowing of the sort that has enriched languages for millennia. What "the users of real or pseudo English words enjoy" is "outlandishness and anarchy of usage." They want "relief from the commonplace."

The second problem, also discussed by Barzun, is the formality inherent in French, compared with the relative flexibility, the casualness, of English. The problem is not merely that the "Anglo-Saxons" have great cultural and economic power, but that English is crisper than French, which often has only a single, rather stodgy word to express something that can be expressed in two ways in English. Think of the informal "to move up" or the more stodgy "to elevate" in English. French has only the rather stiff *élever*, or the equally formal *faire monter*. To move out, to move about, to move away, to move in, to move along, to move back—all have rather less quick and handy equivalents in French: *se déloger, se déplacer, s'éloigner, faire entrer, circuler, se reculer*. Forming catchy new expressions by putting together new combinations of words, which is commonplace in English, is usually impossible in French. Thus, when the 1988 dictionary of neologisms came out, it translated "flashback" (not explaining why it was so slow to get to this rather old movie term) as *retour en arrière*, which simply does not have the same quick power as the English equivalent. "Voice off," another movie term showing the English susceptibility for new combinations, became *voix hors champs*. The war against English, moreover, implied a complicated war, as unwinnable as the earlier wars against Third World nationalism, against a certain kind of modernization of the spirit. Young people, the generation of the future, are creating a whole new style of language in France, which takes casualness and insouciance as the key values. For example, emerging out of the high schools all during the 1980s was a mode of word inversion known as *verlan*, which is itself an inversion of the word *l'envers*, which means "reverse." *Verlan* had a modern, with-it feel (the word meaning "with it," "tuned in," was inverted from the already slangy standard *branché* to the *verlan* term *chébran*).

The use of English words, with their Anglo-Saxon shortness, the hardness of their hit, partakes of the same valuation of informality and breeziness. The seductions are hard to resist, and despite the dictionary of neologisms and the associations of patriotism with the movement against Franglais (witness AGULF), there are many slips—*glissades*, as the French might put it—among those who should know better. During the 1986 legislative election campaign, none other than Jack Lang, the

French minister of culture and thus necessarily a leading exponent of French linguistic purity, described himself as "punchy *et bagarreur*" (punchy and ready for a fight). Why did he use "punchy" rather than the French word *dynamique*, which is its dictionary equivalent in French? Probably because *dynamique* is not so dynamic an equivalent. It is what the young people might call *ringard*—fusty and old-fashioned, neither *branché* nor *chébran; dynamique* is in French what we used to call "square" in English. It lacks the staccato vigor, the youthful, modern association, that M. Lang, who personifies trendiness and youthfulness, was evidently seeking. The phenomenon results not from American cultural power or French slavishness to it (it would be hard to think of a people less slavish than the French). It is a product of a late-twentieth-century search for new modes of expression that are fulfilling to the generation generally younger than those who wage Francophonia.

The fact is, moreover, that even with the rise of Francophonia, the anti-American aspects of Gaullism—or those that can be construed as anti-American—have lost ground. Of European countries, France is one of the friendliest to the United States, the memory of D day and the liberation distant enough for the French to be grateful, rather than resentful over the necessity of being rescued. There is none of that punk hatred of America so common in other European countries. The noisome, Sartrean, fashionably leftist jargon that treated the United States as a bourgeois and therefore philistine tyranny, an "imperialist" menace posing a threat at least as grave as the one posed by the Soviet Union, has become as *ringard* as a brierwood pipe. Even the Socialists, who might, like their rough ideological counterparts in Britain, Germany, or Greece, be expected to want to distance themselves from the American military commitment to European defense, reiterate from time to time their certainty that there can be no meaningful defense policy against the Soviet Union without close cooperation with the Americans. But what about Anglo-Saxon cultural hegemonism? Go to the film retrospectives, and there will be long series on Orson Welles, Clint Eastwood, Frank Capra, Laurel and Hardy, Jerry Lewis (a particular French intellectuals' favorite). There will be jazz in the nightspots, endless American drama series on television, along with the *CBS Evening News with Dan Rather* on Canal Plus, the French pay-television channel.

Despite their prickliness on certain foreign policy issues; despite their defense of the language; even despite a tendency to mock Americans as know-nothings, the French, I firmly believe, have warm feelings about us. They are our oldest allies. They imitate us. The average French person vastly prefers the United States to the Soviet Union, and even among the foolish intellectuals, very few of them anymore believe, with the Sartre of the early 1950s, that the two superpowers are equal menaces. As the French have declined as a world power, as they have come to accept their mid-level status, it is difficult to see any widespread concern that the United States casts too long a shadow. Put most cynically, perhaps, whether the French are anti-American or not means less than it did in the days of Sartre and de Gaulle; and the French know it.

Most important for them, they know that the United States has come to France's rescue twice in this century, and they hope that it would do so again if the need ever arose. In other words, all things considered, the long and difficult period of adjustment to the postwar world in such diverse areas as culture and technology, foreign policy and language, has meant that what the French once thought the rest of the world would suffer in the absence of France, they would now suffer if the Americans were to disappear. Victor Hugo may have said that the world would be "alone" without the French; the plain fact is that now the French would be alone without us.

9

Jews, Arabs, and Other "Foreigners"

I n 1987, I got word from a friend about an obscure quarrel that seemed, wrongly as it turned out, to be a classic example of deep French anti-Semitism occurring at a particularly telling moment. France just then was preparing for the first major trial of a Nazi figure since immediately after the end of World War II. Klaus Barbie, the wartime chief of the Gestapo in the city of Lyon—known for decades as the "butcher of Lyon"—had been found living in exile in Bolivia and extradited to France in 1984. After long and difficult preparations, involving the task of locating witnesses to events that had taken place more than forty years earlier, Barbie stood formally accused of 371 counts of crimes against humanity, notably the deportation to Nazi death camps of many Jews, both French and foreign, and a smaller number of members of the French resistance.

A few weeks before the start of the trial, a friend of mine, an Eastern European Jewish survivor of the war, with more than a passing interest in the Barbie case, told me he had heard of something terrible, unspeakable, unforgivable, taking place in Izieu, a tiny but, at that particular moment, rather well-known village in the hills about fifty miles east of Lyon. Izieu was the site of one of the worst of the Nazis' crimes in France, the seizure of forty-four Jewish children and their several adult caretakers from a refuge where they were being hidden, their shipment to Drancy, the Gestapo's transit camp in France, and their final deportation to Auschwitz, where every one of the children and all but one of the adults were killed. And so Izieu had taken on high symbolic value for the looming Barbie trial. The children were emblems of the slaughter of the innocents, of the fact that some of the worst of the Nazi horrors had taken place in France and had not been reserved for the countries farther east.

What my friend told me was this: In recent months, the Jewish community of Lyon, understandably concerned about appropriately memorializing the forty-four children of Izieu, had noted that commemorative plaques both in Izieu itself and in the neighboring town of Bregnier-Cordon, where the Nazi truck carrying the children had stopped for fuel, did not indicate that the children were Jews. The Lyon committee asked that the word "Jew" be added to the plaques, in this way restoring to the children their religious identity and making the roundup at Izieu a symbol of the specifically anti-Jewish nature of Nazism. Both mayors refused the request. One of them, moreover, the mayor of Bregnier-Cordon, had objected at a ceremony honoring the children when Jewish speakers used the occasion to speak of the state of Israel. Beyond that, when the Jews of Lyon had expressed an interest in buying the house in Izieu where the children had stayed, the present owner had sharply increased the price, reportedly saying, "You Jews have money. You can pay more for it."

These various aspects of the situation, as they were reported to me secondhand in Paris, seemed to reflect good old French anti-Semitism, of the sort that one read about in histories of the Dreyfus case and the vicious far-rightist, pro-Fascist movements of much of French history up to and including the 1930s. When I called the president of the Lyon Jewish community, a doctor named Marc Aron, he seemed to confirm that some dark and evil residue of the old evil had reared its head on the eve of the trial of a major Nazi villain. "They know very well what happened, but they want to forget," Dr. Aron said. "They want to erase all memory of Judaism."

The issue was of immediate interest because of the imminency of the Barbie trial (Barbie would be found guilty by the court on all 371 counts and sentenced to life imprisonment). But it had a larger meaning as well, since one of the underlying questions that are always being raised about France is the extent to which the pleasant garden of postwar life continues to conceal the rusty nails of traditional French xenophobia, anti-foreign hatred, and racism.

This, after all, was the country of the Dreyfus case, in which an innocent officer in the army had been found guilty of treason, largely because treason had been committed by somebody and Dreyfus, as a

Jew, was the handiest "guilty" party. During much of the twentieth century, a period still well within the living memory of many people, the anti-Semitic press was not merely a marginal gutter affair; major writers—Céline, Brasillach, Maurras, all openly anti-Semitic—were among the most admired figures in the French literature of the time. The far-right press, which fed the powerfully Fascist sentiment in France that erupted from time to time in major street fighting, referred to the Socialist prime minister of the country as "Blum-Shylock," his policies as "Talmudic." France, they said, was endangered by *juiverie*, a word that could be translated as "Jewishness" but in a very pejorative sense—"Kikishness" might be a better rendition of the term—meaning the way of life of "this crappy race of usurers," as one magazine put it in 1936, this "rabbinical pontificate." That the Jews were a loathsome foreign element—never mind that thousands of Jewish families had lived in France since the fifteenth and sixteenth centuries and had been made full citizens by the revolution of 1789—was part of the common discourse. It was not regarded as a very extremist view.

And while the war and French complicity in the persecution of the Jews had erased the acceptability of this strain of French thinking and discourse, it was difficult to believe that traditional anti-Semitism had somehow, miraculously, disappeared. More to the point, there were clear indications even now that when other sorts of "foreigners" were concerned, Arabs in particular, but blacks and Asians as well, the racist sentiment did not take the trouble to conceal itself behind the veneer of post-Holocaust civility. During the 1980s, France had become the breeding ground for Europe's most powerful and electorally successful far-right political formation, the National Front party, led by a former paratrooper in the Algerian war named Jean-Marie Le Pen, whose entire program was based on the call for large-scale expulsions of Arab immigrants from France. "France for the French" was the inevitable slogan, but a slogan suggesting fairly obviously that "French" meant having a name like Le Pen rather than something Jewish or Arabic. There was a host of virulently anti-immigration magazines, warning that the ostensible waves of what were called "non-European foreigners" coming into the country threatened the French essence; that there were race wars coming up if the immigrant tide was not stemmed. One of these publications—its name printed in yellow across a black band at the top of the title page—was ominously called *J'ai Tout Compris*. In the 1930s, one of the major anti-Semitic rags was a tabloid named *Je Suis Partout* (I Am Everywhere). The similarity with *J'ai Tout Com-*

pris (I Have Understood Everything) did not seem to be an innocent accident.

But if I went to Izieu and Bregnier-Cordon expecting, though not hoping, to find an unpleasant echo of the past and a telling reminder of present anti-Semitism, my trip, happily, produced no such result. After I had talked to Dr. Aron and to inhabitants of the villages in question, including both mayors, it became clear that there had been a misunderstanding between the Jews of Lyon and the villages of Bregnier-Cordon and Izieu, where a uniquely Jewish tragedy had taken place forty-three years earlier. True, the villages had turned down requests made in the past couple of years by the Lyon community to put the word "Jew" on the plaques commemorating the tragedy. But the villagers had accorded a kind of custody over the plaques to Sabina Zlatin, an elderly Jewish woman living in Paris, who in the 1940s had set up the home in Izieu, miraculously escaping the Nazi roundup (in which her husband was taken to his death) by being away on an errand when the Gestapo arrived. Mme Zlatin, who seemed to be deeply respected by the mayors of the two towns, had not particularly thought to put the word "Jew" on the plaques, though when I called to ask her, she said she would do it after the Barbie trial was over. She expressed considerable affection for the people and the mayors of Izieu and Bregnier-Cordon but a certain impatience with the Jews of Lyon, who, she said, had done nothing to help her maintain the children's memorials during all those decades when the Izieu tragedy was barely known or remembered.

Serge Klarsfeld, the lawyer and Nazi-hunter whose work had located Barbie in his hiding place in Bolivia, told me that at the end of the war, when monuments like those to the children of Izieu were put up, French Jews, who had seen the Nazi and French collaborationist persecutions as at least in part a denial of their Frenchness, were anxious to assert that aspect of their identity—rather than the Jewish aspect. They wanted to be thought of and recognized as French. So the absence of the word "Jew" on the plaques had arisen from a Jewish desire. I remembered going in August 1984, shortly after I arrived as a correspondent in Paris, to the Great Synagogue on the rue des Victoires, where a memorial service was being held to commemorate the fortieth anniversary of the liberation of Paris. It was one of many events in Paris that day held to mark the great occasion. I talked to a man in the synagogue who gave his name only as Jacob. On that day of "indescribable happiness," he said, when General Leclerc's armored division had rolled into Paris in the wake of the evacuating Nazi forces, the first thing he did was tear off the yellow star of David he had been forced to wear during the occupation. He did it, he said, "not because I was ashamed of being Jewish but as an act of liberation." Jacob wanted to be Jewish, but as a Frenchman, he didn't want to have to be Jewish.

Izieu itself is a tiny place seemingly lost in time. It is a small, isolated conglomeration of tumbledown farms, pastures, orchards, masonry walls covered with honeysuckle and moss, reachable on a small, easy-to-miss, winding road that reaches up from the valley below. It has a small church, no café, restaurant, or hotel, a few hundred permanent inhabitants, and magnificent views of the Rhône Valley below and the snowy Alps beyond. The mayor of the town, Henri Perret, was a kindly, gray-haired retiree, who took me to the large, rectangular, stone-terraced house where the forty-four Jewish children had gotten their all too brief refuge, introducing me to the elderly widow who lived there (and who said that yes, she would like to sell the place, since her husband had recently died, but her son was handling the matter for her). The mayor seemed a bit bewildered by the Jewish community's accusations, saying that the whole matter was in the hands of the revered Mme Zlatin. He mentioned talking to a fellow inhabitant of Izieu, a woman of about forty who had four children of her own; she told him one day, after news of the upcoming Barbie trial had become a near-daily affair, that when she looked at her own children, she thought of "them," the forty-four who disappeared; and she understood, she said, the agony of their parents. That attitude, he said, reflected how the villagers felt about the children who had been taken away.

Down the hill, in the village of Bregnier-Cordon, closer to the main provincial road and a bit more commercially equipped, Mayor Robert Mériaudeau, younger than Perret, more politically committed, was angrier at the Jewish accusations and more argumentative than his fellow mayor up the hill in Izieu. Mériaudeau was in his forties, a Socialist party activist with an Abraham Lincoln beard, who acknowledged pro-Palestinian sympathies and seemed generally inclined to believe that the Third World needed liberation from Western imperialism. His argument was that the Jewish community of Lyon had itself only rediscovered the children of Izieu because of the arrest of Barbie and his return to France. He said that every year since the end of the war, on the anniversary of the roundup at Izieu, the town of Bregnier-Cordon has held a memorial ceremony; all the schoolchildren are present, the mayor is there, along with Bregnier-Cordon's organizations. "For forty years we have done our duty with regard to those children, and it pains me to have people coming now to reprimand us," Mériaudeau said. "For forty years we hardly ever saw a Jew at one of our memorial services."

WHILE the French, like the people of Izieu and Bregnier-Cordon, have frequently done their duty as the people who invented the Declaration of the Rights of Man—and who have long seen their country providing an asylum for the persecuted—race relations and ethnic conflicts remain central domestic problems that are unlikely to become less important in the years ahead. There have always been foreigners in France, and the French have always had ways of distrusting them, excluding them, making them uncomfortable, even as these same foreigners (some of them having been in France for generations) have eventually managed to become integrated into French life and to succeed. There are more foreigners than ever before in France today, and unlike many of their predecessor immigrants, they are not Poles, or Serbians, or Portuguese, or Jews; they are not, that is, whites and Europeans. They are, in a majority of cases, Arabs from the former French colonies of North Africa, Asians from the former French colonies of Indochina, and, to a lesser extent, blacks from the former French colonies of West Africa. If anti-Semitism was the major French prejudice of yesteryear, an intense discomfort with, a visceral dislike of Arabs is the widespread problem today. Clearly, some French—as, it is safe to say, some Swedes, some Danes, some Germans, some Italians, some Spaniards, some British, some Americans—hate Jews, in the way Jews have been hated by some for centuries, and they hate also blacks, Arabs, and Asians. If anything, perhaps some of the historic anti-Semitism of the French has been redirected toward these other groups, particularly the Arabs, who of course are also Semites. But the Jews, the Arabs, the blacks, and the Asians will continue to move both toward acceptance and toward equality of rights and opportunity. The race wars predicted by some of the rightist rags will not occur. The fragile, threatened tradition of toleration will prevail over a reinvigorated xenophobia.

But it will not be easy.

First, a look at the brighter side. For the Jews, it is virtually inarguable that despite whatever social barriers and misapprehensions may remain—and they certainly do remain—conditions have never been better, despite the remaining imperfections of the French in this regard. Jean-Marie Le Pen, the National Front leader, for example, never openly says that he dislikes Jews as a people—this, in any case, would be illegal in France, which has laws against such types of public statements—but without ever pronouncing the words, he makes this dislike clear, and it explains some of his popular support. At National Front rallies in Paris, always symbolically held in the shadow of the statue of Joan of Arc, the far right's appointed patron saint, people in the crowd call for the Jews to go back to Israel. In the 1988 election, they shouted, meaning no compliment, "Mitterrand the Jew," not that President Mitterrand is literally a Jew, but that, by definition, the hated thing is the Jew just as the Jew is the hated thing. The National Front's very slogan, "France for the French," has been traced back to 1889, when one Jacques de Biez founded the frankly named National Anti-Semitic League. Whenever Le Pen himself lists his enemies, excoriating them in front of his crowds, they very often just happen to be journalists and political figures known to be Jewish, their not classically French names rolling conspicuously off his silver tongue. My enemies, Le Pen is insinuating, are not really French, and that is why they are my enemies.

I myself do not know whether Le Pen, whom I have met, interviewed, and disliked, is in the classic anti-Semitic mold himself, whether he hates Jews or not—and I have been criticized in private conversation on this subject by some of my friends for what they see as my naive open-mindedness. I once asked Jean-Pierre Chevalier, one of Le Pen's lieutenants, what Le Pen's feelings about Jews were, and his reply was oddly nonsensical. "He's not anti-Semitic," Chevalier said, "but he doesn't feel that you have to like somebody just because he is Jewish, either"—as though Jews or others were demanding that. Certainly, Le Pen and the movement he has created are sly and clever, allowing those followers who want to hear an anti-Semitic message to hear it loudly and clearly, without anybody actually having to pronounce it aloud. And the message resembles the same one less discreetly purveyed in *Je Suis Partout* a half century ago, namely that the foreigner, the Jew or the Arab or the Asian, is a threat to the essence of France.

What is it like to be a Jew in France? After centuries of precarious existence; after being expelled something like four times from France, the first time by the Merovingian King Dagobert in the seventh century and the last early in the fourteenth century, when they were accused of complicity with lepers in polluting water sources; after weathering the vicious and widespread anti-Semitism of the century and more following the Revolution; after surviving the Nazi occupation of 1939 to 1944 and, lest we forget, the shameful collaborationism of the French, which resulted in the deportation, in most cases carried out by French police eager to please their German masters, of some 65,000 Jews, about 10 percent of them French citizens (2,800 of the total survived to return to France), to their deaths in the East*—after this long history of suffering and exclusion, it is no wonder that the Jews themselves, including the members of the Jewish community of Lyon, are inclined to suspect the non-Jewish French of harboring deeply anti-Semitic feelings. (In the case of the children of Izieu, after all, somebody, presumably living in the town or near it, had betrayed the existence of the children's home to the Gestapo.) It is not difficult in France to uncover the chauvinistic strains, the snob's concentration on genealogy and the vague concept of "heritage" that are among the bases of chauvinistic exclusion. I have been told by people who are in positions to know that to have a name like Levy or Blaustein is not an advantage in, say, making a career in the French Foreign Ministry, where there are plenty of people with names like d'Estaing, de Nanteuil, and de Jolibois.

And yet it is safe to say that today, despite certain remaining problems, the Jews of France—and there are 600,000 of them now, the largest community by far in Western Europe—are a free and generally prospering French minority. Their situation seems comparable to that of Jews in the United States, with the difference that in France, when a Jew becomes prominent, it is somewhat more noticeable given the stand-out quality of many Jewish last names—even if most Jews long ago dropped first names like Jacob and Abraham and took on other names—Jacques, Jean-Paul, Philippe, Pierre—which come from the standard lists of the names of the saints. France, at this writing, has a Jewish president of the Constitutional Court, Robert Badinter, whose father, a rabbi from Nice, was murdered at Auschwitz. President Mitterrand's special adviser—who once told me he saw himself in the tradition of famous Jewish advisers, like Abravonel of Portugal, to Christian kings—is Jacques Attali, an Algerian-born Jew. His brother, Bernard Attali, is the president of Air France. Jews are among the most widely read and successful writers and commentators, the likes of Bernard-Henri Lévy, André Glucksmann, Alain Finkielkraut, Annie Cohen-Solal, Elizabeth Badinter (maiden name: Blaustein-Blanchet), and others.

Beyond the conspicuously successful Jews is the simple fact that a rich Jewish life takes place in France today. It is my conviction, for example, that Paris has more kosher restaurants than New York, Chicago, and Los Angeles combined. Jewish quarters of Paris in the Marais, along the rue Montmartre in the Ninth Arrondissement, and in Belleville in the

---

* Robert O. Paxton, *Vichy France: Old Guard and New Order, 1940–1944* (New York: Columbia University Press, 1982), p. 183.

northwest of Paris, are thriving and crowded, with restaurants, kosher butchers, Hebrew schools, and synagogues of every Jewish clique and faction, from Moroccan to Hasidic. It is true that in recent years there have been several bloody terrorist attacks against Jewish targets, most notably a synagogue in the rue Copernic and Goldenberg's restaurant in the Marais. But these attacks were carried out, not by French groups, but by Arab terrorists. The French police and government have made a concerted and, so far, successful effort to provide security for such potential targets ever since.*

To a great extent, the relative ease of Jewish life, and the integration of many Jews, mark the hard-won victory of one side in an ancient French polarity that has for centuries posed the forces of xenophobia, the belief in the existence of a mystical national essence, against those of toleration, the belief in a cosmopolitan, pluralist world. It is one of the chief characteristics of French history for ideas, including seminal, revolutionary, enlightened notions that capture the imagination of millions of people, to lie for decades, even centuries, in the fallow ground of French resistance to change. France, after all, invented the idea of republican government a full century before a durable republic was established on French soil. One might say there was a lag of nearly two centuries between the idea of Jewish liberation, born in the revolution of 1789, and its real achievement in postwar French society. In the present case of Arabs, however, the contest between the two opposing strains in the French attitude toward outsiders faces a struggle equally difficult and, perhaps, more complicated than the one involving the Jews. The general situation of non-European immigrants in France is certainly hazardous today, containing within it the potential for major turmoil for all of French society—something that the "Jewish problem" never did.

Nonetheless, here, too, we can begin on the brighter side, with the fact that the atavistic worry among some that the French national essence is threatened by non-European immigrants has been matched by an extraordinary, spontaneous antiracist movement of youths, political figures, writers, and ordinary people, which demonstrates the accumulated

---

* There are unpleasant and unintended reminders from time to time of that atavistic reflex that refuses to accord French Jews the same Frenchness that belongs to others. Following the attack on the rue Copernic synagogue, in which two non-Jewish bystanders were killed, Raymond Barre, who has never shown the slightest indication of anti-Semitic sentiments, referred to "this odious attack, aimed at Jews who were going to the synagogue, and that struck at innocent French people who were crossing the rue Copernic."

strength of the strain of openness and toleration. An example of the political power of antiracism in France came in 1987, when the Conservative government of Prime Minister Chirac (since chased from office by the electorate) attempted to implement a plan for some reforms of university education. The plan (which, in my view, was a good one, or at least not nearly as bad as many assumed it was) was bitterly opposed by students. There were huge peaceful demonstrations against it, putting the government into a difficult position. But while the students were peaceful, there were also troublemakers on the scene, generally helmeted young motorcyclists—not students—who tried to provoke the police, taking advantage of the general disorder. On one memorable Saturday night in December, the Latin Quarter, that traditional battleground where idealistic radicals clash with the forces of order, was turned into a battleground again, as demonstrators overturned cars, smashed shop windows, set up barricades, and rushed at riot police, injuring nearly sixty of them (about ten demonstrators were hurt).

The educational reform thus turned into a disaster for the government, which, in a humiliating gesture, was eventually forced to withdraw the plan and to accept the resignation of the deputy minister of education who had formulated it. But what provided the coup de grace to the government's effort was the fact that, on that violent Saturday night, the police, apparently trying to get in their licks, attacked some demonstrators in the inner courtyard of a building and killed a twenty-two-year-old student named Malik Oussékine, an Arab immigrant.

By coincidence, the Conservatives had only shortly before the student demonstrations drawn considerable attention to themselves by proposing a new nationalities law that would have made it more difficult for foreigners to become French citizens, a move that was already viewed by many students as a cowardly concession to the racist, anti-immigrant demands of the far right. Similarly, the government was pressing to make it easier to expel what it saw as undesirable foreigners, another move widely seen by its opponents, including most of the students, as yielding to ultrarightist blackmail. With that as the background, the death of the Arab student promised to enlarge an already immense protest movement that had seen some of the largest demonstrations held in Paris since the end of World War II. The government withdrew its reform plan, admitting utter and complete defeat. Two days later, on December 10, 200,000 people marched in a demonstration of "mourning" for young Malik Oussékine, who had emerged, rightly or not, as a martyr, certainly as an innocent victim of both police brutality and racism. All over Paris, and in many provincial university towns, drawings of a prone body were chalked on the street, with the legend *Plus Jamais Ça*—Never This Again—written across them. My feeling at the time was that if young Malik had not been Arab, he would not have generated such emotion as a symbol of all that was wrong with the government's policy, which, with his death, seemed not only mistaken educationally but morally and politically compromised.

There was another slogan that caught on in the mid-1980s: *Touche pas à mon pôte*, which means "Hands off my buddy." Worn as a slogan on a lapel button or a badge made out of stiff paper, it consisted of a yellow hand, palm facing outward in a gesture of resistance. The badge was the insignia of a group called S.O.S.-Racism, formed by a coalition of Jewish, Arab, and black activists to counter the influence of the far-right anti-immigrant movement. There were numerous demonstrations, concerts, radio and television discussions, and other events reflecting the worry that the National Front's "France for the French" slogan, and the party's capture in a very short time of some 10 percent of the vote, were a grave threat to the French enlightened tradition.

I remember one drizzly Sunday in the spring of 1985 when thousands of people moved through the narrow streets of the Marais, after a bomb explosion at a Jewish movie festival had injured eighteen people. There were a few actors and actresses, several political figures, the Grand Rabbi of France, and members of various other civil rights organizations, many of them wearing the S.O.S.-Racism badge. The particular incident that brought out the crowd on that raw, rainy morning was the bombing, but on everybody's mind were other incidents that had got intense newspaper coverage in preceding weeks. In one, an Arab youth had been thrown out of a moving train. In another, an immigrant from North Africa had been shot by a man who, explaining his motive to the police, said simply that he did not like Arabs. Near Marseille, an Arab youth had been shot to death by a Frenchman and a Spaniard after an altercation in a bar.

With incidents like those suddenly getting front-page treatment, a new sort of vocabulary appeared on the scene. The word "racism" became common. So did "banalization of violence." Both expressed the fear that racial conflict was only at a beginning stage, that it would spread. High schools began holding days of "sensitization." S.O.S.-Racism, *Libération* said, "has undertaken the most pressing task: the banalization of antiracism." The article went on: "The worst thing that could happen would be for antiracism to emerge as an individual opinion and not as the mainstream consensus that is taken for granted in a democracy." There is no question that the antiracist movement helped to quell the racist violence that threatened France at that moment and has helped to stifle it ever since, signaling to the bigots that the country as a whole would not rest silent and indifferent in the face of barbarism. The reaction to the National Front showed some of the same idealistic spirit that characterized the United States during the civil rights movement of the 1960s. It led to the conclusion that if the French were guilty of silence and complicity in the 1930s and 1940s, when the Jews were the targets of xenophobic hatred, they are guilty of it no longer. This time, enough French refused to wait or to condone until racism had, as they said, become banalized, part of the scene. It was itself turned into a pariah, chased out of public places, so that while, yes, some of the French are full of hate, a large number of them, a critical mass, hate the haters.

FOR THE other side of the coin, you could go to a place like Toulon, a tough seaport city on the Mediterranean, a grimy, skulking place of sailors' bars and harborside cafés where the whores are out by the late afternoon and you wouldn't want to be found walking alone late at night. If, farther east along the Mediterranean coast, there are gleaming capitals of chic and fashion, places like Cannes, Antibes, Saint-Tropez, Saint-Jean-Cap-Ferrat, Toulon is in the depressed, high-unemployment belt that mingles with some of the Riviera glitter. Behind the port is a part of town known, with none of the flattery of emulation intended, as "Chicago," a grid of extremely narrow streets lined by weather-stained old buildings, darkened courtyards, and small groceries, restaurants, and cafés. The music of North Africa pours out of windows. Swarthy men gather in clusters around rickety tables on the sidewalk. There is an aroma of Levantine spices and an atmosphere of the *souk*, such that one of the common conversational observations among the French, both those who are disturbed by such sights and those who take them with equanimity, is that places like Chicago are replicas of Algiers or Oran (almost everybody, of course, forgets that for the better part of a century the French built up places much like Toulon or Paris in the very heart of Algiers and of Oran). Toulon, moreover, is not the only city in France where such a neighborhood exists. They are throughout France, in the Belleville district of Paris and in the city's scabrous suburbs, in Lille and Tours, Marseille and Sète, and all along the thickly populated districts of the Mediterranean coast. Chicago, despite its name, is the

Arab quarter of Toulon, and, as such, it is commonly the center of attention for the strong far-right political organization that exists in the city.

In September 1986, a group of ultraright fanatics blew themselves up in an Alfa Romeo sedan in the Chicago district. The police said that the men in the car were members of an organization that called itself S.O.S.-France. Their effort to preserve the motherland from the likes of S.O.S.-Racism had led them to set off a series of six bomb explosions in the Arab part of town, apparently part of an effort to accomplish what the French government had refused to do—scare the North Africans out.

There is no question that the terror campaign led by S.O.S.-France was highly exceptional in recent French history, which, despite the existence of plenty of verbal violence against Arabs, has seen only isolated, sporadic, and quickly condemned episodes of physical violence. But Toulon well reflected the way some of the French hate the foreigners in their midst, and why.

First of all, the place has a particularly explosive mix of populations. There are large numbers of Arab immigrants, just as there are throughout the southern French zone stretching from Nice in the east to Montpellier to the west, with Marseille, the fabulously seedy old port, occupying both a geographically and a demographically central point. There are also the so-called *pieds noirs*, the French former settlers of Algeria, who were, against their bitter and sometimes violent opposition, forced to return to *La Métropole* after Algerian independence in 1962. The *pieds noirs*, vast numbers of whom have long since reacclimated themselves to the home country and cannot be distinguished from other Frenchmen by their views on Arabs, provided a core of anti-Arab sentiment in a town of high unemployment and economic dilapidation where both groups had settled. The National Front had gotten something like 20 percent of the vote in recent elections in Toulon. What's more, the town had formed several rightist splinter groups—the Opposition National Front, the New Forces Party, and the Federation for the Unity of Refugees and Repatriated People—which, somehow, tended to view the National Front as too moderate for their taste.

The four men who died accidentally in the Alfa Romeo bomb blast were, according to documents found on them by the police, members of several organizations. One was a secret group called the Commandos of France, intended, apparently, to serve as a military wing of an anti-Arab movement that would, its members hoped, mix a bit of terrorism with open political activities. They also belonged to the entirely open and aboveboard House of Parachutists, a sports and recreation club with headquarters in the center of town, whose members were mostly veterans of France's colonial wars, including the ones in Indochina and Algeria. The clubhouse of this last organization was full of military insignia, war-era posters, banners and flags, and photographs of various military units, and groups of visitors—American visitors, British visitors—belonging to veterans' groups in their countries. The Parachutists' president, the newspapers had reported, was planning to hold a funeral for the four dead "commandos," giving them full "military honors." No matter what the four had done, a club member said, "they were friends, and we are going to remain faithful to them." The Parachutists' vice president, a man named Paul Lopez, summed up the group's carefully formulated political philosophy this way: "If things continue the way they are going now, we're all going to be Arab in five years." When the funeral for the four was finally held, the eulogy was given by a member of S.O.S.-France named Jean-Claude Pelou (a member of the Toulon police, who was fired by the Paris minister of the interior as soon as his sympathies for S.O.S.-France and the Commandos of France were discovered). Pelou addressed the four sarcophagi lying in state in a church in La Seyne-sur-Mer, an industrial dockyard perennially threatened with large-scale closures: "What you thought was your duty, you carried out to the end," he said. "Your fight was ours, and we will continue it."

The fact is that the Toulon branch of S.O.S.-France, the only branch of that organization to come to light, did not continue the fight, at least not in the way the four deceased members were carrying it out, with bombs placed in Arab cafés. It seems to have been a very tiny organization, possibly made up of not much more than the four men killed in the Alfa Romeo. Nonetheless, the sources of their anti-Arab animosity are clear, as are the reasons for France's furtherance of renascent semi-Fascism in the form of the National Front party. It is a rare combination of demographic mingling, economic insecurity, and nostalgia, with nostalgia's role not to be played down. Those men at the Parachutists' Club, with their old badges and insignia, and their firm conviction that they represented what was left of the moral backbone of France, were guided to a great extent by a yearning to recapture a time that, perhaps, never existed—when France was great and prosperous and uncorrupted by foreign blood and the cowardly betrayal of national leaders.

The situation in Toulon was echoed throughout the south of France, where Le Pen's National Front was, in the mid-1980s, getting as much as one third of the popular votes cast in various elections. Even in

pleasant, relatively prosperous places like Grasse, in the hills just behind
the Mediterranean coast—not only the perfume capital of the world but
also a center for vacation houses and tourists—the National Front got
one third of the vote, forcing the classic rightist parties to share power
with it on the municipal council. There, too, the presence of numerous
Arab workers among a population of many *pieds noirs*, and against the
background of a disappearing way of life, was the instigating phenomenon. Grasse had a high unemployment rate. Its perfumeries still pros-
pered, but they no longer used as essences the jasmine and the lavender,
the narcissus and vervain, that once grew there, much of the terrain for
such products having been given over to a certain semiurban sprawl.
And so, in elegant Grasse, too, there was nostalgia and insecurity. Nothing like Toulon in architecture or atmosphere—the center of Grasse,
built on a long hill that rises up from the Mediterannean, is a place of
antique beauty—the perfume capital of the world nonetheless gave off
a similar political odor.

You didn't, moreover, have to go to places like Grasse or Toulon to
sense the widespread French unease. You only had to read the pages of
the national newspapers and magazines. In October 1985, the treatment
of the issue reached a sensationalist low point when *Figaro* magazine,
a supposedly respectable if somewhat middlebrow weekly, published a
cover story with the alarmist headline: WILL WE STILL BE FRENCH IN 30
YEARS? The magazine failed to define exactly what "French" meant, but
the implication was clear. It was not enough to have been born in France
of immigrant parents to be French; Frenchness was considered something
that lay in deeper roots, in names like Raspail or Dumont—who were
listed as the authors of the article—rather than in names like Hassan
or Rosenzweig, Nguyen or Chang. "To govern is to foresee," a preface
to the much-discussed article said. "We don't have the impression that
the magnitude of the disaster is clearly measured in France." Given the
higher birth rate of what the magazine called E.N.E.s, meaning non-
European foreigners, and an expected immigration rate of 59,000 per
year, the E.N.E.s would rise from 5 to 17 percent of the total French
population, and, presumably, the tendency would continue, leading—
to borrow the word of the article—to the inevitable "disaster" of a non-
French France, a France suddenly nonwhite, speaking Arabic, largely
Islamic, eating *couscous* and *tajine* rather than *boeuf bourguignon* and
blanquette de veau.

Is the concern itself a sign that the French hate foreigners? Probably
not in the old-fashioned, racist sense of yesteryear. The French, like

other people, have learned something over the centuries about the moral and practical unacceptability of turning whole classes of people into pariahs. That is what makes the issue so difficult to analyze. One of the frequent boasts of Le Pen, for example, is that he dares to say out loud what ordinary people think but don't dare express (though he ignores a deeper meaning here, namely that their not daring to say certain things is itself a sign of progress). When he claims, "I love Arabs, but I love them in Algeria," there are probably many who identify with the sentiment, believing in their hearts that separate cultures, ways of life, religions, and habits do exist and that their continued existence is threatened if there is too much mixing. And yet racism and open hatred always emerge from such "reasonable opinions." The disservice, the sensationalism, of the *Figaro* article came in its headline, in the suggestion that, somehow, the issue to be grappled with was not simple non-European immigration. The issue was posed as though the very survival of the French nation were at stake. The magazine's editors knew perfectly well it was not. When Louis-Ferdinand Céline—a great writer but not a great human being—claimed in 1936 that "against the Jews, I would well make an alliance with Hitler," some of those who found commonsense wisdom in the remark believed no doubt they had nothing against Jews—outside France. Did they learn the lesson when 65,000 Jews were dragged from their homes by French police willingly doing the work of the Gestapo, and sent away to die at places with names like Auschwitz?

For a couple of days once I spent time talking with customers in some of the old bars of Marseille, places with names like L'Océan, La Gaité, Le Merango, a little reminiscent, with their yellow wallpaper, scarred tiled floors, and brown wood counters, of César's portside café in the famous trilogy by Marcel Pagnol, *Marius, Fanny,* and *César.* The habitués wore leather jackets and thick mustaches and drank glass after glass of sweetish *pastis.* They proclaimed their support for the National Front, but they denied, without being asked—they rather anticipated the suspicion—that they had racist sympathies. It's not racist, they argued, to fear losing your job to a foreigner. It's not racist to be unable to feel at home in your native city because so many people representing a different culture, a different way of life, had settled there. It wasn't racist, they said, to want to control immigration. Every country did it. The United States did it, they pointed out. Why was it racist if somebody in France wanted to do the same thing? They invited me to go to La Canebière, once the commercial center of Marseille. The broad avenue, running from the daily (and still existing) fish market on the quai toward

the interior hills, was once lined with grand hotels and apartment buildings. You'll find that it has become a casbah, a souk, the habitués of
the harborside cafés said. The place smells of *merguez*, they said, referring to a spicy lamb sausage that is a standard part of Arab cuisine. Half
the women are wearing veils. Islamic fundamentalism is taking root in
Marseille. Khomeini already had his agents infiltrated in the city, where
they were ready to support anti-European terrorism. You can't go to
La Canebière at night anymore, they said. It has become too dangerous.
The habitués of the bars were often former supporters of France's declining Communist party who had, because of their worries over
immigration—which the Communist party, for ideological reasons, had
little choice but to denounce as racist—switched to the National Front,
the Communists' supposed opposite on the political spectrum.

Is the issue one of racism? I myself, without underestimating the
dangers involved in the situation, think that it is not. Indeed, a current
of opinion in France that had considerable underground support was
that the mainstream, classical political parties in France, but particularly
the Socialists and even such groups as S.O.S.-Racism, had played into
the hands of the National Front by denouncing virtually any concern
about the North African presence as racist by definition. Once an issue
has been put beyond the bounds of moral acceptability, once an opinion
or a fear has been branded an ethical evil, it can no longer be debated
or discussed as a matter over which reasonable men and women can
disagree. Branding antiforeign opinion as "racist" had pushed the men
at the Marseille cafés into a defensive and angry posture, one whose
only political outlet was the National Front, which certainly did not
represent the enlightened, tolerant traditions of France. Those in the bar
did not have the same opportunity for moral purity as the intellectuals
in Paris who, from relatively secure and comfortable offices, determined
the tone of the national debate. I remember a magazine editor telling
me once that it was relatively easy to be tolerant and to live in Paris's
ever chic and fashionable Sixth Arrondissement, a block or two from
the Luxembourg Gardens, where the only Arabs you see are the ones
who pass through two or three times a week, collecting the garbage or
sweeping the streets. Go to the Stalingrad métro station and see what
percentage of the passengers there is white and European, he said. It
might be a greater test of toleration to try to live in a subsidized housing
block on the outskirts of Paris, where your neighbors, with seven children
each, were all from Algeria, played Arabic music all day on the radio
rather than Edith Piaf or Yves Montand, and in the evening filled the

air with the scent of the *merguez* cooking. You might, he told me, believe in the slogan "France for the French" without being a racist.

The issue for France, it seems to me, is not so much one of traditional racism as it is of facing up to a new situation. The plain fact is that no major country open to the rest of the world, not even France, can expect anymore to remain ethnically homogeneous. One hundred years ago, the French had gone, uninvited, into the native places of Arabs, Africans, and Indochinese, expecting that the inhabitants of those places, all of them with their own rich and ancient cultures, would somehow become French-like without actually invading *La Métropole*. The visit is now being returned, and the only choice is for everybody to learn to live together, to accept pluralism as the richness it is rather than to perceive it as a threat, perhaps to recognize also that if people could become French-like in Abidjan, Oran, and Hanoi, they are far more likely to become not only French-like but actually French if they are welcomed civilly in places like Toulon, Grasse, Marseille, and Paris.

Meanwhile, as the difficult adjustment goes on, the National Front seems, despite prodigious efforts by its charismatic leader, Le Pen, to have peaked at about 10 percent of the vote, a 10 percent that probably always has been, and always will be, in the electorate. In 1988, the French reelected Mitterrand, who, when the tide of anti-immigrant feeling reached a high point, had declared without ambiguity that "foreigners whose papers are in order are at home in France." Mitterrand's unambiguous declaration came as the classic rightist parties were fumbling for a way to draw off support from the National Front, not wanting to dismiss the general unease about immigration, not wanting, either, to risk the racist label by being too outspoken on the issue. Some pundits also saw in Mitterrand's statement less a ringing affirmation than a sly political parry, one designed to split the right, inducing some to get angry enough to vote for the marginal National Front rather than the more sizable, and politically threatening, classic rightist parties, Mitterrand's real foes in the battle to gain a majority in the National Assembly. Still, the president of France said it loud and clear and in plain French, needing only one declarative sentence: "*Les étrangers en situation regulière sont chez eux en France.*" Later, the right gained a majority in parliament as expected, and the National Front got a block of more than thirty seats (which they subsequently lost in the 1988 elections, because of a change in the voting system). But Mitterrand, who had been unpopular, began an extraordinary political resurrection that led to his being reelected as president in 1988 for a second seven-year term.

The entire episode certainly indicated that there was no political fatality, and, it seemed, even a benefit, in speaking out in defense of what *Figaro* magazine chose in its wisdom to refer to as an undifferentiated category, the E.N.E.s. There was no apparent immediate danger that xenophobia was going to sweep the country and gain power.

No, I used to reply to the questions of well-meaning friends back home, France is not going to become Fascist. But the battle is far from over.

POSTSCRIPT: On the métro line crossing town between Belleville and Porte Dauphine, passing through a kind of demographer's cross-section of Paris from modest mixed Arab and black neighborhoods, past the tawdry zone of sex clubs and porno theaters at Pigalle, and on to the quiet elegance of the Parc Monceau and then the imperious wealth of the avenue Foch. A man gets on the car at Stalingrad, and he is muttering something about "Arabs and Negroes." He has skin a chocolate-brown color, is rather short and round, about fifty years old, wearing a soft plaid short-brimmed hat and a well-worn raincoat, and he is saying, "Why don't they like the Negro? I ask you, why don't they like the Negro, these people from North Africa? So somebody is from North Africa. I'm from the Cameroons, and some are from the Antilles. I'm a Negro; why don't they like the color of this skin?"

"Why don't you just shut your trap," a younger man, also black, but a darker black, says. "You got a problem about the Antilles, just shut your trap. I'm from the Antilles. Don't talk about me."

The second man spoke French with one kind of accent; the first spoke with another, using the term *nègre*, meaning the English "Negro" or, when used pejoratively or derisively in French, "nigger." In French, the term *petit nègre*, "little nigger," means "bad French"; *nègre* is "ghost-writer." I can't reproduce the conversation, or rather the argument, that ensued, but in essence, the man from the Antilles was telling the man from the Cameroons that he ought not to complain, that everybody had problems, that his complaints were embarrassing to other "Negroes," that if he didn't like it here in France, he should go back where he came from. And the man from the Cameroons was saying, "Never have I seen anything like it in France," apparently referring to his earlier exchange with a North African. "The Arabs, the Arabs, why they don't like the Negro?" he said. "They are Moslems. I'm not a Moslem. Me, I'm a Christian. Yes, a Christian can have skin like this, ladies and gentlemen. This is France. I never saw anything like it."

The car was crowded, and most of the people on it were black or brown or, at least, swarthy, except for a small group of Dutch tourists, looking at their subway maps, and a scattering of what, for lack of a legally more precise term, I will call French people, white French people. There were Semitic men with heavy shadows of beards and white skull-caps; black men with colored skullcaps; other black men, with that uncommingled blackness that usually comes only from Africa, wearing ski parkas and jeans. One of them was reading a book, in French, entitled, *The Fall of Allende*.

The man from the Antilles got off the train at Pigalle, exchanging a few last words with the man from the Cameroons, who stayed in the car, speaking of the color of his skin, quietly, unaggressively, reaching out with his arm and pulling his coat back from his wrist so the color could easily be viewed, telling each person in turn, "This is France. I've never seen anything like it."

Everybody—the Arabs, the other Africans, the white people—looked on, turning away, slightly embarrassed, when the man spoke to them in a tone that had slowly changed from anger to resignation. In France, you don't talk to people whom you don't know. The man uttered his monologue to a silent audience. There was no applause. No call for an encore. The train stopped, the people of color filtered away; the people who got on were mostly white, reflecting the racial demography of the city above us. Finally, the Cameroonian got out of the train at the station called Rome, a kind of border stop between the modest zones of working-class French and immigrants of color and the wealthier areas of the *haute bourgeoisie*, where few Cameroonians venture. The man stood on the platform and turned back toward the people in the car, saying in his African accent: "I'm really German. Really. You don't believe me? I never saw anything like it."

10

In Praise of Frivolity

THE BRITISH and, to a somewhat lesser extent perhaps, the Americans used to think that the French were frivolous, naughty, immoral, given to erotic and culinary excess, even though that didn't stop these same British and Americans from coming to Paris or from drinking the fine clarets, Armagnacs, and cognacs, from admiring the women or even from helping to rescue the immoral French from their own military incompetence twice in this century. "Furious in luxury, merciless in toil," Rudyard Kipling said of them (he admired the characteristics). Oliver Wendell Holmes, in *The Autocrat of the Breakfast-Table*, remarked that "Good Americans, when they die, go to Paris"—such, he meant, are the luxuries of life there.

The French, though Catholic in the majority, go to the beach rather more than they go to church, to wine bars more than to confession. There are many other signs of their preference for secular over spiritual pleasures, or, perhaps, a confusion of the two. They have—to focus at random on one aspect of their lives—more dogs and other domesticated animals per capita than any other people in the world, which, I suppose, can be seen as a measure of a collective sort of frivolity. What's more, they bring these dogs to restaurants. They dote on them. For several weeks, I lived on the boulevard de Courcelles, where, next door to my building, was a fur-trimming establishment named Crazy Dog (the name was in English). Every day, streams of poodles and Afghan hounds, Irish sheep dogs and other long-haired creatures, stood on tables, held in place by hanging straps, while women in leather pants and silk blouses looked anxiously on. Such scenes take place in other countries as well; and yet there is something about the sleek, well-dressed society matron waiting for her dog to have his hair cut in the window of an elegant shop before she takes him with her on a leash to the Brasserie Lorraine for lunch that seems, perhaps unfairly, a sort of frivolity, a banalized, normative hedonism indulged in by the French.

One aspect of French hedonism widely imitated, certainly forgiven, is devotion to the arts of the kitchen and of the table. Here, it is the Mediterranean part of the French nature that prevails. The French took the cuisine of Italy—a gift of the cooks of Catherine de Médicis, who came from Florence to Paris in the middle of the sixteenth century to marry King Henry II—and subjected it to a kind of northern rigor. This does not mean that the French always eat well. They can eat abominably. I have witnessed meals of greasy sausage, smelly cheese, stale bread, and cheap wine, all consumed without benefit of anything green, leafy, fresh, or, for that matter, prepared outside a factory. Some of the most famous French delicacies are overrated. The bread is one such item. One baker, a certain Poilâne in Paris, bakes a sourdough loaf that would, in any fair contest, have to be deemed among the great breads of the world. It is fragrant and chewy, refined and substantial. Of Poilâne I am a great admirer, but I am a dissident regarding most others. I have always found the standard *baguette* or *pain de campagne*—pleasantly crusty when freshly baked, and smelling marvelous when arrayed on the nice wooden shelves of the neighborhood *boulangerie*—to lack taste, to be insipid and cottony in texture. The tableau of the French lined up in a café at noon and eating what they call sandwiches—meaning a bit of ham or Gruyère cheese in between two long slices of dry *baguette* that flakes off like scaly razor blades in the mouth—does not provide a vision of a people addicted to good food. French sandwiches are not only without moisture or taste; they are without soul or nutritional value.

You can eat badly in France, very badly. There are entire districts of restaurants advertising cheap *formules*—fixed prices—for a fixed menu, listed on artists' easels outside their doors. Many of them, not all, represent the triumph of sheer style over content. A typical such meal would begin with a plate of shriveled tomatoes with some oil and vinegar, perhaps a *terrine de poisson*—meaning a bland, cold cylinder of puréed fish held in place by some flour and egg; you move on to a small piece of nearly unchewable beef with some fried potatoes or, perhaps, a piece of overcooked chicken breast in a gluey sauce; and you finish with a small scoop of ice cream or sorbet or a wedge of *tarte* consisting of a wafer-thin layer of soggy apple and a crust so brittle that you have to turn your fork into a hatchet to chop it into bite-sized morsels. This is all washed down with some thin and sour house wine and then harsh, acid coffee. I have thought in my surly moments of writing a guide to the inedible in France as a service to unwary tourists.

But the French, of course, are very good when they are good in the preparation of things to eat. And, moreover, they have surrounded food with so much commentary, learning, and connoisseurship as to clothe it in the vestments of civilization itself. A psychologist might see in the French cultivation of the oral and olfactory aspects of their lives some deep meaning. I, frankly, do not know what that meaning is, even as I recognize that, if excessive attention to the pleasures of the senses is an indication of frivolity, the French are certainly among the world's most frivolous people. It should be added here, however, that their reputation for this is due in some part at least to the seriousness with which the non-French examine French culinary products. The British and the Americans arguably make more of a fuss over Bordeaux and Burgundy than the French themselves do. I have met many a French person who did not know the difference between a Graves and a Pauillac, while I have rarely met an Englishman or American living in France who was similarly ignorant. In fact, I suspect that the French themselves are more devoted to and knowledgeable about cheese and its varieties than they are about their own wines or liqueurs. The average French family drinks wine with its meals, to be sure, but the wine is bought at the local shop, where the cheaper, more common brands are in far better stock than the higher-priced château-bottled wine. But when they buy cheese, they are more fussy (good cheese, of course, being a far less expensive indulgence than good wine).

But at the same time, the culinary part of life is very important. Rating restaurants is a national preoccupation. There are numerous efforts to do so, the Michelin star system—one star means very good, two stars indicate quality worthy of a detour, and three designate an establishment that justifies an entire trip—being only the best known. The great chefs have the kind of status and prestige that only concert pianists, prize-winning novelists, or movie stars have in other countries. There is a whole area of knowledge in France that consists of restaurant gossip— knowledge of such subjects as who owns which establishment, who stole whose chef, who was a disciple of whom. Cooking is viewed as a major art form; innovations are celebrated and talked about as though they were phases in the development of a style of painting or poetry. Customers spend a great deal of money to enjoy the best. A place like Robuchon in Paris, one of Michelin's three-star establishments, costs upwards of two hundred dollars a person, but it can take months to get a reservation—though here again it must be noted that a large number of the tables will be occupied by foreigners.

The French are not fat. Their devotion to food does not involve gluttony, only considerable expense. They eat discreet amounts. They do not load up on chocolate bars, potato chips, or frozen yogurt between meals. But they do love to eat. Almost every region has its remarkable delicacies, whether cheese or truffles, foie gras, mushrooms, preserved ducks, spices, or the great varieties of wines. A meal at a truly great restaurant is a sort of theater you can eat. The decor and the service are impeccable and the menu so finely crafted that it does represent a considerable accumulated skill and wisdom. The served plate itself is a kind of flower arrangement, an interior decorator's invention. A mere description of the dishes does not do justice to the artistry of the arrangement of edibles on a porcelain plate.

There is no typical great menu; but if you went to G. G. Boyer in Rheims or Taillevent in Paris or Espérance in Vézelay, you might have something like the following. Hors d'oeuvre: sauteed fat duck's liver with grapes or a pastry crust with gray shrimp or perhaps very thin slices of warm sweetbreads in a salad or a lobster-and-crayfish soup. Fish: langoustines with fresh morels, filets of sole with oysters and asparagus tips, scallops forming a ring around a "crown" of celery, roasted potatoes, and watercress and surrounded in turn by a *ruban rouge*, a red ribbon of tomatoes and endive. Meat or fowl: sweetbreads in a truffle crust with two or three vegetable purées, a roasted pigeon with parsley and sweet garlic, thin slices of chicken breast with truffles, rabbit thighs with whole plums, veal stew with corn blinis and foie gras. Then: salad and a selection of cheeses from cow's milk and goat's milk, hard cheeses and soft cheeses, cheeses with crusts and cheeses without, aromatic cheeses, cheeses doused in spices or marinated in olive oil, blue cheeses and yellow cheeses, creamy cheeses and dry cheeses, cheeses that seem to have absorbed into themselves the very breath of the earth. Dessert: caramelized Gascony peaches flambéed in cognac, little apple tarts with apple sorbet and peach sauce, a simple, elegant *tarte* of wild strawberries or a *clafoutis* with apricots and honey. You will have wine with this meal, a white burgundy with the fish, perhaps a Bâtard-Montrachet, or maybe just a nice cool Vouvray from the Loire Valley; and with the meat or fowl, an Haut-Batailley, a not enormously expensive Bordeaux, or maybe a Volnay from the Domaine de la Pousse d'Or, which will cost you a bundle. Is this necessary? No. Is it frivolous? Yes. Is it an illusion of happiness, a kidnapping of the mind, a diversion from the harsh material and spiritual realities of life? Is it art and, as the French might say, the art of living? I suppose it is a little of both.

O F   C O U R S E , when the British complained about French self-indulgence and immorality, they were referring not to *haute cuisine* and not even to the urban ratio of dogs to human beings but to other matters, such as naughtiness in sex; and here, it must be admitted, the French have little of what they like to call Anglo-Saxon puritanism, no laws against any sort of consensual, adult sexual behavior. (It was not by accident that Oscar Wilde, persecuted in Britain, went to Paris after his imprisonment in the Lord Douglas case, dying there in 1900.) I remember the French reaction to a 1987 Supreme Court decision in the United States, which upheld the arrest of two homosexuals for performing an act of sodomy in a private bedroom. The French were scandalized, not by the sodomy but by the Supreme Court decision, which, it seemed to them, constituted a violation of basic human rights (an opinion shared by many in the United States, the difference being that no such case would ever have reached the French courts in the first place).

Whenever the Americans engender some political and sexual scandal, the French scratch their heads with bemusement and puzzlement. Indeed, it is one of the characteristics of French political behavior that the private lives of politicians are never publicly examined. Many is the figure in France whose mistresses and marital infidelities make up the informed gossip of dinners in town, where other men, women, mistresses, and lovers being talked about at some other dinner have been invited. As a correspondent in Paris, I invited members of the beau monde from time to time, and not being Parisian, and not knowing all the ins and outs of social life, I sometimes did not know, when inviting a guest, whether I should ask him to bring his wife or his mistress. These are things that the French talk about with wicked good humor. But if they talk and behave with naughtiness, they do not publicize. No political career in recent years ever suffered because of the sexual indiscretions of an elected or appointed official, no matter how well known these might be to the cognoscenti. Ministers of state have scarcely concealed affairs; they show up at public functions with their wives, with whom they do not live, and then, at the end of the evening, they return to the apartments of their mistresses, by whom, sometimes, they have illegitimate children. Nobody says anything; at least, not in public. The plain fact is that a mistress is accepted as one of the emblems of success for a man—often, but not necessarily, a far younger mistress—and while this may be true in other countries also, the French glorify the fact, revel in it, turn the subject of the mistress into a scholarly pursuit. Great writers are assumed to have them, sometimes in addition to, sometimes instead of, wives, and their identities are established facts for literary scholars. Flaubert's oddly occasional and literarily passionate liaison with Louise Colet is an example known to all serious admirers of the author of *Madame Bovary* (who herself had lovers and suffered grievously because of them).

Probably more ink has been spilled, more words uttered, over the women of Jean-Paul Sartre than over the books of Jean-Paul Sartre. It became a minor literary event in France when one of his mistresses—he is known to have had about four or five of them—named Liliane Siegel, wrote an account of her relationship with the philosopher called *La Clandestine* (The Clandestine One). Mme Siegel appeared on the celebrated literary talk show "*Apostrophes*" to discuss her work and to defend the blessed memory—as well as the other mistresses—of her lover. Another of the guests mentioned having met Sartre in New York with Dolores Ehrenreich, another of Sartre's mistresses—and a married one at that—moving yet a third guest, an Italian writer, to comment sourly: "Did she write a book about her love affair with Sartre?" Mme Siegel's reply was to express the wish that all of the great man's mistresses had written accounts of their lives with him, since, after all, while Sartre was the same with them all, he was also different, so such books would enhance the public's understanding of the philosopher. I thought: What a marvelous idea for the realization of womanhood! Men have mistresses and the mistresses write about their men. There was indeed a small vogue of this sort of thing. The mistress of Albert Cohen, author of *Solal* and *Belle de Jour* (both of them cult novels in France), wrote a book in the late 1980s in which she claimed to have been the model for one of the writer's most celebrated characters; Cohen's wounded widow responded angrily, maintaining that the claim was untrue. The dignified literary supplement in *Le Monde* devoted long articles to this debate, which, indeed, was fascinating and moving, as well as evocative of the character of an important writer. But the point is that the mistress is taken as a part of life, like after-dinner cigars. Wives may not like it; some become resigned, others take lovers. (There are, of course, husbands who remain entirely faithful.) To those outside the marriage, in any case, having a mistress is understandable; not admirable, perhaps, but not particularly sinful, either.

Businessmen with positions to maintain and money in the bank, politicians, commentators, lawyers, bankers, doctors, and other men of means take on what are called *petites danceuses* thirty or forty years younger than they, the designation *danceuse* coming from the days when the members of the corps de ballet at the Paris Opéra, young, sexy, poor, and in need of protection, provided the chief hunting ground for this sort of pleasure. The men don't get kicked off the board of directors because of what is expected to be a costly indulgence, available only to the financially successful and powerful, the sort to whom calculating girls with few ambitions for themselves are prone to give themselves. The plain fact is that the phrase "sexual indiscretion" is practically an oxymoron in France. And in any case, the French argue, what difference does it make if a presidential candidate, or a president, or a minister, has a mistress? It's his private affair. It says nothing at all about his ability to govern the country. François Mitterrand was noted in 1988 to be making occasional, private visits to Venice. The unconfirmed scuttlebutt was that M. Mitterrand—who travels on official visits with his wife but is reported to be no longer conjugally related to her—had a woman friend there. What was unusual was that the French press made allusions to these reports rather than maintaining the usual Gallic silence on such matters. Normally, even candidates opposing each other for office steadfastly avoid the issue of sexual character, for at least two reasons: first, charges of immorality might redound to the benefit of the accused person, who would be admired for his Rabelaisian qualities, his *joie de vivre*; second, as the French say, people should sweep in front of their own doors first.

Homosexuals are commonly elected or appointed to important positions; none of them ever jump out of hotel windows, as they sometimes do in the United States, for fear that someone will disclose their sexual identity, which, in any case, is known without being disclosed.

So, yes, the French are frivolous. They know how to enjoy themselves without guilt or embarrassment. They gorge themselves on oysters and foie gras. They spend freely on their pleasures; they drink well; they enjoy the pleasures of sex and the form of the naked body, which adorns uninhibited beaches, movie screens, and advertising posters. A common expression describing a sort of regular guy, the salt of the earth, is to say: *Il bouffe bien; il boit bien; il baise bien*—He eats well; he drinks well; he fucks well. It cannot be insignificant that the French not only have a female figure as the symbol of the Republic, Marianne, whose facial features adorn coins and city halls all over the country, but officially select an actual Frenchwoman, usually a movie star, to be the model for the symbol. It used to be Brigitte Bardot; then it was Catherine Deneuve; in 1989, it became a model, Inès de la Fressange. I always felt that the attitude of the French toward the female breast was a sign of their skill in incorporating, without fanfare or triumphalism, a certain eroticism into everyday life. The French love breasts, which are photographically and artistically reproduced everywhere. One hundred years ago, it's fair to say, the ideal was for the breast to be rather ample and fruity, as in the paintings of August Renoir. Nowadays, judging from the numerous representations that one sees around Paris, the preferred form is sleeker, smaller, more a fig or a plum than a melon, just as the preferred woman is slimmer. Breasts are pictured, photographed, displayed, even flaunted, but with none of the snickering and gloating that surrounds that part of the anatomy in the puritan countries, where the prurience of the interest is more blatant.

French girls often lose their virginity when they are sixteen or seventeen, usually when they are in the later stages of high school. It does not seem to be a big event, not something that they discuss for hours with their psychiatrists in later years. They are taken by their older sister or by the older sister of a classmate or even by their mother to a doctor, where they are prescribed birth control pills. There is no debate in France over matters that tear the United States to pieces, such as whether doctors should be able to prescribe birth control pills or perform abortions on teenage girls without informing their parents. Put most simply and directly, there is less guilt, less anguish, less fuss, over the pleasures of the flesh in France than there is in most countries. They are taken as an attribute of life, to be appreciated with a certain finesse, like the foie gras and the Bordeaux. Feminists, somewhat behind their American sisters in this regard, have not generally raised the sorts of objections to sexual typing or to the commercial exploitation of the female body that is common in the United States. With the exception of a few largely ignored female Socialist politicians, women in France do not go around demanding that the honorifics used for them eliminate the distinction between *Madame* and *Mademoiselle*. The country that produced Simone de Beauvoir has generally been content to follow traditions in matters of sexual relations, Ms. de Beauvoir's pathbreaking book *The Second Sex* notwithstanding.

In fact, the clever use of sexiness is considered an achievement. In the mid-1980s a new advertising agency displayed a series of posters in demonstration of its own creativity. One day, a nubile beauty appeared on a poster, dressed in both parts of a two-piece bathing suit and viewable from head to toe, saying: "Tomorrow I take off the top." The next day, the same girl was shown with bare breasts of the sleek and plumlike kind currently in favor. She promised: "Tomorrow I take off the bottom." Everybody waited to see the delightful creature in the fullness of her nudity, but when she took off the bottom, she turned around for the occasion, thereby giving an illustration of what was deemed suitable for public exposure. Bare breasts and bare behinds, yes; full frontal nudity, no. Even the government once played an erotic little joke with the image of Marianne, played by an actress diaphanously, translucently clothed and very seductive, who appeared on television to encourage the French to go to the polls, even if voting Socialist or Conservative was not the first thing the beautiful creature brought to mind. And then there was the advertisement for a suntan lotion that pictured what can only be described as a ravishing pair of breasts, suitably summery in color. Posters near the superhighways had to be removed because they were believed to be the cause of a sudden increase in automobile accidents at those spots on the road.

And yet from time to time even the French suspect they have gone too far, particularly in sexual display. Around 1986, for example, there was a move to curb the semipornographic nature of advertising posters and the entirely pornographic nature of certain magazines. The National Assembly, controlled at the time by the Conservatives, did not exactly ban pornography, but in a sensible solution (proposed, it should be noted, by the National Front, most of whose other legislative initiatives were spurned), it passed a law increasing the value-added tax on it—thereby presumably increasing state revenues while expressing moral disapproval of the source of those revenues. Generally speaking, the French in the domain of advertising concentrate on their favorite erogenous zone, the breast, and on a certain coquettish nymphet's allure, or else on the female breast and on the seductiveness of sophistication, manicured blondness, coolness, indifference, and unattainability. Two of the recent models for Marianne would seem to be good illustrations of these types, Brigitte Bardot of the former and Catherine Deneuve of the latter, the one a model of a teasing, ingenue's allure, the other the epitome of classic, icy beauty.

This use of sex in advertising is denounced from pulpits from time to time as yet another sign of the decadence of our time (which it might very well be), and every so often, some restrictions are put on extreme suggestiveness or nudity in advertising posters, these being no sooner imposed than relaxed again. In 1986, one of the ads that went too far showed a woman wearing jeans and nothing else, her hands tied behind her back—a portrayal that did, in this rare case, arouse the ire of women's groups especially. It was the suggestion of sadomasochism in the ad, the portrayal of the woman in a position of compliant, perverse submissiveness, that made it controversial; bare breasts alone would not have evoked any particular opposition, or even any particular notice. For months in 1987, a host of sex and dating services using telephone-computer networks sprang into existence, and at that time, all along the *grands boulevards* of Paris, enormously provocative posters went up, showing young females oozing concupiscence and promising complete satisfaction if you would only dial a particular computer code number. These lustful ads provoked moral concern, but nothing was done about them.

Paris, of course, is the historic center of legendary French naughtiness, and from what I have gathered, it deserved this reputation more half a century ago than it does in the relatively sober 1980s. In the 1930s, when divorce was difficult, prostitution allowed, and the sexual revolution of the 1960s still a mere gleam in the eye, a phenomenon of the future like television, Parisian nightlife—and its provincial imitations—permitted a host of erotic activities more associated with Bangkok now than with a European capital. Painters like Degas and Picasso, and photographers like Brassaï, as well as playwrights and poets like Jacques Prévert, were habitués of the dusk-to-dawn lowlife in every quarter. And that is what it was largely, lowlife, even if the occasional aristocrat—Proust's Baron de Charlus was a famous example, but there were other, nonfictional ones—was drawn to the city's tough, earthy scenes. Brassaï has written a memoir called *The Secret Paris of the '30's*, accompanied by photographs, that takes the reader to the brothels that existed in every arrondissement (they were supervised by the city halls and known as "houses of illusion"). The book includes the *lieux* of streetwalkers and short-time hotels, the more innocent *bals musettes*, the popular dance halls, where the music was provided by a nasal woodwind instrument, the musette, related to bagpipes. Brassaï reminisces about the *bal nègre* in the Latin Quarter, where, in the 1920s, white Frenchwoman—"society neurotics," Brassaï calls them—exercised a passion for black men. When the American Negro Dance Company made a sensation in Paris in 1925 and, later, when the American dancer Josephine Baker became a big star in France, a host of black nightclubs opened in Montparnasse and Montmartre. In addition, still according to Brassaï, there were numerous homosexual and lesbian clubs. Every year, medical students held a famous party called the *bizutage*, during which everybody was naked. The art students had their own occasion, the Bal des Quat-Arts, which Brassaï describes as a "wild, naked horde, fairly drunk," invading "the cafés on the avenue, kissing women and producing general panic."

Much of this—not all of it—has faded away. Those in search of old Paris go sometimes to Balajo, on the rue de Lappe, a deliciously seedy establishment on a deliciously seedy street, which has been enjoying something of a bohemian vogue in recent years, as a place where you can dance with a stranger all afternoon, have an aperitif at an "authentic" old café, and eat the cuisine of the Ivory Coast or Senegal in the evening. The rue de Lappe, not far from the Place de la République, in the eastern part of town, was once famed as a sinful place, where, amid a collection of warehouses, some of the best dance halls and whorehouses of Paris were located. In the 1930s, just as the small *bals musettes* were going out of fashion, an enterprising man known as Jo de France created a larger ballroom, Balajo, designed, as Brassaï puts it, to recreate the atmosphere of the films. Soon the tourist buses started to arrive, and so did the Parisian bourgeoisie, changing the atmosphere. Now Balajo is the only dance hall left that anybody seems to know about. It is a normal young person's discotheque on Friday and Saturday nights and a venue for tinglingly illicit encounters every afternoon, the place where bored housewives from the suburbs come for a Pernod, a *pastis*, a grenadine, perhaps a glass of champagne, and to meet an adventurous, probably married shopkeeper or out-of-work musician or perhaps an accountant or an insurance executive or a dentist, if not for a full-fledged affair then at least to rub and cuddle a bit in the intimacy permitted by the darkened dance floor. I remember sitting there with a friend watching the crowd, which was of a certain age and a certain studied bourgeois homeyness, doing the fox-trot and the tango under the pastel glow of a cityscape projected onto the ceiling. This was Paris, after all, the Paris of discreet insouciance and a dedication to the self, where people feel free to escape their humdrum lives for a while.

The other great holdover from the old days are the spectacular topless revues, the Moulin Rouge, the Crazy Horse, the Lido, and others, where hugely expensive and, in fact, not very erotic extravaganzas are staged, in large part for American and Japanese tourists. Most of the female performers at these places are not French, since, in the choreographer's mind, the French girls are not generally big enough. So these places employ Swedish girls, American girls, Dutch girls, English girls, and have about as much connection with French society as the Alliance Française, the language school, has with French universities.

And yet France is sinful, open to sexual display and experimentation. There are probably more pornographic bookstores and peep shows on Paris's rue Saint-Denis alone—along with dozens of prostitutes, who carry out their activities with virtual immunity from the law—than there are in all New York and Los Angeles combined. There seem to be hundreds of them, and they are devoid of that grim, underworld quality of their counterparts elsewhere. Many of them, no doubt, are patronized by tourists who do not have such facilities back home. It is said in Paris that there is a published map of the city showing where various sexual services can be obtained. At a certain spot in the Bois de Boulogne, for example, is the street for Latin American transvestite prostitutes. These can be seen displaying their wares and soliciting customers as a long line of bumper-to-bumper traffic passes through the dark park until nearly dawn. Elsewhere in the Bois and in the city there are other sorts of prostitutes, including many of the conventional streetwalker sort. Every night, until the early hours, dozens of men can be seen hanging around along the avenue Foch, within a stone's throw of the Arc de Triomphe. They are, or so I have been told, waiting for invitations to orgies, where they serve as paid participants. I once asked a savvy French-woman exactly what so many people were doing in all those parked cars that I had noted late at night in the Bois de Boulogne. Of course, I suspected what was going on in them. And yet, I appreciated the matter-of-fact precision of her answer. "They are fucking," she said.

An episode of governmental intolerance of this sort of thing erupted into public debate in 1987 when, suddenly, the Conservative minister of the interior, Charles Pasqua, announced a list of publications that would thenceforth be banned from public sale—thereby restricting them to the ghettos of the specialty sex shops, which, while numerous, don't have the reach or the respectability of the streetside newsstands. The move seemed designed to transform the easy French acceptance of sexual representation of all types into something covert and sinful, and, as some immediately predicted it would, it turned out to be one of those clumsy and self-defeating gestures of the Conservatives—similar in its imperious, autocratic style to the attempted school reform later in the year, undertaken with very little consultation and not much forethought—that led, eventually, to the electorate's rejection of them in 1988. The banned list included a magazine called *Gai Pied*, which was devoted to homosexuality. There were some soft-core porno magazines, one of them called in English *New Life*. For some reason, after being tolerated for decades, the French version of *Penthouse* was put on the list. Strange, too, a very popular magazine of somewhat salacious cartoons and comic features called *l'Echo des Savanes* was also banned. There were a few others. The reaction was a typically French one of outrage and derision. The *Ligue pour les Droits de l'Homme*, the League for Human Rights, took up the defense of *Gai Pied*. The government rather quickly dropped the threatened ban. Meanwhile, a magazine named *Globe*, which had been started a year before by some of the country's leading writers, particularly several already well known for serious libertarian beliefs, came out with a special issue designed to pour contempt on what it called "the new moral order" and "the obscenity of the censors, who see sex everywhere and examine hair and flesh under the magnifying glass."

The issue of *Globe* was a perfect illustration of the French love of the shocking, in this particular case shocking by appearing to have been shocked. The large-format cover consisted of a chiaroscuro photograph by Robert Mapplethorpe of a distended male member held at midpoint by the hand of an unidentified person. Inside, there were other erotic drawings and photographs and a series of articles that, taken together, treated the interior minister's move as something close in perversity, immorality, and stupidity to the construction of gas chambers. "A state that attempts to regulate conscience is a Fascist state," one of the essays declared bluntly. Striking a somewhat less alarmist tone, Bernard-Henri Lévy, the founder of *Globe* and a philosopher and novelist of considerable visibility in France, wrote: "I have a hard time imagining that such innocent idiocy could still be possible today in France." Charles Pasqua and Robert Pandraud—the two senior interior ministry officials of the Conservative government—were not Fascists, Lévy hastened to assure the worried world. "They aren't even only demagogues," he went on. "They are especially, and first of all, two gross imbeciles," who should be prevented from "behaving like jerks in public."

The issue here, as I saw it, was not so much a matter of sexual liberty or even the defense of free speech. The Pasqua-Pandraud gesture evoked an ancient conflict in France, taking place this time under circumstances that in no way presaged a return to genuine censorship or to a regulation of conscience. The harsh class and political conflicts of the past have always taken on the tones of anger and righteousness, in which each faction tends to turn its opponents into reactionary villains or anarchistic terrorists. And so when MM. Pasqua and Pandraud tried, in essence, to make it more difficult for minors to buy certain highly suggestive and erotic publications, one writer found it appropriate to resurrect the memory of Claude le Petit, burned in the eighteenth century at the age of twenty-three, after the executioner had cut off the hand that had written impious poems. There were reminders that the Marquis de Sade, one of the initiators of the tradition of saying shocking things in order to rouse people out of the stupor of convention, spent most of his life serving out various prison sentences, most of them imposed because of his writings. The minister and the deputy minister of the interior had, according to François Léotard, the minister of culture, committed "an astonishing political mistake" in ordering the ban. But their real crime was not the ban on the magazines; it was in being the exemplars of institutional power itself and of attempting to give lectures on morality to a people who didn't need or want them.

There is another political overtone to this issue of pleasure. In 1936, the short-lived Socialist government of Léon Blum legislated for the first time that all French workers would have a paid vacation of one week. The magazines of the era showed a massive, joyous exodus from Paris, great happy throngs piling into cars and trains, heading for the verdant countryside. The workers had torn a precious concession out of the grasping talons of the bourgeoisie. No longer would the privileged and the rich enjoy a monopoly on leisure time. Vacation for everybody was a Socialist victory, a triumph in the ongoing class war, something that had been yielded unwillingly by the enemy. In 1981, after the Socialists came to power in France again—and far more stably this time—they understood the symbolism of the moment when they decreed another mandatory week of paid vacation, a fifth, for every French worker. Subsequently, nobody seemed to object very much; certainly nobody, not even the Conservatives, after they came back to power for a bit more than a year in 1986, suggested that the fifth week be taken away. But in one of the spasms of self-examination they subject themselves to from time to time, the French did begin asking whether they were collectively lazy. Statistics were published revealing that the French worked fewer hours and took more vacations than their counterparts in Japan, the United States, or Germany. A book called *Lazy France*, by Victor Scherrer, became a sensation in the summer of 1987. It claimed not only that the French worked less than the Japanese and the Germans but that they worked less than the Spaniards and the Italians. That, he argued, was the reason for France's loss of competitiveness, its growing trade deficit. With Scherrer's book, the lazy French became a matter of parlor conversation for a time, and the consensus was that, yes, they did work less and enjoy life more. But what was the underlying issue? To Scherrer, pointing out that the French enjoyed four three-day weekends in May and June each year, it was laziness.

The explanation is more likely historical and political. The underlying element in that extra week of vacation awarded by the Socialists was less laziness or hedonism—though these ancient sins may have been present—than the conviction that to work less is part of the French worker's eschatological vision, his belief that the tide of history is supposed to bring less work, more time for leisure, and by God, if the capitalists won't let him have it, then the only solution is to get it through political action.

The French thus take their pleasure as a political gain, as part of the ritual of the assertion of rights, and in doing so, they embark on a kind of sybaritic crusade where, it always seemed to me, the joys were far more illusory than real and the purpose was more to demonstrate an acquired social advantage—one of what the Socialists like to call *les acquis*—and not simply to have a good time. During Easter week and in August, the Great Exodus from the cities takes place, a lemming-like departure en masse, since the French always insist on taking their vacations all at the same time. "*Les Français sont des veaux*," de Gaulle once said in a despairing, pessimistic moment—The French are calves. (It is virtually impossible to imagine an American leader saying something equally despairing of his electorate and getting away with it politically.) Well, all people have their bovine aspects, the French among them. The pursuit of pleasure, the departure on vacation, seems to bring out their subservience to ritual, their tendency to flock.

"The hallucinatory frenzy of departure has its result in a pitiable monotony," the sociologist and historian of ideas Jean-Paul Aron wrote once in *Le Monde*. "One changes his decor, not his existence." Aron was referring to the practical fact that the typical vacation begins with a traffic jam on the *autoroute* that can last eight or nine hours or more. People sit in their cars, listening to a lugubrious radio recitation of the lengths of the blockages on the main highways. The statistics show ten, twelve, sixteen million people leaving home for the countryside on a single weekend in August. French television carries footage of stalled motorists expressing philosophical resignation over the fact that the holiday begins in an interminable, sweltering crawl. And where are they going? Often to seasonal roadside slums, vast, disheveled camping grounds where the Duponts and the Durands, arriving from opposite ends of Paris, find themselves, each year, at last together, cheek by jowl, or standing on line at the public latrine, enjoying their weeks in the countryside, while on the nearby highway the constant drumbeat of the great, ritualistic mass migration toward supposed enjoyment is taking place. Aron's belief was that the exodus marked the great "illusion that rediscovering the quality of life lies inherently in being idle," rather than in undertaking some rewarding task, achieving a goal. Actually, the illusion is in large measure a political one. If the Protestant, according to Max Weber's famous theory of capitalism, shows that he is among the elect by gaining wealth, the Frenchman uses his hard-won leisure to brandish his political triumph.

The avid pursuit of pleasure turns one of the world's most beautiful countries into paradises of the imagination and Calcuttas of population density. The stretch of beach towns along the Mediterranean in July and August is one of the most crowded zones ever created in human history. It is one of the world's great false imaginings that there is something glamorous or luxurious about this part of the world during the summer. True, there are exclusive preserves, places where the wealthy and famous go, no longer to be seen—since to be seen in places where absolutely everybody can and does go is hardly the height of fashion—but to be known to be hiding out, at, for example, the Hôtel du Cap, on a tree-lined peninsula jutting into the Mediterranean just east of Cannes.

When the empress Eugénie, the wife of Napoleon III, who ruled dictatorially from 1852 to 1870, went to Biarritz to bathe in the Atlantic, it was to make a great and conspicuous show of the privilege of enjoyment. Now that enjoyment has been democratized, turned into something that the travel agencies advertise as "formulas," a product of mass production and consumption, the fashionable thing is to enclose oneself in a private and invisible world inaccessible to the masses. Brigitte Bardot made Saint-Tropez fashionable by being seen to go there and to disport herself on the beach. Since then, the great explosion of activity all along the Mediterranean has begotten an enormous stretch of commercial establishments, fast-food joints, and immense condominium complexes, snapped up by the French but also by numerous Swedes, Germans, Dutch, and Americans, all hemming in the private villas, the places of real comfort and luxury that remain. I don't know whether Bardot goes to Saint-Tropez anymore. Certainly, she is not seen to go.

· · ·

AND SO the French are serious about enjoyment, politically serious about it as well as devoted to it as a matter of fulfillment in life. Before we Anglo-Saxons accuse them of a lack of seriousness, an absence of weightiness, of self-indulgent flightiness, we should consider the fact that if they enjoy the pleasures of the flesh with a certain intense determination, they show the same determination over the pleasures of the mind. It is not that the French these days are creating more than their share of masterpieces in literature, the theater, or the arts, even in that form that we particularly associate with a special French genius, the movies. The plain fact is that, with certain happy exceptions, they have not been distinguishing themselves in art and literature in the 1980s. The midcentury literary giants are gone; the new novel is passé (perhaps it never deserved the attention it got) and has been replaced by no particularly bright trend; films are small, clever affairs, but they have little of the pioneering, visionary aspects of the days of Jean Renoir, Marcel Carné, Pagnol, or, more recently, Truffaut, Godard, Resnais.

But the passion for debate over serious matters remains. There may be a large number of naked breasts in subway ads, but there are also books of philosophy, history, and politics on the best-seller lists, taking the places that, in the nonfrivolous United States, are occupied by that endless stream of how-to books—how to get more sexual pleasure, how to be slim and beautiful, how to make more money. These sorts of books do not sell so well in France. But in 1985, when Annie Cohen-Solal brought out her biography of Jean-Paul Sartre, both she, the author, and it, her book, were sensations. She was on the best-seller list for several months. She was on television, written up in all the magazines and newspapers, invited all over the country to participate in public discussions of Sartre and his work. There is always a significant number of "good" books doing well at any given time in the French bookstores. In 1987, Alain Finkielkraut published his *The Defeat of Thought*, a probing, highly learned exploration of what the philosopher saw as the decline of intellectual standards. The book, which would have been bought by a few university libraries and scholarly individuals in the United States, was the number one best-seller in France for the entire summer. The ultimate numerical index of this unfrivolous behavior is the major French book club, France Loisirs, which sells some twenty-six million books per year, or roughly one for every second French person. Another index is "*Apostrophes*," the fifteen-year-old seventy-five-minute Friday-night TV ritual during which the now celebrated host,

Bernard Pivot, talked with a group of writers before a small studio audience. "*Apostrophes*," which M. Pivot, weary after so many years, has decided to take off the air in 1990, generally got about 15 percent of the television viewers on Friday night.

Given their seriousness about the life of the mind, some French, reacting seriously to the Anglo-American portrayal of them as frivolous —and no doubt thinking there could be no more frivolous a people than the one that spends billions each year on recreational drugs and bakes its collective brain in front of empty TV sitcoms—have done research on the origins of the image. The French historian of Paris, Louis Chevalier, traces the notion of an ongoing French debauchery to the Second Empire, when "Gai Paris" took hold of the British imagination. True, Chevalier writes, in the drawings of Hogarth in the eighteenth century, Paris is already depicted as a center of sin and immorality. Industrial artifacts from the period no doubt contributed to this view. What did the French seem to manufacture at the time when the British were creating the industrial revolution, inventing practical, universally useful things like industrial looms? The French were creating fabulously useless playthings for a fabulously useless class of decadent nobles: intricate clocks, mechanical contrivances that set whole miniature worlds in motion. But the view of Paris in particular and the French by association as inherently naughty comes after the Revolution, the constant political bloodshed of the first half of the nineteenth century, the bungling, comic-opera reign of Napoleon III, the Great Napoleon's nephew, and, finally, the rise of neighboring Prussia, which seemed not only powerful by comparison with France but stable, politically enlightened, vigorous, and wholesome.

On the Prussian side, after all, was Bismarck, a colossal figure of unquestioned force and vigor, a worthy heir to the eighteenth century's Frederick the Great. In beautiful, ornate, decadent Paris was the vain, narcissistic, inauthentic Napoleon, Napoleon le Petit, given the nickname Krapulinsky by Karl Marx, the man whom Bismarck said could be dealt with via a policy of *pourboires*, or tips. And so, Chevalier says, "Paris takes on the image of a city of perdition, and by contrast to the good Germans and the virtuous Berliners, the Parisians are merely people without morals." They "pass their time in love, in games and in politics, with women, with wine, with talk and, for recreation, on the barricades." When Edward VII, Chevalier notes, went to Paris following his abdication for the sake of the divorced Wallis Simpson, the image became indelible.

There is today a telling equivalent to the French eighteenth-century fascination with pretty toys, music boxes, frilly clothes, and foppish manners. In more recent times, the French skill at producing great perfumes, jewelry, wines, pâtés de foie gras and other culinary delicacies —such as de Gaulle's hundreds of cheeses—has infuriated some, who believe a slander against other French skills is being perpetrated, that the French are not taken seriously, as the Japanese or the Germans are, with their electronics and cars, their steel mills and computer chips.

French industrialists do not like their country to be thought of as a fuzzy-headed place given over so much to *joie de vivre* that they are not capable of running a modern, competitive economy. They say that French technology is not taken seriously, not even by themselves, because of what might be called the foie gras complex, even though, in addition to making the world's best foie gras (no insignificant accomplishment), they have the world's fastest high-speed trains, one of its most advanced airplane industries, a vigorous space program, a supersonic airplane in passenger service, advanced battlefield communications systems, bought by the American military, the globe's best nuclear power technology, more nuclear weapons than any other countries except the U.S. and the U.S.S.R., and medical laboratories that were the first in the world to isolate the AIDS virus. Even in the nineteenth century, the French textbooks like to point out, more than porcelain dollhouses were being manufactured. In 1823, a Frenchman, Nicéphore Niepce, invented photography, a technique later developed by Daguerre and, at the end of the century, by the Lumière brothers, who created motion pictures. Barthélemy Thimmonier invented the sewing machine; Pasteur a method for killing bacteria in milk and immunizing human beings against plague; Charles Tellier refrigeration in 1867; and Aristide Bergès the first hydroelectric station in 1869.

And on it goes. Chevalier tells the story of one Francis Croisset, an aristocrat of the early part of this century, who, having rented the Tir aux Pigeons club in order to give a party there, and having ordered eighty thousand Venetian lanterns to illuminate the Bois de Boulogne, where the club was situated, went with the Prince de Sagan, his uncle, to the president of the municipal council of Paris in order to obtain a detachment of mounted cavalrymen. When the president of the municipal council asked de Sagan what the purpose of the occasion was, the prince "adjusting his monocle, replied: 'This festival will be held for pleasure,' repeating each word three times with an impertinent insistence: 'For pleasure, for pleasure, for pleasure.' "

11

The Revenge of the
Bourgeoisie

WHY DO they keep their homes so gloomy, so crepuscular, filled
with dark upholstered Louis XVI chairs and sofas, royalist cloth
wall coverings in purple with gold-threaded designs, dark paintings of
ancestors or ancestral lands—or, more likely, of somebody else's ancestors or ancestral lands—encased in heavily ornate, dusty gold frames?
True, they don't all live like that. There are light and airy apartments
also, and even places of ultramodernity, full of glass, chrome, molded
plastic, furniture upholstered in leather. I remember one dinner at the
home of an editor in the Sixth Arrondissement, where the squeaking
and grinding of the off-white molded plastic chairs around the dining
table practically drowned out the conversation.

But the haute bourgeoisie of the Seventh or the Sixteenth Arrondissement seems, often, to dwell in the architectural twilight. I have visited
former ministers with magnificent genealogies in their third-floor apartments on the rue de Grenelle, where every step brings you to another
stage in the archaeology of haute bourgeois French style. First you walk
up to one of those ornate buildings of cut stone, arabesques, wrought-
iron railings, massive carved window frames, slanted slate roofs with
skylights or dormers. Then you push through the heavy outer door on
the street below; you take the gilded wrought-iron elevator upstairs, or
you climb the stone stairway, covered in a patterned red carpet, that
spirals around the elevator's straight vertical line. You are let through
large double doors into a sparsely furnished foyer with creaking floor-
boards. After a decent interval, the host appears and leads you into a

dim drawing room, whose single light bulb can barely illuminate your face because of the heavy ocher-colored, fringed octagonal lampshade that frames it.

For many years, the bourgeoisie was the class that everybody, including other members of the bourgeoisie—who excluded themselves from the category—loved to hate. "France?" wrote the humorist Pierre Daninos, in *The Notebooks of Major Thompson*, a book that presents the French through the eyes of an imaginary English officer. "A nation of bourgeois attacking other bourgeois because that is what they are." As a class, the bourgeoisie was urged on by Louis XIV's minister of finance, Colbert, who encouraged merchants and manufacturers to create the commerce and goods that would add to the national wealth, the expansion of which was his ultimate goal. In the beginning, however, the aristocracy's disdain for commerce led it to its historic contempt for this Colbertian class, which, after all, was to triumph politically over the nobility, the clergy, and the king himself when the revolution of 1789 came along. The bourgeoisie, Guy Sabatier has written, was the class that "preferred money to the saber"—a tasteless preference, the aristocrats felt. Strangely, this disparagement of the moneyed class, the trading class, the industrial class, was adopted not only by the later working class and, of course, the Marxists but, along the historical road, by intellectuals and writers of the nineteenth and twentieth centuries as well, though certainly these later antibourgeois detractors obviously did not see themselves as the inheritors of an aristocratic prejudice. Twentieth-century writers like Sartre, Merleau-Ponty, Camus, made their hatred of the bourgeoisie an article of literary faith and moral philosophy. And so the bourgeoisie in France was thought by just about everybody, including itself, to be snobbish, pretentious, formal, unfriendly, and crassly materialistic. The bourgeoisie made the Revolution, according to the academically dominant Marxist historians, but they made it for themselves, using the short-lived restorations and the even shorter-lived republics to advance their own commercial instincts. One writer, Émile Keller, a late-nineteenth-century monarchist, accused it, variously, of being "Voltairian, Jacobin, imperialist, royalist, Orleanist, and Republican—of having betrayed all and sold everything, beginning with its soul, in order to continue to eat gold and dividends."

If France is seen as a contentious society, a place that loves intense debate and political speculation, much of the contention has centered on this class, one of whose worst features—or so goes the charge—is that having overthrown the old nobility in the Revolution, it then set about to imitate it, in part out of a striving to gain, not just money, not only power, because these it has had since early in the nineteenth century, but acceptance as well. France, which set the standard for royalist splendor and aristocratic panache for the rest of the world, became the country of bourgeois splendor, bourgeois panache. Hence the imperious, forbidding style to be found in those apartments on the rue de Grenelle in Paris's Seventh Arrondissement, the rue de la Faisanderie in the Sixteenth, the gloomily pretentious home furnishings, the attempts to create *chez soi*, at home, small reproductions of life in the palaces of the great. The misdirected aesthetic principle here seems to be an obsession for formal perfection, for everything to be just so, in its place, parts of a precisely ordered whole—microcosms, that is, of Versailles. Indeed, just as those who dwelt in Versailles came into their possession by birth, the grand apartments of Paris or Lyon, Toulouse or Nice, are more often than not inherited by people who could not have afforded them otherwise, a fact that may well increase the desire to keep up appearances. It is tempting to suppose that even the French city dweller's insistence on a country house, a kind of manor reproducing the family châteaux of the families with particles—Jean-Antoine de Sardines-en-Boîte is a made-up example, the *de*, meaning "from," being the *particule*, the particle, and Sardines-en-Boîte the name of a former feudal fief—derives from this emulation of the aristocracy. If American urbanites buy homes in the country in order to recapture an imagined lost rural idyll, the French love of their *maisons secondaires* (and 10 percent of the French have them, a world record) arises out of a kind of feudal nostalgia.

But this is unfair. I am drawing a kind of negative ideal type here. It exists. I have been to these stuffy dwellings with somebody's ancestor's oil portrait on the wall and the imperfect of the subjunctive coming out in stiff conversation; and for some reason I never quite understood, the rooms are but feebly illuminated—perhaps merely to save electricity in a country where electricity is very expensive. But of course, the French middle class, like other middle classes, is varied in taste. There are several main stylistic types. One of them is that of the intellectual who lives on the Left Bank in a sunny apartment looking over a quiet, charming courtyard, his setting one of studied informality, utilitarianism, and anti-snobbishness, with books on the shelves, on the tables, piled on the floor, and the dormer-style windows open to views of the Paris rooftops. Then there is the new arrival on the middle-class scene, the thirty-something deputy manager of an insurance office from modest origins, perhaps the young doctor just starting his own private office—while working nights at the clinic to make ends meet—who has taken over a former working-class flat on the rue Mandar or the rue Tiquetonne or, perhaps, farther east near the Place de la République, stripped the Versailles-imitation wallpaper, framed some posters for the walls, and installed chairs, tables, and bedroom sets from Habitat, the French yuppies' furniture dealer. Finally, another broad category consists of the sons and daughters of the older, better-established bourgeoisie, starting out in life for themselves. They have been given the name *bon chic bon genre*, BCBG for short, a brilliant linguistic invention, meaning, literally, "good fashion good type," whose closest American equivalent would be "preppie." The BCBG's are studiously casual, wearing cashmere sweaters and foulards and driving BMWs—or the most souped-up Peugeot 205, red with a convertible black top—and they live on the rue du Cherche-Midi near the Luxembourg Gardens or, often, in Paris's most fashionable suburbs, Neuilly or, perhaps, Saint-Germain-en-Laye.

The point of this sketch of the different types of bourgeoisie, describing a society that is extremely and entirely aware of its division into social classes, is that things are changing in France. Whenever there is a strike on the public transport system, or among nurses in the hospitals, or of postal workers, or within the ateliers at Renault, the press and politicians talk about the situation of "social conflicts"—*les conflits sociaux*. There is an implicit Marxist assumption in the term, suggesting that disputes over wages are the manifestations of underlying conflicting interests among social classes, the oppressor class being the bourgeoisie. But despite the continued use of the language of social conflict, much of the antagonism toward the bourgeoisie has diminished in recent years. It has become acceptable to want to make more money (it was always desirable, but it was rarely fashionable to be born with it), to accumulate material possessions, to buy that BMW, even to practice some imitation of the old aristocracy, which, in any case, has made something of a social comeback, no longer being regarded with mixed contempt and envy by the rest of society as privileged anachronisms, necessary evils. And this, in part, is due to the democratization of French society, the leveling effect of more or less equal opportunity conditions, where birth counts for less and less and skill, ability, and hard work for more.

The change here is remarkable. When various French writers, mostly of the nineteenth century, used the phrase "to shock the bourgeoisie" —*épater les bourgeois*—as an acceptable motive for some outrageously silly and otherwise profitless behavior, the fullness of French class combativeness was being asserted. "Why are you beating your head against the wall for something that you yourself recognize as absurd?" the Goncourt brothers asked a friend, as recorded in their *Journals* of 1879. Answer: "*C'est absolument pour épater les bourgeois*"—It's only to shock the bourgeoisie. For much of the late nineteenth century and the first half of the twentieth, whole intellectual worlds were based on an idealistic hatred of the class of stuffiness and aristocratic pretension. The great Flaubert, who lived, aside from occasional adventures abroad and his quadrimensual visit to his mistress, a quiet life at home with his mother, once said that "Hatred of the bourgeoisie is the beginning of all wisdom." For him, the uncomprehendingly smug pharmacist Homais in *Madame Bovary* is the model of this detestable creature, a man whose overbearing self-satisfaction, his utter confusion between egotistical drives and the social good, lead him to a blissful unawareness of the human tragedy around him, in much the same way that his supposed opposite but actual twin, M. Bournisien, the priest, is spiritually the most insensitive of human beings.

Beyond Flaubert, who once remarked rather sourly, showing a politically ungenerous spirit, that "the entire dream of democracy is to raise the proletariat to the level of bourgeois stupidity," the writers and artists of the late nineteenth and early twentieth centuries represent an ongoing disparagement, a continuous attempt to pour abuse and scorn on what was regarded as the joyless, uncomprehending self-satisfaction of the stereotypical bourgeois. Witness the portrayals in Balzac or the drawings of Daumier, showing the "typical" bourgeois as a bloated incarnation of greed and stupidity, dressed in a frock coat and leggings, a horrible, monstrous deformation of the elegant, slender aristocrat he made so poor a job of emulating. The progenitor of this negative image was probably Molière, whose seventeenth-century *Bourgeois Gentilhomme* —Bourgeois Gentleman—is a model of ignorant snobbishness, trying to learn all the fine arts practiced by what he calls "quality," meaning the nobility, but utterly failing in his endeavor. "It's true that he knows them badly," the music master tells the dancing master of the bourgeois M. Jourdain's efforts in the fine arts. "But he pays well, and that's what our Arts need now more than any other thing." When the dancing master replies that the best payment is an "enlightened praise," the other replies, sadly, that praise alone does not make for an artist's ease. "He's a man whose lights are, it is true, rather small, who speaks ignorantly about everything and whose applause comes always at the wrong moments, but his money corrects the judgments of his Mind. He has discernment in his pocket book. His praise is moneyed; and this ignorant bourgeois is worth more to us, as you see, than the great enlightened Lord who gave us our introduction here."

I N *The Banquet Years*, Roger Shattuck explains that the avant-garde flourished in France during the *Belle Époque*, the period from the 1890s to the beginning of World War I, precisely because of the deep, resisting conservatism of French society as a whole. The great French artistic movements, impressionism and postimpressionism (remember the scandal that was created by Manet's *Déjeuner sur l'Herbe*), Fauvism, Dadaism, Cubism, as well as the militantly bohemian life-styles of the artist class, are understandable only against the backdrop of bourgeois resistance. There could be no avant-garde in American society, Shattuck argues, because of its habit of absorbing and sanitizing today's outrageous innovation, packaging it, selling it to millions of consumers as tomorrow's fashion. Only in France did the avant-garde have the ability to shock and to disturb, to appall and to discomfit, without running any real risk that the hated society would collapse, something the members of the avant-garde did not, in their heart of hearts, wish.

There is only the slimmest residue of the old avant-garde in France today, and part of the reason is that the middle class is no longer so conservative—at least not in its artistic styles. There are occasional remaining efforts to *épater les bourgeois*, but finally, what would be the point of shaking up a class that is rapidly becoming obsolete, or, at least, evaporating into a kind of imagined classlessness? One of the striking things about France, in the overall context of social styles in Europe today, is the relatively small number of young people out to *épater les bourgeois* by, in that goal's latest incarnation, being punks or skinheads. To be sure, these subcultures exist in France; you only have to spend an hour around the Pompidou Center in Paris to see that. But my impression is that they are far less conspicuous as a whole than they are in, say, London, Amsterdam, or Frankfurt, where these styles of appearance and dress blend with angry protest movements against nuclear power and NATO—protest movements that scarcely exist in France. The French spent more than a century shocking the bourgeoisie, most recently in the violent student protest movement of 1968, and the desire to continue shocking it seems to have been smothered in the gentle fogs of a postmodern, post-protest tolerance. The plain fact is that it is very difficult for your actions to have any real capacity to disturb, to annoy, to derange, when the society has acquired the capacity to embrace you in a treacly, uncritical, unshakable forbearance.

To some extent the emerging situation represents an extension of the erosion of real class antagonisms that some writers on the subject trace back to World War I, when, as Guy Sabatier has written, all men, noble and bourgeois, peasant and worker, "found themselves in the trenches of Verdun or in the cemeteries of Picardie," the squabbles among them suddenly erased by something far more menacing than mere civil conflict, namely the destruction of all civilized life. This fracturing of class divisions continued in World War II—after a vigorous resurrection in the period between the wars—when France split, not along class lines, but between the supporters of Pétain and Vichy and the supporters of de Gaulle and resistance. "The Unknown Soldier," Sabatier writes, "buried under the Arch of Triumph, before whom flags and men bow with respect, is, perhaps, a bourgeois. It's entirely possible. It doesn't matter."

The absence of antibourgeois fury these days is a continuation of this process, an illustration of the change in French preoccupations. In a world where the country itself fights to remain weighty and influential, what matters is not the old class antagonism but France itself, the Frenchness of everybody and the greatness, or the desired greatness, of the country. The reason there is no movement against nuclear weapons of the sort that exists in Germany, Holland, or Britain is that the French do not question the possession of the weapon that makes them a force to be reckoned with in the world. There are no moral qualms aroused by the imperative to be great, or to strive to be great in the way that de Gaulle, ever hopeful, ever despairing, imagined.

A century ago, when a vast Prussian army was laying siege to Paris, the threat to the nation exacerbated class conflict. The proletariat, led by rabble-rousers who were generally not themselves proletarians, accused the bourgeoisie of cowardice and treachery, of willingness to yield to the insulting German demands (namely the cession of Alsace and Lorraine). In the face of the siege of 1870, Paris became fragmented; the Commune, the short-lived radical government that became an object of reverence for all later revolutionaries, arose and was then destroyed in one of the century's great bloodlettings. But France at that time was not used to a loss of greatness. Only a few months before, the French had considered themselves, militarily, the supreme power on the European continent. And so if today there is no debate about national policy, about the role of the country in the world, it reflects the classless solidarity born of a loss of national status. There is no tendency to confuse different policies with different class interests. To hate the bourgeoisie is too great a luxury when the country is struggling for a historic mission.

At the same time, there has been a genuine change in values, whose overall effect has been to upgrade the bourgeois image. The French, who once made money covertly, the way they kept mistresses, now make it openly. During the 1980s, new slogans appeared, the most important of them being *La France qui gagne*—The France that wins. Competition in the international business world is what is meant by this, and there is a great appreciation that the competition can only be won by industriousness and entrepreneurship. Words like "dynamism" have become popular, again, in the commercial sense. Earning money is a sign no longer of moral weakness but of success, thereby, of course, weakening one of France's unique contributions to Western civilization, one of its attributes—the special status accorded a certain kind of activist intellectual, *l'homme engagé*, a phrase perhaps not spoken by but associated with Jean-Paul Sartre, whose prestige came from his moral and intellectual stature rather than his wealth. Thus, in the 1950s and '60s, Sartre himself, novelist, philosopher, and *homme engagé*, emerged as the country's most renowned private man (as opposed to a quintessentially public figure like de Gaulle). His counterparts today are figures like André Glucksmann and Bernard-Henri Lévy, writers on philosophical questions who also march in demonstrations, speak before crowds, traveled to Afghanistan when it was occupied by the Soviet Union. But a new sort of hero has at least partially dimmed the philosophers' light. It is the entrepreneurial dynamo, exemplified by two men in particular, Francis Bouygues, a construction magnate—known as the cement king—and Bernard Tapie, whose fame is owed to his skill at buying failing businesses and reinvigorating them.

Bouygues, a large man with a broad, florid face and graying hair combed straight back, came into the limelight when he became the buyer of a major national television network privatized by the Conservatives in 1987. The sale into private hands of the television company provoked intense debate, centering around the worry that culture itself, the possibility of quality programming, would come under attack once commercial interests had taken over. And when a quintessential *homme d'affaires* like Bouygues (pronounced Bweeg) won the competitive bidding for the network, this fear increased. The cement king was suddenly in charge of France's most important television station. Alarm bells went off, and not without some reason. After making assurances that he would not interfere with the contents of programs, Bouygues fired a Saturday-night talk show host named Michel Polac, who had a flair for controversy and a habit of getting under the skin of comfortable political convention.

Polac went; there was a bit of a protest; then the issue died away. France became accustomed to Bouygues's not only building but broadcasting as well, and within a year or so his station rocketed far ahead of the single remaining state-owned station. You have to think that France, in the days of Sartre and Camus, when the antibourgeois images of Balzac predominated, would have reacted differently. The country has finally accepted the ultimate consequence of Colbertism. Money is not only money, it is power. Moreover, by contrast with Molière, the French today in no way associate money with ignorance, or with the urgent desire among those who have made it to be accepted by "quality." It *is* "quality."

While Bouygues helped to effect this revolution in values quietly, discreetly, Bernard Tapie, another man of business and money, made his contribution with *éclat*, with messianic enthusiasm. He wrote books, cultivating his image as a businessman, not an intellectual. He created and starred in his own television program. Some of the intellectuals took note. In 1987, Bernard-Henri Lévy wrote *In Praise of Intellectuals*, a book that lamented their decline. Whom, he asked, do the French people turn to these days for guidance? No longer is it to figures like de Gaulle, Sartre, Raymond Aron, he said. It is to rock stars, comedians, and businessmen, like Bernard Tapie.

"To be bourgeois has always been pejorative even if it has also made people dream," Bernard Cathelat, a member of the Center for Advanced Communications, which monitors cultural changes, said in the magazine *L'Express*. "What's completely new is that suddenly people are becoming proud of the label. They are demanding it." Material consumption is "in," the magazine claimed, noting this sea change in attitudes. "From now on, one can be both socialist and bourgeois," it averred. Most important of all, perhaps, youth dropped its antimaterialistic, antibourgeois attitude and moved into a new era of bland self-acceptance. Many noted in France what was called "the apotheosis of the BCBG look," the triumph of a bright, young, casual, colorful style, with an accent on pastel cashmere sweaters, tweed jackets, silk scarves, far less formal and forbidding than the earlier fake-Versailles affectation it is in the process of replacing. I felt that the use of the word "look," a borrowing from English for which no fashionable French equivalent was ever found, contained its own message of what the French used to consider petit-bourgeois modishness. You almost cannot imagine an English word like "look," full of tinsel and flash, reeking of artificiality, having all the slickness and suddenness of a good advertising slogan (like the phrase *prix choc!*—incredible price!—that shouts from department store displays during sale times), gaining currency in the "serious" publications of the French 1950s or 1960s, springing from the lips of "serious" Gaullists or student rebels of that era. The word marked the triumph of the bourgeois "look" as the predominant style. The connotations of class, of a certain morality, a particular, previously despised ethic, were crushed under the enormous weight of the "look," which was becoming universal. Everybody had become bourgeois, and the bourgeoisie had become everybody. Why keep on fighting the old, lost battle?

12

The Noble Residue

THE NOBILITY was abolished long ago, but the aristocracy, which gave its taste to the bourgeoisie while losing power to it, still exists, in social if not legal reality. The French attitude toward the *noblesse* is almost as complicated, and as contradictory, as the one it holds toward the bourgeoisie. But while, until recently, all French both hated the bourgeoisie and were bourgeois, they massacred the aristocracy even while they imitated it, adopted its *savoir-vivre* as its own. One of the elements in the standard disparagement of the business class, as exemplified, say, in the drawings of Daumier, was that the bourgeoisie had appropriated the nobility's standing without managing to master the elegance of its style. In a sense, the greatest sin of a Frenchman was not to be stupid or greedy but to lack finesse, to be ridiculous. And whatever you said about the inhabitants of châteaux, about those who had the particle *de* standing like a heraldic coat of arms in the middle of their names, no matter how much you chastised them for emblemizing reaction, absolutism, and obsolescence, the one thing you could not accuse them of was a lack of finesse.

The aristocracy is so absent from public life in France that it is surprising there are something between 3,500 and 4,000 "noble" families still in the country, including one prince, 40 dukes, 146 marquises, 194 counts, 37 viscounts, and 406 barons. There are also a large number of families falsely claiming aristocratic descent. The confusion may come, in part, because the particle *de* is often taken to indicate an aristocratic lineage, when in fact, before the revolution of 1789, it could also be used by commoners who owned certain lands. In any case, many from both categories, the true nobles and the false nobles, seem to be doing quite well, thank you, give or take a few instances of *la noblesse désargentée*, "the impoverished nobility," occupying with desperate pride an underheated corner of the patrimonial estate. To be an aristocrat meant, when there were, juridically speaking, aristocrats rather than people with aristocratic names, that you served the king, bore arms, did not go into commerce, and, most important, were granted a title of nobility by the monarch or, after the Revolution, by Napoleon (who betrayed the Revolution in this sense by creating 2,130 titles) or one of the restored kings, Louis XVIII, Charles X, Louis-Philippe, or Napoleon III, who together created about as many nobles as Napoleon did.

Aristocratic privileges were abolished in 1789, when the Declaration of the Rights of Man and Citizen determined that there should be no distinctions based on birth. The Constitution of 1958, establishing the current Fifth Republic, has a similar provision banning noble privileges, and while these privileges were restored at various times in the nineteenth century, today if you rent out land to a tenant farmer you no longer have the right to ride your horses through his fields while you hunt, even if your great-great-great-grandfather was a marquis and took *le droit de chasse*, hunting rights on his tenants' lands, as a matter of course.

Theoretically, in fact, any person in France today can call himself a count or a marquis or a duke or a prince. There is no law against it, just as there is no legal standing conferred by being a count, a marquis, a duke, or a prince, even though, if you go to a charity ball, perhaps a glittering dinner in one of the great halls of the palace of Versailles, the elegantly printed guest list will veritably teem with such titles. The master of ceremonies will fawn over dukes and countesses. If an event—say, a huge formal party to celebrate the Burgundy harvest—is held under what is called "the patronage" of the princesse Napoleon, this royal personage will be referred to as *son altesse*, "her highness," and treated with the utmost respect by the multitude unfortunate enough to have been born common.

So obviously, even if the nobility is a thing of the past, noble titles continue to have a certain usefulness. Holders of the *particule*, people who have inherited a château someplace in the countryside, even if they often do not brandish an aristocratic title by having it printed on their calling cards or emblazoned on the pages of the *Bottin Mondain*, France's social register, are quick to admit that the little *de* does carry with it certain advantages. It sounds elegant; it opens doors; it makes a good initial impression; it is something of a head start to be called Jean-Baptiste de Vaison-la-Romaine rather than Jacques Martin or, perhaps, Jacques Hussein, though the head start is far from decisive. Despite it, Martin and Hussein might well end up far ahead of de Vaison-la-Romaine in the ultimate professional and even social competition.

The most celebrated illustration in recent years of aristocratic allure, or, more accurately, the striving for aristocratic status, concerns the case of Valéry Giscard d'Estaing, the former president of France, whose particle is known to have been an artifice, arising out of either snobbery or a cold, calculated desire to add some luster to his name in the service of political ambition. The various, generally snickering, press accounts of this issue, most of them apparently based on a solidly researched book called *The Saga of the Giscards*, written by one Pol Bruno, which is pseudonymous, have attributed the initial drive for a noble moniker to René Giscard, an uncle of V.G.E., as the former president is called, who, presumably, believed that René Giscard de Fromage de Chèvre, or something along those lines, would sound better than plain old René Giscard. The Giscard family after all was wealthy and successful; its various members came from the Republic's best schools and served in its most prestigious posts. Why not a particle and what the French call a *terre d'apanage*—a noble estate, a fief? The quest for these adornments to a fine name follows a standard procedure. The seekers of noble titles attempt to locate and revive some name fallen into disuse, its onetime holders having all died out, in the way one might find an abandoned castle deep in the countryside and simply take it over. René Giscard, or so the accounts go, first toyed with de la Tour-Fondue, which would have made him René Giscard de la Tour-Fondue, but unfortunately, an obscure but genuine claimant to that name raised objections, forcing René to abandon his manufactured claim. René then discovered d'Estaing, the last holder of which name, an admiral who had fought with French forces against Britain during the American Revolution, had died in 1794 (he was guillotined). Uncle René in 1923 obtained from the State Council, which has jurisdiction in such matters—and of which he was a member in good standing—the right to add d'Estaing to his existing name.

Giscard d'Estaing, as president and ex-president, has taken a terrific beating in the form of Parisian mockery for this quest for aristocratic status, which was seen as an example of the highest form of snobbery and social-climbing pretension. This shows that not everybody is impressed by noble titles. A clever little pun was applied to the newly minted d'Estaing—Valéry Giscard de Puispeu, he was called, Valéry Giscard of Since-a-Short-Time-Ago. But that did not stop Valéry Giscard d'Estaing from continuing to try to add luster to his name. He claimed on his grandmother's side descendance from King Louis XV, on the grounds that one of his female ancestors was a chambermaid who bore the monarch an illegitimate child. When Giscard d'Estaing, as president, created something of a cult of Louis XV, the Parisian manufacturers of clever insults came up with a new name for the republican president, Sa Sufficance, His Sufficiency, a not so sly reference to his tendency to spend a degree of the Republic's funds on semi-imperial trappings—a habit that may have contributed to his loss of the presidential election in 1981 to the entirely unparticled Socialist Mitterrand. Undeterred, Giscard tried to gain admittance into the very exclusive Société de Cincinnati, an odd organization of people in France that contains 297 hereditary members, who all claim descent from French officers who fought in the American War of Independence. Giscard, trying to establish his credentials for membership, presented his ostensible ancestor the admiral d'Estaing to no avail.

I once talked with Marcel Chereil de la Rivière, descended from an aristocratic family in Brittany, who publishes an unabashedly pro-monarchist quarterly newspaper called *France Monarchiste et Légitimiste*, and the subject of Giscard d'Estaing came up. He said that the ex-president had applied for membership in the Association de la Noblesse Française, a group that, among other things, determines whether a claimed noble lineage is a valid one, thereby decreeing who is a real aristocrat and who is a false one. The president of the French Republic was turned down, de la Rivière proudly said, on the grounds that his claimed lineage was false. He went on to say that the Société de Cincinnati made a similar decision for similar reasons. Giscard just didn't have the right color in his blood. Birth has, after all, to count for something in some things, even in a democracy. You might, by dint of effort, talent, and ambition, become president of the Republic, but genuine nobility cannot be acquired.

De la Rivière, it should perhaps be added, was by no means an imperious, fusty old marquis speaking in the imperfect of the subjunctive. He seemed, particularly for a man with unabashedly reactionary ideas, rather gentle and unpretentious, a retired insurance company executive with some quirky political notions, including, among others less innocuous and anodyne, a love of the old royalist authoritativeness and a sentiment in favor of heraldic insignia. Not all members of the nobility are monarchists; very likely only a small percentage of them are anything but good republicans. And even M. de la Rivière, while assuredly not a republican, not even an advocate of constitutional monarchy but, on the contrary, a firm proponent of a king who rules, believes that the restoration of the monarchy can only come about in France because the mass of the people want it. "To think otherwise would not be realistic," he said. I met M. de la Rivière in the modest office on the rue de Rome where *France Monarchiste et Légitimiste* is edited. A poster on the wall carried the slogan: *Aujourd'hui l'Anarchie; Demain la Monarchie*—Anarchy today; Monarchy tomorrow. A front-page editorial contained a photograph of a very handsome, dark-eyed young man of about ten, named Louis de Bourbon, "the gentle dauphin of France," the son of Alphonse de Bourbon, the duc d'Anjou, who is de la Rivière's preferred de jure, though not de facto, king. "Yes, My Lord," the editorial reads, "on two knees, I ask you to instruct yourself, to nourish your spirit, your soul, and your heart . . . you will have to understand, to judge, to inspire, to decide, to defend, even at the peril of your life."

The fact that since the monarchy was first abolished in 1792—Louis XVI was guillotined in January 1793, proclaiming his innocence to the large crowd assembled in today's Place de la Concorde—there have been two monarchical restorations plus two Napoleons lends credibility to de la Rivière's argument that the monarchist idea is not yet dead. In fact, it is. The small bands of monarchist nostalgics, often allied to the fundamentalist Catholic Church, reflect only that no idea or preference ever really dies out completely in France. Their organized existence, and even a certain support they have from members of the fundamentalist church, does not mean that the monarchists have significant appeal, or that there will ever again be a king on the French throne. Nonetheless, out of curiosity and for the record, I asked de la Rivière why he was a monarchist. Didn't he think that in France it was an obsolete notion? What good would it do to have a king, and a genuine king with real powers, more than a century after the last royalist figure—an "emperor," as Louis-Napoleon was called—was overthrown? He gave two reasons. First, he said, it would recover the "ethics and culture" frittered away by the decadent Republic. Second, it would put an end to all of the parliamentary bickering that saps the national energy and makes policies unstable, the whims of a paralyzing sectarianism. De la Rivière himself at the time of the interview favored Alphonse de Bourbon, who is a cousin of King Juan Carlos of Spain, as the legitimate pretender—"the rightful king," he calls him, not liking the term pretender.

But Alphonse died in a skiing accident in Colorado in early 1989 (oddly, spookily, he was "guillotined" when he ran into a low-hanging wire that nearly severed his head), leaving the aforementioned ten-year-old Louis as his heir. In any case, he was not the only pretender. The more widely known one is Henri Robert Ferdinand Marie Louis-Philippe d'Orléans, otherwise known as the count of Paris, a courtly octogenarian who, in fact, spent much of his life outside France, the Republic having banned from 1886 to 1950 all direct descendants of the last king, Charles X, from living in France. I once interviewed the count of Paris at the Ritz Hotel and found him, during our half hour together, to be courteous, even modest, more like a retired insurance company executive than the heir to the scepter of the Sun King, Louis XIV himself. I was writing a story on the first millennium of the French monarchy, Hugues Capet, the first generally recognized king of France, having come to the throne in 987. Perhaps because of the arrival of the millennium, there seemed to be a revival of interest in the monarchy in France, at least as a subject of public curiosity and scholarly inquiry. A few books had been published, including a new one by the would-be Henri VI, in which he made his argument for a constitutional monarchy along the lines of Britain's, one that would give what he believed to be a much needed symbolic focus to the French nation, which was currently, in his opinion, painfully bereft of one.

The count of Paris represents the Orleanist branch of the French royal family, and out of ignorance, I failed in my article to mention the Bourbon branch, represented at the time by Alphonse de Bourbon. Within a few days, I received a most polite, good-humored four-page letter, written in excellent English, from a Daniel Hamiche, who described himself as "accredited to His Excellency the duke of Anjou," meaning Alphonse de Bourbon. He argued that the count of Paris was, contrary to the widespread misconception, not at all first in line to the throne. Complicated genealogical charts were included in the envelope, showing that this pretender was descended from the line of Louis XIV's younger brother, while Alphonse de Bourbon's line went directly to the Sun King himself, via Louis XIV's grandson, Philippe, who became King Philippe V of Spain. Easily lost in the charts and the complicated rules of succession, I couldn't figure out the important question of who was the rightful pretender. Finally, however, Henri-François de Breteuil, another aristocratic scion, who owns a beautiful château outside Paris and who, educated at Georgetown University Law School, is a modern, secular individual inclined to look askance at the whole pretender business, explained to me the basic issue. The Bourbons were disqualified from the throne in the early eighteenth century, when, as part of the settlement of the War of the Spanish Succession, it was decided that nobody who had a claim on the Spanish throne could occupy the French one. That determined that the French king had to be an Orléan, not a Bourbon. Recently, however, the duc d'Anjou, the Bourbon pretender, had generously renounced the Spanish throne—occupied, in any case, by his cousin Juan Carlos—thus making him eligible for the French one.

It is fair to say that not many of the French follow this sort of thing too closely. The one thing that France seems safe from these days is another king on the throne. Meanwhile, the monarchists, even rather courtly, affable monarchists like M. de la Rivière, seem to associate themselves with some rather far-right views. They tend to be Catholic fundamentalists. They thus are followers of Archbishop Lefevre, the leader of the fundamentalist movement in France, who ordains his own priests and runs churches where the ancient rites are observed. *France Monarchiste et Légitimiste* speaks in alarmed tones of the large numbers of non-European and non-Christian immigrants coming into France these days, an alarm that seems to align them with the National Front party of Le Pen, about whom the publication has rather kind words. They are angrily anti-Revolutionary; de la Rivière's newspaper denounces the events of 1789—the disavowal of the king and even such products as the Declaration of the Rights of Man—as an "explosive cocktail of the fermentation of all the license and disintegration of the national unity and identity." Every year certain members of the nobility gather in a group to celebrate the birthday of Louis XVI. They make pilgrimages to Spain to lay wreaths on Franco's tomb, pointing out in their accounts of this event that Franco not only restored the Spanish monarchy but also made a contribution to the Allied victory in World War II by refusing permission for Germany to cross Spain to take Gibraltar from the British.

In these senses, the conservative monarchist groups take their place alongside other diehard nostalgics in France, such as the veterans' groups who believe the colonial wars in Indochina and Algeria should have been fought to victorious finishes, or those far smaller groups—an old aristocrat here and there among them—who favor outright military dictatorship rather than the current puerile, decadent parliamentary democracy. As indicated above, no idea ever dies out completely in France. But the monarchists are obviously small in number and politically insignificant. The real importance of the aristocracy in France is social and aesthetic. They represent the country's undying attachment to a certain notion of elegance and exclusivity, and the members of the noble families take full advantage of it.

There are still enough families around to be photographed by the glossy magazines inside their castles, decorated with old bluish tapestries and wainscoting and inlaid armoires and silver chandeliers, and thereby credence to the idea of an aristocratic *savoir-vivre*, which remains a kind of social ideal for the French—even if the owners of many of the châteaux rent them out to Japanese tourist groups for banquets or to the sons and daughters of French businessmen for wedding receptions, because without such income-producing ventures, an old château is hard to keep up. The marquis de Breteuil, who gave up his law practice some years ago to run his château outside Paris as a business, has had wax figures made to show what human activity was like in the good old days. He has scenes from his own family, which included a minister to Louis XV; he also has Marcel Proust, looking sickly and lying in bed surrounded by a manuscript of *À la Recherche du Temps Perdu*, since Proust was an occasional visitor to the château in lost time. Entry to the château and its impressive grounds is six dollars a person. It is open 365 days a year. De Breteuil says that he personally greets 80 percent of the visitors. He is president of something called Demeures Historiques—Historic Homes—and publishes a glossy magazine of that name destined for people who own châteaux and manors and are faced with the costs of keeping them up. Indeed, if a family in financial need wants to sell a château, it is very difficult to find a buyer, he said, because upkeep is so expensive. There are some wealthy Americans, Japanese, and Arabs who come into the market from time to time; but you don't get a very high price for your château anymore.

De Breteuil belongs to what might be called the discreet, republican aristocracy. He doesn't use his title. His card carries only his name, giving no indication that, by lineage, he is a marquis. He sums up the political attitude of most aristocrats by saying that even while they are entirely assimilated into the Republic, they are monarchists at heart—that is, monarchists of sentiment, republicans of necessity. De Breteuil acknowledges that, like other aristocrats, he has a particular interest in royal history and artifacts, in family lineages and heirlooms, but it is the same sort of interest that another person might have in old postage stamps or timepieces. He himself follows none of the standard aristocratic pursuits. He does not keep horses on his château, even though the place is equipped with a handsome antique stable. He does not play polo or collect vintage cars or even hunt deer on his three-hundred-acre domain. He does play tennis. He has two daughters and a son, all of whom have attended what the French call *rallyes*, which are high-society coming-out parties by which the children of the aristocratic families learn the social graces and meet one another. "It's a must in aristocratic society," he said.

Indeed, aristocratic society is a remarkable survivor, given the bloody history of France, the country's savage internal wars, during which class and privilege, often allied with the church, fought bitterly against the ideas of democracy, opportunity, and secularism. It was these bitter conflicts that gave rise to the heavy dose of the unreasonable in French history, the sense that the country was irremediably and forever *coupé en deux*, "cut in two." But the ultimate triumph of the Republic, and the fact that the aristocracy no longer poses a real political challenge, has finally tamed both the conflict and the antagonism. France has become like any other country in this regard, a place that adores its "beautiful people" as embellishments, glamorous objects of reverie.

And so the aristocratic society that de Breteuil belongs to, even as he maintains a bit of distance from it, has a certain critical mass in France, its social weight. There are at least three magazines that specialize in reporting on events within the worldly set and on other aspects of the supposedly royal comings and goings—*L'Éventail, Dynastie*, and *Point de Vue et Images du Monde*. The aristocrats are automatically admitted into the most exclusive of the Paris clubs—the Jockey Club (an English imitation that blackballed—the French term is *blackboule*—Giscard d'Estaing while he was president of the country), the Automobile Club, the Tir aux Pigeons (a target-practice and sports club in the Bois de Boulogne), the Cercle Interallié, with its vast lawn and swimming pool, situated right between the American ambassador's residence and the British embassy on the rue du Faubourg Saint-Honoré. Remnants of manorial life abound in France. Small villages where a noble family resides are more than likely to elect one of its members as its mayor, election after election. Even aristocratic families that are not rich go through the ritual year after year of inviting the entire village to a formal reception in the château, however dilapidated it may be, the host and hostess standing in the doorway to greet each guest who arrives.

There is a certain self-help involved in the aristocratic life, embodied in an organization on Paris's rue Richepanse called Association d'Entraide de la Noblesse Française, Mutual Help Association of the French Nobility, which is presided over by Count Jean de Bodinat. Founded in 1932 by the duc de Lévis-Mirepoix, the association was designed "not as the dead museum of defunct privileges and the vanities of another age, but as the conservatory of the real nobility . . . serving as another authority on a subject where ignorance, confusion, and fakery often prevail." Eight scholars in the organization's library research lineages, making certain that claimants indeed have noble blood. But the organization also provides scholarships; it gives unsecured loans; it helps members to rent out their châteaux for the summer; there is even a closet containing ball gowns, wedding dresses, morning coats, and other accessories so that young aristocratic debutantes from *familles désargentées* will be able to attend the *rallyes* that are, as the marquis de Breteuil said, so important in aristocratic society. The purpose, Count Jean de Bodinat told the weekly magazine *L'Événement du Jeudi* in 1986, is to "give moral and material help to our members, and in particular to enable them to raise their children in the service of the country."

What do young aristocrats do for a living? How do they make careers? Given their heritage of serving the country (can it be a coincidence that the expression *noblesse oblige* came to us from the French?), the scions of noble families often go into diplomacy and the military. *L'Événement du Jeudi* reported, in an issue devoted to the aristocracy two hundred years after the Revolution, that fully 40 percent of the posts in the Ministry of External Affairs were held by nobles. Loving uniforms and the "image of an elite founded exclusively on service and merit," they also are well entrenched in the French officer corps. Two thirds of all aristocratic families have at least one member serving as an active officer. Five percent of the students admitted into the École National d'Administration (Éna) are from aristocratic families, which clearly has helped get them in such large proportions into the good posts at the Quai d'Orsay. And indeed, it is often whispered in the corridors of the Quai, one of the bastions of old French conservatism, that it is a clear and undeniable advantage in getting promotions to have the particle in your name. Or is it a coincidence that the present French ambassador to Great Britain is named Luc de la Barre de Nanteuil, while a recent holder of that post in Washington was Emmanuel-Jacquin de Margerie? This observation is not intended as a slight on the merit of these two friendly and solid individuals. Still, it seems clear that the country whose most famous diplomat ever was Charles-Maurice de Talleyrand—who managed to serve as foreign minister to both Napoleon and the post-Napoleonic monarch Louis XVIII—still finds a certain comfort and security in being represented abroad by men perfumed by the noble essence, those who, as Jean de Bodinat once put it, have a certain "poetry to their names."

What does it mean? France is a country of castles. The Socialist president of France governs from one whose main entrance is on the rue du Faubourg Saint-Honoré, and his prime minister administers the state from another on the rue de Varenne, both places of slightly gloomy, just a bit tarnished, Baroque splendor. After many years of experimentation with a government of a strong parliament, hamstrung by party politics, shifting coalitions, repeated elections, the French have finally settled in the Fifth Republic on a government with a powerful president, a head of state who rules more like a king than do any of the other heads of state in the other Western democracies, even when that head of state is a real king. He is a man of genuine, decisive power and influence, but one whose style is to remain aloof, at an Olympian distance from day-to-day affairs. He does not hunt or maintain a private art collection. He is well off but has no immense inherited fortune. Yet there is something of the Sun King in his bearing and in the way the nation expects from him a certain degree of pomp and ceremony. The temptation to think of France as a sort of elective monarchy is strong, irresistible. That is not at all the same thing as a hereditary monarchy or even a constitutional monarchy. But in the country's styles and preferences, the kings are not dead, not yet.

13

Elegance and Anarchy

YOU MIGHT overcome any notion that the French are models of elegance and good taste if you have ever been, say, in Avignon on a Saturday night at midnight and wandered down the boulevard Juan Jaurès between the hoary Place de l'Horloge, where the Palace of the Popes is situated, and the railroad station, just beyond the city's medieval wall. Here is not so much stylishness on parade or even, strictly speaking, bad taste; here is an imitative, sheepish young nihilist's aversion to color, to grooming, to shape. The entirely ungilded youth of Avignon seems to be present, not the kids that go, eventually, to the prestige academies in Paris, some of whom, surely, originate in Avignon, but the more ordinary types, who will work pumping gas or selling used car parts, parading in a hairy, leathery, unkempt, self-conscious sort of antistylishness, which of course is, in its way, as much a style, and a chosen one, even a calculated one, as any other. They congregate in the quick-hamburger joint, in front of the movie theaters, in a few cafés, on a street given over at other times to retail commerce, travel agencies, one of France's best restaurants, flocks of tourists eager to see one of France's prettiest towns, solid burgomasters going about their affairs; on Saturday night, the youths take it over. They are not menacing, these young people, dressed, in some cases, like Darth Vader; they don't intimidate; they mind their own business; but there is such a critical mass of this particular human genre on the streets at a certain hour of night that you wonder if the nice kids who wear tweed jackets and pink shirts, yellow sweaters and blue skirts, ever go out to the movies or cafés in Avignon on Saturday nights.

The Saturday-night crowd struck me—admittedly more comfortable with the tweed than the leather-jacket set—as a bunch of tarnished, bored spirits, a bit undereducated and undermotivated, particularly out of place amid the picturesque, antique refinements of Avignon, whose sycamore-lined avenues, twisting narrow streets, old stone houses, distinguished monuments, charming hotels, good restaurants, and France's most important summer theater festival make it one of the centers of *savoir-vivre* in southern France. I once spent an entire night in the open-air theater inside the Palace of the Popes—built during the thirteenth-century schism in the church—watching a ten-hour performance of *The Satin Slipper* by Paul Claudel, a dreamy, phantasmagorical, otherworldly play if ever there was one. But that was August, when Avignon devotes itself to the arts and to artists and to the significant portion of the Parisian *beau monde* that fills up the hotels and occupies the tables in the outdoor cafés in front of the Baroque city hall. The Saturday night I am talking about here was in late October, when the cool wind known as the mistral rushes up the Rhône, and Avignon is left to its restless natives, in particular the hundreds of young people shifting around the boulevard Juan Jaurès for something to do.

They make a good contrast, given the reputation of their city for elegance, with those who carry France's renown for stylishness and taste. Later on in life, these young people will be among the lumpy, dumpy men of a certain age seen playing cards in the local Café du Commerce or hunched over their games of *pétanque* on some dusty ground beneath the plane trees, helping to give French towns, villages, and even the less heavily commercial parts of cities like Paris two of their more famed features: first, a sense of conviviality, the feeling that life is best lived as a conversation with the other guys about the Formula One race or the soccer match, and second, a high alcohol consumption. The young people on the streets of Avignon, like young people in many other cities these days, tend toward nihilistic black, though not necessarily an inexpensive one. They wear short black leather jackets, black leather or cotton pants, thick-soled heavy black shoes; they often carry shiny black motorcycle helmets and, in the case of the young men, favor some state of partial unshavenness, a mustache, a Yasir Arafat stubble of beard (never a full, trimmed growth but always a careless one, one that just happened, that wasn't planned), accompanied by long, greasy hair. In recent years, as in other parts of the world, single earrings for men, small gold loops sparkling under unkempt locks, have become fashionable, a sole and, I always felt, somewhat forlorn male concession to cosmetic adornment, a little spot of daintiness in an undainty setting.

The stress here is on a defiance of conventional grooming, on any appearance of paying attention, on any sort of trimming, polishing, brushing, or combing, though, of course, the perceptive observer will not fail
to note that the style seen on the boulevard Juan Jaurès is as carefully
constructed, fabricated, designed, calculated, and, ultimately, narcissistic
as any other. It is James Dean or Mick Jagger inside the medieval cren-
ellations of Avignon (even though many members of the throng cannot
afford to dwell *intra-muros* and only come into town on their "motos"
at night from the antiseptic, impersonal *banlieue*, to which they will
return in the wee hours). There is a certain rebel-without-a-cause affectation involved in this style of dress of the young Avignonais, a questing
for a separate identity in a society that bores them even as they refuse
in any concrete way to strike out against it.

And so are the French the globe's avatars of good taste and discrimination? They are a people who pay attention to dress and who spend
a good deal of money on clothing. Go to any recreational spot and you
will see large numbers of people, not particularly wealthy and not necessarily very skilled in the activity in question, but, certainly by comparison with more casual Americans, dressed for the occasion. At the
Gymnase Club on the rue Chazelle, where I went to exercise from time
to time in my tattered sneakers, my college gym shorts, and a well-worn
tennis shirt, I always used to feel a bit outclassed by my fellow exercisers,
who came in color-coordinated sweatsuits, purple with yellow vertical
lines, white with red stripes. Those were the men. The women rode the
bicycle machines and pumped iron in snazzy one-piece suits with black
tights and snug green bottoms easing into a green-and-black top, and
either green sneakers with black shoelaces or black sneakers with green
shoelaces. Or, shifting to another form of athletic recreation, take the
Sunday cyclists touring through rural villages in their very professional
outfits, looking like members of the French Olympic team, or as though
they are about to set out on a segment of the Tour de France bicycle
race, wearing their nylon shorts, their striped polo shirts, their hard,
flat, light, rather expensive narrow shoes. I've been to the shore in France
where catamaraning and wind surfing are the rage; nobody, whether
beginner or expert—except the occasional British or American tourist
—undertakes these activities without first donning his wet suit with
racing stripes, or his yellow slicker with all the hooks and snaps in the
right place. And of course, there are the ski slopes, where the beginners
learning the snowplow come in their five-hundred-dollar mauve-and-
yellow outfits, more prepared to be photographed than to ski. I have

been to French riding stables in otherwise unpretentious Normandy or in the Loire Valley for purely recreational promenades; everybody arrives in jodhpurs and knee-high boots and those stiff black hats with short visors and chin straps that you might see on television during the Olympic equestrian events. The children, little tots of seven or eight learning how to ride, are small versions of the adults, equally equipped with helmets, jodhpurs, boots, even riding crops brought from home.

It could be said, of course, that all Westerners these days are attentive to their recreational duds in this age of serious and ample leisure time —just witness the fashions on the beginners' slopes at Vail or Sun Valley. But we are talking here of matters of degree, of the scrupulousness of the attention paid to the appropriateness of dress; and my belief—based, admittedly, more on subjective impressions than on any scientific survey—is that the French, the holders of a reputation for style, attempt mightily to live up to it. There is a heritage here, one coming down from the feudal, aristocratic past, when, in a society of high degrees of stratification and little social mobility, dress was a sure index of status and position. A nobleman dressed with imperious elegance, as was expected of a nobleman; his tenant farmers humbly and roughly, like tenant farmers; workers appeared in clothing suitable for workers; capitalists dressed in capitalists' garb, as though they were imitating the portraits of themselves in Balzac. It's intriguing that in the Revolution the common people came to be called the san-culottes, those without the breeches worn by upper-class men. Today, to dress properly and in a style expected for the occasion when you are riding your wind surfer or manipulating the pectoral muscle machine at the Gymnase Club is both part of the formal social ritual and an index of status. To appear at the health club as some do in the United States, in a pair of cut-off jeans and ragged sneakers, would suggest an absence of self-definition, an inattention to the semiotics of clothing; it would be as out of place as hanging around the quick-hamburger joint on Avignon's boulevard Juan Jaurès in a tuxedo.

If the French dress with the care of those creating symbols, does it mean that they are somehow instructed from birth to have good taste, to show a discriminating intellect? I don't think so. But for the French, more I suspect than for other Europeans, style is associated with message. Choices are carefully made. Charles de Gaulle, already sixty-seven and embarking on the creation of the new Fifth Republic in 1958, presented himself, elderly but powerful—powerfully conservative, powerfully sure of himself—in his black civilian suit; holding his hands outward in a gesture of appealing frankness, putting due weight on every word, he said: "*Je suis ce que vous voyez*"—"I am what you see."

I ALWAYS used to make a connection among three apparently disparate, unconnected elements of French life, grouping them together by their common concern with style. One is the French adoration of the black leather jacket. Second is the persistence of the pinball machine as a form of recreation. Third is the popularity of the singer Serge Gainsbourg, now a fading, middle-aged man with a cigarette always drooping from his lip and a stiff, live-dangerously whiskey generally close at hand.

The style that joins together these three items—an article of clothing, an industrial artifact, and a well-known individual—is not difficult to discern. The common element is an association with a studious sort of antimodishness similar to that of the young causeless rebels on the boulevard Juan Jaurès. All partake of an antimodernist ethic or association, of a "real man" authenticity. They manifest a repugnance of the ornate, the decorated, the pretty, the adorable, the chic—all of which are highly valued elements of more conventional French style. They represent a sullen and yet, somehow, admirable repudiation of all that is frilly, new, glittery, sleek, and trendy; they are a reaffirmation of the old French attraction to a defiant sort of drabness, a safe and cozy nihilism rooted perhaps in certain tough-guy images from the old days, when men were loners of the sort played by Alain Delon or Jean-Paul Belmondo (in his early films), or, to go back even earlier in cinematic history, of the genre of Louis Jouvet in *Quai des Orfèvres*, Jean Gabin in *Quai des Brumes*.

The guys in the black leather jackets, often with two-day stubbles of the sort sported by certain with-it movie directors and, usually, M. Gainsbourg himself, are to be seen in the dusky corners of neighborhood cafés, where the pinball machine murmurs and glows like a small shrine, a shrine to yesteryear, a bulwark against the new. The shame is that eventually, even hold-out cafés in little towns along the national highways, or in Parisian areas of authentic seediness like the rue Oberkampf or the rue Montmartre, might well succumb to the temptation of higher-tech electronic games. For the time being, however, there is a comforting correlation between the preference for black leather—not the softer, friendlier brown leather of the bourgeois type but forbidding motorcycle-gang black, often with metal studs, suggesting a proletarian origin—and the somewhat sinister, sulky, lugubrious gathering around the pinball machine by the guys with glasses of *pastis* in their hands and cigarettes drooping from the corners of their mouths. Gainsbourg, or the stylistic message of Gainsbourg, comes into the picture as a model, an illustration of the philosophy of the genre.

The important thing, since we are asking a question here about the French as the arbiters of taste and fashion, is that, taken together, all three of these items are elements in a clearly defined and very French preoccupation with style, the notion that fashion determines not only social position but a certain worldview, an outlook, an attitude toward society. In this case, it is a pose of hard-bitten cynicism, a pretense of repudiating the conventions of politesse, of the lusting for money and comfort, of reverence for God, country, and phony sociability. One of Gainsbourg's most controversial musical successes was an antipatriotic rendition of the "Marseillaise," which he sang in concert and recorded in the 1970s. It was the national anthem sung with a sneer, sung to stress the ultimate hollowness not only of patriotic symbols but of all attempts at significant association, at the delusion of belonging to anything larger than the basic, instinctual self, and it was, significantly, sung by a man who looked the part, whose very appearance was a calculated act of indifference to the decent opinion of mankind.

Gainsbourg's "Marseillaise" outraged many, delighted many others. Its appeal, for those to whom it appealed, lay, of course, in the very outrage it inspired in those who found it offensive. There is something very close to the French soul in this nihilism of style. Lying beneath the smooth surface of more conventional French stylishness, the stylishness of international fame and big business, whose centerpieces are on the avenue Montaigne and the rue du Faubourg Saint-Honoré and in the big tents set up in the Tuileries for the spectacular semiannual fashion shows, is this leather-jacketed Gainsbourgian snicker, this reminder of contempt.

The French, including those who make fortunes from the country's reputation for trendsetting tastefulness, love it—hence the success of Gainsbourg and others who cultivate the same image. Once, the singer was invited to present one of the awards at the televised French "César" night, the rather precisely copied equivalent to the American Academy Awards, identical right down to the creation of that moment of suspense when an actor and an actress stand before the cameras, open a sealed envelope, and cheerfully announce the winner. Gainsbourg, unshaven as usual, shuffled up to the podium, seeming to slump, to droop, like an unwatered houseplant, in front of the camera; then, slowly, he took a cigarette out of his pocket, put it between his lips, slowly extracted a lighter, lit his cigarette, inhaled deeply, and blew out smoke, all of this performed with the deliberation of a man alone, bored, with nothing else to do, conveying an Olympian indifference to the impatience of the live audience, which chuckled knowingly at this minor insult to itself, and to the millions of *téléspectateurs*, as the French call those looking on at home. Finally, he glanced outward as if to say: "Oh, have you been waiting for me?" On the boulevard Juan Jaurès, I would imagine, the performance won applause.

N O, T H E French are not always very stylish, but dress is an insignia, a statement, conscious or not. Nothing so marks the elderly man dwelling in a little village, a one-belfry town, so much as his soft, short-brimmed cap and his dark suit jacket worn with dark trousers, more often than not from a different suit. The town's stout women are in flowered housedresses, with black sweaters, pullovers or cardigans, and carrying capacious straw baskets for their rounds of the butcher, the baker, and the greengrocer. Around the red belt of Paris—so called because of a now weakening but earlier robust affiliation with the Communist party—class status is broadcast by the creased blue work shirts and overalls, the round-neck sweaters and the cotton windbreakers, that the men wear not only to the factory but to the café bar afterward. At the Parisian elite academies like the École Nationale d'Administration, we are back to tweeds and cashmere sweaters of the BCBG type.

The bourgeois, too, display several distinctive and distinguishing styles, but here there are gradations. A degree of gentle rebelliousness against convention, partaking modestly of the spirit of Gainsbourg, is seen in the determined tielessness of many intellectuals, generally younger ones, who are apparently trying, whether consciously or not, to set themselves off from the more readily identifiable modes of their elders. In a sense, the great antibourgeois war, waged by members of the bourgeoisie who dislike the category, has been reduced to this. Turn on any of the prime-time television discussion programs—those living exemplars of the French avidity for verbal exchange, serious public conversation taking place at a level of sophistication and articulateness rarely seen in the American media—and there will be two types of clothing, particularly among men; the tied and the tieless. Some guests will be dressed in immaculate banker grays or academic tweeds, with ties. Those without ties, showing their freedom from bourgeois convention, wear old sweaters and corduroy pants, or perhaps velour jackets and open collars, sometimes heavy leather jackets and sunglasses, even an occasional man's earring. The tied guests will wear tortoiseshell glasses and hair slightly oiled and combed straight back. The tieless ones are more varied, with hair to the shoulders, in ponytails, or falling in heavy curls over the forehead. The bohemian dress style peacefully, cozily coexists alongside conventional garb, but it proclaims something different. It is an audacity, a desire to flout and to be seen to flout the conventional.

I once asked the novelist-philosopher, Bernard-Henri Lévy, pioneer of the new tielessness, why he chose that style of dress. Lévy, it should be added, has a couple of dress styles. One is a white shirt covered by a crew-neck sweater. I have seen him dress that way at the best parties and television shows. He made a point of telling me that he has been received by two presidents of the French Republic dressed that way. The other style, the one he is often photographed in, consists of the white shirt coyly opened to the lower part of the chest. At first Lévy did not philosophize on my question, claiming that he dressed like that because he was comfortable. "I don't like to be cinched or corseted," he said. Then he admitted: "Not wearing a tie reflects something of the way I function intellectually. It is an exterior and derisory sign of my liberty, derisory because there are more important ways for me to show my liberty." His dressing style was then, consciously, an amalgam of outlook and appearance.

The same could be said of the opposite end of the sartorial spectrum in France, represented by the standard uniform of the members of the French Academy, a self-perpetuating group that is supposedly the literary elite. The Academy's forty members meet in an antique domed chamber, each of them wearing a white tie, a sword, and a long black coat embroidered in green or yellow silk. Lévy, by contrast, as one of the so-called new philosophers—along with André Glucksmann, another writer rarely seen in a tie—values a casualness of dress that is a living reproof to the formality of the establishment, whether represented by the Academy or by some other traditional organization, such as the Communist party. In France, the old-left stalwarts dress in respectable suits or jackets and ties, as do the members of the Soviet politburo. The new philosophers, like Lévy, appear tieless, and so does the new bourgeoisie.

T HE FRENCH, then, do not really have better taste than the rest of us; they are guided by the same historical models, the same need to signal personal identity by outward appearance. Whence, then, comes the French reputation for connoisseurship—an anglicized version of a French word, after all—in dress as well as in various nonsartorial areas of life, in food and scents, in what might be called, using, significantly, another French term, *savoir-vivre*? Much of this, like the dim living rooms of wealthy government ministers, is a heritage of the aristocratic past, furthered by pure commercial hype. The nobility knew how to live in France, its privileged members surrounding themselves with a gorgeous sensuality and a refinement of manners that showed France's favored geographical position between the Atlantic and the Mediterranean. It was the royalty in France that demanded finery, silks from Lyon, perfumes from Grasse, wines from Bordeaux, and variations on the complicated, highly developed cuisine that came originally from Italy. When the revolution of 1789 dislodged the nobility and confirmed the already growing power of the bourgeoisie, the alleged aristocratic refinement of France became part of the business trademark.

By now there is little doubt. The French do not have worse taste than anybody else. And, thanks to general prosperity and the heritage of Catherine de Médicis's cooks, they eat well, usually. But is their taste any better than anyone else's? The proliferation and success of McDonald's and its local imitators in Paris and elsewhere indicates that the French do not feed only on haute cuisine. They love the industrial hamburgers that come from America; they adore, too, the dungarees that come from there. They shop for clothes in stores with names like Old England and Westons, French establishments that, in imitating a British retailing style, paid the highest of compliments to the "taste" of their neighbors across the Channel, the compliment of emulation.

Paris, that crown in the world's urban jewel, seems to have lost its aesthetic sensibilities in recent years. Modern projects like the Montparnasse Tower, the Forum des Halles, the row of high-rise hotels and apartment houses along the Seine in the Fifteenth Arrondissement—looking like nothing so much as vast sheets of Christmas wrapping paper stretched over huge steel frames—have desecrated the town, while showing that the French are as capable as anybody else of vulgarity. Look at the Champs-Élysées these days, once a broad avenue lined with the mansions of the wealthy. It has become a haven for the Parisian version of the unkempt crowd seen in Avignon; they ride the fast trains in from the suburbs and hang around the crass shopping malls and even crasser fast-food places that now crowd each other along the once-fabulous avenue, jostling for space with the movie theaters.

And speaking of vulgarity, is there anything more lacking in taste than a poorly mastered aristocratic manner, an ill-educated imitation of refinement? If there are in France, and especially in Paris, some of the best-dressed women in the world, there are plenty of pathetic failed attempts as well, marked by the ultimate vulgarity of gaudy, bejeweled, and heavily powdered self-satisfaction of the sort to be found in the lobby of the Hôtel Georges V or the nightclub Maxim's at night. I am thinking of the fat society dame surrounded by her things, her small dog with its hair tied up in a ribbon, and her pretensions, a modern-day Mme Verdurin, one of Proust's greatest creations, wearing expensive fashions, conspicuously platinumed hair, and skin, exposed by a grotesque, indelicate, sexless décolletage, rendered copper by her local tanning studio. This is France too, this deformation of good taste. The young people on the boulevard Juan Jaurès are stunning by contrast.

14

A Contentious Solidarity

A SCENE on the streets of Paris: At the busy intersection of the rue du Colisée and the rue du Faubourg Saint-Honoré, one of Paris's busiest commercial districts, the traffic police have begun the sad task of towing a car, when the owner runs out from a nearby building and tries to stop them. The man, portly and middle-aged, plaintively contends that he had only stopped for five minutes or so. He points to the fact that in the car's back seat is a German shepherd, as if to say that a car with a dog in the back cannot be towed away no matter what the parking infraction. He pleads long and loud and with much body language to be allowed to drive away, his palms held outward in furious supplication, a look of amazement in confrontation with stupidity on his face.

The police are unsympathetic. They have heard this before. Besides, they have their orders. To combat the epidemic of illegal parking in Paris, headquarters has devised a new blitzkrieg approach, arriving on the scene with three or four or even five tow trucks at once and swooping away that many violating automobiles within a few minutes, before word can spread through the streets that *les flics*, the cops, have arrived. I always felt, even at the risk of losing my own car to *la fourrière*, as the place where towed cars are taken is called, that it was an appropriate response by the forces of order to an intolerable situation. Parking in France is another part of the R5 complex. The French put their cars wherever they will fit—on traffic circles, doubled up next to legally parked cars, on sidewalks, on median dividers, on pedestrian islands, straddling the white line in the middle of an avenue, in bus stops, in taxi and bus lanes. The only things they will not do, as a rule, is knowingly to block traffic and to park in front of driveways. And so, as part of the general effort to govern a people widely rumored to be nearly ungovernable, the police had declared war—unsparing, total war—on illegal parking. The gendarmes working the intersection of Colisée and Faubourg Saint-Honoré were not going to be stopped because a German shepherd was occupying a back seat.

A sidewalk spectator, a rare sympathizer with the traffic police, offers the skeptical opinion that the owner of the car travels with his German shepherd as a ruse, believing that the police will decline to tow a car with a live animal in it. In fact, as it turns out, they are ready to tow the damned thing with a human being in it. Having lost his argument, the portly owner defiantly gets into his car, plants himself behind the steering wheel, and dares the police to take car, dog, and himself all together to the violators' garage. The police, no doubt having seen this tactic before, proceed to put the heavy cloth straps around the car, a kind of sling by which, in the clever French towing technology, it can then be hoisted up and onto the flatbed of the tow truck. Just before the car is raised onto the truck, the car owner, not wanting to be trapped inside, gives up. His bluff has been called. He manages to open the door just enough to squeeze out, though he leaves his dog behind. The incident seems to be over. The forces of order have triumphed. At just that point, however, a deus ex machina intervenes, and the situation suddenly gets serious.

It is in the form of a kind of Mme Defarge—named here for Dickens's revolutionary matron in *A Tale of Two Cities*—who emerges from the gathered crowd of spectators to challenge the police. He was only there for five minutes, she says to the surprised cops and to the several dozen onlookers, who seem, with some variations of opinion, generally sympathetic to the car and dog owner. You can't tow away a guy who has only been there five minutes, and with a dog in the car, no less, she says. What kind of behavior is that? Don't we have rights in this country? The woman is fiftyish, large, not particularly stylish, a redhead holding a big purse. To the general amusement, she sits down in front of the tow truck in an act of civil disobedience borrowed from Martin Luther King, Jr., and defies the police to run her over.

Not to be outdone, another Dickensian figure, heretofore unseen, makes his presence known. He steps out of the crowd and in front of the tow truck, gesturing to the onlookers to follow his example. And they do. Suddenly, the incident has taken on the aspects of a popular uprising, a spontaneous rebellion against the symbols of authority, a selfless, angry defense against a small person confronted with the awesome power of the state. The police do not know what to do. Obviously, force is out of the question; so, too, is yielding to the demands of the mob, who, in any case, have chosen a dubious issue on which to make their stand. The problem is that traffic is beginning to back up on the rue du Faubourg Saint-Honoré; horns are being honked; an entire quarter of Paris is being paralyzed by a fat man with an R5 and a German shepherd.

Needless to say, the incident did not become the opening blow in a new revolution, a mob uprising, an effort to sack the National Assembly or the headquarters of the police—though these sorts of incidents have happened numerous times in earlier, less harmonious periods of French history. Just down the street in the Place de la Concorde, there once gathered the notorious right-wing mobs that stormed the National Assembly in 1934. But this time the crowd, many of whom were probably getting hungry, eventually chose not to sacrifice themselves for the sake of an illegal parker. A small number of police reinforcements arrived. The woman instigator was gently lifted from the scene and stood on her feet on the sidewalk. The man was persuaded to remove his dog from the car, which was duly taken away and, no doubt, redeemed by its owner a few hours later, upon payment of about a hundred-dollar fine.

It could have happened anywhere, this small and, ultimately, amusing confrontation. But because it happened in France, the temptation is to use it as a starting point to examine one of the oldest and most cherished aspects of the French self-conception, and the image of them held by others—namely, that they are contentious and quarrelsome, that they inhabit a country of class war and civil conflicts, which, in turn, echo something significant and deep in their nature, the indelible historical flaws but also the admirable collective passion of a people.

The French do love to argue. And they have plenty to argue about. In French political life, there is almost never a spoken, explicit consensus. Every issue provokes a debate, waged in angry and often eloquent language and riddled with historical memory and references to the past. I have witnessed bitter quarrels in academic life that take on a dimension certainly unusual where I come from. A friend of mine once had postcards printed up of a former professor of his with whom he had broken, both personally and intellectually. On one side was a not very flattering photograph of the unfortunate professor. On the other side was a biting, sarcastic text, in the form of a parody of the usual tourist postcard, identifying the individual and his crime—mainly that he was a monument to Stalinism within the university. They were scattered around Paris by the thousands, these postcards.

Once, in academe, I witnessed a discussion in the lobby of a building in a southern university between two professors who disagreed over whether a particular student should be allowed to formally defend a controversial thesis that he had written in pursuit of his diploma. The conversation ended as a shouting match, or, more properly, with one professor shouting repeatedly to the other: "You are abject, abject, abject," and the other saying, also repeatedly, "You have lost your sangfroid, sir, and that's very bad"—all this while students and other faculty members were looking on. When, finally, the professor accused of being abject had left, the one who had lost his sangfroid availed himself of a favorite French image. "If somebody is giving it to you in the ass, are you supposed to hold your behind up to him to make it easier?"

And yet the question remains. Are the French today a contentious and quarrelsome people? My theory is that behind the smoke screen of angry debate and exchanges, the clever repartee, the slash and parry of verbal conflict, the bursts of anger at authority, behind the attitudes that de Gaulle complained produced an ungovernable people, behind all that lies another concept, born of the aftermath of the Revolution, which counterbalances the love of a certain controlled acrimony. The concept is called "solidarity." It actually exists. And so there is a paradox here. The French do adore to think that issues carry within them great significance, that they should, almost by definition, engender bitter battles. They are accustomed to such issues as urban uprisings, decolonization, collaborationism, and resistance, and it is the memory of these seminal questions that seems, in combination with a love for verbal jousting, to fuel the mental violence in French life, a capacity to transform a cartowing incident into a confrontation with the symbols of power and authority. At the same time, there is a ritualistic aspect to this. It conceals a soft, sweet core lying just beneath the briny surface of contention.

I'VE OFTEN been struck in some examples of French culture by the existence of a cruelty, an appreciation of an understated sort of sadism, which occurs particularly in films. The French hate (and with good reason) the blatant sort of scowling violence exemplified in American culture by, to take an example current at this writing, the *Rambo* movies (although all the *Rambo* films played in France with commercial success, it would be hard to imagine a character like that being portrayed in a French-made movie). In France, the violence is less physical and certainly less cathartic than it is in the American versions. In 1988, a film called *Un Drôle d'Endroit pour une Rencontre* (A Funny Place for a Meeting), with Gérard Depardieu and Catherine Deneuve, the country's biggest male and female stars, played to critical success in France. It's the story of a woman, played by Deneuve, kicked out of her car at night by her husband at a superhighway rest area, where she meets the character played by Depardieu. He first tries to persuade her to leave; then he falls in love with her, a feeling that she at first encourages and then repudiates. At one point, a group of truck drivers appears on the scene. One of them seduces Deneuve, and she accepts his overtures in the very face of Depardieu, who is, literally and figuratively, shut out. As the truck driver and Deneuve climb into the spacious cab of the tractor-trailer and the driver pulls a privacy curtain in front of the windshield, Depardieu is sitting in his car just in front of them, reduced to honking his horn in impotent fury and jealousy. The next morning, the cold cruelty involved in the human connection takes a new turn. We see the truck driver in the café, getting his breakfast tray. Deneuve appears with hers. The driver, having no further use for her, ignores her entirely, treating her like the whore she has become, so that she has no choice but to sit at a table by herself. The result is that all three are left unhappily or happily alone after the agonies and pleasures of the night.

French films of the 1980s often display this coldness, this metaphorical presentation of the impossibility of consoling human contact, as though the filmmakers are striving to realize Jean-Paul Sartre's famous formulation: "Hell is other people." I don't think these cinematic portrayals have much to do with real life, where the French are no more or less emotive in their relations than other people, no more or less isolated from emotional contact. Yet lurking in these movies is some sense, ultimately, that the Other is to be distrusted, is a potential enemy, cannot be relied upon; that there is, in the relations of human beings, a repressed reptilian savagery, an underlying meanness of spirit, even if that meanness is bathed in the ointments of cultivated behavior. *Les Liaisons Dangereuses*, which, after all, was written by a Frenchman in the eighteenth century (even if made into modern-day plays and movies by Britons and Americans), is an extreme statement of cynicism in human relations, the idea that love is a form of insanity that can be manipulated for sadistic advantage over others.

In a similar vein, the French often talk of their humor as being of the destructive, sometimes not very funny kind, and this, too, seems to illustrate the collective anger simmering just beneath the surface. Humor, of course, comes in many forms in France, much of it relying on cleverness, on intricate, even erudite wordplay, for its effect. But there are, broadly speaking, two basic kinds of satiric humor—that is, a humor based not on an intrinsic playfulness but on the existence of a target for ridicule or parody. One is inner-directed; it aims its barbs at oneself; the humorist is his own target. The other, the French kind, targets others; it attacks the imbecilities of people around the humorist but not those of the humorist himself. It is plainly aggressive, a humor that erupts well beyond the border of plain hostility. It is a humor of mockery, disdain, absurdity, exaggeration.

For several years, until he died in a motorcycle accident in 1987, the biggest French comedian was Michel Colucci, who went by the single name Coluche. He was Rabelaisian, coarse, intentionally vulgar, overweight, outrageous, often clothed in costumes of a bizarre extravagance that were parodies of parodies—as a fat, out-of-shape Tarzan, or a devil in a red costume with a tail, or a stupid platinum-blond society dame, or a news anchorman who suddenly issues a jungle cry and leaps across his desk after some imaginary prey. Coluche was, for several years, perhaps the most recognizable single living person in the country, or, if not first, second after the president of the Republic. *Le Monde* once called him Saint Colucci; *Liberation* said he was "public entertainer number one." "Coluche Uber Alles" was the headline of another newspaper story. He was interviewed on the serious programs on the serious subjects—racism, immigration, the nationality law. As he put it himself, he wanted to be "a pain in the ass to just about everybody." His target was what he saw as the smallness, the narrowness, the meanness of the French xenophobic spirit. He attacked racial and ethnic prejudice with the raucous instruments of ridicule and exaggeration. In one sketch, for example, he was a timid Arab immigrant approaching a policeman to ask directions to the police station so he can replace lost identity papers. The policeman is grotesque, arrogant, bigoted, swelled with self-importance. He imperiously demands the very papers that the immigrant says have been lost, thereby demonstrating his cruel and arbitrary power over him. Once, Coluche showed film clips of Prince Charles of England giving a speech and used a voice-over technique to make the speech bawdy, tasteless, and pornographic. Derision was the key to Coluche's often cruel humor, a stinging, remorseless contemptuousness for the symbols of authority.

He was enormously popular. He had a daily fifteen-minute television show, which was watched religiously by people who apparently got vicarious pleasure from the blunt instrument of satire he wielded. I once visited Coluche in his hotel room in Cannes during the annual film festival there. He received me cordially and warmly, but I was nonetheless disconcerted during the conversation, because heavy-set, hairy Coluche appeared at his door dressed for a performance that was to follow our appointment—in a frilly, gauzy bonnet and oversize woman's lingerie. I asked him how much of his daily television routine was ad lib. His answer: None of it. Every word, every gesture, was planned and rehearsed. Nothing was left to accident. His was an entirely premeditated derision, a derision built on a sort of fury arising from the frustrations of life.

The clearest expression of this humor on the stage came in the phenomenon of Thierry Le Luron, a young comedian who had an uncanny knack for caricature and imitation of virtually all the major national figures, teasing them, mocking them mercilessly. Le Luron's greatest invention, however, was a certain Adolph-Benito Glandu, a far-right bigot full of stupidity and rancor, who, supposedly, stood for all the parochialism, the narrow-mindedness, and the general stupidity of a certain type of Frenchman, one in less bloated form still recognizable. Le Luron in style was very different from Coluche, the latter being fat and cultivating a certain physical ugliness, the former being slim, handsome, and elegant. But Le Luron's jokes and parodies seethed, they boiled over; this was humor as sharp as a needle. The French adored him.

When he died late in 1987—the cause of death was officially announced as intestinal cancer, but it was widely assumed that the real disease had been AIDS—women cried in the streets, and the television news programs were given over to retrospectives and discussions of the deceased. Almost every major political figure in the country, including most of those who had been savagely lampooned by him, issued sanctimonious statements mourning the death of one whom, in less charitable moods, they had probably often wished dead. Actually, it had become a left-handed honor to be lampooned by Le Luron, a sign of status in what one French journalist, *Libération*'s Serge July, called "the tragi-comedy of power." A writer in *Le Monde*, ruing the "unfurling of superfluous messages and excessive sorrows" that came in the wake of Le Luron's death, half-seriously suggested that perhaps the comedian should be buried in the Panthéon, next to the likes of Voltaire (whose Candide was a precursor of Le Luron's scalpel satire), Victor Hugo, and Émile Zola. He was buried in Brittany, not the Panthéon, but he lay in state at the vast Madeleine Church in Paris, where thousands filed past the catafalque, paying their last respects, as if the dead man had indeed been not a nightclub comedian but a social critic of the historic stature of a Voltaire, a Hugo, or a Zola. Le Luron's death had produced such an outpouring of grief because he, along with Coluche, had broken down many of the barriers of the previously unacceptable. In reverent and reverential France, the two comics had made it possible to laugh at anybody, to exercise a certain muscle of contempt and derision at the cost of those normally treated with the solemnity and respect previously reserved for kings and princes.

THE SOCIOLOGIST Jean-Paul Aron believed that the proneness toward derision and satire in French life was the cultural expression of a brooding latent dissatisfaction with the shallow materialism of modern times. Humor is, as he put it to me once, "the meeting place of bitterness with style, where impertinence is required as a ritual of dissatisfaction." The reflex toward reverence in France mingles with a contradictory inclination to ridicule, just as altar boys may appear angelic during the Mass but scarf down wafers as blasphemous snacks afterward to express their independence from the system in which they are called upon to play a sacred role.

The most popular cultural form in France is what the French call the *bande dessinée*, the comic strip, known as B.D. for short. Borrowed originally from such American prototypes as Mickey Mouse and Superman, B.D. has become a national French cult, in which an attraction to the grotesque, the ridiculous, the absurd, and the cruel mingle with more ordinary, cuddly objects of sentiment, such as Asterix or Tintin, the enormously popular child detective, actually a Belgian creation but considered an aspect of French culture. Tens of millions of hard-cover volumes of B.D. are sold in France each year. There is a huge annual B.D. festival in the city of Angoulême in the southwest, where thousands congregate, including, at times, the president of the Republic and the minister of culture, who have decreed these comic books to be art. The truth is that they are remarkable. The graphic designs break new ground in every issue. But what has always struck me is the powerful attraction to the grotesque in them, not the grotesque that is plainly monstrous, the Frankenstein grotesqueness or the grotesqueness of science fiction, but the grotesqueness of human beings and their behavior. The characters in the more outlandish of the B.D.s are twisted and deformed into monsters of stupidity, coldness, or cruelty, such as the revolting married couple the Bidochons, who live with a huge, ungainly dog of surpassingly sardonic powers of observation. Again, there is that mental violence in them, a rage smoldering within, that, in my theory, is loosely linked to the broader French anger, their anarchistic spirit, their stifled tendency to want to tear things apart, which are, in turn, the sublimated products of Europe's most violent and contentious history.

On the other hand, the French pull together. They behave like a family, quarrelsome but aware of their commonality. This is probably a late stage in their history, made possible by the fading away of many of the seminal issues that divided them, of such things as the wartime conflict between resisters and collaborators or the violent acrimony that erupted as France dealt, not brilliantly, with the demands of its colonies in Indochina and North Africa for independence. There is also the factor of diminishing importance in the world, the sense, born of lightning defeat in 1940—though slow to sink in during the course of the 1950s—that the country could no longer squander its resources in internal conflicts. Finally, there is the success of the institutions of the Fifth Republic and the selection of a very powerful, almost kinglike, president elected, not, as before, by the fractured parliament but directly by the people, all of them. The French have gotten used to a certain stability in national political life. But the concept of national unity, the notion that the French had to pull together as a society—the idea they call solidarity—came in the wake of the Revolution and evolved during the course of the violent nineteenth century.

It is remarkable today how often that word—*solidarité*—crops up in French public life. In 1986, Laurent Fabius, then the Socialist prime minister, was being asked on television to define the nature of socialism—or, as a right-wing critic of the Socialists liked to put it, what was left of the left in France. The question came in the context of policies of economic austerity that the Fabius government, with the approval of President Mitterrand, was following, including the reluctantly undertaken shutdowns of inefficient industries, which involved the dismissals of thousands of workers, many of whom felt bitterly betrayed by a government supposed, on ideological grounds, to be furthering their interests. Those who were expecting some classic formulations in M. Fabius's answer, such as the need to control the major means of production and distribution to guarantee the public good, were disappointed. Socialism came down to "solidarity," Fabius said. In other words, socialism, the doctrine inspired by Saint-Simon and Marx, fought for in the First and Second Internationals, assailed and defeated in the epoch of Léon Blum in the 1930s, had been reduced to that bland formulation. Socialism is not the laissez-faire spirit, the assumption that unhindered competition will produce the greatest good for the greatest number; it is rather the engineer's concern that all parts of the mechanism operate well, that nobody be harmed or left out.

This doctrine, which could come out of the pages of the Democratic party platform in the United States, was not exclusive to the left in France. The right used it too. In the bitterly cold winter of 1987, when strikes were crippling the transportation system and France was experiencing a sudden rise in the numbers of homeless people, the word on the lips of the political leadership—at the time Conservative—was, again, *solidarité*. In a country with very little knack for private charity, where, it is assumed, the state will take care of all problems, a new organization was created, actively inspired by the very comedian whose trademark was a gross sort of derision (and whose death in that year had caused national consternation). Coluche's "Restaurants of the Heart" were set up all over the country, mostly in circus tents placed in empty lots and fields, where, with the help of an impressive flow of private donations, people in economic difficulty could come to collect free food that they would then prepare by themselves at home. The appeal, needless to say, was to "solidarity."

The term first arose in the late nineteenth century, when France was about to celebrate the hundredth anniversary of the 1789 revolution. Léon Bourgeois, the leader of the Radical party, the reformist formation whose most famed member was George Clemenceau, came up with the notion that the rights of man needed to be supplemented with a declaration of man's duties. Expressing a concept whose roots were in Rousseau's Social Contract, Bourgeois proclaimed that the laissez-faire individualism that had been one of the early Revolution's principles was "an evil and a delusion." Combating the triumphant ideas of Social Darwinism common at the time, especially in Britain with the work of Herbert Spencer, Bourgeois's idea was that the law of nature was "cooperation, not hostility; solidarity, not individualism." Every individual had a "social debt" to pay, a debt he summed up in a political doctrine that he gave the name "Solidarity," which took its place alongside the terminological trio of the Revolution—Liberty, Equality, and Fraternity.

The idea was not a socialist one, contrary to M. Fabius's later assertions. Indeed, it was regarded at the time as a kind of liberal reformism, a way of assuaging social agonies without changing the basic, capitalist structure of economic life. In other words, it was the French way of framing the debate in favor of what, in other countries, is called social welfare legislation. In 1892, some restrictions were put on child and female labor, prohibiting labor for children under thirteen years of age. In 1893, a law was passed by which every Frenchman without financial resources should receive medical aid at home or in a hospital. In 1898, workers got accident benefits, even if they themselves were responsible for the accidents. In 1901, the government, calling it an "act of solidarity," gave workers the right to pensions. The tradition that the Socialists later followed, providing for universal medical insurance, paid vacations, the thirty-nine-hour workweek, emerged from the political tradition established in the last century. Nobody in France today, whether of the left or the right, disputes these social provisions. They are a part of a consensus.

SOLIDARITY in action—or, perhaps, in reaction—was seen in 1987 at the shabby, ramshackle collection of buildings, laboratories, amphitheaters, and classrooms that constitutes the vast French university system. Solidarity was seen there, but also the penchant for contention, the deep distrust of authority. French general-purpose universities, from the Sorbonne in Paris to the large campuses of the provinces, are arguably among the least brilliant, the most unkempt of any in the Western world, despite the prestige many of them enjoy. They are very different from the *grandes écoles*, the places like the Éna and the Polytechnique, which admit about 10 percent of the entire university class each year on a highly competitive basis. The rest of the system, open to all without competition, is an obvious poor cousin to the elite portion of it.

The Sorbonne, the oldest and most highly reputed, is an example. Outside, it has a certain splendor, its domed building occupying a commanding position in the Latin Quarter, its entryway containing touches of earlier grandeur, an inner courtyard of cobblestones and arcades, ancient mosaics and sculpted columns. Then shabby reality takes over —yellowed, peeling walls, dingy corridors, exposed wires hanging around doorframes, naked light bulbs dangling from ceilings, overcrowded, badly lit classrooms, neglect, decay, atrophy, despair. Elsewhere, the twelve universities in the Paris area and the fifty-nine in the provinces are often sprawling, tarnished arrays of the worst in shopping center architecture, signs of great quantities of money spent without adequate planning or forethought. I remember one student at the Sorbonne telling me that French universities were what he called a "myth." "They are seen," he said, "as a kind of patrimony of the nation. Actually they are dilapidated, underequipped, and old-fashioned." And yet when the government came up with a plan for changes in the university system that might eventually have led to some improvement, to less dilapidation and neglect, the students overwhelmingly rejected it. The impulse toward solidarity was the reason.

The government's plan would have imposed a higher degree of selection at the university level, taking away what students had come to see as a right to guaranteed entry for all those with high school diplomas, what the French call the *baccalauréat*, which actually represents a somewhat higher level of attainment than an American high school degree. In addition, the government wanted to enable the different universities in the system to be able to issue their own degrees. The system, as it existed then, was for a single diploma to be awarded by the state, with the name of the university attended affixed only as a bit of fine print on the document. The system still exists, for the students paraded by the tens of thousands in the streets and forced the embarrassed government to withdraw the plan.

The university-reform incident was front-page news for a while and then was forgotten as the French moved into a new year. Still, it illustrated two important things about France, both its contentious side and its solidarity side. The government, made up largely of those who had gone to the *grandes écoles*, accustomed, perhaps, to solving problems by administrative dictate, had made the mistake of simply announcing the reform, without attempting to discuss it beforehand with students or even faculty. The attitude of the Conservatives—and also the tone of some of the debate—was well summed up by an editorial in the rightist, progovernment newspaper *Figaro*, which argued that the students "are afflicted by a mental AIDS; they have lost their natural immunities; all crippling viruses can strike them." The idea behind the reform plan seemed so clear and simple to the Conservative ministers, so obviously good, that consultation did not seem necessary. They wanted to add luster to the university experience, making it more of a distinction to get into one of the large universities in the first place, giving individual institutions a bit of a say in the students they would select, and, by having the institutions issue the diplomas, inciting some competition among them, rather than allowing them to exist as an amorphous, indistinguishable mass.

But the students objected. Suddenly, the atmosphere was full of contention. There were confrontations between students and the police. Others got into the act, nonstudent troublemakers trying, successfully, to provoke the police, who responded excessively, thereby giving rise to further protests, this time not so much about university reform but about police behavior. Underlying the entire incident was student frustration, a dislike of government ministers who, they found, condescend to them, failing to speak their language. Charles Pasqua, the interior minister, who emerged as a kind of public enemy number one in the eyes of the students, defiantly declared that the reform would go through. "Laws are voted on in parliament, not made in the streets," he said.

But this one was unmade in the streets. In the space of a few days—and for a few days—a carnival of protest took over Paris streets, as demonstrations were mounted almost every day. In Paris, always the center of this sort of thing, but also in the provinces, the odor of insurrection could be smelled. The French were enjoying an outburst of political passion as only they can enjoy it. The government, clearly alarmed, withdrew the reform plan in haste, just as the labor unions, always nostalgic for the barricades, announced a readiness to join in the protest. A cartoon in *Le Monde* summed up the atmosphere. It showed two government ministers dressed as riot police, rifles slung over their shoulders, helmets over their heads, while in the background there is the fury of a battle between students and cops. One of the ministers says to the other: "One thing is certain. We've got to keep in close touch with our young people."

But what were the underlying reasons for the students' protest? They found the reform elitist. The idea of selection at the entry level was unfair, they said. The idea that the universities might get to pick the students, rather than the students the universities, struck them as implicitly unjust. It would enable some universities to pick the better students. There would be a hierarchy. And if, in the end, the universities themselves were responsible for issuing the diplomas, some of them would emerge in the free intellectual competition as prestige places, some diplomas would carry more weight than others, just as, in the United States—whose educational system is no model for the French—a diploma from Harvard opens more doors than does one from a local branch of the State Teachers College. The students in France were even against the idea, encouraged in the government plan, that individual campuses could attempt to lure private money for specific projects or programs. "In France," one student at the dilapidated Sorbonne told me, "no private company is going to give unless the universities train students for them. We would become adjuncts to the companies and would no longer be universities at all." I never understood in this the implicit contradiction in the students' overall argument. The *grandes écoles* were already highly selective and reeking of prestige. To introduce selection, and the possibility of prestige, elsewhere in the system would, I thought, narrow the gap between places like the Sorbonne, regarded in France as a far less sure instrument for personal advancement, and the *grandes écoles*.

The students seemed to be giving a demonstration of one of the most oft-repeated paradoxes of French life, the passion for revolution and the abhorrence of change. The government is seen as the guarantor of solidarity, not of individualism. The highest student political value—and strangely, no students emerged to contest this point of view—was based on the notion of an indissoluble community, a band with a common interest. It is the idea, as a labor union leader once told me in the very different context of an industrial walkout—that everybody should rise together, even if it means that the merits of particularly meritorious individuals go unrewarded.

So the French have it both ways. They are individualists but not rugged individualists. They spew forth anger, but their political values call for togetherness. Hell is other people, but other people, especially other French people, is all they've got.

III

THE REASONS
AND THE MYSTERIES
OF STATE

It is never possible to rule innocently.

Louis Antoine Léon de Saint-Just,
address to the Convention,
November 13, 1792

15

A Country Cut in One

THE HISTORIC problem with the French was that they never understood, or, certainly, they never observed, the concept of gradualism or natural, evolutionary change. They were for the better part of two centuries a people compelled to fight bitterly and with excessive violence against one another, allowing events to take place twice or more, the second time sometimes as farce but usually as tragedy. The often conservative holders of power have tended to see themselves as the instruments of God or, if not of God, of the Nation itself, allowing for no opposition or change. The advocates of something different have entertained the self-defeating notion that everything can be made over at a stroke, constitutions and kingdoms overturned in great paroxysms of utopian violence and revenge. The French have for centuries been violent idealists, impatient conceptualizers.

"The study of our Revolution," Alexis de Tocqueville wrote, "reveals that it was carried out precisely in the same spirit as the writing of abstract books on government, with the same attraction for general theories, for complete systems of legislation, the exact symmetry of laws, the same contempt for existing facts, the same confidence in theory, the same taste for the original, the ingenious, the new in our institutions, the same desire to remake the entire constitution at once following the rules of logic and in accordance with a single plan, instead of seeking ways to amend it in its parts."

The corollary attribute of the French is that because they have a tendency abruptly to call everything into question, to veer from one system to another and back again, no principle, no institution, no political way of life, has been safe from assault. Unlike relatively peaceful England, where deep social conflicts have been edged by reasonable men toward compromise, the French have been neither compromising nor reasonable. Monarchists have refused to accept elections and parliaments; republicans have rejected kings, including constitutional kings. In the 1930s, after more than half a century of unbroken republican government, the historian Leo Ferrero wrote that "the parties and leagues continue in their programs to pose issues that seemed resolved and even outdated: the Republic, freedom, authority, religion." Even in the 1980s, governments tinkered with basic procedures. What the French call the *mode de scrutin*, the system of elections, went through three phases, from a majority system to a proportional system and back again to a majority system—depending on the political interest of the party that was in power. That, of course, is minor, a faint echo of earlier, far more monumental and sanguinary quests to wreak fundamental changes in the way things were. All you have to do is list the various stages of the last two hundred years of French history—comparing them to the history of Britain or the United States—and you have displayed before you a record of instability that, in turn, makes clear the unprecedented nature of the stable situation that prevails in France today.

Between 1789, the beginning of the Revolution, and 1955, when de Gaulle created the Fifth Republic, France has lived under two empires, two types of monarchy, and five different republics. It has had a total of thirteen written constitutions. The monarchy was abolished in 1792, only to be restored in 1814, after the abdication of the emperor Napoleon Bonaparte, who had overthrown the first Republic in the coup d'état of 1799. For sixteen years, first one and then the other of the two younger brothers of the executed Louis XVI ruled France; then, after new anti-royalist street riots in 1830, came the July Monarchy—otherwise known as the "bourgeois" monarchy—of Louis-Philippe, a collateral relative of the newly deposed Bourbon king, who, accepting the constraints of a constitutional system, called himself "king of the French" (rather than king of France) and displayed the revolutionary tricolor, not the Bourbon fleur-de-lis.

Eighteen years later, there were barricades again in Paris, as the class and civil wars renewed, leading, after much confused carnage, to the creation of the Second Empire when Louis-Napoleon Bonaparte, having been elected by universal suffrage as president, followed the example of his illustrious uncle and mounted a coup d'état in 1851. Napoleon III then was eliminated by the debacle of the Franco-Prussian War of 1871, when Paris, besieged by Prussian armies, fell, not into anti-German unity, but into civil war instead—class struggles, according to Karl Marx, observing events from London. The famed Paris Commune, one of the country's patented occasional experiments in radical popular government inspired by the revolution of 1789, emerged from the defeat at the hands of Bismarck. Again, barricades were thrown up across key intersections. The Commune, in fact, while goaded on by intemperate radicals and guilty of several small-scale atrocities, never reinstituted the wholesale terror of 1789, even though some of its leading radical intellectuals called for doing just that; it did unwisely recreate a Committee of Public Safety. But the bumbling, incompetent, virtually comic-opera Commune inspired fear that the beheaded Robespierre would rise from his grave, inducing the fledgling republican government of Adolphe Thiers to slaughter more people in crushing the Commune than had ever been destroyed by the hated revolutionary tribunals of 1793. The radicals wiped out, a durable republic did then emerge out of the ashes of the calamitous Prussian war, and there has never since been a restoration of the monarchy. Nonetheless, instability under a parliamentary system, fueled by near-constant threats of either radical uprisings or monarchist restoration, remained rife and persistent up through 1958.

From 1875, when the Republic was permanently established—in fact as well as in French political culture—until the outbreak of World War I some thirty-nine years later, the country had forty-nine governments, each lasting an average of nine months. Between 1918 and 1940, when the Germans defeated the French in a mere six weeks, there were forty-three governments, or, on the average, one every six months. Between the liberation of 1944 and the new Gaullist constitution of 1958, there were nineteen more governments. The Fourth Republic, it has been calculated, spent about one tenth of its time—that is to say, a total of 375 days—trying to resolve ministerial crises.

This parliamentary instability does not mean that France was paralyzed, that it was not governed. Institutions continued to function; taxes were collected; the trains ran, often on time. As a French essayist once pointed out, the acrid whiff of the unreasonable in French history did not absolutely prohibit the country from having a certain success. "Let's admit," he went on, "that there is a French manner of mutual detestation." During the Fourth Republic, as during the July Monarchy and the Second Empire, there were achievements. And yet the record of the past, the habit the French have of hating one another even more than they hate the external menace, seems to justify the historian Mark Ferro's bitter observation: "France is gifted not so much for battle as for civil war."

More significantly, perhaps, the contentiousness of the French past reflects the enormous difficulty that the country has had in establishing durable political institutions. Unlike Great Britain, where the monarchists accepted the parliament and the republicans the monarchy, and reform was more likely to take place than revolution, in France the opposite was the case. When de Tocqueville returned to Paris after the elections of 1848, he found "a society cut in two; those who possessed nothing united in common greed; those who possessed something, in common fear. No bonds, no sympathies existed between these two great classes. Everywhere was the idea of an inevitable and approaching struggle."

Until recent years, that Tocquevillain phrase, a country "cut in two," characterized the country's political life—at least since the revolution of 1789. Unity always eluded the French because they always fell on different sides of some great polarizing question. In the beginning, there was the revolution versus the counterrevolution, the republicans against the monarchists; later there was the Commune and its opponents; and after that, the Dreyfusards against the anti-Dreyfusards, the World War II *résistants* versus the *collaborateurs*, the supporters of Algerian independence against the diehard advocates of Algérie Française, the Gaullists versus the anti-Gaullists, the classic left, representing labor, versus the classic right, representing capital. These polarizing disputes have fed on the long history of mutual fear, the sense that the interests of one group were not only incompatible but absolutely irreconcilable with the interests of the other. "Pluralism is impossible," Maurice Duverger, a historian, writes, "when royalists are haunted by fear of Red Terror and republicans by fear of White Terror." "Division," wrote Fernand Braudel, speaking mostly of the past, "is within the house, and unity is no more than a facade, a superstructure, a shout in the wind."

In a similar vein, the English historian Alfred Cobban has written that the French political system emerged devoid of "moral and ideological bases." In a context of clashing interests where compromise seemed impossible, the only solution was warfare against the class or political enemy aimed at installing an alternative political doctrine, one that, as de Tocqueville noted, arose not from the practical experience of governing but out of the minds of dissatisfied dreamers. "In this intensely conservative society," Cobban writes, "ideologies proliferated. Their number and their wildness bore witness to their remoteness from practicality." The picture, he goes on, "is a depressing one, of a society which had forgotten most of the ideals inherited from the age of the Enlightenment and the earlier days of the Revolution and from which all who held to these, or to newer ideals, felt themselves alienated."

Naturally, France paid a terrible price for this, a price not only in lives lost and property destroyed, though this is great indeed. Between 1792 and 1795, the most radical and violent phase of the Revolution, an estimated 16,600 people were guillotined. In *Le Coût de la Révolution Française* (The Cost of the French Revolution), the historian René Sédillot estimates a total of two million deaths as a result of the Revolution and the wars of the Napoleonic empire, representing nearly 10 percent of the entire population of France at the time, believed to have been about 27 million. Cultivated land diminished from 33 million hectares in 1790 to 25 million hectares in 1821. In seven years, Sédillot points out, the Revolution, ending nearly a century of fiscal stability in France, saw the amount of paper money in circulation increase twentyfold, meaning a near collapse of the value of the currency.

Sédillot's conclusions have been criticized as excessive, as instances in themselves of a deep hatred of the Revolution, less a description of French politics than an act of partisanship. Nevertheless, there is virtually no question that the colossal losses of the Revolution and the deep divisions of civil society badly wounded France in the later competition for power and influence in Europe and the world. The pattern, moreover, continued during other episodes of conflict and bloodletting. In Thiers's anti-Commune reprisals of 1871, there were probably about thirty-thousand executions. That gave France, the country of the Enlightenment, that beacon for all mankind, the distinction of having hosted on its territory the largest massacre in nineteenth-century Europe.

The chronic fragmentation of French public life cost the country its very goal of national grandeur. It is ironic that even as the country believed itself to represent the higher ideals and aspirations of humanity, it remained, until recent years, utterly deficient in creating institutions that allowed for domestic peace and tranquillity. The *gloire* so precious to the French has often eluded them, not primarily because of confrontations with outside powers—though outside powers took advantage of French weakness—but because of confrontations among the Frenchmen themselves. Traditionally the largest and the richest country of Europe, France permanently lost its paramountcy with the very quest of Napoleon, acting out the messianic impulses of the Revolution, to spread

French power from Paris to Moscow. While France was expending its energy, spilling the blood of hundreds of thousands of its young men in faraway Napoleonic battlefields and in its stupid civil wars, Germany was uniting behind Prussian militarism to become, in the second half of the nineteenth century, Europe's most powerful state. Earlier still, England was developing the industrial revolution and the naval power that would enable it to outstrip all of the other European countries in the scramble for overseas colonies.

"England," Sédillot writes of the years following the Revolution, "less populated than France, outdistances it in all the domains that count for the future: It has more children, more coal, more iron, more steam engines, more manufacturers of cloth, more external markets. Its ships are on all the seas, its currency is going to dominate the century." France, the country of "frenzy," whose armies in the seventeenth and eighteenth centuries were the terror of its enemies, failed to win any of its wars since that great string of Napoleonic battles commemorated still in the names of Paris métro stations. Destroyed at Waterloo by the duke of Wellington, defeated at Sedan by Bismarck, almost overrun in 1914–15 by the Kaiser (though, in the end, managing via a series of strategic retreats and territorial concessions to fight the Germans to a stalemate, until Britain and the United States tipped the balance), crushed in little more than a month by Hitler, defeated by Ho Chi Minh at Dien Bien Phu in 1954, France, more than any other major Western country, has managed to prepare for the last war and to lose the next one. There is more in this record than mere political instability, internal conflict; but French contentiousness has played its debilitating role.

AND THEN on the night of March 16, 1986, something happened to signal the end to this long and deeply flawed two centuries of French political history. In fact, I dramatize. What happened was not a sudden event. The main political development of France did not show itself on a single night. Since the end of World War II, a less contentious national fabric was slowly woven, taking its final form on the loom of the Gaullist constitution of 1958. Slowly, for the past four decades, France has gradually healed its wounds, despite continued rhetorical flourishes, becoming a country that, one might say, is cut in one. But what happened on March 16, 1986, removed perhaps the last unanswered question about the ultimate stability of the Gaullian edifice. It showed that after two hundred years of trying and failing, the French had finally figured out a way to live in freedom and stability at one and the same time.

De Gaulle himself had never resolved what would happen if a president and a prime minister in power at the same time belonged to opposing political formations. The possibility stemmed from a peculiarity in the 1958 constitution. This interesting and, in places, vague document provided for a president to be elected for a seven-year term, this president, among other things, to appoint a government headed by a prime minister. The president would preside over ministerial meetings of the government, which would run the day-to-day affairs of the state, but he would not be a part of it. The president was the president; the government, the government. The latter had to be headed by a figure who had the confidence of the parliament—in other words, somebody who came from the majority party there. But if the president came from one party and another party controlled the parliament, it seemed, given France's history of deep cleavages, that political paralysis could result. In France, the parties traditionally represented the two irreconcilable camps into which the country was split. And so if a president of the left governed with a prime minister of the right, there would be civil war at the very apex of the government. Until 1986, no doubt in part because of this very specter, the French electorate always gave a majority in parliament to the party of the president. National unity prevailed.

When, for example, the Socialist Mitterrand, after numerous failed attempts, won the presidency in 1981, his first step was to dissolve the parliament and call for new elections in the hopes that, for the first time in half a century in France, the left would govern in an unhindered fashion, free to realize its program. The polls and the actual votes cast in the presidential election would seem to have indicated that Mitterrand's chances of getting an absolute Socialist majority in the parliament were extremely slim. He had won the presidency by a bare majority, only with the help of the 10 percent of the vote that otherwise went Communist. The Socialists by themselves did not seem generally to be able to count on more than roughly 38 percent of the total popular vote. Nonetheless, the electorate not only gave the Socialist-Communist electoral alliance (dissolved in 1984) a majority; the Socialists all by themselves controlled the National Assembly by a significant margin.

Mitterrand appointed Pierre Mauroy, a stout party stalwart and Socialist traditionalist, as prime minister, and under his guidance, and with Mitterrand's approval, the government enacted a radical program, reducing the workweek, granting an extra week of vacation to all workers, nationalizing a slew of industries and banks, granting amnesty to the members of extreme leftist groups who had been caught robbing banks and engaging in other criminal activities. Maurois changed the rent law to favor tenants over landlords, legislated a new tax on the very wealthy, put new men in charge of the state-owned radio and television networks, clamped down new and stringent controls on the export of currency—installed, in short, a recognizably Socialist program and, not surprisingly, provoked the classic divisions in French society, as the supporters of the right—the moneyed bourgeoisie, the landowners, the capitalist entrepreneurs, and others—took alarm. There were well-publicized departures from the national territory, the most well-publicized being that of Baron Guy de Rothschild, whose family bank had been nationalized by the incoming government. Rothschild declared, angrily, before moving to New York, that he was: "Under Pétain, a Jew; under Mitterrand, a pariah."

Many alarmed people, less famous, less symbolically important than the baron-banker, without making any announcements merely put their cash into leather satchels, hid them under the spare tires in the trunks of their cars, and drove the stuff across the border into Switzerland, where it would be safe from the ravages of the revolutionaries. Throughout the first several years of Mitterrand's first term, the attitude toward the Socialists on the part of those who had voted for the right was not merely one of normal opposition and discontent. It was venomous. It reflected the French propensity for thinking of their country as *coupé en deux*.

I remember a visit in 1985 to the champagne country, where I was graciously hosted by a wine grower and his wife. Their lives were clearly blessed; they were well off and comfortable. When the conversation, taking place over many glasses of champagne, turned to politics, it became verbally violent. To this pleasant, reasonable couple, Mitterrand was not just a man with Socialist ideas. He was the Enemy, the Red, the Mortal Danger to our liberties and our way of life. Mitterrand and the Socialists had by this time all but abandoned their ideological program. Maurois was gone, replaced by a thirty-eight-year-old technocrat named Laurent Fabius, who bore no greater resemblance to Karl Marx or Lenin than he did to Genghis Khan. Austerity was the policy of the moment; French freedoms were in no evident jeopardy; foreign policy had, with a few small adjustments—most of them in favor of a more pro-American policy—been a continuation of that followed under the ancient regime. And yet that conversation over champagne made me think of the bitter, intractable, near-irrational opposition that had faced the last full-fledged Socialist government of France, that of the unfortunate Léon Blum of 1936.

Then came March 16, 1986, and for the first time, the unimaginable possibility contained in the Gaullist constitution became a reality. The Socialists that night lost their parliamentary majority. Control over the National Assembly reverted to the coalition of rightist parties whose most prominent figure was Jacques Chirac, a former prime minister, the current mayor of Paris, and a man who wanted, ardently, passionately, to replace Mitterrand as president. Chirac himself may not have believed it, but he embodied to many the notion, common among French conservatives, that the right was created to rule and the left to remain in opposition.

Thus, for many, when Chirac regained a parliamentary majority, thereby virtually requiring Mitterrand to name him prime minister, the victory seemed a first step toward a restoration of the correct order of things. The foul left would be chased from the rococo seats of power reserved for the rulers of France; the right would occupy them again. All would be as it should be. There was only one difficult and unpredictable stage to go through first. The right and the left, those immemorial adversaries, those two irreconcilable poles of attraction in contentious, perpetually divided France, would share power in a governmental arrangement given the name cohabitation. Journalistic pundits were predicting its short life. The country would be paralyzed, they said. There would be a constitutional crisis the first time the leftist president and rightist prime minister, both strong-willed men, clashed over some matter of state. A perceptible tremor of anticipation swept a country for whom politics is, in any case, the major national spectacle. Millions looked on, waiting to see what would happen.

Nothing happened. Or, certainly, nothing very dramatic happened, nothing to justify the anticipatory delectation of unsettling events that accompanied the installation of the government of cohabitation. The atavistic expectations simply failed to be realized. True, there were some ruffles on the surface of the political calm. There were insider disclosures about the mood of cabinet meetings, which were short and cool. Mitterrand and Chirac were known not to like each other. On occasion, Mitterrand unsettled the prime minister by expressing public reservations about some of his initiatives—such as the privatization of some of the nationalized banks and industries, or the decision to sell the major state-owned television station into private hands, or the move to strike from the books the special tax on great wealth legislated during the Socialist control of parliament.

But within a few weeks, it became clear that the unusual situation would endure until the scheduled presidential elections two years later, that there would be no constitutional crisis, no paralysis of state policy. The Conservatives pushed ahead with much of their program. They withdrew parts of it, not because of Mitterrand's reservations, but because they sensed opposition from the public. The pundits who had predicted a quick death for cohabitation predicted now that it would prove durable, if only because the public wanted it to last. Chirac and Mitterrand were going to be opponents in the next presidential election; the one perceived to have sabotaged the unusual political arrangement was going to be punished by the electorate.

That is to say that the French public seemed to have lost its taste for combat, for the tumultuous political tradition of France. Skeptical in any case about the ambitions of the political class, the French wanted to be spared more speeches and campaigns, more posters and television advertisements, more debates and proclamations by politicians whose lives, everybody knew, were devoted as much to power as to the national good. After living through 111 governments in little more than a century, the French were not eager to live through yet more. They appreciated the relative stability of the Fifth Republic, and they were not in any mood to see that stability, that unaccustomed predictability, wrecked by yet further expressions of personal ambition.

That, too, depended on a deeper change within the French state. Perhaps the oddest thing about cohabitation was the absence of real and sharp disagreement within the two wings of the government, Mitterrand's Élysée Palace on the Right Bank and Chirac's Hôtel Matignon on the rue de Varenne on the Left. The great cleavages of French society, the cleavages that had endured for two hundred years, had not entirely disappeared. But they had mostly disappeared, or, at least, the French had reached the point where the differences among them were no longer worth the price of constant battles. The French tended still to think of themselves as divided into right and left, into Conservative and Socialist camps, and in the way they voted, they were. But the differences between the two sides had over the years dwindled. The durability of cohabitation was the proof. The system had not broken down in quarrels and recriminations for the simple reason that Mitterrand and Chirac had little to quarrel about other than who would emerge as president at the end of the route.

In short, an underlying consensus had come to rob French political life of its previous endemic nastiness. There was during the two years of cohabitation no basic difference on foreign policy or defense. There was not even any debate on such matters as the country's nuclear deterrent, the size of its defense budget, the votes it cast in the United Nations, its arms sales to Iraq, its bitter quarrels with Iran over its help to Iraq, the various crises it experienced because of Middle East terrorism carried out on French soil. When France denied the United States the right to overfly its territory during the American bombing run against Libya in 1986, the two sides of the French government made clear their agreement on the issue. Whether Socialist or Conservative, there was going to be no kowtowing to American might. On domestic policy, disagreements were greater, but again, the area of consensus had come to obscure the disagreements, to render them, not exactly innocuous, but tolerable. There is no debate in France over the principles of a mixed economy, over the paramount role of government to solve problems, over basic freedoms, the separation of church and state, the independence of the judiciary, the heavy degree of social welfare spending, which, while seemingly Socialist in inspiration, has more often been legislated by the right in France than by the left.

The news was thus that despite the minor cohabitationist hitch, the 1980s had finally brought France to the sort of political life enjoyed in the Anglo-American countries for more than two hundred years. It seems, finally, that the Fifth Republic was not the "permanent coup d'état," as Mitterrand had called it before coming to be its president, but simply the permanent French government, a system whose principles and functionings are no longer subject to deep questioning and quick overthrow. The development, while widely noted, occasioned little celebration; there were no fireworks, solemn declarations, or ceremonies, even if it did mark the end of two hundred years of strife. Serge July, the editor of *Libération*, attempted in a book to explain the significance of the first five years of Socialist government. France had become "normal," he said. For the first time, he pointed out, it had become possible for the country to be ruled for a time by the right and then, for a time, by the left—much the way the United States can be ruled by either the Democrats or the Republicans—while remaining largely the same, preserving its institutions and its basic policies and programs intact.

A STRIKING element of the public discourse in France is the frequency with which political leaders reiterate what ought to be an unarguable fact: that France is a democracy, that its system of government, by contrast with the system of two hundred years ago, is a republic, in which the sovereignty of the whole people is enshrined as a first principle. French leaders commonly preface remarks with the formulaic phrase: "*Dans une démocratie comme la nôtre*"—In a democracy like ours—as though they are not absolutely sure that the people of France fully understand and appreciate the implications of their slow, blood-drenched political evolution. The civics lesson is a reminder that democracy in France came to be accepted by virtually all the powerful groups and forces in the country only a short time ago. The country's history is a lesson in the difficulties of establishing durable and predictable political institutions. It shows how hard won French freedom was.

The French have a word, *décalage*, meaning a shifting, a discontinuity, a disordering of the normal flow of things, a gap. *Décalage horaire*, "a shifting of the hours," for example, means jet lag. The country, because of the violence of its inner conflicts, has long experienced a *décalage* between principle and the realization of that principle. The Declaration of the Rights of Man and Citizen, promulgated in 1789 by the revolutionary National Assembly, was fully realized in law and in practice only a century later, when the French established the shaky but durable Third Republic. The republican principle itself, first created in the Revolution and constituting the Revolution's primary legacy to the rest of the world, a legacy that today makes the average Frenchman swell with pride, remained a political wallflower for a century, as those who called themselves republicans did battle, open and secret, explicit and symbolic, with the often more powerful forces who saw in the Republic a denial of Frenchness itself, a repudiation of the possibility of national greatness, which, they believed, required an authoritarian government. One hundred years later, French political orations, addresses to the nation, politicians' stump speeches in city halls and party headquarters, always end with those other formulas: "*Vive la République! Vive la France!*" It is possible to see these stirring affirmations as pure formulas, habits, ritualistic expressions of national allegiance, as routine and spiritually devoid of meaning as the playing of the national anthem at American sports events. I cannot prove otherwise; but my observations and my intuition tell me that the French ritual reflects something of the historic fragility of the republican concept.

When they shouted "*Vive la République!*" in 1871, they could not be at all sure that the Republic was going to endure. When de Gaulle, exiled in London, declared "*Vive la France!*" on the radio, speaking to his countrymen under Nazi occupation, it was because France itself was in peril. When, in 1986, terrorist thugs had set off a series of explosives in crowded downtown commercial districts of Paris, in an attempt to force the country to change its policies in the Middle East, Mitterrand, displaying his penchant for the simple, elegant phrase, declared: "*La France est attaquée*"—France is under attack—thereby recalling that rallying cry, first seen in 1792, of "*la patrie en danger*"—the fatherland in danger. And when, having lost parliamentary elections that year, Mitterrand went on television to announce that he was appointing a prime minister of the opposing party, he explained that this was the way things were done "in a democracy like ours." Are these phrases mere patriotic forms? My suspicion is that the French, remembering collectively the battles they have fought, are not yet quite confident enough to take the concepts of democracy and the Republic for granted. They have battled over them far too long for that.

In the nineteenth century, a century after the Revolution, the hardy band of republicans who finally succeeded in establishing democracy on French soil fought for their concept openly and secretly, explicitly and symbolically. We Americans have in New York Harbor one of the major tangible signs of the long and complex struggle. In the early 1870s, one Édouard-René Lefebvre de Laboulaye, a republican partisan, envisaged the gift of a statue of liberty as a republican emblem, as a way not merely of showing respect for the well-established American democracy but of attempting to beam the idea back to France itself, where, though Louis-Napoleon Bonaparte had been overthrown, the nascent republic that had emerged was still beset with enemies. De Laboulaye, no revolutionary, a rare moderate in French history, wanted to avoid excess and violence, and this desire was part of the very iconography of the statue whose beams of liberty would shine back toward France. The statue was not to be like Delacroix's famed *Liberty Leading the People* of 1830, that bare-breasted maiden waving her flag while, around her, the republicans are falling. She was to be a mature lady, "advancing with the light but sure step of progress," de Laboulaye said. "She should emphasize the Order of establishing, rather than the Order of tearing down."

The dream of de Laboulaye and the small band of hardy republicans of the late nineteenth century—one of the few groups in France not eager to take to the barricades—has slowly been realized as the twentieth century has proceeded apace. That is what Serge July's "normalization" means. I think of it as the creation of a national consensus, the end of fundamental strife. It will, I believe, be seen by later historians as the great, if unintended, consequence of the Socialist government that came to power, amid great nervousness among non-Socialists, in 1981, and by the success of "cohabitation" kept order and stability.

The "light has replaced the darkness," the Socialists' newly installed minister of culture, Jack Lang, declared after the left's electoral victory, the first one it ever had that gave it real, undisputed power to govern France as it saw fit. As it turned out, the Socialists brought not so much the light as a rather welcome shade of gray, one that was acceptable to the French, that dissolved the terrors—though perhaps not the resentment, certainly not the ambition for power—of the Conservatives, one that was not all that different from the acceptably innocuous shade of gray of the right. And so, one hundred years after de Laboulaye, two hundred years after the first republican constitution, there is no *décalage* anymore. *Vive la République!*

A ND YET, of course, there is a French difference. The country cut in one still reflects the silent history lying behind its institutions and habits of mind. Even if the French do not quarrel as much as they once did, they nonetheless, as we have seen, love to quarrel, as though they are expressing an atavistic urge to destroy the hated enemy, the imaginary oppressor, the illusory menace. And the country is governed unlike any other, as though it were still a kingdom rather than a republic. History has made them an odd and admirable people, the French, given to do things in their own way, fighting all the way the powerful, anonymous force of homogenization—or, as July put it, "normalization." They are odd and different in the way they organize things, in the way they look at their leaders, in the way they rally around them when the call to national greatness is made, even in the way they remember the past, which glowers at them like a bearded prophet, reminding them that, if they aspire to greatness, they have not always done great things. There is Frenchness everywhere, especially in the way the French have waged that sometimes farcical, sometimes operatic, always absorbing endeavor known as political life.

16

The Sardonic Worship of
the Political Class

EARLY in 1987, the major state-owned television station in France broadcast a two-part series that was advertised as a new kind of programming. Called in French "*Auto-portrait,*" it was hosted jointly by a journalist and a psychiatrist (one supposedly the expert in programming, the other in the study of personality). The first program was devoted to Jacques Chirac, who, as the newspaper accounts of the event put it, talked of "everything but politics"—that is, of running barefoot as a boy in the countryside, of acquiring his belief in God, of the great love he felt for his father and his mother. The next program was an *auto-portrait* of François Mitterrand, who disclosed, among other things, that he used humorously to imitate General de Gaulle during the war and that from time to time he got angry and tired.

The programs were interesting in their choice of subjects—the prime minister and the president, already the two most talked-about and visible figures in France. Presumably, the producers had considered other possibilities—famous figures in literature, members of the French Academy, Claude Lévi-Strauss, the father of structuralism, which is one of the major intellectual revolutions of our time. They could have done a film director, an actor, perhaps Claude Simon, who won the 1985 Nobel Prize for literature, or Luc Montagnier, the head of the famed Pasteur Institute and one of the world's leading AIDS researchers. One self-portrait might have been of Francis Bouygues, who had just acquired control of the newly privatized first television station, or Jean-Luc Lagardère, the chairman of the Matra-Hachette arms and publishing network, or perhaps Georges Kiejman, France's most celebrated trial lawyer, or François Furet, one of the country's most popular and prolific historians.

But no; the choice was to portray Mitterrand and Chirac, the very two figures already most written about, most photographed, and best known in France. It was a telling illustration of a striking phenomenon: the worship by the media, and, presumably, though far more ambiguously, by the public, of members of the political leadership. "*Autoportrait*" as a programming idea emerged from the fulsome, adoring (and sometimes contemptuous) attention paid to what is called, with a tone of paradoxical resentment, the "political class." If in private life the French are fascinated with artifice and intellect, public existence is dominated by an absorption with power and its uses, especially political power, governmental power, which is in turn a reflection of the paramount role that the holders of political power have always played in the life of the nation.

Perhaps it could be argued that the choice of Mitterrand and Chirac arose because there are no nonpolitical figures remaining in France of sufficient stature to compete with them—not since the deaths of such greats as Sartre, Raymond Aron, Malraux, Truffaut, and others. In fact, the inverse is true. The concentrated, near-obsessive media attention paid to political candidates has crowded the field to the exclusion of figures from intellectual and cultural life. The dominance of politicians in most of the "slots" available for public attention is not an index of some higher degree of intrinsic interest or importance of the national scene. It is a reflection of the centralized state, the paramount role played by government and bureaucracy in France, and a concomitant public expectation that if problems exist, if there is insecurity, unhappiness, misery, suicide, even natural disaster, they are going to be taken care of by the political figures.

In short, the political power game has become so much the primary public spectacle that all else has been put into a relative shadow. This, of course, does not exclude other fascinations—the yearly national rugby championships, the annual Tour de France bicycle race, the Cannes Film Festival, and other events. When, each year, the French Open Tennis Championship takes place at Roland Garros stadium in the Bois de Boulogne, it leads the evening news report every night, eclipsing the gesturings of the politicians. Moreover, members of the French public —who show a rather low abstention rate of about 15 to 18 percent in elections—have deeply mixed feelings about politicians, loving them and hating them. It is the media, rather than the public, whose attention seems exaggerated and obsessive. But even if politics is not the exclusive preoccupation of the French, it always seemed to me that the comings and goings, the declaimings and arguments, of the members of the political class were followed with an attention and an absorption far greater than anything I have witnessed in any other country, particularly my own—far in excess, it always seemed to me, of what the majority of the political figures deserve.

What does it show? The French, since before the days of Louis XIV, have always defined themselves in relation to the holders of political power—meaning, in essence, that they were either for it or against it. The struggle for power in France was identical to the struggle for the implementation of vision, and while relatively peaceful in recent decades, it has been particularly vicious and sanguinary over the longer period of time. Indeed, it is only relatively recently that the French have finally reconciled those two cardinal principles of a happy national life, democracy and order. And so when the French adore and despise their leaders with a greater intensity than we Americans, who are not indifferent to ours, normally experience, it is more than a quirk. They are giving expression to one of the essential qualities of their history, unconsciously (or perhaps consciously) commemorating and reliving the passions of yesteryear; they are reflecting several of the qualities that make them and their history different from any other.

HERVÉ DE CHARETTE is a distinguished government bureaucrat who, several years ago, as the minister of something called *Fonction Publique*—Public Administration—was the man responsible for hiring and firing in the vast state bureaucracy. Reflecting once on the subject of monarchism, he told me: "The French are both monarchists and regicides." He was conducting me on a brief tour of the lovely garden behind his jewel box of a ministry. "They loved in the past to prostrate themselves before their king, and then they loved cutting off his head," he went on. "It's the same now, though now we have a president instead of a king."

M. de Charette was referring to another paradox of the French. It is that they crave powerful leaders, particularly in times of insecurity, and then they love to behead them (in earlier days) or throw them out of office (the democratic method) when they have seen them around too much. The French are fascinated by power, and they are deeply cynical about its holders. In the past, especially, they wanted peace, but they commonly provoked civil war. And all the while, the focus of their national life was on the single main symbol of authority in Paris (or, sometimes, Versailles), whether Louis XIV or Napoleon, de Gaulle or Mitterrand.

The common explanation for this goes back to Louis XIV and Colbert, his celebrated finance minister, who during the course of the seventeenth century collaborated on imposing the first truly centralized administration on the entire country. When Louis XIV uttered his famous formulation "*L'état c'est moi*"—I am the state—he could have meant several things: one, that he was the supreme ruler, all powerful, not to be thwarted or limited in authority; two, that he and his person represented sovereignty, legitimacy, the very right of France to exist, an idea that was overthrown during the Revolution but flickered back to life again over the next century as France several times restored its monarchy. But Louis was also making a pronouncement about the state itself as the agent ultimately responsible for private, civil society.

The habit of not merely big but worshiped government was enhanced by the revolution of 1789, one of whose first acts was to claim, in defiance of Louis XIV's great-grandson Louis XVI and his captivating wife, Marie-Antoinette, that sovereignty resides in the people, not in the king, which is the opposite of what the Sun King meant in his celebrated identification of himself with the state. The revolutionaries created a legislature, the National Assembly, whose laws—and not the king's decrees—were supreme in the land. Still, if the king could no longer say that he was the state, the Revolution did nothing to discourage the idea that the state, and its apparatus, was paramount in the life of the nation. The Revolution gave birth to the notion of the state, not as arbitrary and absolute, but as the guarantor of enlightenment itself. It became responsible for the creation of a just society. The key here, as many have pointed out, was the Revolution's inclusion of *Égalité* as a goal. *Liberté* and *Fraternité* are stirring concepts and mean many things. Liberty, in the French sense, meant such things as freedom of religion, speech, the press, and assembly. In the revolution of 1789, it also meant freedom from the exactions of the king and the nobility—that is, freedom from the caprice of government. In this sense, liberty in France could have led to a belief in government as a necessary evil, with such a powerful tendency to grow new tentacles that it can easily stretch into the domains of private life, endangering the right to property, which is the principal bulwark for the autonomy of the individual. In France, however, equality, the notion that led to much of the extremism and bloodshed of the Revolution, required Big Government, to which the French were already accustomed.

This is the major difference with Anglo-American tradition, whose main goal is individual liberty. The American Constitution, particularly the Bill of Rights, is a protection against the authoritarian tendencies of government. Liberals and conservatives divide over just how big government should be, conservatives generally preferring it to be smaller, liberals favoring more government for the sake of certain social benefits. The Anglo-American right wants individuals to assume responsibility for their welfare; liberals also believe in individual responsibility, but they trust in somewhat more government to ensure that everybody has a fair chance—that is, to assure equality before the law.

In France today, by contrast, both liberals and conservatives, Socialists and members of RPR, the main conservative party, believe essentially in Big Government. Left and right in France have had more bitter quarrels than they do in Anglo-America over such questions as whether government should be democratically elected or chosen via the rules of aristocratic succession. The question of individual liberties, which were guaranteed early on in the Revolution by the Declaration of the Rights of Man and Citizen—which states simply that everything is allowed except for those things that are specifically prohibited by law—has been hotly debated over the decades, with their suspension coming far more easily than in the Anglo-American world. Indeed, only a few months after *Liberté* was enshrined in the stirring document of 1789, the revolutionaries, goaded by the mob and acting on the grounds that the Revolution itself was the supreme good, promptly put it into abeyance, turning to the guillotine to silence those whom they saw as the enemies of *Égalité*, and silencing them far more ruthlessly and efficiently than the *ancien régime* had silenced those who called for *Liberté* in the first place. And so it went throughout much of the nineteenth century, until, finally, after the twin debacles of the Franco-Prussian War and the Paris Commune, liberty came, permanently, to have equality with equality. Before that, the classic right believed in monarchy; the left in the Republic. But either way, monarchy or Republic was going to serve as the expression of the enlightened self-interest of the entire society. It was going to have primary responsibility for assuring a fair, if not an equal, share for everyone.

This point became very clear in recent years over the question of nationalization of property. The Declaration of the Rights of Man and Citizen does recognize the right to property, but it allows for nationalization, with fair compensation, in case of urgent national need. One would think that French Conservatives would be far more reluctant to put property into the hands of the state than the Socialists, whose doctrine led them, until a recent moderating trend, to think the major means of production and distribution ought to be publicly owned, whatever it may say in the Declaration. Certainly after 1986, when the right came to power after a five-year hiatus, they accused the Socialists of, in essence, stealing the property of others through the ambitious nationalizations of 1981, and they began to sell off some public companies, some banks, and a television station into private hands. What the Conservatives disliked remembering was that the first round of nationalizations—the abrogation of the right to property—was undertaken by Charles de Gaulle just after World War II. True, de Gaulle's nationalization of such giants as the car manufacturer Renault was punitive; he did it because of their record of collaboration with the German occupiers. Nonetheless, his means of punishment was very French. Presumably, if the United States were faced with a similar situation, the offending individuals might be prosecuted and sent to prison. It is difficult, however, to imagine that any American government would want to put an industrial giant like Renault under permanent state control (where it remains in France to this day, more than forty years after de Gaulle's punitive measures).

The assumption that government will take care of everything is one that recent French Conservatives have set out to combat, saying that the society needs to place more reliance on individual initiative and free enterprise. But it is an idea that failed to catch on. In the presidential elections of 1988, after two years of restored rightist government and several major denationalizations, the electorate overwhelmingly rejected the Conservative candidate, Chirac, in favor of the Socialist Mitterrand, who had all along opposed removing companies from state control, arguing that they were among the *acquis*, the things acquired by, in his opinion, hard-won progressive legislation devised in the service of equality. Even the Conservatives, while in power, did little to reduce government's size or the expectations citizens had of it. Certainly, there was no diminution in the idea that there should be a "political class," professionally concerned for life about the functions of government. It continued to seem perfectly normal and necessary, as did the tendency of the whole country to pay its members a kind of homage, symbolically dressing them in public in the way that Louis XIV used, literally, to be dressed by aristocratic court attendants.

It is not simply that the French, like other people, are aware of and even knowledgeable about the identities of their political leaders and what they represent. They have been transformed into statesmen—matinee idols, into an elite of the elite. They have been given practically Napoleonic significance by the press, including the serious newspapers, which furnish them with almost unlimited opportunities to air their views and condemn the views of others. The French press reports speeches and statements of politicians and bureaucrats that would go entirely unremarked in, for example, the United States. They appear regularly as guest stars on a host of television and radio programs that seem to go on forever. There is "*Questions à Domicile*"—Questions at Home —which consists of an interview with a political figure in his living room, along with taped film clips showing, perhaps, his collection of seventeenth-century drawings, or his Chinese porcelain, his library or his kitchen. There is "*L'Heure de Vérité*"—The Hour of Truth—which is actually ninety minutes of questioning, billed in advance as the television event of the month, of one or another of the dozen or so politicians who are, by some mysterious standard, deemed of great public importance. There is "*Sept sur Sept*"—Seven on Seven—which is a review of the previous week's news events, commented on, usually, by a politician guest.

The media attention, and the skill shown by some political figures in using the media to their own advantage, has increased the tendency, built into French institutions and practices, to accord a supreme role to politics. The dozen or so major television and radio forums for political discussion are open to various presidential candidates, declared or undeclared; to numerous serving ministers and a smaller number of ex-ministers; to the chairmen of the seven major political formations, from the Communists on the left to the National Front on the right. The frequency of their appearances is in part a function of their ability to solicit them—with both the journalists and the political figures cooperating to leave the impression that it was the former who sought out the latter, rather than the other way around. They talk seriously and weightily about matters of state on the serious programs. But they are not on the scene merely to talk about national and foreign policies. Their personal views, their tastes, their preferences, their ruminations about the meaning of life, their views on sex, marriage, literature, and leisure time, their hobbies, their foibles, their favorite movies, songs, jokes, and things to eat and drink are also sought after on the less serious, entertainment programs, where they tell anecdotes and stories and describe personal feelings and experiences. One popular Sunday morning radio variety show on the state-run national radio network, France Inter, called "*L'Oreille en Coin*"—The Cocked Ear—often invites, as a kind of special guest commentator, ex-presidents and would-be presidents, ministers and ex-ministers of all political persuasions, to chat away the brunch hours; just about all the figures invited, from former presidents to the head of the National Front party, accept, and are treated in the unremittingly bright and cheerful fashion of guests on game shows.

One morning, for example, the program's first guest was Alain Savary, the former minister of education under the Socialists. Savary talked amusingly and learnedly about the French language; he laughed during a little skit that showed in satiric fashion the presumed differences between elementary schools of the right and those of the left—the concepts left and right are deeply ingrained in the minds of every Frenchman. Savary then made a few serious remarks about national education, and it was time to break for the hourly news. A subsequent guest was Philippe de Villiers, the deputy minister of culture in the Conservative government. Also with great charm and humor and skill as a raconteur, showing enormous ease and comfort in front of the microphone, the deputy minister told stories and jokes, including how he had learned in the course of his job to breathe fire (meaning the circus act). Then he turned the conversation briefly into a kind of political joke, naming "left" and "right" political figures and declaring which of them would be physically and constitutionally capable of breathing fire. Breathing fire? The deputy minister of culture of the French Republic? In France, ministers and deputy ministers, ex-ministers and ex-deputy ministers, play the role that is played by the guests on American nighttime talk programs—but, I hasten to add, they play it with great and admirable shows of cultivation, charm, and grace.

The average Frenchman may not know who his parliamentary representative is—a minor figure in the presidential system of the Fifth Republic, whose votes are determined entirely by political affiliation, not by personal conviction or conscience—but he is likely to be familiar with a host of political figures at the Parisian center of things, whose counterparts would be known only to specialists in the United States. The bureaucrats who head France's political parties are examples of this. How many Americans could identify the chairmen of the Democratic and Republican parties? Probably a very small percentage. But the bureaucrats who run the Socialist party or the RPR are constantly in front of the cameras and microphones.

One Sunday morning, a radio talk show featuring Jacques Toubon, the chairman of the RPR, was on the air. M. Toubon, a warm and intelligent man, talked touchingly of a period of loneliness he went through before his marriage to a woman who had been married before, whose daughter, Sophie Deniau, a press officer in the Ministry of the Interior, was also on the program. Once, he said, two canaries that kept him company in his bachelor's apartment flew out of their cage, and he spent the entire day walking the nearby streets, trying vainly to find them. Sophie Deniau spoke about how she had observed a relationship growing between M. Toubon and her mother; she knew things were serious when one morning she saw M. Toubon's boxer shorts lying around her mother's home.

All this, of course, had nothing to do with Toubon's important function as chairman and chief spokesman of the RPR who frequently, on the major television news broadcasts, argued passionately, and often convincingly, in favor of the government's policies. But political figures, even those like Toubon, who at the time held no government office and was not a member of parliament, become objects of the general interest. This alone marks a sharp change in the style of French politics, a move toward what some French might disdainfully call Americanization. It would be hard indeed to have imagined de Gaulle, or Pompidou, talking of fire-breathing or pet canaries on a national radio program, or, in fact, of virtually any aspect of their sentimental lives. When Giscard d'Éstaing was president of the Republic, he was known for his haughty and imperious manner, but, probably because times have changed, Giscard, who would like to be president again, recently made frequent, bubbly, amiable, good-humored appearances on *"L'Oreille en Coin"* several Sundays in a row, chatting brightly and gaily with the program's evercheerful hostess. De Gaulle would not have done so.

The plain fact is that French political candidates in the media age can no longer appear to be reserved and aloof as de Gaulle was—not before they have been elected. Some twenty years behind the United States in this, the French have only in very recent times (most conspicuously during legislative elections of 1987) begun to market themselves in the fashion of soap powder, using television advertising, humor, catchy slogans, to attract the eye of the electorate. These days, no political figure can afford to pass up an opportunity to be worshiped, no matter how silly and remote from issues of state the contents of the worship may be.

In part, the worship of the political class is encouraged by a sort of unspoken complicity between politicians and the members of the press, particularly in television, who specialize in reporting on them. This is complicated in part because, paradoxically, the press is less subject than ever before in France to political pressures. De Gaulle and Pompidou pretty much assumed that the state-owned television stations, whose directors they themselves appointed, would behave in conformity with their wishes. This is no longer the case, particularly with the advent of several channels that are not run by the state. Nonetheless, even if the press is critical and independent of political power, the press as a corporate body has gained by helping along the various media events that surround the political class. In any event, the newspapers and television stations follow all the twists and turns in the political contests with what always seemed to me exaggerated attention. Elsewhere in the world on any particular day, there may have been battles and floods, summit meetings and massacres, but on the hourly radio news broadcasts in France, if there has been some sign of tension inside the parliamentary majority, particularly involving one of the dozen or so superstars of the political arena, that is what will get chief attention.

There is a paradox in this, for the fact is that the worship of the political class coexists with a powerful streak of resentment and contempt for its members. The French are cynics, and nothing makes them more cynical than their view of the very politicians they worship. Nobody, after all, would accuse the French of being conformist, worshipful, unduly reverential. Nor are the French particularly law-abiding when it comes to squaring the demands of the state with personal interests. They cheat on their tax returns and go through red lights with reckless abandon. They enjoy satire against their politicians that is so sharp it suggests the anarchistic, regicidal tendencies that lie buried not so far beneath the surface of the collective mentality.

Polls published in Le Monde in the mid-1980s showed that 82 percent of the public believed that politicians lied as a matter of course. That no doubt helps to explain the immense popularity of Thierry Le Luron, whose comic stock-in-trade was his imitations of the politicians. "The Bebete Show," appearing every weekday just before the main evening news program, features puppet caricatures of seven or eight of the major political leaders, usually sitting at a bar and talking hilariously with one another. President Mitterrand is shown as a frog; Georges Marchais, the Communist party chief, is a pig. Jean-Marie Le Pen is shown as a peasant woman from Brittany. (He was originally depicted as Frankenpen, wearing a Prussian military helmet and speaking with a German accent, but he sued, and the producers of "The Bebete Show" gave him a new identity, modeled on a certain Becassine, a stupid Breton girl featured in a well-known children's comic strip.) The program, in fact, is not cutting or overtly disrespectful, at least not nearly to the extent that Le Luron was. Nonetheless, it shows the tendency to portray politicians in an irreverent, cartoonist's light that adds little to their dignity. And it also shows that the politicians themselves prefer this sort of portrayal to no portrayal at all. When Giscard d'Éstaing was running for president in 1988, he complained that he was depicted on "The Bebete Show" as a caricature of himself, not as an animal, like most of the other major figures. He publicly let it be known—though to no avail—that he wanted to be shown as a dog.

And then there is the role in French society of *Le Canard Enchaîné*, a weekly newspaper that has no exact, or even very near, equivalent in the United States, unless one thinks of it as a strange cross between the *New York Times* and *Mad* magazine, presented in a racy tabloid format. *Le Canard Enchaîné* specializes in exposés and scoops, many of them accurate. It exposed, for example, Giscard's habit of accepting gifts of diamonds from the African dictator Jean-Bédel Bokassa. Its tone is one of unrelenting disrespect and satire, and its appeal is to two sorts of readers. One is the person who savors the gossip-columnist tone of the paper, its ability to convey the impression that its reporters are particularly in the know. The second is the reader whose resentment is powerful enough to enjoy a heavy dose of aspersion and innuendo directed at politicians.

The popularity of "The Bebete Show," of Le Luron, *Le Canard Enchaîné*, and other artifacts of French political culture, is commonly attributed to a deep strain of skepticism among the population toward the politicians. But rather than show a reduced importance, a lessened public ardor toward their actual and aspiring leaders, the programs indicate that the political game has been swept up stylistically in the past few years by the world of popular entertainment. The politician remains the center of attention, but the nature of the attention has altered considerably, as the French themselves are less prone to an unalloyed public gravity toward their political figures and have adopted a far more casual, lighthearted mood.

A major figure in this was Coluche, the fat, intentionally vulgar comedian, who died a few months before Le Luron. In 1981, in perhaps his most celebrated gag, he declared himself a candidate for the presidency and then led a show business campaign that was a parody of the campaigns of the more solemn major candidates, Mitterrand and Giscard. Coluche ran as the antipolitician, the man who would utter truths that the classic candidates refused to utter, poking fun, along the way, at the hypocrisies, the pretensions, the vanities of power. The campaign was a joke, and everybody took it that way, many tiring of it when it dragged on for several months. But before Coluche brought his candidacy to an end, his point having been made, something like 16 percent of the population in one poll said they had "a lot of desire" to vote for him, another 22 percent said they had "some desire" to do so.

The irony is that to allow for reputations to be built on ridiculing politics, politics has to be deemed very serious business. The French may have acquired a certain lightheartedness toward politicians, an attitude of easy irreverence, but the politician is still at the dead center of national life. The full paradoxical attitude of the French is summed up in another common expression used to describe political life—*la politique politicienne*, "politicians' politics," meaning the habit of attributing significance to events or quarrels that really matter only to the careers of the politicians themselves and have no bearing on real life. The phrase reflects a deep conviction, supported by much historical experience, that the political game encourages national divisions and weakness but that it is played by the politicians anyway because, in the final analysis, they are out for themselves. *La politique politicienne* is viewed as a means by which the political figures attempt to surround their words and activities with import and meaning, when, as everyone knows, they are merely inventing issues and magnifying differences of opinion that, according to the conventional wisdom, are of no real interest to the public. And yet the public shows interest, or at least it pays attention, because it pays attention to everything the at once useless and indispensable, self-interested and dedicated, political class does.

And at the same time, the public feels this class it worships is not only failing to advance French glory but sits at the top of an immense and unwieldy bureaucracy that no longer serves the needs of the society's individuals. The great, swollen state bureaucracy includes grammar school teachers, university professors in the entire system of state-run universities, researchers in the sprawling Centre National de la Recherche Scientifique, railroad workers, postmen, policemen, airline pilots, bank tellers, members of the prestigious French Academy, and many others, including, of course, the tens of thousands who work as secretaries or department chiefs in the Ministry of Foreign Affairs, the Ministry of Transport, or the National Commission for the French Language.

The *fonctionnaire*, like the political leader, is an object of mixed feelings. The public—which is, of course, made up largely of fellow *fonctionnaires*—perceives him as lazy and self-serving, while protected by a system of lifetime employment, social security, and easy work rules that make him an emblem of inefficiency and rudeness.

There is a story that expresses the common French attitude. A woman villager earned her livelihood by loaning out her ram to mate with the sheep of the other villagers, the ram having particularly good breeding qualities. ICI, LE BOUC, a sign on her cottage read—the ram is here. The income she earned was so good that the mayor decided to buy the ram and make it communal property, so it could add to the local treasury. The signboard reading ICI, LE BOUC was transferred to the town hall. But as soon as the purchase was made, the formerly active ram became unwilling to perform his service, preferring instead to spend the day eating grass, ignoring the females that were brought to him. How can this be? the perturbed mayor asked the woman who had sold him the ram. "It's simple," the woman replied. "As he is now a *fonctionnaire*, he doesn't feel he has to work anymore."

E VERY analysis of French society points out that this vast, elaborate, and, until now, relatively smoothly functioning system has its origins in Louis XIV, the Sun King himself, whose minister of finance, Jean-Baptiste Colbert, centralized the state. It is ironic that when the Conservatives returned to power in 1986, vowing to reduce the role of government, the top cabinet-level official, a man enjoying the title Senior Minister, was Édouard Balladur, the minister of finance and denationalization, or, roughly speaking, the counterpart to Colbert, three centuries later. M. Balladur, a composed, beautifully tailored, trim, discreet, and courtly man, who had a great talent for convincing explanations of complicated economic questions, was an important spokesman for one of the major stated goals of the Conservative government, which was to reduce the size of the Colbertian state, putting more responsibility into the hands of private people.

Despite this task, a kind of war apparently raged inside M. Balladur's anti-Colbertist heart. It happens that his ministry had occupied since the days of Napoleon III huge and splendid offices in the north wing of the Louvre, the great imperial palace whose other wings serve as France's greatest art museum. In 1984, President Mitterrand announced a major renovation and expansion of the Louvre, involving the transfer of the Finance Ministry to modern quarters being built in a renovated area in the eastern district of the city, well outside the traditional domains of the major captains of the state. Mitterrand's finance minister, Pierre Beregovoy, took his office to a temporary site on the boulevard Saint-Germain, on the Left Bank. M. Balladur created a minor scandal when, despite the plans for the Louvre, which at the time was a vast construction site, he moved back into the former finance minister's quarters there, expensively redecorated the place, and let it be known through spokesmen that he had no intention of vacating the premises, ever. Reports filtered out of the ministry that the minister himself, the great privatizer, the reducer of the dominant role of the French state, thoroughly enjoyed the splendid trappings of the Ministry of Finance, always the primus inter pares of the French administrative institutions. The Parisian press talked about how he had his ministry footmen wear white gloves, how he decorated his office with antiques from the Louvre storerooms, how he was called "arch-minister" behind his back. In the end, it seemed, M. Balladur, who never spoke in public on the Louvre issue, accepted a compromise, worked out in 1987, three years after the project began. His ministry would remain in the Louvre for some ten years, until what the text of the agreement (signed with the minister of culture; significantly, in the vast and powerful French state, there is a minister of culture) called "suitable quarters in the center of Paris" could be found. In fact, when the Conservatives were voted out of power a year later, the new finance minister, a Socialist, naturally agreed to Mitterrand's master plan, which included vacating the Louvre. But while he was in power, M. Balladur had his way. The very finance minister whose public ideology was for a kind of withering away of the all-powerful state led a successful battle to retain the prestige and centrality of that state's most central institution.

That a man like Balladur wanted to remain in the old king's palace rather than move to an antiseptic near-suburban office complex seemed an understandable arrogance, but it was also an obsolete arrogance. And indeed, there is a healthy element of the imaginary country in the public's attitude toward men like him. If France were still a great power, the white-gloved foibles of a Balladur might seem normal and justifiable. But when ministers who behave like latter-day Colberts preside over a shadow of the former France, the foibles seem mere pretension. Here is the great divide between the public and the political class. The latter strive to maintain the glory that attended them when France itself was glorious. They are, after all, not merely ministers; they are French ministers, representatives not only of a country but of an idea. The public, on the other hand, not convinced of the special prestige attendant on being a minister of France, wonders what all the fuss is about.

Being the bureau chief of the *New York Times* in Paris sometimes put me into an awkward position in this regard. I would not infrequently get calls from a press secretary of a minister or the chairman of a political party requesting a meeting with the editors of the *Times* during M. le *Ministre*'s upcoming visit to the United States. My task became telling the press secretary that, actually, the envisaged meeting was not easy to arrange, the editors of the *Times* being busy people not able to stop the work of producing a daily newspaper because of the visit of some cabinet minister or party leader from a country that just wasn't quite that much of a presence on the international scene anymore. "*M. le Ministre* is not seen as quite important enough" is what I would have said if I had felt myself free to be entirely honest, which I wasn't. It is not even that French government officials, individually, are any more prideful or pompous than their counterparts from other countries. It is that their entourages, if not they themselves, seem, perhaps unconsciously, to partake of a certain reflected Gallic grandeur, as if they say, in unison: "The state, it is we."

President Mitterrand's habit of turning up late, even to official functions and meetings with foreign leaders, seems very likely a sublimated expression of French officials' attachment to the concept that they represent something more than a middle-sized country, that they emblemize the historic grandeur, the cultural eminence, the genius of the France that is, somehow, larger than itself. Once, Mitterrand agreed to an interview with A. M. Rosenthal, then the executive editor of the *Times*, who was planning to come to Paris for the occasion. The day before the scheduled meeting, one of Mitterrand's aides called to tell me that the president did not want the talk to be for publication. He preferred an off-the-record chat, and was looking forward to Mr. Rosenthal's visit. Rosenthal had other ideas. There was no point, he felt, in coming such a long distance if there was not going to be a printable outcome. The Élysée officials seemed to have difficulty understanding that the editor of the *New York Times* would not fly across the Atlantic for the honor of a private chat with the president of the Republic. I thought—but, politely, did not say—that had de Gaulle still been at the helm, Rosenthal might very well still have come. With Mitterrand, however, the trip was out of the question. Rosenthal canceled his trip. France, I thought—again not rudely uttering the thought—was in itself not quite that important anymore.

What this means is that the peculiar political system of the French, including the attitude of worshipfulness toward the political class, is something more than an administrative quality. It reeks of the French self-image. Worship implies a certain divinity on the part of the worshiped object, the divinity in this case being the national grandeur, the idea of France. If that fades, then reverence becomes mere form, only ritual, its object a target of parody. The public attitude is held in purgatorial suspense between ridicule and admiration, which is the French public's attitude toward France itself.

17

The Way to Power

YOU MIGHT say that the political elite gets its foundation, its sense that it was formed to rule, in the basement of a building on the rue de l'Université in Paris's Sixth Arrondissement, where the École National d'Administration (Éna) is rather modestly situated. On the upper floors of the recent-vintage, glass-encased building, teeming with purpose and ambition, are photographs of classes, or promotions, as they are called, each named after a great event, a great concept, a great, usually French figure. "France Combattante," was the first, in 1946; it was "Promotion Robespierre" in 1968, the year of the student rebellion; "Promotion Solidarité," in 1981, honored the Polish labor union; other years were designated "Promotion Voltaire," "Promotion de Gaulle," "Promotion Descartes." There are classrooms and conference rooms and faculty offices, all of them characterized, not by the shabbily genteel, country-squire decor that one expects from great European centers of learning (and that actually exists at Harvard or Oxford), but by a certain waxy green and brown and beige linoleum texture of the sort that you might find in a midwestern American high school or a new airport corridor.

Never mind. This is the most exclusive and prestigious school in France, a place that takes only a fraction of the number of students that Oxford or Cambridge takes, gives them a state salary right away, and then, after two and a half years of intense study, launches them on careers that bring most of them to the top of the bureaucracy and the political system. The basement, and the Éna itself, are crucial elements in the essential feature of the French political system. It is that politics is a profession, the pursuit of power and the right to govern, the activity—sometimes the obsession—of a lifetime. Rare is the amateur in French political life. Power is never the interest or passion or activity into which one is thrust because of skills or fame in some other area of life. This is the key ingredient in the nature of the "political class." Its members are professionals in the pursuit of political power, individuals who have done little else in life but seek office. And the quest begins right here, in the gleaming, tiled corridors of the Éna, the place that stamps out amateurism in politics, encourages the professionalization of the members of the political class.

What is ironic in this is how very similar in background, life-style, education, and outlook are the members of the bureaucratic elite. These are men and women, after all, who, according to the common perception, are deeply divided into two or more opposed camps, whose struggle for power is deeply rooted not merely in philosophical differences but in different origins. There are, to be sure, genuine disagreements between Conservatives and Socialists, though they are, I maintain, not nearly so profound or irreconcilable as many of these very same Socialists and Conservatives themselves believe. Nonetheless, it seems strange and ironic that these members of the elite believe themselves to be so different from each other when they are manifestly so similar.

There was, of course, a long day in France when class differences among individuals practically required that they line up on different ends of the spectrum. What, after all, did the Jewish intellectual Léon Blum have in common with the aristocratic Édouard Daladier during their long competition for power in the 1930s? But what really makes for a basic difference now between Laurent Fabius, the 1984–86 prime minister and the scion of another French Jewish family, and Valéry Giscard d'Estaing, the former and would-be future president with the aristocratic name? Despite their difference in heritage, they were both formed by essentially the same experience, an experience whose major element consisted of going to the same school.

I N T H E Éna basement there is a complete, high-tech television studio. Why? Demosthenes, recognizing the importance of oratory in ancient Greece, practiced speaking with stones in his mouth. Churchill practiced his speeches, even his "extemporaneous" ones, in front of the mirror. The assumption in France is that the important oratory will be done in front of the television cameras. At the Éna, not all students avail themselves of the basement facilities; not all students intend to try to become prime minister. But the administration of the Éna makes much of the fact that students there have the opportunity to practice and perfect their skills in audiovisual communication, their ability to declaim before the masses that, presumably, they will one day lead.

Charles de Gaulle, who founded the school in 1945, may not have imagined that the TV studio would be part of the elite's training—though even he, in later years, became a mightily effective user of the television address to the nation, looking into the camera and beyond it to the destiny of France. But believing in the need for a professional core of leaders to take charge of the central state bureaucracy, he did, shortly after the liberation of France from the Nazi occupation, create the Éna as a superelite school with the express purpose of forging a national leadership. The Éna joined several other *grandes écoles* already in existence, legends in the world of higher education, including the renowned École Normale Supérieure, which trains teachers and intellectuals (Louis Pasteur, Jean-Paul Sartre, Léon Blum, and Raymond Aron went there), and the École Polytechnique, called for short "X" (pronounced "eeks"), which trains engineers and mathematicians.

But while the Écoles Normale and Polytechnique remain exclusive and prestigious, with "X" continuing to produce its share of cabinet ministers and bank presidents, the Éna has become the high church of the technocratic class, the nerve center of the very idea of big government, whose leading figures will be taken seriously indeed by the public. In fact, the elite technocratic schools are not supposed to produce political leaders; they are designed theoretically for the training of teachers in the case of the École Normale, engineers in the case of "X," and elite government functionaries in the case of the Éna. But there is some cynical lore about this. When interviewing for admission, you are supposed to tell your panel of jurors that your goal is to serve as a state functionary, that your deep and abiding interest and passion is administration. But everybody knows, including the examiners, that the real goal of many candidates is to become prime minister one day. The father of a friend of mine who was about to go to the Institut d'Études Politiques, the famed Sciences Po—a kind of preparatory academy for the Éna—used to say only half jokingly that the students' main task there was to learn to manage the great fortunes they would marry into after graduation. The École Normale Supérieure, said Paul Nizan, the philosopher and friend of Sartre, is an institution that calls itself "normal but believes itself superior."

The graduates of the Éna, known, naturally, not as anarchists but as *énarques*, seem, along with smaller numbers of *normaliens* and *poly-techniciens*, to float by the natural functioning of their specific gravity to the very top, not only of the bureaucracy but of the political class itself. If you look at the presidents of the major state-owned and private companies and the ministers and cabinet chiefs in any government, there is going to be an extraordinary concentration of *énarques, polytechni-ciens*, and *normaliens* among them, even though these prestige institutions are very small. "X" takes about two hundred students a year, the École Normale about the same number. For many years, the Éna admitted one hundred sixty students into each class, about the same as are admitted each year to the Yale Law School. Over the years of its existence, the Éna has begotten something like five thousand *énarques*, not a very large number in a country that, in any given year, has just under one million students in institutions of higher learning. Yet in 1986, when Chirac (Éna 1959) was forming his government, no fewer than thirteen of his ministers were *énarques*. Chirac succeeded Laurent Fabius (Éna 1973) as prime minister when the Conservatives won control of the National Assembly, and was succeeded by Michel Rocard (Éna 1958), who promptly named fifteen other *énarques* to be ministers in his new government. Usually, the chairmen of the main political parties, the Socialists and the RPR, went to the Éna, so that while they may now be opponents in the political arena, they may well have sat next to each other in class. Mitterrand, the president of France, did not; nor did Raymond Barre, the economics professor who is a former prime minister and a perennial presidential contender. But these two figures on the political scene finished their schooling before the Éna existed and so could not have gone in any case.

Giscard is an *énarque*; so is François Léotard, the head of the rightist Republican party and a likely presidential candidate for the future. So are Mitterrand's two top advisers and several other senior figures at the presidential palace, and so too, at least in 1987, were the heads of leading private and state-owned companies, such as Air France, the Union des Transports Aériens (UTA), Canal Plus (the pay television station), the Havas advertising agency, Radio France, Bull, the computer company, and the Banque Nationale de Paris. A career in diplomacy is highly sought after by bright young Frenchmen and Frenchwomen, but if you do not go to the Éna, your chances of ever making ambassador are extremely slim (France has far less of a tradition of political appointees as ambassadors; most who reach that post rise up through the foreign ministry ranks). The 1987 Éna yearbook reveals that fifty-three of France's ambassadors posted in foreign countries were *énarques*. Generally speaking, the *énarques* cluster in the major, classic parties grouped around the center of the political spectrum. They eschew such extremes as the Communist party and the National Front. But leaving those aside, when you watch television or listen to the radio and hear one of those smooth and elegant figures talking about national politics or education or environmental protection or, perhaps, merely about two lost canaries, you will more often than not be listening to a person who has had the Éna experience. This fact explains more than the confident, smooth, unruffled, commanding, and, at the same time, highly personable public styles of the members of the elite, the sort of style that manifests itself on *"L'Oreille en Coin"* on Sunday mornings. It is also at the heart of a big change in the nature of political life in France, the shift from rule by politician to rule by technocrat.

In the old days, there was a technocracy, to be sure, constituted in large part by the *normaliens* and the *polytechniciens*; it was centered in industry and commerce and the military and, to a lesser extent, in the governing ministries. Georges Pompidou, for example, de Gaulle's successor as president, was a *normalien* (like Mitterrand and Barre, he was too old to have gone to the Éna). But Pompidou also had to come up through the political ranks during the parliamentary Fourth Republic, when unstable party coalitions competed for power. Until the Éna took hold of political life, a politically ambitious person would start by being a municipal counselor; then a local mayor; then he might be elected to the National Assembly in Paris, where he might eventually become a minister, possibly prime minister. This was what might be called the political route. To be sure, having gone to one of the *grandes écoles* was a major help in a political career. In the 1930s, the common phrase *la République des lettres* referred to the fact that much of the political leadership of the time were *normaliens*. But the *normaliens*, trained to teach school, people who did teach school wherever they were sent, still had to go the political route if such was their ambition. becoming active in local or party politics and, in some cases, eventually rising to the top.

The Éna established a technocratic route by which some of the arduous political stages are skipped. The brilliant student first finishes the Éna. In fact, what has become very fashionable in France is for the most brilliant students to have degrees at two or three of the *grandes écoles*, the École Normale and then the Éna, or the Polytechnique followed by the Éna, with Sciences Po, a virtual requirement for admission to the

Éna, sandwiched in between. Then he (those that enter politics in a big way are mostly men, even though more than a third of the Éna *promotions* in recent years have consisted of women) gets a job in the bureaucracy, goes to work for a cabinet minister while attaching himself to one of the main political formations, and finally, if and when his party comes to power—and perhaps after an intermission as the director-general of a private bank or a state enterprise—he becomes one of the forty or so state secretaries and ministers serving in a governing cabinet.

This prototypical figure, already enjoying a national reputation, will then sometimes be required, in order to justify his political role, to win a seat in the National Assembly from a parliamentary district, either his own or one that his party selects for him and sends him to—the latter phenomenon known as *parachutage*. It is extremely common for one of these candidates to become the mayor of his town, since townsfolk tend generally to select a person who has some weight to throw around in Paris. For a long time, visiting villages and towns in France, I heard the phrase *député-maire* and thought, a bit stupidly, that it meant deputy to the mayor. The phrase refers to someone who is both a town or city mayor and a deputy in the National Assembly. These are men and, on rare occasions, women who finally, after much very fancy formal schooling, learn to slog it out on the field of election battle, spending campaign weeks trudging through farming villages on snowy nights, two or three or four meetings each night, giving speeches, mingling with *le peuple*, trying to win votes. But strangely, for the parachuted *énarques*, the hard local waging of a campaign comes, not as a first step toward a political career, but well after it has been launched. For the *énarque*, political power begins with success in the Éna entrance exam. It tends to precede standard political activity.

From time to time, there are voices raised in France to complain about "*énarchie*," which, I would imagine, is a phenomenon representing perhaps the highest degree of social engineering at the top existent in the non-Communist West. True, the countries of planned economies and little political freedom have party schools, for the training of cadres to run the state apparatus. But even the all-powerful politburos do not have so heavy a concentration of memberships of people belonging to the same alumni association as the top of the French bureaucracy has. The strange thing is that France, which has an abundance of political freedom and only a minimal amount of economic planning, does bear this superficial similarity to the East bloc. It always seemed to me a sign of the importance that the French attach to government—and a reflection of their contemptuously worshipful attitude toward their political leaders—that the most prestigious institution of higher learning in the country, the one most difficult to get into, does no scientific research, produces no Nobel laureates, invents no new theories about literature or art, publishes no books, and is certainly not a center of political unrest. It is a place whose sole and only function is to draw in bright young men and women, generally in their twenties, and to ready them for careers in state service that will last over the next forty years.

And so, particularly when the Éna is combined with the École Polytechnique and the École Normale, the complaint that France is governed by an arrogant elite that sees itself as, if not born, then, at least, raised to rule does have some apparent validity. And the point is that the *énarques* do—unlike, perhaps, the graduates of Oxford or the Harvard Law School—possess the conviction from the beginning of their studies that they have been carefully selected to run the French government. The Éna, it should be added, is not the only educational experience they have in common. Because the vast majority of the entering students have graduated from Sciences Po—located, conveniently, only a few blocks away from the Éna, on the rue Saint-Guillaume—when they begin at the Éna, they are already considered functionaries of the French state, joining stewardesses on Air France and teachers in the *lycées* in this status. They get a salary of around twelve thousand dollars a year to cover their living expenses. Tuition is free. They spend something under three years in the school, doing case studies of hypothetical problems —writing a memo, for example, for the construction ministry on lower-income-housing needs in the next decade, or figuring out likely petroleum import needs for the Bouches du Rhône district. They also spend a few months working in local governments or French embassies abroad, getting some practical experience. Then, at the end of their studies, they are ranked in order of performance, with the highest of them getting what are presumably the best jobs. These best jobs are, moreover, very clearly demarcated—they are in the Conseil d'État, the Cour des Comptes, and the Inspection des Finances, all supervisory organs of the government. Each takes in about three or four *énarques*, and only *énarques*, a year.

A similar phenomenon exists at the Polytechnique, where the top ten students in each class are automatically admitted to the Corps des Mines, a prestigious engineering academy. Some bright young graduates then stay on these bureaucratic perches, where the work is not too demanding and life is easy, for the rest of their lives, but many use them as launching pads to go elsewhere. The interesting thing is that even after one of the more ambitious *énarques* becomes, say, the chief of staff to a minister, or a minister, or even the president of the Republic, he will likely remain a member of the Conseil d'État, the Cour des Comptes, the Inspection des Finances, or the Corps des Mines, enjoying leaves of absence that extend forever, continuing to draw at least parts of their salaries. This custom began in the nineteenth century as a way to allow bureaucrats to participate in political life, and it continues with what seem, at times, to be odd results. While president of the Republic, Giscard was an *inspecteur des finances* on extended leave. Now, as an ex-president and current member of the National Assembly, he is still an *inspecteur des finances*, though I would imagine it highly unlikely that he ever shows up for work at his old desk. Fabius, who finished first at the Éna in his *promotion*, remained a state counselor when he was prime minister. If you graduate at the top of your class at the Éna, you have it made for life. And so it is no wonder that the institution on the rue de l'Université manages to attract so many of the brightest young people of France.

Take Laurent, for example, a twenty-three-year-old Parisian of the sort who devours the world of knowledge and ideas. He won prizes in Latin and Greek when he was at the *lycée*. He knows everything about European philosophy, is adept at discussing the intricacies of the political situation in Portugal and Turkey, and has read everything there is to read about Georges Clemenceau and Raymond Poincaré. He understands English and speaks French rapidly, articulately, commandingly. Laurent, obviously an academically gifted and ambitious young man, illustrates the route to the top, where doubtlessly he will one day end up.

He went to the Lycée Louis le Grand in Paris, one of the two or three best secondary schools in the city, graduating when he was sixteen. Then, along with about a thousand other top high school graduates around France, he was accepted into an intensive, pre-university preparatory course for the École Normale, with the odd name *hypokhagne* (the second year is simply called *khagne*). The name comes from Napoleon, who noted once that the candidates trying to get into the Polytechnique, which the emperor founded in 1794 (making me wonder whether de Gaulle didn't have his great predecessor in mind when he founded the Éna in 1945), looked a bit frail and unhealthy. They are *cagneux* "knock-kneed," Napoleon said, giving rise to the cleverly Hellenized spelling *khagne* (*hypo* means "under"; hence it is used for the first year) to designate the preparatory stage. (The terminology has changed a bit since Napoleon, however. Now the *khagneux* are preparing for the École

Normale's division of letters. Students wanting to get into "X" or the scientific division of the École Normale do a two-year preparatory course called *hypotaupe* and *taupe*—*taupe* meaning "mole.")

To get into *hypokhagne* is already a mark of achievement and a tough course to follow. The idea, the students are told, is that after two years, and when they are about nineteen or twenty, they will have achieved a master's degree level of competence in all the major subjects—history, literature, foreign languages, philosophy, and so on. Only the one or two top students from each *lycée* around the country are admitted into the course, so already the *khagneux* are members of a certain elite in this country whose special political value, supposedly, is *Égalite*. Laurent has had his membership in the elite drummed into him numerous times. He won a national prize for essays in Greek and Latin, and when received by Giscard at the traditional presidential reception for the winners of these high school distinctions, he and his fellow prize-winners were told, "You are the elite of the nation." Then Laurent got into the École Normale Supérieure, where, meeting the director, he was told, "You are the elite of the nation." And when he was admitted into the competitive exam for the Éna, once again he heard the same line—"elite of the nation."

Actually, when I talked with Laurent, he was waiting to hear whether he had passed the written exams for the Éna, which would then admit him into the oral exam, in itself one of the legendary events of elite French schooling. He decided, he said, to go to the École Normale because he wanted to be a classics professor. Then he decided that "the university and I don't get along," so he embarked on an effort to get into the Éna. Why? I asked. Aren't there more interesting things to do with one's life than be an *inspecteur des finances*, a civil servant, a dull, gray member of the Nomenklatura? Laurent, decidedly not gray and not dull, not a nerd and not a prude but rather attuned to the possibilities of life, replied in his playfully ambiguous way. "I'm not interested in private industry. I'm not interested in public service. I'm not interested in state management. But I am interested in all three," he said. "That's why I want to go to the Éna.

"You see," he continued, "if you become an *inspecteur des finances*, you stay there for two years; after that you can do anything you want." Moreover, he went on, you just have to look at the Éna yearbook to realize the extent to which going to that particular school is the only way to reach the top in the main domains of French public and private life.

It is not easy to get there. You have to be good, well prepared. Even today, many members of the elite will attest to the fact that the long training that preceded the Éna, beginning, perhaps, in a Jesuit boarding school where the food was plain, the discipline harsh, and the bathwater icy cold, is far from luxurious. In the old days, moreover, the *grandes écoles* were often more grand in intellectual reputation than in physical fact. Sartre described the École Normale, where the philosopher studied to teach philosophy in a *lycée*, as a violently unhygienic locale. "The dormitory is practically never aired or swept out," he wrote. "Dust grows under the beds, impregnates our clothes, saturates the air we breathe. Our morning ablutions take place in the most primitive conditions: lucky are those who manage to keep a small washbowl on their windowsill . . . the food is acceptable, but the service isn't; the plates and forks are poorly washed and caked with dark sediment—a marvelous vehicle for germs."*

The Éna, and the École Normale, somewhat faded in reputation, are more hygienic these days, with the Éna, in particular, housed in a building and bathed in an atmosphere of unrelenting architectural antisepsis. But to get into these places requires a certain degree of character. You have, in essence, to be among the best in a series of entrance exams that tests less your ability to write technical memos for an imaginary future minister than what the French call *culture générale*. The exam questions reflect, in fact, the French tendency to drift into the higher regions of philosophical speculation, to appreciate more the workings of the mind than a mastery of facts. (Pierre Nora, the nonfiction editor at Gallimard, once talked about Sartre as the last of those major French intellectual figures who loved to talk at great length on just about every subject without bothering to gain any knowledge of it.) Simone de Beauvoir talked of long conversations about such topics as the difference between the notion of concept and the concept of notion, and these sorts of playful and airy issues make up the kinds of things that students are expected to be able to do well if they are to rise to the top of the French state.

There are some important differences here between the various schools, with the École Normale stressing cultural brilliance and the Éna allowing more mastery of governmental technique into the picture, but both schools have enough of a whimsy about their entrance exams to justify the image of the French, even the government bureaucrats; as, first and foremost, philosophers and literary aesthetes. I once collected

* Cited in Annie Cohen-Solal, *Sartre: A Life* (New York: Pantheon, 1987), p. 58.

lists of questions asked of students trying to get into these places. One on the philosophy portion of the written exam at the École Normale consisted of one word—*voir*, "to see." The students had five hours to compose an essay on the subject. Another was: "Can one interpret creation?" Then there was: "The sciences: Do they describe reality?" For the oral exam at the École Normale, students choose a slip of paper out of a basket. They look at the question inscribed upon it, have ninety minutes to prepare an answer, and then are required to give a fifteen-minute oral presentation of it, followed by questions from the admissions interviewers. One student I know drew a question consisting of a three-word phrase: "The first time."

Parts of the written exam for the Éna are somewhat more down-to-earth and yet show the same sort of intellectual whimsy, the similar expectation that the candidate will be playfully, creatively erudite. Laurent told me all six of the questions that appeared on his written exam in 1988. The question in international relations consisted of two words: "Regional conflict." The economics question was: "What remains of American economic domination?" The law question consisted of two words: "*l'État impartial*," the impartial state, which, Laurent helpfully explained, clearly required the student to "discuss the juridical norms by which the presumed impartiality of the state can exist." In history, the question was: "The German question from 1945 to 1973." Then there was a question testing "general culture." It was "*l'Homme providentiel*," which means, roughly, "the right man at the right time." It seemed an invitation to discuss some great figure, such as Clemenceau or de Gaulle, and to answer whether the man created the times or the times the man. Finally, there was a "legal problem." Students were given the text of a law passed at one time or another by the National Assembly. They were then asked to write a memo for an imaginary minister, giving an opinion about some problem relating to that law. In Laurent's case, it was: "What are the respective duties of state representatives and local authorities in environmental protection?"

Thus, it is not all that surprising that the *énarques* and other members of the elite speak well when invited to appear on "*L'Oreille en Coin*," that, if a generalization can be made about this, they tend to be more engaging, less self-important and stuffy, than the former political elite, which was less one of merit than one of wealth or inherited advantage. There is a certain similarity here with the old Chinese ethos by which Confucian gentlemen, the class of cultivated men who excelled in poetry and painting and moral philosophy, were believed to be the best civil servants. Indeed, to carry the comparison a bit further, in the old Confucian examinations, what was tested was refinement of expression, philosophical knowledge; the idea was that the superior man governs by virtue of moral example. The Confucian scholar took an exam lasting three days, during which he was locked into a small cell; sometimes he tied his topknot to a ceiling beam so he would be jolted awake if his head fell in sleep. The series of written and oral exams that you take to get into the Éna have been humanized a bit; you don't tie your topknot to a ceiling beam in Paris. But their stress on humanistic cultivation and philosophical knowledge bears some similarity with the old Chinese model—except that in France, the country where solemnity has always coexisted with a sense of, an admiration for, the absurd, there can be moments of rewarded levity.

The most intimidating part of the admissions process at the Éna is an oral exam given by a jury of half a dozen questioners, often themselves alumni of the school serving in important government posts, and held in front of the public. Anybody can attend, including the other candidates for admission. Nervousness is common, presence of mind, sangfroid, highly valued. The questions can concern anything—Babylonian architecture, Latin American literature, the Greek playwrights, or the foreign policies of Aristide Briand. There may be more technical questions—say, on the modalities of foreign-exchange control or on the relationship between inflation and interest rates. One *énarque* friend of mine listed all the questions he was asked, starting with a demand that he deliver a ten-minute talk on Balzac. That was followed by: "What do you think of the British royal family?" Then: "What major international market is Renault trying to get into?" and "What happened in February 1954?" (The answer to this factual question was that Prime Minister Guy Mollet sent French troops to quell the first independence uprising in Algeria.)

"A lot of people make gaffes," my friend told me. "You're so nervous you can't help it. Mine came when they asked me about French nuclear submarine policy. During the answer, I called a dolphin a fish. Everybody knows that a dolphin is not a fish but a mammal. For days afterward, I said to myself, 'How could you have said that a dolphin was a fish?'" Ever whimsical, the French examiners throw in trick questions from time to time, questions it would be absurd to attempt to answer. The business of getting into the Éna is serious indeed, and the trick questions are in that spirit, measuring quickness of response, sense of humor, presence of mind. There is, for example, the legend of one candidate who was asked: "How deep is the Seine under the Pont-Neuf?" He did well by asking back: "Under which arch of the Pont-Neuf, sir?"

· · ·

THERE are complaints in France that the system of elite formation is undemocratic and excessively technocratic, that the privileged few who squeeze past the numerous barriers placed on the road to "*énarchie*" are masters at talking well, writing memos, handling Cartesian discourse, but they have no real experience of life, no sense of the human heartbeat. There are complaints of a kind of social brain drain caused by the Éna; it siphons off many of the best students, who end up doing work in the middle levels of the bureaucracy—because not every *énarque* goes to the top—rather than giving free rein to their talents.

Sometimes, in response to these criticisms, there are efforts to make changes. The Socialists, coming to power in 1981, wanted to open up admissions to new types of candidates—in particular, members of local governments and labor unions. Since there were already two ways of getting into the Éna—attending Sciences Po and, frequently, first occupying posts in the state bureaucracy—the Socialists' creation was called the "third way," and the students thus admitted were known as "*énarques* of the third kind." There weren't very many of them. When the Conservatives in 1986 won parliamentary elections and came to power, they decided to reduce the number of new *énarques* altogether, bringing the size of entering classes down from 160 to a mere 40. Thus, when Laurent applied, 1,100 candidates were let into the written exam. Of them, 80 would go to the oral. Half of those would be admitted. The reduction was part of the effort to reduce the statist nature of France, *moins d'état*, "less state," having become a kind of neo-Conservative slogan. "The Éna's disease is its very success," said Hervé de Charette, the government minister in charge. "It has colonized the French bureaucracy and even French society. It has become the symbol of the permanent expansion of the state."

But whatever the criticism, and whatever efforts have been made to change this ultra-Gaullist institution of a manufactured elite, one thing is never done. Nobody in France suggests abolishing it, creating a newer, freer system, allowing some who do not get into the Éna when they are twenty-five to rise nonetheless to the top of the bureaucracy. The Éna, which is a symbol for the state-sponsored creation of a pampered, privileged, technocratic elite, has become an element of consensus in France. Virtually nobody, left, right, or center, opposes it.

There are several reasons for this, among them the simple fact that the Éna produces topflight bureaucrats for the state machinery at a very small cost. When, for example, the economics ministry needs a new PDG—*président directeur-général*—for state-owned Renault or Saint-Gobain, it can get an *énarque* at a civil service salary rather than have to pay a Lee Iacocca $2 million a year in salary, plus bonuses. Moreover, even if the system of bureaucratic training does seem to turn the running of the country into an arid, nonexperiential, academic affair, with perhaps a too heavy dose of Cartesian logic and not enough of the stubbornness of human nature, the truth is that the *énarques* are far from a dull, stodgy group. France being France, those who get into the Éna are well-educated individuals in the classic Gallic sense of the term. They tend to be lively. They make good impressions. The plain fact is that France, unlike the East bloc countries, has managed to create a privileged elite caste without producing obedient, reverent, boring bureaucrats. *Énarques, normaliens*, and even *polytechniciens* are encouraged to be philosophers and belletrists. Like my young friend Laurent, they are far more likely to know Greek or Latin, Plato and Kant, Rousseau and Heidegger, than are their American or European counterparts.

Most important, however, the Éna, like the other *grandes écoles*, paradoxically satisfies the French requirement of *Égalite*. Getting into the Éna is a matter of pure merit. It is seen in France as what it probably really is, an elite academy open to all comers who succeed in the tough competition for entrance—to women, Jews, blacks, rich and poor alike. In the real world, of course, those who come from advantaged backgrounds compete better for admission than those who do not. If your father was an *énarque* or a *normalien* or perhaps just a descendant of the comte de Charente and thus the scion of a well-connected family, your chances of having gotten the sort of preparation that might lead to the Éna are far better than if your father was an immigrant from Senegal or Tunisia. Nonetheless, in theory at least, the Senegalese immigrant—assuming that he has become a citizen, because French citizenship is a requirement for the regular Éna program—is treated the same as anybody else. If there are preadmission machinations behind the scenes, if there is favoritism or corruption by which certain members of the gilded youth get into the school and ungilded youth do not, they have certainly never been exposed. Nobody, not even the cynical, seems to believe that they exist. And so while the Éna may be elitist, it is viewed as the opposite of aristocratic.

This is a significant development for a country like France, which, believing itself to be a historically and culturally homogeneous place, has always had some difficulty integrating into its midst those whose roots do not seem to lie deep in the country's past—people, for example, with names like Hussein, or Rosenzweig, or Cjaja. There is a well-known, perhaps apocryphal, story about a man named Bloomfeld, an *énarque*, who was presenting himself to his boss. "Bloomfeld, Bloomfeld," the superior bureaucrat muttered uncertainly under his breath, knowing that since the said Bloomfeld was an *énarque*, he had to be French. "Well, M. Bloomfeld," he said finally, "since when have you been French?"

The Éna and the other prestige schools have erased some of these kinds of problems, and there are certain illustrious careers that illustrate the phenomenon. Jacques Attali, a Jew born in Algeria of wealthy parents who came to France when he was twelve, went to the Polytechnique. He graduated first there and was thus automatically admitted into the Corps des Mines. After that, he decided to go to the Éna, where he finished third in 1970, getting a job in the Conseil d'État. Meanwhile, he wrote books, including a rather philosophically airy volume called *La Figure de Fraser*, a history of timepieces (he collects hourglasses), and a biography of the English-Jewish banker Sigmund Warburg, which was a best-seller in France. Attali then became the special adviser to Mitterrand, occupying an office next to the president's in the Élysée Palace, where he remains to this day.

Other, more recent examples, involve Arab immigrants, who, if anything, have to overcome far deeper and heavier layers of prejudice and discrimination to be accepted as Frenchmen in France. But to do well at the Éna is almost a guarantee. Jean-Claude Hassan, the son of a Tunisian grocer, finished first in his *promotion* in the early 1980s, an event that made some news in France. He became a member of the Conseil d'État. Then, in his early thirties, he became the director of the Banque Stern, an important private bank.

It should be noted here that the ideal is not always attained. The Jean-Claude Hassans are rare; even rarer are Éna success stories among theoretically admissible sons and daughters of Senegalese immigrants. It is rare indeed for a black to be in a regular *promotion* at the Éna, which, after all, reflects the social and economic realities of the society itself. Even inside the Éna, success, some argue, is helped by social position, by being acclimated to a certain milieu. "At a place like the École Normale," a somewhat disgruntled *énarque* named Henri-François told me, "what counts is science, and that takes place in books and in your mind. But at the Éna, other things besides knowledge, in particular knowing how to handle yourself amid the political elite, count in what you do, and these other things lead to power."

Henri-François finished in the bottom third of his class and thus did not get into the Conseil d'État or the Inspection des Finances, though he ended up with a good job in a government ministry, involving regular contact with the minister and the prospect of greater responsibilities in the future. But he is not happy about his decision to go to the elite academy. He makes less than forty thousand dollars a year, lives in a rather small apartment, not in one of France's best districts. Uninvolved in politics, for which he lacks both an interest and an aptitude, he does not see a future as an elected official, and not having finished at the top of his class, he is unlikely to be seen by his superiors as a candidate to be a minister or a secretary of state in a ministry. He is likely to labor anonymously, and for something less than a grand salary, in the upper middle echelons of the bureaucracy for the remainder of his career. He sees that as a flaw in the French system. Having done brilliantly at the École Normale, he decided to enter the competition for the Éna, and when he got in, the irresistible lure of the institution, its fame and prestige pushed him to attend. Now he wishes he had chosen a different course. He feels he would have done better if he had stayed with his original intention of pursuing an academic career.

My young student friend Laurent, the candidate for admission, may feel differently, but he, too, sees going to the Éna as a calculated risk. If you finish among the top ten or so, the future is brilliant. If not, the future can be rather ordinary. If you succeed, you could well be prime minister, even if your social origins are humble. You might even be a guest on "The Hour of Truth" or "Questions at Home." All those hours of practice before the basement television cameras might just pay off someday.

18

Above the Laws of the Republic

CLAUDE MAIGNANT, gray-haired, distinguished, sixtyish, had taught French with apparent success for twenty-eight years at the Military Academy of Aix-en-Provence when, at the end of 1985, an odd, right-wing cabal whose goal was his expulsion emerged out of the opaque mists of local resentments. Suddenly, within ten days or so, some forty parent and student letters arrived on the desk of the army colonel who commanded the school, an institution of a sort virtually unique to France, which largely prepares the sons, and a few of the daughters, of both civilian and military officials for careers in the army. The forty letters all made the same argument, most of them using the same words. The instruction in history and French at the school was of poor quality; it was "too academic." It was the reason some students did badly in competitions for entry into higher-level military schools. Two professors, M. Maignant and a history teacher named Roland Warion, should be instructed to change their methods or they should be asked to leave the academy.

The letters, so many of them in so short a time, were clear evidence of a plot, a concerted action to get the two teachers expelled, and they came as an astonishment to the professors, like knives in the chest. The letters also inaugurated a small version of one of those remarkable events that the French call *une affaire*, meaning not an illicit romantic encounter—though *affaire* also means that sort of private event in French—but something that goes conspicuously wrong in public life, a scandal, a political misadventure, a moral transgression, malfeasance in office leading to scrutiny by the press, denunciations, accusations, questions and statements in parliament—in short, to a national event replete with the French reflex that favors a lusty debate about legality and morality.

Of course, every country has its scandals, its *affaires*, but there is something special about the French variety. The French affairs have a ritualistic aspect. They are the expected unexpected, the predictably unusual steam that rises inevitably out of the bubbling caldron of national life. They come along every year or so, large affairs or small ones, shredding a bit the fabric of political life, providing amused and bemused conversation at dinner parties, public expressions of consternation and rage, since the French throw themselves into their affairs with moral fervor, with the passion that can only come from a people committed in the ideal to living morally and according to certain inviolable principles—even if, paradoxically, deep in their hearts they don't really care all that much about the particular affair of the moment. There is something about the nature of French life and French concerns that gets them regularly into this kind of difficulty, something about the way they revel in their various scandals that is peculiar to them. And yet in the end, despite the palpable emotions that the affairs arouse, they also bring out a disabused, cynical side to the French, which says to itself, *sotto voce*, what can you expect, anyway? Human beings are like that, *n'est-ce pas?*

In the end, what is particular about France's affairs is that they expose one of the deepest contradictions of the French, a people given, like others, to quite a few contradictions. Classically, they involve conflict between a moral or legal principle on the one side and the perceived interests of the state on the other. They put the French in a bind. As a people, they want to observe the principle that has been flouted, and it is the urge toward examination that produces the *affaire* in the first place—rousing the national emotions, eliciting all of the French instinct for intellectual and moral combat (otherwise why make a fuss about malfeasance in the first place?). But the French revere also the concept of the interests of the state—what they call *la raison d'état*, "the reason of state"—which is, after all, the vehicle by which the national pride and grandeur are to be achieved. This reverence for two often competing values, the interests of principle against the interests of the state, lands them in that most modern of dilemmas—the desire to act morally and openly in an amoral world while at the same time recognizing the need to behave immorally in the service of the national interest. The dilemma works itself out almost always in more or less the same fashion. The *affaire* becomes the event of the moment, generating an undue portion of noise and commentary; then, just as suddenly, it disappears, still unresolved, from public view.

And that is yet another enduring characteristic of the French *affaires*. They leave behind them a thick residue of mystery, a fog of unanswered questions, sometimes even unresolved crimes, certainly tangles of loose ends. Recent French history is heavily weighted with the burden of the unknown, with this tenebrous quality to political life. And perhaps because the unknown things, the unresolvable mysteries of French life, stem from a secrecy, an unshakable discretion, on the part of public figures, there is also a residue of cynicism on the troubled, but not too troubled, collective conscience. Given some time, however, the mysteries disappear into a willed forgetfulness, an implicit recognition that certain contradictions cannot be resolved but must be lived with in all their messy vagueness. The grandeur of France, real or imagined, requires it.

THE MOST famous, but by no means the most typical, *affaire* in French history began, as any schoolboy would know, in the fall of 1894, when a certain Captain Alfred Dreyfus, a graduate of the Polytechnique, a military officer, and the scion of a well-to-do Alsatian Jewish family, was arrested for passing military secrets to Colonel Maximilien von Schwartzkoppen, the German military attaché in Paris. Von Schwartzkoppen had indeed been receiving classified information from a secret French agent, a traitor. But the colonel was one of the few people in a clear position to know that the guilty person was not Dreyfus, with whom he had never had any contact whatsoever, but a dashing, well-connected playboy-officer, Marie Charles Férdinand Walsin Esterhazy, who was furnishing the Germans with information in exchange for some cash badly needed to sustain a very expensive style of life. Nonetheless, given his position as the German military attaché, von Schwartzkoppen was obliged to watch silently as a French military court sentenced Dreyfus to imprisonment on Devil's Island, a bitter place off the coast of South America. Then he watched as a few good men in France refused to let the verdict—supported by fake testimony, fabricated documents, a willed moral myopia on the part of the military court—pass unchallenged, launching a movement that, eventually, became one of the most renowned in the history of man's insistence on justice.

Von Schwartzkoppen watched, in particular, as the French army, eager to defend what it widely called its "honor," went from one lie, one fabrication, one arrogant deception to another in an attempt to vindicate its conviction of Dreyfus. The anti-Semitic press maintained a virulent campaign against the captain, whose Jewishness seemed to many in anti-Semitic France to make his guilt all the more obvious and irrefutable. When the novelist Émile Zola published his celebrated "J'Accuse" in the newspaper *l'Aurore*, in which he asserted Dreyfus's innocence and the army's guilt, the unfortunate Jewish captain had already been imprisoned for nearly four years. Zola himself was dragged before the courts and convicted of slander against the army, whose officers brazenly cited forged documents as evidence but refused to produce those documents for inspection, on the grounds that the security interests of the state would be jeopardized. More years passed. Dreyfus was for months at a time chained to his bed in his prison barracks. French society divided among two groups: the *Dreyfusards*, who had come to accept a growing mountain of evidence that Dreyfus was not only innocent but known by senior army officers to be innocent; and the *anti-Dreyfusards*, the groups who, out of either conviction, anti-Semitism, or calculation, refused to believe in, or admit, his innocence. Even the senior officials who knew the truth about the roles of both Dreyfus and Esterhazy refused to admit the mistake, since, given their odd perception of things, they believed the "honor of the army" was at stake.

It was only in 1906 that the *Dreyfusards* won their case, nearly twelve years after Captain Dreyfus's unjust conviction. Dreyfus was exonerated and restored to his rank. Esterhazy, who was determined to have been the traitor, fled to England and changed his name. The case has lived on in the French collective memory for all the generations that have followed, first as an example of the triumph of good over evil, of truth over lies, of justice over arbitrary power, and second as one of those defining events of history, an event that clarified and brought into sharp relief the deep cleavages that already existed in French society.*

The Dreyfus affair was perhaps the first in which *la raison d'état* was invoked under the rules of the Republic in order to justify governmental secrecy and, in this case, wrongdoing. When France was a monarchy, *la raison d'état* prevailed without formally being invoked. When France became a democracy, the doctrine became, as it remains, the standard recourse when governments wish to behave monarchically without hav-

---

*Among the best of many books on the Dreyfus case, and the one I have relied on in this brief summary, is Jean-Denis Bredin, *The Affair* (New York: George Braziller, 1986).

ing to justify themselves to the electorate. The fact that in the Dreyfus affair the army was discovered to have used it to cover up a multitude of vicious lies caused any invocation of the reason of state to be viewed with suspicion forever after. And yet, a powerful device at the turn of the century, it has remained a powerful device ever since.

What distinguished the Dreyfus case was the very fact that despite powerful efforts to hide the truth, it was in the end completely resolved. Virtually all of the relevant facts, the complicated details of the anti-Dreyfus, honor-to-the-army conspiracy, eventually came to light, while the injustice perpetrated by the state, and encouraged by xenophobia, anti-Semitism, and militarism, came to be fully recognized. In this sense, the Dreyfus affair was an exception to the rule in France, where, usually, the concept of *la raison d'état* intervenes before there is a full disclosure of all the details of a case. The usual affairs provoke all the indignation of a free people who deeply believe that nobody and nothing, not even the state, should be above the law. They show France's free press in action, the country's penchant for uninhibited debate. But they show as well a tendency to stop short of an invisible frontier where the desire to advance the national interest could be harmed. The refusal to cross the line makes up part of the consensus lying behind the imaginary country. The French, ever anxious to be a major power, reflexively permit whatever government they may have to pursue the goal of greatness, even if it means that certain of the mysteries of public life never get resolved.

CERTAINLY, what came to be called the "Affair of the Military Academy of Aix-en-Provence" never had, or deserved, the status of a Dreyfus affair. Nobody was sent unjustly or otherwise to jail. Nobody involved was persecuted, as Zola was, for speaking undesired truths. Lives were adversely affected, but none were destroyed beyond repair. The "honor of the army" was touched only in a small way. And yet the event, though not a particularly well known one, remains instructive. What happened to Professors Maignant and Warion provides an illustration of the French affair syndrome. The whole matter rings with faint but perceptible echoes of the history of Captain Dreyfus, showing that some of the reflexes eventually defeated in that Great Event still existed but were not defeated in this Little Event.

In the "Affair of the Military Academy," two professors and four students were unjustly expelled from a school, with repercussions for their emotional well-being and their reputations. Certain acts of minor violence and intimidation by a few actors in the drama went unpunished, apparently because of protection by figures in authority. The event gave off an acrid, unpleasant odor of the sort normally smelled in the darker crannies of the national character, involving an unreasoning sort of xenophobia and some undercover anti-Semitism. A movement was organized by some of the leading Socialist politicians of the country to protect the rights of the injured parties, but these politicians, having the interests of harmony within the state in mind, shied away from the case when they obtained the necessary power to rectify the injury that they earlier had been convinced was done. And all during the case, the prevailing value shown was to avoid actions that would interfere with the smooth functioning of the system, that would upset the army, embarrass the state, cause disarray and discomfort, since, with just a little reasonableness and forgetfulness on the part of the victims, everything could be arranged à l'amiable, as the French say—in a friendly, out-of-court sort of way.

Aix-en-Provence, where the military academy is situated, has a well-deserved reputation for being one of the most beautiful and gracious small cities in France, or in the world. It is a middle-class town, a place of commerce, banking, the liberal professions, good schools, nice restaurants and cafés, handsome homes lining quiet, narrow, antique cobblestoned streets. On the broad Cours Mirabeau, the tables and chairs of the cafés are set out under the lofty canopy of the plane trees for eight months of the year. The clientele that sits out there is comfortable, well dressed, stylish, and full of gaiety. Aix provides a striking contrast with tarnished, boisterous Marseille, reachable via a twenty-minute drive on the *autoroute*. In Aix, the *notables*, the recognized gentlemen of influence, education, wealth, and presumed good sense, take care of problems quietly, skillfully, before they reach the point of scandal or even of public notice.

Except that if Aix is stylistically at the other extreme from its large neighbor, Marseille, the two cities share one characteristic. There has been a significant rise of far-rightist power in both towns since the early 1970s, when Le Pen formally constituted his National Front party and called for the large-scale expulsion of immigrants from France. In Marseille, where there were many disaffected Communists ready to give their support to some other pole of attraction, the National Front got upwards of 30 percent of the vote in some elections. In quiet, wealthy Aix, where many *pieds noirs* from Algeria settled in the 1960s and where there is considerable Arab immigration in suburban districts, the anti-immigration appeal of the National Front got the party something in the neighborhood of 25 percent of the vote, about twice the national average.

The growing ultrarightist component of the Aixois mosaic rarely ruffled the placid, sunny surface of daily life in the town, but from time to time, as if by accident, it burst into view like a kind of return of the repressed. Once, in October 1988, *La Marseillaise*—a pro-Communist newspaper but one without the cloying, relentless party-line deadness of the Communists' official organ, *L'Humanité*—published a story describing an exhibition in a building belonging to Saint-Sauveur Cathedral, Aix's most notable tourist attraction. The exhibition, held with the apparent approval of church authorities, seemed to bring together several rightist strands in contemporary France—the National Front, some fundamentalist Catholics, and the small national monarchist movement, the group known as France et Royauté.

There were banners reading VIVE LE ROI (Long Live the King) at the exhibition. There were tables displaying the books of Charles Maurras, the monarchist, anti-Semitic writer whose name has been transformed into an adjective, *maurrassien*, to describe a certain persistent ultrarightist point of view, as well as books by several leading figures in the National Front. There were records, produced by a company owned by Le Pen, of patriotic and military songs. There was a young man in charge of the exhibition, unnamed by the newspaper but quoted by him as saying: "Le Pen is the only man who defends the true values of Christian civilization. When we have reestablished the monarchy, the Jews, the Protestants, the Moslems, will have to convert to Catholicism or leave French territory."

Clearly, the organizers of this small exhibition were extremists representing nobody but themselves. Neither the Aixois—the people of Aix—nor the French in general can be accused of subscribing to these concepts in anything more than the tiniest of numbers. Moreover, it is unclear whether the diocese of Aix, in one of whose buildings the exhibition was held, had any real connection or affinity with its dominant ideas. Yet, only a few days before the exhibition, Aix was the only city in France to yield to the demands of Catholic groups who wanted a certain controversial film, *The Last Temptation of Christ*, by Martin Scorsese, to be banned. The mayor's office forbade the local movie houses to show it, a move that provoked counterdemonstrations by other Aixois, who were quick to accuse city hall of censorship. In an earlier incident, in 1980, a few years before the affair of the military academy, the city aroused the opposition of World War II resistance groups when it hosted a reunion of the 1940–42 class of Saint-Cyr, the West Point of France, which moved temporarily to Aix during the war. The class had given itself the name Promotion Maréchal Pétain, a rather remarkable designation to brandish in later years, given that Pétain, while the hero of Verdun in World War I, was the leader of the collaborationist Vichy government of World War II, found guilty of treason in a trial after the war and sentenced to death (though, in fact, never executed).

Some of the right-wing mood of Aix existed at the military academy, on the outskirts of town. There are six such military academies in France, generally better financed than ordinary civilian high schools and run, not by the Ministry of National Education, as are these other schools, but directly by the Ministry of Defense. A study done for the National Assembly in 1980 indicated that 93 percent of the students ultimately admitted into higher-level military schools, notably Saint-Cyr, come from these six academies, where students are sponsored by career officers, wear uniforms, have rank, and are subjected to strict discipline. Teachers, who also wear uniforms and are subject to military discipline, are, in theory, on leave from the Ministry of Education and under orders of the minister of defense. In practice, they are often chosen from among reservists attached to various military units. And since the students at the military academies are by and large the sons of currently serving or retired military officers, they are furthering the virtually hereditary nature in France of a military career. Eighty percent of the students are the sons—or, in much smaller numbers, the daughters—of active officers in the French armed forces. The schools represent "a microcosm of a military society, displaying as an ideal an exaggerated conception of the notions of honor, sacrifice, and the defense of Western civilization," said Antoine Sanguinetti, a retired admiral, in 1988, during an interview with a French human rights magazine called *Celsius*. "The sons of senior officers and generals, considered to be the most powerful of the leaders, naturally provide the tone and serve as models."

At the Military Academy of Aix-en-Provence, where about seven hundred students were registered, there is no doubt that certain proto-Fascist incidents had taken place. The one that attracted the most attention, once the *affaire* began getting national publicity, was the singing by students in German-language classes of notorious Nazi songs. In one tragicomic incident, a visiting military officer of the Federal Republic of Germany was greeted at the school with a refrain from "*Ein Helter und ein Batzen*," a song of sinister Hitlerian memory. The astonished German officer believed at first that the song had been sung as a provocation. As the *affaire* developed momentum, one defender of the school, a retired soldier named Thomas Schroeder, wrote to the magazine *L'Événement du Jeudi*, arguing that the singing of Nazi songs was actually anodyne and innocuous. M. Schroeder contended that the songs preceded the Nazis and were sung in the French army, "because they are beautiful and they serve the purpose." He did not specify what "purpose" he had in mind. In any case, he went on, "if certain elements of German militarism please young people heading for military careers, it is not, from the evidence, Fascist ideology but the fact that that regime, however detestable it may have been, created the best army of its time—and in a certain sense, all the armies of the world resemble it."

In a less comic, more tragic incident than the German songs, one that was reported in a letter by a former student to a French television interviewer, students at the school once staged the mock gassing, death-camp style, of a fellow cadet, whom they suspected of being a Jew. He was pushed into a glass cage in a physics lab, and the gas normally used for the Bunsen burners was pumped inside. That incident may have been an aberration, a sick joke, but there was strong evidence not only of anti-Jewishness but of a yearning for Fascist orderliness and discipline making up a part of life at this academy. Four students, all of them later expelled, wrote a letter to the school's commandant, complaining that they were being harassed because of their support for the two beleaguered professors. They said there existed a "parallel hierarchy" of students, distinguished by "shaved heads or very closely cropped hair," who "strive to rule over the school." The four students, who talked of physical assaults against those who did not accept this domination, asked whether "an establishment that costs so much to the nation and whose vocation is to train responsible officers for the army should be a nursery for totalitarian and Fascist ideologies?"

When the French press became intensely, if briefly, interested in the affair, it ferreted out various unpleasant incidents, such as the time when a mathematics teacher began discussing the theories of a German mathematician named Riemass and noticed a stir in the classroom. He asked what was going on, and a student, surprisingly well informed, replied: "He's a Jew, sir." The reports had it that certain students were fond of listening to the recorded speeches of Hitler; among the so-called parallel structures at the institution was one called the "Attila network," charged with sifting the ideologically "good" students from the "bad."

Maignant and Warion, accused of being bad teachers, did not fit into this political environment. "Starting in the 1970s, the school became a fief of the hard right," M. Maignant said when I visited him in his home outside Aix. He seemed to me a gentle, cultivated man, proud that he had, in his twenty-eight years of service, at one time or another had a quarter or so of the present officer corps of the French army in his classroom. "The students who weren't in the mold either left or were very uneasy," he said of the school. Some of the student ringleaders, including a few who played an active role in the effort to get him expelled, were openly involved with the National Front, he said. M. Maignant, who is originally from Orléans, in central France, was no leftist. He had all his life been an ardent Gaullist and had directed the local campaigns of several Conservative office seekers, including Georges Pompidou, de Gaulle's handpicked successor as president of France. Once, when several members of the OAS, the "secret armed organization" that violently opposed de Gaulle's plan to give independence to Algeria, turned up on the local election lists of the major Conservative political formation, he resigned from the group and supported its opposition. (It should perhaps be added here that the French military, while by no means monolithic in its political nature, has by and large found Gaullism, particularly de Gaulle's sensible abandonment of the fight to maintain French Algeria, a difficult pill to swallow.) And so, while a declared adherent of the Conservative parties, Maignant was not necessarily the sort of Conservative beloved of all the army brass.

Academically, moreover, he enjoyed a special status, known as a *chaire supérieure* in France, a distinction conferred by the Ministry of Education on a total of fewer than six hundred teachers in the French education system and held by only six instructors in the entire system of military preparatory schools such as the academy at Aix. He hadn't always gotten along well at the military academy, that was true. Among other things, he had presided over a national organization of teachers one of whose main purposes had been to encourage recruitment by merit at the military academies, where academic qualifications were not always given the highest priority. The organization favored a reform of instruction at the military schools and at Saint-Cyr that would have aligned them more closely with other *grandes écoles*, but these reforms were generally resisted by the army hierarchy. Apparently because of these activities, there had been pressures aimed at forcing Maignant out of the *école militaire* before, but when those forty letters suddenly arrived on the desk of the commandant, it was the first time there had been any complaint about his teaching. Indeed, a report by the school's provost—kept secret, like other key documents, including the critical batch of letters, by the Ministry of Defense—admitted that Maignant's official evaluations had always been excellent.

But there had been other sorts of problems. In 1979, Maignant had refused, with good reason, he believed, to give passing grades to a couple of students, both of them sons of ranking military or police officials. The two, known for their ultrarightist sympathies, led a crowd of vigilantes to the Maignant home outside Aix and sacked it. Brought to court, the two were convicted of minor offenses and, in consideration of their ages—even though at twenty and twenty-two they were not all that young—given suspended sentences. At the military academy, however, despite Maignant's formal complaints, not only about the wreckage at his home but about anonymous death threats he began to receive after that incident, no disciplinary action whatsoever was taken against them. Maignant did, however, receive a letter from one Battalion Chief Perolini, apparently an alumnus of the school, making the point that professors shouldn't make nuisances of themselves. "The virtues of a soldier," Perolini wrote, "owe little enough to any university teaching. Our chiefs, the true ones, those whom we would follow anywhere, need to take action on the trail more than they need to keep the seats of their pants in class." M. Maignant lost his battle to get the students who had wrecked his home punished at the military academy itself.

Then, a few months after the letter-writing campaign, both Maignant and his colleague Roland Warion were relieved of their teaching duties by the minister of defense on the grounds that their behavior "was harmful to the pedagogical mission of the school." The two teachers were told they would be sent elsewhere—in Maignant's case, to the Institute for Political Studies, a university-level institution in Aix, where he arrived, after two years of idleness, in the fall of 1988. The four students who had opposed his dismissal were also expelled from the school, the disciplinary action taken against them seeming rather harsh in contrast to the treatment of the two students who had sacked Maignant's house, for whom the school administration had neglected even to convene a meeting of the disciplinary committee. The four pro-Maignant students, whose chief crime was that they had refused to participate in the letter-writing campaign that began the entire affair, were not only expelled but required to pay the equivalent of several thousand dollars to compensate the state for the education they had until then received (some of this money was refunded on appeal).

The two professors appealed to the administrative court of the city of Marseille, asking that they be reinstated. The court decided, on rather technical grounds, in their favor. When Maignant and Warion received the decision of the court, they conveyed the document to the school superintendent. They were locked out of the military academy and had to hand the court order through the closed metal grille at the entrance. The school refused, with the support of the Defense Ministry in Paris, to reinstate the two professors despite the court order, leading the judge involved and many others to remark that the army apparently felt itself free—and not for the first time in French history—to put itself "above the laws of the Republic."

And so it was that, echoing the Dreyfus case, the "honor of the army" required that the two professors not be allowed back into the military academy to teach, despite what had been juridically determined, by the court set up specifically to adjudicate such matters, to be an illegal dismissal. The official reason given was that reinstating them would have disrupted the functioning of the school. Maignant and Warion went to the State Council in Paris, which upheld the decision of the Marseille court. Still the Defense Ministry refused to reinstate them.

With the two professors attempting to appeal their case, the *affaire* finally, in the middle of 1987, got its first notice in the national press, in the form of an article in the weekly *L'Événement du Jeudi*, as well as coverage on two evening news broadcasts. Major attention to the affair came after a popular Saturday-night political discussion program known as "*Droit de Reponse*" (Right of Reply) devoted an entire broadcast to what was now called the "Affair of the Military Academy." But the affair really became an *affaire* when several former ministers in the Socialist government, men at the very top of the party that was to return to power a few months later, formed a Committee of Support for Truth and Justice in the Affair of the Military Academy of Aix-en-Provence. These latter-day *Dreyfusards* included, among others, Pierre Beregovoy, previously minister of finance, and Jean-Pierre Chevenement, the minister of education in the prior Socialist government. A senior Socialist deputy, Georges Sarre, in a speech in the National Assembly—given despite loud heckling by both the National Front members and some others in the "classic" right—harshly criticized the minister of defense for failing to reinstate the two professors, as the court order required. He detailed the whole history of the case, including the letter-writing campaign, the apparent proto-Nazi incidents, and the power of a small group of "extreme rightists" in the school. It was "stupefying," M. Sarre thundered, that the authorities at the school "could have yielded before such pressures." He directed a question at the minister of defense: When are you going to obey the law and reinstate the two professors? The reply was that Maignant and Warion's removal had been an administrative decision, not a punishment, that attention had to be paid to the ability of the school to carry out its educational mission in a serene atmosphere, that it was wrong for the Socialists to be trying to make political hay of a group of administrators and teachers that was carrying out its tasks "with the utmost conscientiousness and for the honor of their establishment."

The minister of defense did not explain how the military academy's "honor" had been served by an expulsion deemed illegal by the court. But in any case, it seemed soon thereafter as though the *affaire* would be resolved. In May 1988, the Socialists came back into power. Chevenement, one of the members of the Committee of Support that only a few months before had taken the trouble to make an issue of the *affaire* in the National Assembly, suddenly became minister of defense. Logic indicated that the decision of the previous government would be reversed, and this because the question of the reinstatement of the two professors was not the only issue involved in the case. There was the conspiracy against them, led, or at least acquiesced in, by the school administration. There was the question of the two unpunished students who had sacked Maignant's home. There were the death threats against Maignant. There were the four students expelled for refusing to go along with the plot against the professors. There were the Nazi songs, the mock gassing of a student, the claims, reiterated by Sarre in his speech to the National Assembly, of an "unhealthy and subterranean climate" reigning at the school. The Socialist members of the Committee of Support had talked about the dismissals as "unjust." Even when, shortly after the Socialists' return to power, the Marseille court that had dismissed the Defense Ministry's action suddenly deemed it legal, there seemed every reason for a full examination of the situation at the school, of the question of compensation for the dismissed students, perhaps even of the inconsistent court action, as well as help for Maignant and Warion.

But that's the point. After returning to power, the Socialists dropped the matter, apparently satisfied that the reversal of the court decision in Marseille—itself something of a mystery—had resolved the problem for them. Sarre, the leading accuser of the military academy—and now a minister in the restored Socialist government—resigned his chairmanship of the Committee of Support. The new defense minister, Chevenement, wrote a letter to Maignant saying merely that he would "study your request with the greatest concern for equity." Meanwhile, the press, which had taken up the affair with alacrity two years earlier, let the issue remain fallow. Nothing was done.

It's hard to know why. Nothing was said, nothing explained, not by Chevenement, not by Sarre, not by anybody involved on either side of the affair of the military academy.

The only group in France that continued to evince any interest whatsoever in the once-hot issue was the French League for Human Rights, a generally pro-Socialist group, whose president, a lawyer named Henri Nogueres, is the author of a five-volume study of the French wartime anti-Nazi resistance. Admiral Sanguinetti, another member of the group, had this to say about the Affair of the Military Academy: It showed "a troubling distrust among the officer corps of republican values and the preoccupying weight of the far right and the departures of its thought in a system just as secret and closed in on itself as is the military milieu. It isn't, of course, that the officer corps is made up of extremists in power. But it reveals the permanence of the historic gap between certain values transmitted by military society and those that form the basis of our democratic republic. The stakes are serious enough for us to have the duty to ask whether the system of military training does not contribute to the development of this extremism."

But Sanguinetti, widely regarded as something of a human rights fanatic in the Republic whose founding document was the Universal Declaration of the Rights of Man and Citizen, did not get attention. The affair of the military academy faded into public forgetfulness and indifference. Nobody would ever say that the issues it raised were momentous, but neither were they insignificant. Principles were involved, and so, too, was the classic incompatibility between justice to an individual and that handy abstraction *la raison d'état*. It is an incompatibility to be seen in other affairs, and in other of France's late-twentieth-century confrontations with itself.

19

The Shadowy Paths
of Grandeur

THE OCCASION was a lunch with Charles Hernu, a bearded man
of about sixty, who had only a few months before, on September
19, 1985, resigned in disgrace as France's minister of defense. Despite
his resignation, Hernu was waging a campaign for a National Assembly
seat in the March 1986 election in his district, near Lyon, and he had
stopped off for some *blanquette de veau* and a glass or two of Côtes du
Rhône at a local countryside tavern, kindly inviting the dozen or so
journalists, both French and foreign, who were accompanying him for
the day.

Hernu, a lifelong Socialist, was an unusual man. He had enormous
charm and grace. I met him twice and observed him closely over a period
of several months, and I found him to be something of a ministerial
model, unpretentious, extremely intelligent, open-minded, sincere, committed to republican values. Because of his charisma and his attachment
to the idea of a strong defense, he had also performed something of a
miracle as the minister of defense, making himself popular in an army
that had regarded the victory of the Socialists in France in 1981 as a
mortal danger to the security of the nation. Hernu was no weak-kneed
intellectual, no fuzzy-headed ingenue. He believed strongly in the Atlantic Alliance, understood the need for a strong defense. He liked to
visit the troops wherever they were. He loved the military as an institution. He was honest and above reproach. Every country in the world
should have a defense minister like Charles Hernu.

But he was no longer the defense minister, and therein lies the story of an *affaire* far more devastating than the little affair of the Military Academy of Aix, but instructive in some of the same ways, similarly revealing as to the nature of France's vigorous attachment to a certain idea of itself. M. Hernu, as the leader of the army, had presided over a kind of terrorist operation during which French army agents had sunk, in Auckland Harbor, New Zealand, a boat belonging to the Greenpeace environmentalist organization, which was determined to attempt to interfere with a series of underground nuclear explosions France planned to carry out at its testing site in the Pacific, tests that France saw, and sees, as essential to its place in the world as a power to be reckoned with.

And so the sinking of the boat in July 1985, by a secret French team operating clandestinely on the sovereign soil of a friendly nation, was aimed at crippling the expected Greenpeace effort. If, as was likely, some people in the world suspected a French operation, so what? As long as there was no proof, it might even be advantageous to France for its enemies to suspect the lengths to which the country would go to protect its interests. But unexpected problems caused the scheme to go badly awry. The operation was bungled. A Greenpeace photographer was killed, a native of Portugal who was a citizen of Holland, an ally of France, whose passport holders should be free of danger from French secret agents. The photographer was on board the boat when the first of two explosive devices, attached by French frogmen to its hull, went off. The first explosion was intended as a warning to any on board to scurry ashore. But the photographer went into the hold to investigate, and he was there when the second explosion went off, killing him and sinking the vessel. A couple of days later, two of the French agents involved in the operation—a man and a woman, pretending to be married, who had carried out surveillance and logistical work—got caught by the New Zealand police before they were able to make good their escape from the island.

The capture of the agents led to the unraveling of the affair and to the embarrassing disclosure that the unintentionally murderous sabotage of the vessel had been carried out by the French government, with the highest approval. Ultimately, Hernu took responsibility. Just two days after a crowded press conference in the Ministry of Defense in Paris, during which he proclaimed himself innocent of all involvement in the Greenpeace matter, Hernu announced he was stepping down.

This did not mean that he suddenly became the goat of the affair. Indeed, he was publicly acclaimed, spontaneously applauded on the streets, in restaurants, on the Paris–Lyon high-speed train, whenever he made an appearance. At a congress of the Socialist party in Toulouse, held a few weeks after the affair, a loud roar of acclaim greeted him when he entered the hall. I visited him once in a set of new offices near Montparnasse, which he had occupied following his resignation. His suite was just across a narrow street from a small hospital, and Hernu, who received me with his usual charm and grace, said that the day he arrived at his new place of work—a research institute on defense matters—the patients, nurses, and doctors in their various costumes had lined up at the windows of the clinic and applauded him. Ironically, the Greenpeace affair, and his no-nonsense decision to step down, had made him more, not less, beloved in France, so that when he had that little lunch outside Lyon, he was virtually sure of election, and indeed, not only did he win his own seat but he ensured the entire Socialist ticket in Lyon a far stronger showing than had been expected. Hernu had been the man in charge during the most serious *affaire* in France in several years. He had bravely taken the rap. He couldn't have expected to sit together with reporters only a few months later and not hear questions asked about the matter. It was much too much on everybody's mind.

And so there were some questions, the ones others in France were asking. Will we ever know all the details? Why the decision to sink the boat rather than use other means to prevent it from getting within a thousand miles of the test site? M. Hernu provided little new information, but he accepted the questions as normal and inevitable. Then a journalist from Spain sitting at the table across from Hernu asked M. le Ministre whether he expected that eventually there would be any indictments of French military officers for their role in the affair. It was, to be truthful, a harsh question, since after all, intentionally or not, what the journalist was suggesting was that M. Hernu, having taken responsibility for the operation, was himself criminally liable. And yet, harsh or not, I thought it was within the bounds of the permissible, a legitimate and politely expressed journalistic inquiry. Hadn't somebody been killed? Didn't it seem as though the crime of involuntary manslaughter had taken place? Wasn't the Greenpeace episode carried out on the soil of a friendly, sovereign foreign power, the sort of thing that France, the bastion of Enlightenment values, condemned when some other country undertook it? Didn't the operation represent what one expected from the KGB or the Palestine Liberation Organization, not the law-abiding, democratic French Republic?

Legitimate or not, the question produced a near-violent reaction on

M. Hernu's part. He got visibly angry. His face darkened. If harsh glares from government ex-ministers could destroy the careers of indiscreet, impertinent journalists, the Spaniard across the table would have been finished. How dare you, Hernu said, in essence. Why don't you go sit someplace else? How could you be so rude and impolite as to make a statement like that during a congenial lunch? The room grew silent and still with embarrassment as Hernu continued to rage. I can't reproduce here his exact words, but the peroration was something like this: I will not sit quiet and still while somebody has the temerity and the bad taste to slander in my very presence the honor and integrity of the French armed forces.

Let there be no mistake. Charles Hernu was the kind of man who would have sided with Dreyfus, not against him, just as Jean Jaurès, the creator of the modern Socialist party, had been one of the Jewish captain's most determined and courageous champions. By "the honor of the army," the phrase used over and over again by the senior officers in the matter to justify the cover-up of the truth, Hernu clearly did not mean its capacity to cheat, to forge documents and to engage in racist slurs against French citizens, all of which had occurred during the Dreyfus affair. And yet the phrase "honor of the army" rings with meaning both in the nineteenth century and in the twentieth. It is a verbal sign of the imaginary country, of the yearning for France to play a role of major importance in the world, which is the perception of things that lay behind the anti-Greenpeace operation in the first place.

Ultimately, what Hernu was defending was the concept of *la raison d'état*, which the French see as essential for the fulfillment of the country's historic mission. What is different from days gone by is that in this age of reduced French power and international public opinion, it is necessary to carry out certain activities in the service of the national interest in secret. And when one of these secrets is revealed, the French fuss publicly for a while. They delve into the matter rather far. But not too far. Unlike the United States, there are no indictments, no congressional investigations, hardly any public demands that all the facts, every one of them, see the light of day. And when, as happened in the Greenpeace case, some reputable investigator does come up with a cogent, well-sourced explanation of the affair, in which the responsibility of those until then carefully protected is revealed, there is no interest on the part of the public to pursue very many of the implications. On the contrary, the defense minister who took the rap for the affair was lionized; those who carried it out were treated as heroes. The search for the truth came to an abrupt end. It was what gave the fascinating and disturbing Greenpeace affair—and many other affairs before it—much of its special character.

T HE CHRONOLOGY of the event alone is a clear lesson in the contradictory tendency in France, first to insist on full disclosure, then to shy away from it, and, in the end, to do nothing at all even when a clear pattern of governmental deception emerges. The sinking of the boat, known as the *Rainbow Warrior*, took place on July 10, 1985. A French-speaking couple carrying Swiss passports and going by the names Alain Turenge and Sophie-Claire Turenge were arrested by the New Zealand police a couple of days later. The suspicion that the French had carried out the affair was strong. France seemed to have the strongest interest in crippling the Greenpeace fleet. But for a month or so, the issue lay fallow. The suspicions were unsupported by any solid information. Journalists like myself seemed to have very little to write about.

Then suddenly, in August, the obscure matter of the sinking of a boat in faraway New Zealand got catapulted to the status of national obsession in France. The first impetus was the publication in two French magazines—neither of them of the absolutely dependable kind—of articles that linked the couple named Turenge, now being held in a New Zealand jail, to the French intelligence service. They were intelligence agents, the magazines said. Very quickly, the government of Prime Minister Fabius, acting on behalf of President Mitterrand's demand for a "rigorous inquiry without delay," announced that an investigator by the name of Bernard Tricot, a former senior aide to Charles de Gaulle, would carry out an investigation to determine whether any link existed.

In retrospect, it is difficult to imagine what the Fabius government intended by the Tricot investigation. Even if Fabius and Mitterrand themselves had not known about the Greenpeace operation in advance, they could very well have guessed that such a move by French intelligence agents would not have been undertaken without high-level approval. The French way in these sorts of things would normally have been a quiet, internal investigation, a determination of exactly what had happened, why, and who was responsible. If Tricot discovered that the French government had carried out the operation, Fabius and Mitterrand were going, at best, to look stupid for not having known it in advance. The cynics—or, perhaps, the realists—would have a different interpretation. They would think that in a country like France, certainly Fabius as prime minister and very likely Mitterrand would either have been in the know before the boat was sunk or have learned rather quickly who was involved. And so if Tricot declared the French innocent, his "rigorous investigation" was going to smack of a cover-up. At worst, it would appear as though the government, knowing itself guilty, had had itself investigated, controlling the information fed to the investigator, in order to have itself declared innocent—and nobody would believe it.

That is what happened. Even before Tricot released his anodyne report, further leaks to the French press confirmed the earlier stories to the effect that the Turenge couple were indeed French army officers. The government did not deny it, knowing, in any case, that the couple, who were not really a couple, would be certified as members of the French secret services in New Zealand when their trial in the killing of the Greenpeace photographer took place. There was no point in rejecting a claim that would later be proved true. And so, with Tricot's report still in the preparatory stages, the word got out that the Turenges, whose real names had not yet been divulged, had been sent to the region to collect information on Greenpeace's plans to attempt to interfere with French nuclear tests in the Pacific. Word further leaked out that four other French agents had been on the island at the time. But there had been no official French attempt to sink the boat, the leaks maintained. Perhaps, the speculation went, French agents had sunk the boat without authorization. The leaks to the press seemed rather to encourage the opinion that the operation had been carried out by a third country, bent on embarrassing the French. After all, virtually all the countries of the region, including New Zealand itself and Australia, were fiercely opposed to the underground tests that France had carried out for decades at a site on Mururoa atoll, a few hours' flight from Auckland. Wasn't it possible that the sinking of the boat had been a frame-up manufactured by one of those countries in order to rouse local public opinion even more against the French?

While these possibilities were considered, Tricot, committing an act either of subterfuge or of naïveté of a rather high order, went ahead and exonerated the French government. His report came out on August 26, after a rapid two-week investigation: Neither the two French officers already being held in custody in New Zealand, nor the four other French officers known to have been in the area at the time—all of them being sought by New Zealand—played any role in the sinking of the ship. The four included a woman named Frédérique Bonlieu, who infiltrated the Greenpeace group in New Zealand, and three other intelligence officers, who had sailed to the island aboard a yacht called the *Ouvéa*, which had since disappeared without a trace. These three men, Tricot confirmed, had been spirited back to France by the secret service. They happened all to be frogmen of the very sort who one might think could provide valuable services to anybody trying to sink a ship in the middle of the night by attaching explosive devices to its hull. Nonetheless, Tricot said that all six officers were merely on an intelligence-gathering mission. This mission, moreover, had been approved both by Hernu, the defense minister, and by a senior army officer named Jean Saulnier, Mitterrand's chief military aide.

It was hard to believe. The newspaper *Libération* greeted the Tricot report with one of its patented sarcastic headlines: TRICOT LAVE PLUS BLANC—Tricot washes whiter. In New Zealand, Prime Minister David Lange said that the report was "so transparent it could not even be called a whitewash." He predicted, correctly as it turned out, that both Tricot and the French government "will live to be embarrassed" by the report. A rightist French parliamentarian, Alain Madelin, said that the Tricot report took the French people for "idiots." He said: "We're being asked to believe that you dispatch frogmen to take pictures."

The next day, the freshly self-exonerated French government carried its aggrieved innocence one step further. M. Fabius, in a statement to reporters, asked New Zealand to turn over all the information it had at its disposal on the sinking of the vessel. "If," Fabius solemnly claimed, "it appears that criminal acts have been committed by French citizens, legal action will be taken immediately. The French government is determined that no elements remain in the shadows." I thought about that statement by the French prime minister after the Hernu tirade at the restaurant months later. In asking his question, hadn't the Spanish reporter merely been recalling the very words of Hernu's prime minister? Wasn't it clear that criminal acts had been committed by French citizens? Was there no question of credibility here, the credibility of the French government to follow its words with actions?

Actually, the issue was not credibility but national esteem, pride, a role in the world, and that issue led the French, after a paroxysm of self-scrutiny, to bury the affair beneath numerous layers of *raison d'état* and to avoid at all costs that any French citizens involved be punished in any way.

Following M. Tricot's credulous account of the Greenpeace operation, two simultaneous trends appeared. The Socialists' rightist opposition reacted discreetly, criticizing the government's handling of the affair but not the goal of the operation. The Conservatives implied that if they had been in power, rather than the group they like in any case to portray as light-headed leftist bunglers, the job would have been done right. Nobody in France, except for the Communists, who were experiencing a historic decline in popular support, criticized the fundamentals of the affair. The Communists said it was an act of "international terrorism." But few in France were prone to that sort of self-incrimination. A rightist figure like Giscard only commented that he was declining to comment. "Right or wrong," he said, "it's my country." The Socialist government, meanwhile, led by M. Mitterrand, took a conspicuously prickly attitude. Whereas an American government might have become embarrassed over a clearly illegal and botched operation, the French virtually brandished it as a blow in the national interest. Mitterrand himself announced a few days after the Tricot report that he would be present at the French testing site on Mururoa for the next series of underground explosions. Fabius, in a television interview, declared "no country or group can dictate French defense policy to us." There was no apology to New Zealand, nor any to the family of the man killed aboard the *Rainbow Warrior*. Aside from some verbal sniping from the Communists, nobody among the public raised serious criticisms. There were no demonstrations, no parliamentary investigations, no hand-wringing about morality in foreign policy. The French, including the French of the 1960s student demonstrations, have never been tempted to believe that the pursuit of the national interest contains within it ethical dilemmas. The national interest is a sufficient explanation. Still, there were a few voices being raised, or, at least, admissions being made, that the Greenpeace affair was not turning out to be the country's proudest moment.

"France," the sociologist Alain Touraine wrote in *Le Monde*, "this country of great enthusiasms and bursts of anger, sensitive to human rights and suspicious of power, has kept quiet even as its agents are accused of having attacked the *Rainbow Warrior* in a friendly country." I called Alain Richard, a young and very bright Socialist deputy in the National Assembly, asking him why the parliament had remained utterly silent on the affair. "The dominant reaction of the political world," he said, "is representative of what the French people think, which is that we have to do things like that to maintain ourselves in the world." *Le Monde*, which was about to publish the pathbreaking articles on the affair that led to M. Hernu's resignation, said in a front-page article that the government's haughty approach to the affair was "a shoddy sort of Gaullism," consisting of "arrogance, false Napoleonic superiority, grandeur in the form of isolation, and *raison d'état* in the form of a fig leaf."

The other trend came from the press, which launched itself on an unaccustomed fury of persistent investigations, laced with sensational scoops and disclosures, establishing beyond any doubt that the conclusions of the Tricot report were opposite the truth and that the *Rainbow Warrior* affair was a government operation from the beginning. In September, roughly a month after the Tricot report and a week after Mitterrand's highly visible, defiant visit to Mururoa, *Le Monde* reported on its front page that the Greenpeace operation had been carried out by military saboteurs working for the DGSE—France's spy outfit—and that the Defense Ministry had approved the operation in advance. M. Hernu, responding immediately, dismissed the *Le Monde* report as part of "the campaign of rumors and insinuations being waged against French military officials over the attack on the *Rainbow Warrior.*" But the *Le Monde* story had the ring of truth about it. It provided intimate details. There had, it said, been three French teams on the island. The falsely named "Turenge" couple, arrested shortly after the incident and still being held in a New Zealand jail, were there for reconnaissance and logistics. The three men on the yacht, the *Ouvéa*, had smuggled into the country the explosives and other equipment, such as a motorized rubber dinghy, needed for the operation. A third team, which escaped from Auckland undetected, actually attached the explosives to the hull of the *Rainbow Warrior*.

The disclosures caused painful embarrassment to the government. Mitterrand, returning from the Pacific only a few days before, had called the operation "an absurd and criminal act." Hernu, after the *Le Monde* story, categorically denied that he had given the order to sink the vessel, declaring at the same time—and no doubt to his later regret—that everything would be done to find out the truth, and if anybody disobeyed orders, he would "ask the government to take appropriate action." The next day, at his press conference at the Ministry of Defense, he repeated his denial of responsibility in the affair, saying he would be "intransigent" in his search for the truth about it and "pitiless" if he discovered that any French officers had taken part in the sinking of the ship. This was "in the interest of the credibility of our system of defense," he said. These statements seemed to be reiterations of Fabius's promise of a few weeks earlier to prosecute any French citizen who had committed criminal acts. Moreover, Fabius himself announced after the *Le Monde* story appeared that he stood by his earlier pledge.

As it turned out, the defense minister was more pitiless with himself than he was with any of his subordinates. Two days after his rejection of the *Le Monde* story, he admitted implicitly—though never explicitly—that the newspaper's report was correct. He announced his resignation, claiming that it had become clear to him that "authorities within my ministry have without doubt concealed the truth from me." One such "authority," Admiral Pierre Lacoste, the head of the French intelligence agency, was asked to step down on the grounds that he had refused to answer questions about the Greenpeace operation. Hernu's resignation did not immediately end the furor in France. Two days later, Fabius, appearing on television, admitted, finally, that French agents had sunk the Greenpeace vessel, though, he added, he did not know who had given the order. Later still, on September 25, the prime minister said that Hernu bore "political responsibility" for the operation, which, he said, had been a "bad decision." Adding a twist of mystery, Fabius went on to note the inexplicable bungling of some of the French agents on the scene, saying: "I ask myself questions. Is it possible that there was a sabotage of the sabotage?" The idea was that somebody—perhaps some right-wing military officers—had decided to botch the operation in order to embarrass the government. Or else they undertook the operation in defiance of orders, then leaked the information to the press, their actions, again, designed to make political trouble for the leftists running the country. Fabius, who gave no details to elucidate his suspicion, never talked about it again; it was never investigated by the press; it always remained a tantalizingly Machiavellian hypothesis.

And yet hypotheses are not enough. Everything that had happened until then—Hernu's resignation, Fabius's admissions of French responsibility, the suspicions of a sabotage of the sabotage—still left basic questions unanswered. Who gave the order for the sinking of the boat? Why were the leaks to the press so selective, incriminating France, claiming that senior officials were responsible, but never specifying exactly who they were, never really resolving all the mysteries of the affair? Whatever happened to all those vows that "criminal acts" would be prosecuted? The plain fact is that the Greenpeace affair was dropped; it faded out of sight, almost as quickly as it had emerged into view in the first place. A parliamentary investigation was announced. It was never carried out. The only people punished in the affair were four military officers arrested at the end of September and indicted for having leaked information about the operation to the press.

And so the "criminal acts" turned out to be not the sinking of the

Rainbow Warrior or the unintended killing of the photographer aboard, not the cover-up, not the pattern of government deception and lies that had crumbled before the onslaught of revelations in the press. The only criminal act ever punished by France in the entire affair was the leaking to the press of the information that had embarrassed the country in the eyes of the world.

The Greenpeace affair as a national obsession came to an odd end at the very end of September. The new director of the DGSE, a former army chief of staff named René Imbot, unexpectedly got on all the major national television stations one evening and made an astonishing declaration. Since taking over the intelligence agency, Imbot declared, "I have, to my deep stupefaction, discovered—and I weigh my words carefully—a truly malicious operation to destabilize our secret services: I would even say to destroy our secret services." Imbot, a former foreign legionnaire, anti-Nazi resistance fighter, veteran of France's wars in Indochina and Algeria, a man of rustic appearance who stands ramrod straight and exudes toughness, determination, loyalty, and discipline, went on: "I have also found people who had to be punished." This reference was apparently to the four men arrested and charged with leaking information. "I have cut off the rotten branches," he went on, not specifying what branches he was talking about, but continuing: "I tell you right now that I have locked up this service, and when I say locked up, those who have served with me, the officers and soldiers who will hear me tonight, when I say locked up, they know what that means."

Imbot, whose white hair seems to stand straight up like the bristles on a brush, announced by his very appearance that this was no man to be trifled with. If France half wept over the spectacle of ineptitude offered by its agents in the field, here was a tough old bird who seemed to know what he was doing. "I am the rampart of this service," he said. "I will be the rampart of this service. That means that starting now, all information that anyone claims to hold or to receive from this service is a lie, because I have locked up this service." He concluded: "And if I have accepted this mission, it is for the honor of our armies, and I will do the job well." Again, the honor of the army.

There were a few questions from the journalists present. Those who "destabilized," he was asked, "are they the four soldiers who have been indicted?"

"Oh, those poor guys, no," Imbot said. "Others have a load of rotten branches, and I was making an allusion to them. I have cut off the rotten branches."

"Others have been implicated?"

"No. I have cut off the rotten branches."

"Were any foreign powers implicated in this undertaking?"

"I'm saying nothing more. I am the chief of the secret services."

It would be difficult to imagine a head of the American CIA appearing on every major television channel in the country and announcing the discovery of a "malicious operation" to destroy the American spy agency, using words like "rotten branches," without immediately launching the scandal of the century. It would be difficult for him to announce that certain officers had been "punished" and never be required to disclose exactly which ones and for what reasons. There would surely be congressional clamorings for details. The press and commentators would scream for full disclosure. There would be televised hearings. In the United States and elsewhere, a declaration like the one made by Imbot would have marked a new beginning to the scandal, an entirely fresh and fascinating stage, a whole unprecedented arena for aggressive investigative reporting of the sort that had unleashed the scandal in the first place. And for a day or two, it seemed that such would also be the case in France. I remember awaiting with a keen sense of anticipation the next stage of a story that just didn't want to come to an end. Everybody in France—the newspapers, the public, the politicians—were talking about Imbot's appearance, wondering exactly what this malignant operation was, who the "rotten branches" were. Were heads going to start to roll at the DGSE? Was the Greenpeace affair far bigger than it had originally seemed? Had somebody tried to destroy France's secret service?

These questions were never answered. The French, as the country's two leading investigative journalists, Jacques Derogy and Jean-Marie Pontaut, noted in a book later published on the Greenpeace affair, were no longer looking for a continuation of the affair; they wanted somebody to come along "and save the national honor." This is what Imbot had done with his highly theatrical, extremely compelling, admirably succinct appearance on the air. The no-nonsense old soldier achieved a brief epiphany as a resurrected de Gaulle, putting an end to the intrigues of politicians and the press, taking charge, slamming the door shut on a kind of national farce. That was what the public and the governing bureaucracy wanted. Nobody said much more about the Greenpeace affair again; or, more accurately, nobody, except the pair of persistent journalists, whose thorough volume on the affair was ignored, cared about getting to the bottom of it anymore. M. Imbot's announcement came like a final punctuation mark on the last page of an unfinished novel. After it, there was nothing more, nothing except the unsatisfying sense that always accompanies a plot with no denouement, a story without a climax.

I T W A S Bernard Barral, a bartender at Le Café Maryland in a working-class neighborhood near the Bastille in Paris, who, among others, shared a clear vision, not of the unresolved mysteries of the Greenpeace affair, but of the meaning of the silence that followed it. I went to the café, a brass-counter establishment with a pinball machine in what is known as a *quartier populaire* in Paris, looking for some grass-roots commentary, and I asked Barral what he thought. "Why are they making such a fuss about the sinking of a boat?" he said, clearing the counter of used demitasse cups. "So many other boats have been sunk." He went on: "The affair has been exaggerated, and when the press stops talking about it, so will the people."

A poll in the right-wing daily *Figaro* supported this point of view. It showed that 78 percent of the French thought that the Greenpeace operation was "unacceptable," meaning, presumably, that it had been morally wrong, an inappropriate way for a great nation like France to advance its interests in the world. The *Figaro* poll showed 52 percent of the population believing that President Mitterrand, despite his denials, had advance knowledge of the plans to sink the boat. But it also showed 65 percent of the respondents believing that he should remain in office (a painful finding for *Le Figaro* to report, since the newspaper, owned by a Conservative parliamentarian named Robert Hersant, ardently hated the Socialist president).

In the end, the Greenpeace affair showed several things about France, including a few things that were new. For one, the press had shown far more independence, far more of an investigative peskiness, than ever before in France, and this alone was significant. It was commonly noted as the Greenpeace affair unfolded that in bygone days, the newspapers and, particularly, the television and radio stations would have been dealt with by a call or two from the prime minister's office or the Élysée Palace. That was the way things had been handled before. Nobody believed that in a country where all the television stations were owned by the state, their directors appointed by the government, the media were truly and entirely independent of the political will of those in power. In the Greenpeace affair—constantly compared in France to the American Watergate affair—the press had been the protagonist. A new class of journalists, defiant of authority and jealous of their role as monitor of political power, had emerged as a genuinely independent force, one welcomed by a public less reverent than ever. That was the reason the Tricot investigation, engineered by a government hoping foolishly that the formality of an explanation would serve as a convincing explanation, had provoked such widespread disbelief. "The government didn't understand Montesquieu," Jean-François Revel, the author of numerous polemical volumes, told me over lunch, referring to the philosopher who first devised the theory of the separation of powers. "They didn't understand that the public would not accept the political leadership itself appointing the power that would investigate it."

Indeed, the Greenpeace affair underlined the absence of any nongovernmental agency available to investigate the government. The parliament, controlled, in any case, by the party in power, showed no will to look into the affair. There were no special prosecutors, no hearings, no courts to be appealed to. France, despite the greater friskiness of the press, remains a country where all real power lies in the hands of a few figures at the apex of the system. The country has no mechanism by which apparent wrongdoing can be truly and impartially explored. It is, rather, a country where a head of the secret services can impose an end to an investigation with a tough, three-sentence statement on national television.

That is an institutional fact, a judicial reality. But the Greenpeace affair showed something deeper still about France. Presumably, only mass popular demonstrations would have ensured that the affair have real political effects. Only that in the French democracy could have provided the impetus to a full disclosure of the operation, perhaps to put pressure on the president of the Republic to explain his own attitude clearly. Certainly, in recent French history, such demonstrations have taken place, and had clear and demonstrable effect. In 1984, a million people took to the streets, protesting a Socialist plan to remove some of the independence of France's religious schools, following which the government wisely withdrew its initiative. A few years later, after the Greenpeace scandal, students marching down Paris's broad avenues had stopped dead a university reform plan that they didn't like. In the Greenpeace affair there were no demonstrations, and there was no desire for demonstrations, even though the affair had mesmerized the country, providing it with a kind of multimedia dramatic serial featuring a new disclosure, yet another sensational event, almost every day for two months. Despite that, there were hardly any calls in the press, whether leftist or rightist, for the matter to continue, for an impartial investigation to take place, for the top leaders to explain what they knew and when they had known it. Most surprisingly, the very press that had pursued the affair so relentlessly during August and September suddenly let it drop. I called André Fontaine, the editor of *Le Monde*, to ask him why. He referred briefly to the American penchant for moralism in politics, which did not exist in France. He did not seem to want to talk much about the post-Greenpeace role of the press. He didn't appear to have agonized much about it. I had the impression that this one newspaper editor viewed it already as a matter in the past.

What the Greenpeace affair revealed was the absence of any significant questioning among the French of the absolute right of the elected leadership to act in an untrammeled fashion in the international world. Very soon, in fact, the French themselves, both the people, the press, and the government, took on an interesting new stance, particularly with regard to New Zealand. Gradually, France emerged, in the French conception of things, as the aggrieved party—the *offensé*, the "insulted one," as the old language of dueling used to have it. The country that had committed involuntary manslaughter and sabotage on the soil of another country suddenly began seeing the other country, New Zealand, as the real villain of the piece. The *affaire* that started out as the Socialists' worst political crisis since their taking power in 1981 got transformed into a rallying cry for national unity against, not exactly an enemy, but an adversary nonetheless.

The issue that provoked this reaction was the status of the people who had come to be called *les faux Turenge*, the pair of intelligence agents, posing as husband and wife, who had been arrested by New Zealand in the wake of the Greenpeace operation. The two agents, whose names were actually Dominique Prieur and Alain Mafart, originally charged with murder, were allowed in New Zealand to plead guilty to the lesser charge of manslaughter, the guilty plea meaning there would be no trial and thus no awkward presentation of the facts. Versions of this plea-bargaining arrangement differed. French officials openly claimed that they were the result of delicate negotiations over the fate of the two officers that had been taking place for several weeks. The French press reported that France, eager to get the two soldiers off as easily as possible, was threatening to use its weight inside the European Economic Community to restrict New Zealand's sales to it of butter and other products. New Zealand officials, eager to protect the image of their independent judiciary, denied that negotiations had taken place, Prime Minister Lange proclaiming, "This is a process of law—not some sordid haggling."

In November, the two agents were sentenced to ten-year prison terms. French officials said they would try to convince Lange to give them amnesty so they could return home quickly despite the sentence, which was deemed harsh in France, where the two prisoners were being lionized, treated as martyrs—which, in a way, they were, since after all they had only been following orders. The French quietly, in negotiations sponsored by U.N. secretary-general Javier Pérez de Cuéllar, did finally issue an apology to New Zealand, and they agreed to pay a $7 million indemnity. The French also made a financial settlement with the family of the photographer killed when the *Rainbow Warrior* was sunk. The New Zealanders, presumably understanding that the two French agents were not ordinary criminals, agreed to let them go. But there was a condition. Both had to remain for three years on a French military base on Hao atoll in the South Pacific. They would not be able to go to France before that time was up.

But they did go. In December 1987, after remaining on Hao for less than a year, Mafart was flown to France for medical treatment. It seems he had a stomach ailment. No New Zealand doctors were allowed to examine him. New Zealand's prime minister, again speaking with a certain degree of logic, declared the repatriation "a blatant and outrageous breach" of the agreement between the two countries that had already spared Mafart ten years in prison. Prime Minister Chirac lamely defended the French move—which was popular at home, where it really needed no defense—on the grounds that the agreement allowed for repatriation if either of the agents fell ill, or if Captain Prieur, a married woman, should happen to get pregnant.

Captain Prieur did get pregnant. She was flown back to France in May 1988, two days before France's presidential elections, M. Chirac evidently hoping that her return would win him more votes. Perhaps it did. Probably it did not, since the move's electoral motive was so blatant as to appear hypocritical. Chirac lost the presidential election to Mitterrand, the man many suspected of having known about the Greenpeace affair in the first place. Back in New Zealand, David Lange reluctantly accepted Captain Prieur's repatriation. She was, it seems, indeed pregnant. But he continued to demand that Mafart bring his bellyache back to Hao atoll and serve out his three years of exile. In a way, it was a ridiculous request. Mafart was no more guilty than any number of others involved in the affair, including the higher-ups who had ordered it in the first place. His punishment would have been purely symbolic. After the May 1988 elections, when a new Socialist government came into power, Prime Minister Michel Rocard asked Mafart to return to Hao voluntarily, "in the superior interest of the country." It seemed, as of this writing, unlikely that Major Mafart would follow the suggestion.

THERE still remained at least one judicial possibility that further details of the Greenpeace operation would come to light. Even if Imbot had been vague about the "rotten branches," the new DGSE chief had after all discovered some people whom it had been necessary to punish. And four men, all of them DGSE officers, were under indictment. It seemed possible, though not certain, that their trial, if there was a trial, would force new disclosures in the affair. Any good defense lawyer would try to prove the criminal responsibilities of higher-ups in the government as a way of exculpating his clients. That being the case, it seemed likely the government would try to avoid a trial, disposing of the case of the four arrested intelligence officers in some other way. But if the four refused to plead guilty, a trial would have to take place, unless the charges against them were dismissed. And if the charges against them were dismissed, wouldn't the press and the public want to know why they had been arrested with such fanfare in the first place, with all that talk of "destabilization" and "malignant operations"? At the very least, it seemed that the four officers posed a problem for the government. This was wrong. The four officers also faded into the mists of national forgetfulness.

In fact, no details about the four were ever given publicly, though the Derogy and Pontaut book on the Greenpeace affair contained a credible account of their arrest and interrogation. The authors say that beginning in late August 1985, when the leaks about official French involvement in the Greenpeace matter began appearing in the press, there was shock and consternation in the offices of the DGSE, whose internal security services began to tap phones and monitor the movements of the service's own agents. In this way, four men, including the colonel who was in charge of the DGSE's antiterrorist operations, were picked up, questioned, and charged with leaking secrets to the press—their arrest itself leaked to the same press to which they, presumably, had leaked. Derogy and Pontaut alone raised the ethical issue surrounding these arrests that the French as a whole seemed inclined to ignore. They reminded the reader that the secret services in general had apparently lied to the man designated to carry out a "rigorous" investigation of the affair, concealing from him the true nature of the involvement of French officers. And so, while the rest of the agency lied and prevaricated with impunity, the four arrested officers stood accused of telling the truth. "The moral of the story is this," Derogy and Pontaut wrote. "It costs more dearly to tell the truth to a journalist than to lie to a counselor of the state appointed by the prime minister and the president. We are a curious republic."

Months went by. The four officers remained in a military stockade, sometimes, according to the two investigative reporters, kept in solitary confinement, treated as traitors, even though the investigating judge, unhappily appointed to pursue this unhappy case, had declined to charge them with treason, indicting them instead for the crime of passing classified military information to unauthorized persons. Among the state's problems, however, was the absence of a good case against them. They had been observed by the DGSE internal security service talking about the Greenpeace operation to each other but not to any journalists. At one point, the investigating judge had the houses of the suspects searched, but nothing incriminating was found. For several months the investigation dragged on, while the four men remained locked up. Finally, in 1986, the new minister of defense, André Giraud, had them released and restored to their ranks, dropping the ridiculous charge of their having been the only people in the affair to tell the truth.

By then, the French had put Greenpeace behind them. The closing of the book on the four intelligence agents was hardly noted.

Shortly after that, Derogy and Pontaut cast a vapor of light on the Greenpeace affair when they published the findings of their investigation. The two journalists, it should be noted, were celebrated in France for their investigative teamwork. They had published numerous reports in the newsweekly *L'Express* and in nearly a dozen books on the various earlier *affaires* of the French government. Their reputations and their sources were both excellent. Moreover, their conclusions regarding the Greenpeace affair were potentially explosive. Mitterrand had indeed been informed of the operation. It had been approved by the highest authorities of the government, the same government that then mounted the charade of a self-investigation. It didn't matter. The public had forgotten. There was no interest in Greenpeace anymore. The book made hardly a ripple on the surface of French life. *Raison d'état* had triumphed.

20

Gaullists and Bonapartists,
Presidents and Kings

THE CONVERSATION, held with two journalists in the rather disheveled precincts of the Aix-en-Provence office of *La Marseillaise*, the tabloid-sized, Communist-owned newspaper, was about Charles de Gaulle and the political legacy that the tall, gangly, arrogant, self-assured, prideful, and often cynical resistance hero of World War II left to France.

The heritage is called, as everyone knows, Gaullism, a term meaning so many things to different people that I always wondered exactly what, if anything, it really did mean. To most Americans, clearly, the term refers to the conception the French have of their relationship with the rest of the world. It has to do with the French quest for *gloire*, national glory, a quest seemingly indistinguishable from the image that foreigners had of de Gaulle himself. The general's single most significant act was his insistence on making France a nuclear power. He built the French bomb not so much out of military necessity—though it could be, and was, justified by the evocation of just such a necessity—but for the sake of national prestige. It was a kind of shortcut toward the acquisition of weightiness in the world, and the French cling to that policy with an emotion that could only come from deep love of national glory. To this day, they are deeply suspicious of the superpower attempts to achieve sharp reductions in nuclear weapons, lest that force the French themselves to reduce their far smaller arsenals. The second most significant act, the one remaining in American eyes de Gaulle's most characteristic, notorious, and outrageous gesture, was to remove France from the co-ordinated military command of the North Atlantic Treaty Organization

(NATO), thereby at once seeming to weaken the defenses of the democratic West against the undemocratic East while gratuitously snubbing the great ally that had twice rescued France from its frequently demonstrated inability to defend itself unaided from its enemies.

While in the eyes of the rest of the world de Gaulle's main characteristic was a reflexive haughtiness, a persistence in behaving as though France were a great power in its own right when, in fact, it was a recently defeated nation whose very survival was utterly and inextricably tied to that of the rest of the NATO countries, in France itself, both the general and his heritage mean something different. If the United States and its allies saved France twice from its own military inadequacy, de Gaulle, in the common view, saved French democracy twice from its political foolishness—once, in the years immediately after the war, when, in agreeing to head the government, he prevented the Communists from coming to power, and, again, in 1958, when, coming dramatically out of retirement in his home village of Colombey-les-deux-Églises, he announced that he could, if the French people so wished, be of service to his country again. The French people did so wish, and de Gaulle promptly pulled them out of a dual crisis, thereby consolidating the Republic, making its functioning both more predictable and more stable, and even taking some small steps in the direction of that ultimate Gaullist goal, enhancing French prestige in the rest of the world.

Indeed, if there were one factor that had to be singled out to account for the unitary and generally harmonious nature of France today, that factor would have to be called Gaullism. The French often remind themselves of a statement made decades ago by André Malraux, the author of *Man's Fate* and other novels, who became de Gaulle's minister of culture in the first government of the Fifth Republic in 1958. Everybody, Malraux said, "either was, is, or will be a Gaullist." Many in France violently disagree. To ask a Socialist to agree to the label Gaullism, for example, would be to ask a Capulet to become a Montague. And yet Malraux was right. To understand France in all its glorious political particularity, to comprehend the way it has grappled with the overwhelming challenge of the twentieth century, you have, perhaps, not to begin, but to end with that odd and gutsy genius from Colombey-les-deux-Églises.

F RANCE in 1958, when de Gaulle emerged from what has come to be called his political wilderness, was paralyzed by parliamentary factionalism and instability, as a host of small parties constantly bickered and maneuvered in an attempt to gain influence and power within the parliamentary system established after the war and known as the Fourth Republic. Graver still, the country was rapidly becoming bogged down in the second costly and, apparently, unwinnable war that it had been called on to fight in less than two years, both of them against independence forces in what had only a few years earlier been its extensive colonial empire. In 1954, the French had been defeated at Dien Bien Phu by the Vietnamese, who thereby gained their independence from France after a century of colonial rule.

Now it was the turn of the Algerians, colonized since the early nineteenth century, whose struggle for independence carried far higher stakes than that of the Indochinese war, not that there were no colonial settlers in Indochina, no national pride at stake. But Algeria was the jewel in the rapidly shrinking French imperial crown. Geographically, it was right there, just across the Mediterranean from *La Métropole.* More important, a million ethnic French citizens lived in that North African colony, and they deeply yearned—indeed, they were willing to go to almost any lengths—to keep Algeria French. Algeria and the emotions it involved, the desperate, quixotic effort to maintain it inside the French sphere, the accusations of torture and inhumanity directed against the French army and the corresponding charges of treason and betrayal directed against those who were ready to let Algeria go, were elements of the last of the colossal struggles that divided the French and posed for de Gaulle his greatest challenge.

Eventually, after surviving a series of assassination attempts by hardline anti-independence military officers who created the OAS, whose near-exclusive though unrealized goal was to shoot the general-president and take control of the French government, de Gaulle got France out of Algeria, signing an independence agreement in the Swiss city of Évianles-Bains in 1961 and seeing to the repatriation of hundreds of thousands of French citizens from North Africa, the groups that came quickly and somewhat sorrowfully to be called *les pieds noirs,* "the black feet."

De Gaulle, arguably, was the only figure in the country who possessed the prestige and authority essential to end the Algerian conflict, particularly since the French withdrawal from North Africa signaled the definitive collapse of France's once-great empire, from which much of the national *gloire* had derived. At the same time, the generally conservative general, whose roots seemed to lie in the sort of soil that in the past had begotten the country's fiercest antirepublicans, its *anti-Dreyfusards,* its most Catholic monarchists, was the same man who, by standing above the parliamentary maelstrom generated by dozens of committed republican parliamentarians, saved the Republic from its own inner turmoil.

He came back to power in 1958 empowered by the National Assembly. He promulgated a new constitution, affirmed by a national referendum in which 80 percent of the electorate voted in favor. The result of the constitutional redaction was the Fifth Republic, which de Gaulle made into a powerful presidential system, dismantling the parliamentary prerogatives and producing a near-monarchical executive, elected for a seven-year term, who, presumably, would rule in consultation with the only other power that really counted in France, the whole, sovereign people.

The arrangement caused rage and consternation among many of the politicians, particularly those on the left, who saw their means of making their presence felt taken away from them. François Mitterrand, a wily master of the parliamentary game who had voted in the National Assembly against the return of de Gaulle to power, charged in a famous book, *The Permanent Coup d'État*, that the Fifth Republic was highly authoritarian and deeply antidemocratic. But the new arrangement stuck. Compared to the nineteen governments that had succeeded each other during the fourteen-year existence of the Fourth Republic, in the thirty years following the adoption of de Gaulle's constitution there have been four powerful chief executives elected to that office. French democracy, which in 1981 brought M. Mitterrand himself to the near-monarchical presidency, seems to have survived, even flourished. Mitterrand these days would have to agree, even if his agreement is conditioned by the claim, made on his behalf by his closest advisers, that only he has the kind of republican temperament to allow the Gaullist constitution to function without posing a threat to the democratic freedoms of the French. The Fifth Republic is still, thus, a permanent coup d'état, but under Mitterrand, it is nonetheless benign.

If abroad de Gaulle represented a haughty, prickly, stubborn, and yet somehow admirable Gallic independence—it is, of course, far better to have truly independent allies than sycophantic ones—Gaullism at home was, first and foremost, a unifying spirit, one that, in itself, drew sustenance from the general's own overweening ambitions for France, the urgency of his desire that it quash its quarrelsomeness and restore its national greatness. "It is necessary to know whether the French want to remake France or lie down," he told André Malraux in 1969. "I can't do it without them. But we are going to reestablish our institutions, gather together around us what is called the empire, and restore to France its nobility and its rank."

With greatness itself his rallying cry, rather than this or that policy, this or that leader, the general fashioned his acceptance by the vast majority of the French on the very concept of the imaginary country, the France that was a "particular idea" more than a reality. He was thus one of those few political figures who, at least in retrospect, seem to have stood largely apart from routine political tussles and ambitions. The organization he created was something called the RPF, for Rassemblement Pour la France. The word *rassemblement* is key. It means a collecting together, a reassembly. It suggests an ingathering of the French around a few great patriotic themes: national greatness, solidarity, unity. There have been other such efforts by the contentious French to put aside their debilitating quarrels and be reassembled around some colossal figure, a *grand homme*. One could certainly imagine Richelieu and Louis XIV in this category. The most unfortunate of the *grand homme* precedents was no doubt Marshal Philippe Pétain, the hero of World War I who called on the French to throw down their arms, yield before the inevitable German victory of 1940, and build a new unity of purpose around three great values, summed up in the oft-repeated phrase "*famille, travail, patrie*"—family, work, country. De Gaulle, the hero of World War II, presented himself, like Pétain, as a figure above politics, pleading with the French to set aside their petty differences and stand for something great again. Pétain, like de Gaulle, appeared as a near-monarchical figure, a father of the nation, one whose interest was not personal political gain but France itself.

The difference—and what a difference—is that Pétain's appeal came in the service of defeatism, dictatorship, and barbarism, and de Gaulle's on behalf of national independence and the Republic. De Gaulle used his prestige to advance rather than humiliate the French cause. And he bolstered his image as *grand homme* by his readiness to retire from the scene when his authority was questioned, rather than cling to power at any cost. When early in 1946 the parliamentary maneuvering around him reached a new point of intensity, he simply stepped down, complaining publicly of the "exclusive regime of the parties." He went back to Colombey-les-deux-Églises and waited to be called again. He was called in 1958, and he spawned a whole new concept for the French, summed up in that word *rassemblement*. The student riots of 1968 cast a shadow over his prestige, and when in 1969 he stepped down, again having lost a referendum on government restructuring that in no way obligated him constitutionally to resign his office, the claimants to his mantle continued to use the same word. The powerful neo-Gaullist party, forged and led by Jacques Chirac, was named the Rassemblement Pour la République, or RPR, a designation aimed at draping around its own shoulders the ample cloak of Gaullism.

A ND YET being aware of this history does not necessarily enable one to specify exactly what Gaullism is today, and that was the subject of my conversation with the two reporters in Aix-en-Provence. If Gaullism was primarily a belief in French greatness, then, surely, every French political figure had to be, or pretend to be, Gaullist. The Conservative writer Jean Dutourd once described Gaullism, with a bit of cynicism that the general would have shared, as a refusal to confuse France with the French. "The latter are the means," Dutourd wrote, "France is the end, that is to say, a work for whose beauty no effort should be spared." And yet if that is the essence of Gaullism, what political leader would dispute it? Roughly fifteen years after de Gaulle's death and ten years after the founding of Chirac's ostensibly neo-Gaullist party, I went around talking to renowned old Gaullists to try to discover the essence of the Gaullist concept in France today. In what way were Gaullists different from the Socialists who were ruling the country? Was Gaullism really a political concept, or did it refer entirely and exclusively to the particular historic role and the special, imperious personality of de Gaulle himself? I betrayed my own belief during this short-lived quest of mine by asking the question: Is there anybody in France in a position of power today who is not at heart a Gaullist? Hadn't Malraux's famous formulation been correct? Gaullism, it seemed to me, was not so much the creation of de Gaulle as it was the expression of the French political culture, a meeting of a certain aristocratic demeanor, aloofness, and imperiousness of personality with an ability to serve as a centralizing force, a magnet for *rassemblement*.

I talked to men like Maurice Couve de Murville, de Gaulle's foreign minister, who, silver-haired and distinguished, received me in the study of his town house in Paris. I interviewed Jacques Chaban-Delmas, avuncular, feisty, self-possessed, in the huge, crepuscular office used by the president of the National Assembly, which he was. Chaban-Delmas, a former prime minister, had been de Gaulle's military representative on the wartime Resistance Council in London. I went to see Jacques Toubon, the young, affable secretary-general of Chirac's RPR, in a small meeting room at the party's headquarters on the rue de Lille in Paris. I asked them all the same questions, feeling always dissatisfied with the answers. No, they all said, not everybody is a Gaullist, certainly not the

Socialists. Gaullism is not a doctrine but an attitude, not an ideology but a pragmatic approach to problem solving, they said. I never managed to pull together a story from their comments, so vague and general did they seem to me.

And now, similarly, here I was in the run-down office of a Communist newspaper, offering the opinion, yet again, that everybody in France is a Gaullist, and encountering the same opposition to that notion. Weren't the Socialists as much the champions of French *gloire* as de Gaulle had been or as Chirac would have been had he been president? Didn't they refuse, in classic Gaullist fashion, the American request to overfly French territory on their way to bomb Gaddafi's Libya in 1986? Hadn't they kept France out of the NATO military command while continuing to build up the country's independent nuclear deterrent? Didn't the Socialists insist, as de Gaulle had, on keeping a certain distance from both of the superpowers, adopting a certain defiant prickliness toward the Americans, insisting on being the leaders of the European Community, seeking influence in the Third World by, among other things, stationing troops in several African countries, building up the concept of Francophonia, striving to play a major role in the Middle East by, for example, serving as the major arms supplier to Iraq in its war against Iran? And back home, wasn't President Mitterrand, after pursuing a few months of ideological politics in the beginning of his first term, becoming ever more the grandfather of all the French, no longer pushing a program but attempting to exemplify the nation, standing for a vague sort of national unity more in the fashion of England's Queen Elizabeth than of a Socialist politician with a particular leftist vision to implement?

Absolutely not, came the answer. The reporters' conviction was that I overlooked key changes in French policy since de Gaulle's day. De Gaulle had indeed been prickly toward the United States, but since him, France had become slavishly Atlanticist, ever more closely tied to the United States and NATO, following Washington's lead on the most important foreign policy questions. And in Europe, the move toward a fully integrated economic community, one in which France will lose elements of its sovereignty as well as its position of political leadership, did not represent what the general had in mind. For him, Europe was an instrument of French greatness, a coalition of nations, excluding the British, whose membership in the organization de Gaulle had vetoed precisely because he did not want their rivalry. The Common Market, according to de Gaulle, was to be an organization whose cooperation and policies would be inspired by a French vision—namely, that of a third great power bloc in the world buffering the Soviet-American antagonism.

What Europe has become, the journalists said, was an unwieldy customs union that had the effect of diluting the original Gaullist vision. The Socialists, under Mitterrand, had presided over this non-Gaullist trend, but the same would have happened under the classic rightist party, which is, not coincidentally, the neo-Gaullist RPR. Gaullism to the two gentlemen of *La Marseillaise* was in this sense a particular set of policies. It remained "*une certaine idée de la France*," meaning a grand idea, if also an idea that, de Gaulle himself admitted in his gloomy, pessimistic moments, made more of France than it did of the French, about whom he tended to be skeptical and even contemptuous.

Yes, I had to agree that policies, and times, have changed. I nonetheless remained convinced that Gaullism was what my journalist friends said it was, and something else as well, something close to the heart of the imaginary country. It was not so much the creation of a philosophy and a personality as it was the matching of a philosophy and a personality with the deepest cravings of a troubled nation. If de Gaulle had not existed, the French would have had to invent him. It was not so much the lanky general who shaped France to his specifications but France that was the mold out of which the *grand homme* was cracked.

D E G A U L L E died in November 1970, and a sharp dispute, what the magazine *L'Express* called at the time "a mediocre affair," erupted immediately, serving now, nearly twenty years later, as a kind of basis for comparison of the general's image. The day after his funeral on November 12, even as the newspapers published their lengthy eulogies, a fierce debate broke out within the political world over what now seems to be the most trivial of issues—the renaming of the Place de l'Étoile for the general. On November 13, the Paris city council quickly and unanimously passed an ordinance giving the name Place Charles de Gaulle to the great circle around the Arc de Triomphe, which itself rises over the tomb of France's Unknown Soldier. The decision came with little debate, but as word of it spread to the country as a whole, the uproar was tremendous.

The death of de Gaulle showed that there was no grace period in contentious France, no episode of mourning during which reverence and sanctimony would get general acceptance. Questions were raised, arguments made. The renaming of l'Étoile seemed to give greater honor to one man—not beloved of everybody—than it did to all the dead of World War I and World War II, who were collectively symbolized by the Unknown Soldier. General Gilbert Rémy, who served with de Gaulle during the resistance, declared that the defunct president "would never have permitted this sacrilege—because that is what it is—perpetrated against the Unknown Soldier." A newspaper editorial, agreeing with this sentiment, averred that the French needed to maintain l'Étoile as a place where they can "encounter each other in a spirit of national unanimity, forgetting their partisan quarrels." An anti-Gaullist, Pierre Pujo, wrote in December that de Gaulle had been little more than a "harmful political adventurer." Many French, he noted, including many "still fooled today, will ask themselves tomorrow how the Paris city council could, on a day of collective craziness, give him l'Étoile." The satirical weekly *Le Canard Enchaîné* published a banner headline above a drawing of the Arc de Triomphe: "After l'Étoile: why not rename France de Gaulle?" And when on December 15 the renaming ceremony did take place, the city council's decision not having been revoked, there were cries of "assassin," "Fascist," "swine," emanating here and there from a partly worshipful, partly hostile crowd.

The context of the moment has to be taken into account. France was in the final stages of its long period of domestic turmoil, its last days as a nation cut in two. The bitter heritage of the Algerian war was still powerfully felt, de Gaulle looked on by the anti-Gaullist right not as the savior of the national esteem, who had eased the country out of a quagmire, but as the traitor who had come to power vowing allegiance to "*l'Algérie Française*" (or so they thought; actually, de Gaulle never used that phrase) and then sold out the colonial settlers for the sake of expediency. The 1960s had, moreover, just ended, and to an entire radical generation, including the members of that alliance of students and workers who had created turmoil on Paris's streets in 1968, de Gaulle was still the villain, a pompous archconservative, an instrument of the moneyed classes, the big bourgeoisie, and the militarists. His great intellectual rival in France was Sartre, who had opposed him for years, seeing in him all that was stuffy, rigid, dehumanizing, in French political culture. "All our impotence and our contradictions converged in him," he wrote, opposing de Gaulle's return to power in 1958. "Since the sovereign is a general, the country obeys an army, which only obeys itself. Yes, indeed, our state is in bad shape." In the realm of politics, the Socialist leader Mitterrand had been his constant detractor, the man who asked: "And what is he, de Gaulle, the Duce, the Führer, a caudillo, a conductor, a guide?"

THAT the mood has changed, that the polemical aspects of the Gaullist legacy have shriveled away, that the specific, controversial measures he took have gained general acceptance—or been forgotten, replaced in the memory by his charismatic authority—are all revealed in the France of today in three things: a book, a television program, and a presidential style, that of Mitterrand himself.

Over several years, one of the major literary events in France was the publication of a definitive three-volume biography of de Gaulle by a well-known journalist and biographer, Jean Lacouture, a man who would earlier have identified himself as being on the anti-Gaullist left. The Lacouture work was magisterial, lofty, dispassionate, respectful. When de Gaulle died, *Figaro* had predicted that those who had tended to reproach the general would praise him in the future, and while Lacouture did not set out exactly to praise de Gaulle, he did install him among the French demigods, as one of the untouchables, a man no longer signifying certain specific policies but, as Malraux long before had put it, "the man for whom the appellation French signifies those who want France not to die."

Similarly, in 1988, one of the major television networks presented an immense ten-part series on de Gaulle, based largely on Lacouture's book. The series, produced under the Socialist government—that is, under de Gaulle's former sworn enemies—further advanced the sanctification of the general, his transformation from figure of controversy, lightning rod for discontent and oppositionist politics, into a national idol, part of the patrimony. "De Gaulle, the great oak cut down nearly twenty years ago, has become an old chestnut," Michel Richard wrote in the magazine *Le Point*, recalling the great-oak image of de Gaulle commonly invoked at the time of his death, the image itself coming from a poem by Victor Hugo: "Oh, what a fierce noise the oaks make when at dusk they are cut down to serve as logs for Hercules." Richard went on, speaking, now, not of oaks but of chestnuts: "It is the term used in the press to describe the perennial subjects, such as the return from summer vacation, the onset of cold weather, the traffic accidents of the All Saints weekend. De Gaulle is still the chestnut of our references, of our comparisons, and of our memories. He is always the precision scale with which we weigh and weigh again the things that we are and that we have become together. He is everywhere."

After François Mitterrand had been the president of France for eight years—which was only two years less than de Gaulle's tenure—it was hard, in style and in substance, to distinguish the onetime Socialist detractor of the general from the general himself. Mitterrand himself emerged from the maelstrom of *la politique politicienne* in France, from the nonstop maneuverings of the Fourth Republic and the ceaseless oppositionist posturings of the Fifth. He was the polemicist par excellence, the man whose career was built on arousing discontent with the way things were, or, to put this in a more positive vein, on inspiring a following by contending for power. He was an opportunist, in the great French tradition of political opportunism, taking on adversarial positions for the sake of being adversarial, becoming a Socialist, and taking over the foundering party when it seemed to offer his best hope of arriving, one day, at the seat of power itself. He did arrive there, and despite the denials of his supporters, who thrust away the Gaullist label as though it were some fatal virus—only understandable given the *patron*'s long anti-Gaullist bibliography—it is remarkable how Gaullist he has become during his years in power.

It is not necessarily that Mitterrand has eventually come to adopt the majority of de Gaulle's policies, though he has made some of the most important of them his own. In the areas of defense and foreign policy, the country, under him, has achieved greater comfort inside the Western alliance, no longer so forcefully declaring its independence of it. It is not even that Mitterrand has comfortably taken on the semi-monarchical style, the reserved, aloof, serene, detached, magisterial, above-the-common-fray presence that the French expect of their chief executive. In this, I thought it was amusing that early on in his second term, Mitterrand came under heavy criticism in the French press for, allegedly, assuming a bunch of royalist pretensions. The man who scalded de Gaulle for having mounted a "permanent coup d'état" had come, a series of articles said, to embody the behavior and the atmosphere of the defunct monarchy, following, in this regard, his rightist predecessors, de Gaulle included.

At the time—around the end of 1988—France was undergoing a tough series of labor disturbances. Nurses were on strike; so were workers in the Paris métro and bus system, the post office, and elsewhere; Paris and other cities were enduring daily rounds of inconveniences, normal lives snarled by the interruptions of municipal services. It was reminiscent of the time when unionized workers, spurred on by the very Mitterrand who had become president, were out on strike demanding higher salaries and other concessions from President de Gaulle. Mitterrand himself had once lambasted Giscard, his eventual predecessor, for being "a monarch with absolute power, arbitrary, authoritarian, arrogant." Giscard's ceremonies and pretensions—at state functions his children got priority over his ministers—cost him dearly in the higher dictatorship of public opinion, just as did his pursuit of his noble heritage and his acceptance of gifts from an African potentate. Now it was Mitterrand's turn. While Paris choked on labor disturbances, the president was accused of self-indulgent frivolities, of taking off frequently in what *Le Point* called "helicopter ballets," departing on gourmet expeditions, rapid, luxurious visits to the châteaux of rich friends, midweek excursions to Venice, moving the usual Council of Ministers meeting from Wednesday to Monday for the purpose.

In the United States, where there is no monarchist, and thus no antimonarchist, tradition, these sorts of displacements would hardly attract attention. In France, where the antimonarchical battle is still remembered in the collective consciousness, where the traditional French leftist groups in particular repudiated the more gorgeous trappings of power as a reactionary affectation, the accusation against Mitterrand hit home, serving for a time as the most titillating stuff of Parisian dinner parties and numerous articles in the newspapers. Thiérry Pfister, a former adviser to the prime minister, wrote a book entitled *Open Letter to the Mitterrand Generation, Which Is Out of Its Mind*, a leftist diatribe against Mitterrand's royalist habits. "It's an uncontrolled reign of technocrats," he said of the second term of Mitterrand—referring, apparently, to the presence of so many *énarques*, rather than Socialist theorists, in top positions—"under the rule of a monarch who looks after himself." Pfister's book, and a couple of others like it coming out at the same time, led *Le Point* to remark that Mitterrand's imperium had now generated its Voltaire—that is, its courageous critic, its gadfly. History was repeating itself 250 years after Louis XV. Mitterrand, in *Le Coup d'État Permanent*, had been a kind of Voltaire, complaining that in France there has always existed what he called "a solid bonapartism where the vocation for national grandeur, the monarchical tradition, meets up with the passion for national unity, the Jacobin tradition." Now it was Mitterrand himself, according to Pfister, who had become the meeting place of the two traditions.

The resurgence under a leftist like Mitterrand of the antimonarchical sentiment showed the staying power, the irresistible charm within the political class, of the old noble fragrance at the heart of French political life. Napoleon, the prophet of the revolutionary idea, married a niece of Louis XVI, thus becoming, through marriage, a relative of the Bourbons. De Gaulle, once explaining how he selected the foreign visitors that he would receive at the old kingly palace of Versailles—as opposed to those who would come to the more republican Élysée presidential palace in Paris—said: "I receive at Versailles only the sovereigns of ancient dynasties." "Everything counts when it comes to the prestige of the state," the *grand homme* also declared. Inevitably, it seems, every French presidency takes on some of the flavor of a royal court, particularly given the enormous, unquestioned power granted the chief executive by de Gaulle's constitution of the Fifth Republic. But what, besides the French love of making a dazzling impression on less well-endowed foreigners, does it mean? It means, in essence, that under the Fifth Republic, every president is, and will be, a Gaullist, not only in his choice of policies to pursue, but in the very nature and style of his rule.

In his book, Pfister, the discontented Socialist purist, complains that under Mitterrand socialism had lost its ideological thrust. The objective, he contended, changed from implementing the leftist idea to staying in power at all costs, which meant implementing the idea of consensus, being motivated by the desire to rally as much electoral support as possible, to offend nobody, to appeal to every constituency both rightist and leftist, and, thus, to get elected. A less politically partisan view of things would see Mitterrand and de Gaulle linked in the paramount need of the French to express the national grandeur through their choice of a man who ingathers the French by virtue of his character and prestige, his ability to embody the national ambition in his person and to remain remote from the infernal daily political fray—made up of such things as strikes of postal workers and the dull quarrels of politicians echoing through the rotund chambers of the National Assembly. The French feel most comfortable with the very sort of *grand homme* that Mitterrand spent much of his career repudiating and then, when circumstances so dictated, became. And as he became it, he seemed to embody more and more the very qualities that had made de Gaulle, if not beloved, certainly revered by the French.

True, the two men, Mitterrand and de Gaulle, do not look like each other. The one was tall, bony, and almost comically lanky, the other small, trim, inclined toward a slight roundness. De Gaulle was the quintessential soldier, Mitterrand is the epitome of the civilian, the armchair intellectual. And yet, even physically, the dissimilarities are mingled with some odd resemblances. Both have a certain austerity of appearance, accentuated by an austerity of gesture and mannerism. De Gaulle's is obvious. Mitterrand is a de Gaulle shrunk to a more normal dimension. His face is a picture of stony serenity. He seems physically stiff, his movements drawn from a highly limited but classic repertory. He is a man of great formality. He seems to arrange to be photographed standing alone, an expression of near-disdainful composure on his face. Often, he wears a long wool coat, his neck entirely wrapped in a dark scarf, the ensemble giving him a monkish look, as though he were the denizen of some remote monastery dedicated entirely to a deeply important mission.

The editor Pierre Nora once listed the qualities that any French leader needs to succeed with the French, and both de Gaulle and Mitterrand had all of them. The French adore the political leader who shows a mystic identification with the French soil, with the countryside, the nation's rural roots. De Gaulle himself was identified with Colombey-les-deux-Églises. Mitterrand makes his annual pilgrimage, faithfully shown every year on the television news, to a hilltop at Sologne, where he is pictured looking out over the marvels of the French countryside, integrating himself with the mountains and the villages that the nostalgic French still believe retain a wholesome national essence.

The second quality is a taste for literature. De Gaulle's memoirs are among the masterpieces of twentieth-century French literature; like Churchill's, they are grand, sweeping, stylistically elegant in the old-fashioned way of sturdy houses in the country, models of the kind of workmanship you can't get anymore. Mitterrand has written nearly a dozen books; he is a great master of spoken French, eloquent in the spare and understated fashion of de Gaulle, a student of the same rhetorical school, with its stress not so much on argumentation, the technocrats' skill, as on the stirring of fine and deep feelings, on the light fingering of the more honorable of the heartstrings, using a resonant, near-poetical French to do so, replete with many references to *La France* and *les français*, uttered, incanted with reverential intonation, as though spoken against the background of organ music. And that rhetorical gift combines with a third, and perhaps most important, quality. The political leader has to communicate a deep sense of history, to intone the great themes of the French nation.

When Mitterrand first came to power in 1981, he made a ceremonial visit to the Panthéon, the immense domed structure, atop an ancient hill in the Latin Quarter, where many of France's great men are laid to rest. The Panthéon is one of those symbols unique to France, etched with historical meaning. It was a church, the church of Saint-Geneviève, until turned by the revolutionaries into a great memorial for those who served the revolutionary ideal. Mirabeau was the first of the major figures of 1789 to die, and thus he was the first to be interred among the old, cold stones of the Panthéon, whose use and function was a highly accurate mirror of the struggle both for ideas and for power that took place in France over the next century and more. In one of the striking essays in the volumes edited by Pierre Nora, *Les Lieux de Mémoire*, the historian Mona Ozouf traces how, over time, and particularly with the establishment of the Third Republic in the 1870s, the monument became eventually and irrevocably a hecatomb for men whose greatness is owed to personal achievement rather than to birth or privilege. There were never any kings, queens, cardinals, or emperors buried in the Panthéon, though it did on a few occasions—under Napoleon, Louis XVIII, and Napoleon III, whenever the monarchy or the empire was reestablished and the Republic itself put into a tomb—revert to its original status as a Catholic church.

Today it is a symbol of the aristocracy of merit and a denigration of the concept of an aristocracy of blood. As such, it is an emblem of an ideal of republicanism, one of those principles that the Revolution created in France, which were late in being established in fact. The republican *grand homme* is an exemplar of secular and common virtue. He is the figure whose greatness is owed exclusively to his own capacities. He is an illustration of the belief, strong in the nineteenth century but still enduring, in the possibility of every man to attain to the heights, provided that he benefits from the blessings of liberty and equality. The remains of Voltaire and Rousseau and others who died well before the Revolution but were seen as early examples of republican attainment were transferred there. Victor Hugo and Émile Zola are there, as are a host of other great republicans. De Gaulle, who saved the Republic, is not in the Panthéon. He willed that he be buried in Colombey-les-deux-Églises, and he is. De Gaulle's absence was handy for Mitterrand. The left in France has always tried to integrate such events as the revolution of 1789, the creation of the Republic, and the heroes of the Panthéon, into their own tradition. Thus, when Mitterrand paid an early presidential visit to the Left Bank monument, he seemed to be trying to appropriate it in support of the Socialist programs that he wanted to launch.

Still, though he is not buried there himself, de Gaulle represented the heroes of the Panthéon well both in his personal history and in his creation of the Fifth Republic, the most stable and smoothly functioning of all of the many French experiments with democratic government. But de Gaulle had another attribute as well. He was the first to use the symbolism of the *grand homme* to bolster the notion of democracy. He was different in this regard from certain of his predecessors. Indeed, ever since Napoleon, the French have had a special weakness for their own brand of Duce, even if they have the good taste not to call him that. Sometimes the examples are more comic than heroic, more puffed-up bigots than genuine political-military geniuses like Napoleon. In the 1880s, a certain General Boulanger threatened to overthrow the fledgling Third Republic in a coup d'état, but he ended up fleeing to Belgium. Boulanger was a prototypical antidemocratic, antiparliamentarian charismatic figure. So was Pétain. In a country that has often been undecided between democracy and authoritarianism, whose political institutions have undergone numerous upheavals and alterations, the attraction of the antidemocratic *grand homme* has always been powerful.

De Gaulle's achievement in creating the Fifth Republic was to allow the French to be led by a democratic *grand homme*, by a figure who embodied a certain authoritarianism, a certain royalist panache, while being unmistakably committed to the values of the Republic, as figures like the two Bonapartes, Boulanger, and Pétain had not been. This pulling together of two heretofore incompatible strains is the essence and the genius of Gaullism, allowing France for the first time to be both stable and democratic. Given the French propensity for partisan violence, for undermining their own republican principles by their yearning for a king, it is not a slight achievement.

What, then, is the difference between Gaullism and what will someday, no doubt, come to be called Mitterrandism? The Gaullists and the Mitterrandists, if asked to explain, will harrumph indignantly, while proclaiming that the vast gap between the two is so apparent that only a fool would not see it. And yet when Mitterrand began appearing in caricatures as a bewigged monarch, wearing a red frock coat, scepter in hand, the gap had considerably narrowed. It was the royalist-Bonapartist tradition, the aristocratic-imperialist strain of French political culture—perfected by Louis XIV and last glimpsed in its formally constituted form at the moment just before the abdication of Louis Napoleon Bonaparte III in 1871—melding with the Republican tradition of the *grand homme*, the colossus of democracy.

Mitterrand, though a Socialist, will, if he finishes out the second seven-year term to which he was elected in 1988, have served in the monarchical presidency created by the preferences and the personality of de Gaulle for four years longer than the general did—even if he did launch the political debate of the Fifth Republic with an attack against what he saw as its implicit authoritarianism. Part of de Gaulle's political genius had been to create a powerful executive that did not threaten the freedom of the French. Somehow, almost miraculously, the French, with the help of the tall general with the immense nose, created the institutions by which they could govern themselves and be free as well. He was one of those paradoxes that spatter the consistency of French history, the man from the same background and even initial ideology of a Pétain who, once and for all, consolidated the French republican tradition. Meanwhile, Mitterrand the Socialist has continued the tradition of the deeply conservative general, showing that France's mode of politics is forged less by the will of single men than by the collective will of the French.

An Elegy for the
French Difference

CAPTAIN Alfred Dreyfus of the great *affaire* that separated good from evil in France is commemorated by a bronze statue in Paris. It is not exactly hidden, this statue; nor is it particularly conspicuous or easy to find. You go to the Tuileries Gardens and wander around just east of the Orangerie, and there, in a quiet area of the park, holding his broken sword amid the young locust trees, his head bowed with grief, stands old Alfred, disconsolate, the embodiment of miscarried justice.

The fact is that the relative obscurity of the Dreyfus memorial is not particularly noteworthy in Paris. The visitor to the city might have difficulty locating the monuments to less ambiguous heroes and heroines, such as the statue of Joan of Arc, situated in the Place des Pyramides on the rue de Rivoli—where the far right tends to hold its rallies—or that of Charlemagne, the grand progenitor himself, mounted on a glorious steed in a seldom-visited shadow of Notre-Dame Cathedral. France is filled with small plaques and memorials that testify to the variety and complexity of its past. Here and there, etched on building stones on broad avenues or in hidden passages, are little signposts saying: "Here was killed So-and-so, resistant, by the Germans, *Mort pour la France*"—who died for France. Again, near Notre-Dame is a small memorial tablet dedicated to the Jews and others who were deported to German death camps or concentration camps during World War II and never returned.

This question of statues is a constant, small vexation for the French, reflecting the various twists and turns of their past, their tendency to destroy heroes and, sometimes, to resurrect them, as they maintained their long quest to be great and free, unified and democratic, at the same time. Those who endure in bronze or marble are those who have stood a certain test of time, become part of the national consensus. Clemenceau, who is one such figure, is halfway up the Champs-Élysées; Léon Blum, less unanimously anointed but nonetheless within this pantheon, is, like Dreyfus, amid the trees in the Tuileries. Kings, too, are included. Henry IV sits on the Pont-Neuf; Louis XIV rides a rearing horse in the Place des Victoires. It is interesting to note in regard to this latter personage that the present statue is a replacement for one torn down by the revolutionaries of 1789.

The first work, done in the seventeenth century, portrayed the Sun King standing in the center of the Place des Victoires on a pedestal and surrounded by four captives, each representing a nation subdued by France during his reign—Spain, Holland, Prussia, Austria. It was toppled in 1790. The bronze was melted down. The figures representing the subdued nations were brought to the Parc des Sceaux, where they are still on view. A new statue, of the Bonapartist general Louis Desaix, was put up in the Place des Victoires in 1806. That was melted down in 1815 after the defeat at Waterloo, the bronze, not to be wasted, then used to cast the statue of Henry IV that remains to this day on the Pont-Neuf. Finally, in 1822, with the Bourbon monarchy temporarily restored, Louis XIV, again cast in bronze, took his present position in one of Paris's most exquisite squares. Unlike the great column put up by Napoleon in the Place Vendôme (where another equestrian statue of Louis XIV had been torn down in 1792), the new bronze Louis XIV was left unmolested by the Communards of 1871, whose rage was directed more against the Bonapartist vestiges than the monarchist ones.* Still, the point is clear. The French have always had difficulty reconciling their past with the present. The monuments that fall and those that are erected are indexes of the collective historical mood. It is

---

* The famous Vendôme column is another marvelous illustration of the French tampering with the symbols of the country's past. The original column, made from cannons captured at Austerlitz and melted down, was built by Napoleon and surmounted by a cast of himself. The column remained after his defeat in 1814, but he was replaced by Henry IV, who was knocked down during Napoleon's brief return to power in 1815. The restored monarchy put up a fleur-de-lis; the July monarchy of Louis-Philippe replaced that with another Napoleon, this one in the guise of a common soldier, that being replaced in turn by Napoleon III with a copy of the original statue of his uncle. After the entire column was destroyed by the Communards in 1871, it was put back together in something close to its original form by the Third Republic and left unchanged ever since.

the French way of evaluating and reevaluating the moral content of the past.

And so it was with Dreyfus. His statue, put up only in 1987, is symbolic not only of the *affaire* that shook France, helping to forge its conscience, but of the aftermath of the episode itself, the fact that four generations later, it still managed to trouble the national spirit. The statue was commissioned by the Socialist minister of culture, Jack Lang, who apparently intended to place it inside the courtyard of the École Militaire in Paris, where, on January 5, 1895, the unfortunate captain was stripped of his rank, his sword broken before the eyes of his fellow officers as a sign of his shame.

To place the symbol of the reversal of an unjust verdict in the very place where the verdict had been carried out seemed, morally, a suitable decision. But with the statue ready, Charles Hernu, the minister of defense, exercised his authority over military properties by refusing to have it placed in its intended berth. Hernu gave a plausible reason. The École Militaire was not open to the public, he argued, and would thus be inappropriate as a site for the statue of Dreyfus. Only founders of the school could be honored with statues there, he added. Jean-Denis Bredin, a lawyer and historian, who wrote the definitive work on the Dreyfus affair, complained, despite Hernu's unobjectionable reasoning, that the incident revealed France's continuing spiritual unease. The unprovable but ineradicable suspicion remains that Dreyfus inside the École Militaire would have been a constant offense, at the very least an embarrassment, an unwelcome return of the repressed, to some in the army. Certainly, if there had to be a statue of Dreyfus, let it be put someplace where it would not roil spirits, stir up past animosities. The École Militaire was not the spot if the past was ever to be buried. The Tuileries, it was decided—though not before Dreyfus himself seemed to reach out from the grave and pinch the raw and tender nerve of the nation—was a better, more serene spot.

THERE are many episodes that pinch the tender French nerve, too many to treat in detail. History, the maze of the past, stares down at the French like a bad conscience, its gaze often avoided and, when met, met with such a powerful taste for partial interpretations that a certain generalization is warranted. Every people struggles with its past, of course, trying to reconcile the way it perceives itself with the indelible record of events. But the French struggle is particularly acute, its list of embarrassments unusually long. There is the Terror of 1793; the repression of 1848; the coup d'état of 1851; the massacre of 1871, the Dreyfus affair, interwar anti-Semitism, World War II capitulation and collaboration (the worst blots ever), the torture used by the French expeditionary force in its attempt to quell the independence movement in Algeria.

A senior official in the French government once told me that the wartime experience had forever robbed the French of their moral distinction. True, he said, the French were defeated in six weeks. It was a terrible shock. But they then made all the wrong choices. Rather than remain in formal resistance, sending a government into exile to represent the French people and their will to be free, they voluntarily entered into a formal collaboration with the Nazis. Their police chased after the Jews with as much, and sometimes more, ruthlessness as the Nazis. Thus the French are now not merely a people that was defeated: They are a people who transformed their defeat into a moral abomination, becoming subservient allies of their conquerors. Morally speaking, the official told me, the French have never recovered from that mistake.

The sometimes troubled conscience of the French shows itself in various ways. When Klaus Barbie, the wartime Gestapo chief in Lyon (and a German), was extradited from Bolivia and put on trial in France in 1987, charged with crimes against humanity, Barbie and his lawyer, Jacques Vergès, were able to play on French fears that still-unknown moral transgressions could be exposed. They threatened to expose acts of treason and betrayal committed during the war by figures today at the highest level of French society. When in the end the trial took place and Barbie was convicted and sentenced to a term of life imprisonment, not a single unknown misdeed had been exposed, not a single current French reputation tarnished. And yet the very credibility of the empty threat was significant. The French live in a cloudy and vague world. They spin endless tales over such questions as the betrayal of Jean Moulin, the highest resistance official in France, tortured to death in Lyon by Barbie after an informant from within the ranks of the resistance had ensured his capture. There are things they will never be sure about. How many *résistants* were there really, how many collaborators? Who was courageous and who cowardly? How many among them who hold respectable positions were Pétainists at heart half a century ago?

The French, an ancient and a modern people, are still seeking their identity, their footing. How else can one explain the persistence of their self-scrutiny, the intensity of their quarrels? As this is being written, the French have just marked the two hundredth anniversary of the Great

Revolution, that formative event of Western history during which all the political anguish of the twentieth century was foreshadowed. The commemoration revealed that after two hundred years, it was still difficult to determine whether the Revolution was a good event or a harmful one, whether it was best represented by the Declaration of the Rights of Man or by the Terror, by the Tennis Court Oath or by the Committee for Public Safety, by Condorcet or by Robespierre. A school of rightist historians staked out new territory, depicting the Revolution as the first instance of modern totalitarian ruthlessness, a realization of a cautionary epigram from Voltaire: "Those who can make you believe absurdities can make you commit atrocities." The Revolution showed the French in all their genius and unreasonableness. It showed them creating principles that endure for all mankind while wrecking the very edifice that would make the implementation of those principles possible for themselves.

And so, when it came time to commemorate the event, the French were not sure how to do it, whether as a dirge or as a celebration. The Socialists, who claim the event for the left, wanted to hold another Exposition Universelle, of the sort that had been held on the centennial of the Revolution in 1889—and of which the Eiffel Tower, representing the possibility that civil perfection could be attained through Reason and Science, remains the principal symbol. But the idea of another Exposition Universelle was opposed by the right, as not only too expensive but inappropriate. New books were published stressing the horrors of the *dérapage* of the Revolution, the slide into chaos and terror, calling it an inevitable outcome of the inherent radicalism of so dramatic a break with the past. The rightists' books seemed to be more numerous than the books that celebrated the Revolution, which seemed to have a brittle, stereotypical, defensive quality. In the end, a certain compromise prevailed, made possible, perhaps, by a public indifference to the matter. The Revolution would be marked by a host of activities. The bicentennial would be a Big Event, but not so big as to suggest unalloyed acceptance of the Revolution itself as a good for all mankind.

Underlying the debate was this self-conception: The Revolution, no more than the Dreyfus affair more than a century later, was never in the French view a mere discrete set of events stretching over the years 1789 to, in the broad view, 1815. The Revolution was not a national event, a French affair. It was the first conscious gesture by any group of men and women to create a political principle of universal, rather than particularistic, value. It was a secularization of the Christian faith, this forging of the idea that what we are creating here should embrace the entire human race. It was, in short, the first great episode in which the French declared themselves to be the moral vanguard of mankind. It was a resounding echo of the country's global mission, the one they have—despite the bloodshed, the collaboration, the echo of the Nazi boot in a hundred villages—striven to maintain even in this century of their relative decline.

No wonder the interpretation of the Revolution remains an important event. The event was not merely the crucible of modern times; it was the flowering of the concept of French grandeur, of the idea that this is a nation that is greater than its parts. Or do the French still look at it that way? Perhaps they don't. I remember an article in the American press on the preparations for the bicentennial. *The New Republic*, where the article appeared—its title was "Liberty, Equality and Have a Nice Day"—felt it had detected a certain formality to the alleged concern for the evaluation of the Revolution, an indifference, a fatigue, perhaps, with the requirement that all things French have a special meaning, a desire to be caught up, like other people, in the humdrum, inglorious, commonplace, and undramatic pursuit of happiness and prosperity. Or perhaps, in the end, the French, still aware of the events that took place on their soil roughly half a century ago, quietly abandoned the French moral burden. Perhaps, despite the vigorous, Promethean struggles of the national leaders, de Gaulle primary among them, despite a formal public rhetoric that echoes the ideas and phrases of centuries past, there are simply too many frightful memories disturbing the collective sleep for the French as a whole to aspire to Greatness.

I don't know. The French pollsters, ever ready with their questionnaires, have not measured that particular aspect of their countrymen's consciousness. It is unmeasurable. How do you place in the balance the separate weights of bad conscience and normal human indifference, fatigue and the preoccupation with a high standard of living? In any case, there can be only one conclusion: The French are rapidly becoming like other peoples, losing the many things that, for two hundred years and more, made them different. Modernity has leached out their particularity, modernity and the accumulated devastations of a difficult past.

The French will be like us, and as they become like the rest of us—Americanized, prosperous, modern, complacent—a great historical epoch will vanish from the earth, the epoch of Frenchness. After all, if the French themselves are no longer willing to fight bitterly and en masse over the heritage of the Revolution, doesn't that indicate the end of an era? Perhaps, as you hold this volume in your hands, we will be experiencing the last few minutes of the existence of the French difference. It has been a long time since the eighteenth century, when Antoine de Rivarol, speaking of literature and civilization, could announce, "The time has come to call the whole world French." You can be sure that when the urge to be different fades and the need to make that difference a common property disappears, the world will feel a bit relieved and deprived as well. For, as Victor Hugo said, without the French we will be alone.

INDEX

———